UPON DEA

The True Story of a Mother's

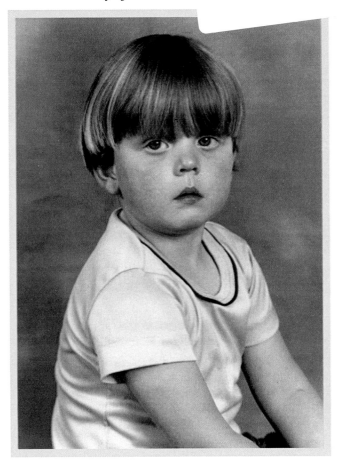

By

Susan Green

CREMER PRESS

3

First Published in Great Britain in 2009 By
Susan Green
C/O Cremer Press, Blackburn. BB2 2JE.

Copyright © Susan Green 2008
First Edition 2009
ALL RIGHTS RESERVED.

ISBN NUMBER 978 1 898722 80 9

Printed and Bound by
Edmund Mercer, Cremer Press,
45 Harrison Street,
Blackburn. Lancs, BB2 2JE

"I promise you mum, I will write my story".

I have made this promise to my dear mum who is 84 years old and totally blind, because she wants this story to be told before she dies.

I HAVE HAD TO FIGHT FOR MY SON ALL HIS LIFE!

As I write this book I do not even know if my son will be alive before I finish it. I will complete it though, and it will be true and from my heart, and although it will be hard to write, I will do it for my mum and Neil.

I NEVER BREAK A PROMISE!

This is a true story that you really have to read to believe.

Susan Green

Many of the names of people and places in this book have been changed, in order to disguise those doctors and establishments that unfortunately we have personally come across, who were either not able to diagnose our son's condition, or not willing to listen to all of his symptoms or problems, despite knowing that there were indeed other members of his family who had suffered from mental illness, and had actually even been treated in the past by the VERY SAME 'specialist' that our son was now seeing.

However in this specialist's personal opinion, mental illness did not run in families, as it was not a hereditary condition. Yet he already knew this to be untrue, as he had personally treated more than one member of this same family himself.

This 'so called Mental Health Specialist' diagnosed that our son Neil was 'BAD' and was simply 'SEEKING ATTENTION' but had no mental illness at all.

Even after Neil had seriously attempted not only to self harm on numerous occasions, and had also tried to kill himself several times, this same 'so called specialist' refused point blank to admit that he was wrong, change or re-check his original diagnosis, or refer Neil elsewhere for a second opinion. Even after Neil had been cut down after hanging himself in prison, and had only just managed to be revived, this same 'Specialist' STILL refused Neil any medical help for his mental illness.

He also absolutely refused to allow Neil onto the mental health wards when he was desperately ill after yet another near death attempt on his life, when he drove a car at speed into a lamppost. This was despite the fact that the paramedics had written that Neil still had suicidal tendencies after this serious attempt to end his life on their incident report, but the Psychiatric Ward refused point blank to admit Neil. Instead he was discharged at weekend, with a full length pot on his leg due to shattered bones and kneecap. He had a broken jaw and other facial injuries which meant that not only was he in extreme pain, but he could only eat pureed food. He was put into an unfurnished house after only one week, at weekend without any suitable medication and left to fend and struggle on alone.

I ASK YOU, HOW CAN WE MAKE A DOCTOR, DOCTOR?

6

NOTE FROM THE EDITOR

*If you are able to bear with me for just a little while at least, then I can assure you that whilst at first sight it appears that this note has NOTHING at all to do with the subject of this book, I can assure you that it **truly does.***

*I know from personal experience that many years ago when I had my own two children, and sadly my second child a son, was diagnosed as suffering from chronic epilepsy right from birth, I was very worried. Naturally I wondered whether or not I would be able to cope properly with this condition, so whilst I read up a lot on the subject, I also placed **my complete trust** in both my GP and the Specialist Paediatrician whom my son was assigned to at the hospital. I had complete confidence in them both as I thought that **they knew what they were doing** whilst I was a complete novice on this topic, so I followed their instructions to the letter.*

Thankfully David my son, had only Petit Mal fits, which are the smaller, shorter lasting ones, yet as he grew bigger he would quite often move on from one fit to several others consecutively, sometimes having up to a hundred a day. This meant that he always needed to be carefully monitored.

If he had one fit I could very easily deal with it. When he had fit after fit, I would ring our GP and be told to bring him down to the surgery. Whilst the doctor would always see him, we would have to wait until the end of the surgery and take our turn AFTER all the other patients had been seen. At that time I admit I accepted that as normal; I was simply following medical orders.

As we had no transport of our own in those days, I would

have to carry my child to the bus stop, wait for a bus, brave whatever weather there was, and travel the couple of miles to the doctor's with David fitting and throwing himself all over the place. Then sometimes we would have to wait for up to ninety minutes before we were seen by the GP. It was always the same, the doctor would then send for an ambulance and David would be admitted after being examined in casualty and being found a bed. The whole thing could take three or four hours, and David would often still be fitting throughout.

I had read in a medical book that the heart could be affected if fits continued for so long. Anyway the hospital staff would simply watch David, but naturally as they always had other things to do they could NEVER watch him all the time, so I would always stay there myself to do so.

One day I decided that I would NOT wait in the surgery for up to an hour and a half. Instead I went to the front and asked the receptionist if David could go in next? My son was now seven years of age, and whilst he was indeed small for his age, after carrying him for over an hour just to get to the doctors I was struggling to keep hold of him.

The receptionist replied, "Well only if the next patient will allow it."

I therefore asked, "Who is due to go to see the doctor next?"

A man answered that it was his turn.

I asked if he or anyone else minded if we went in next as my son had by now been fitting for an hour and a half.

I was encouraged by EVERYONE in the surgery to take him in next. So we entered the surgery and as usual the doctor rang for an ambulance for David.

I asked the doctor, "In order to cut down on the waiting time for my son to get into hospital if this happens again, was it possible for me to just ring for an ambulance myself as David was getting far too heavy for me to carry like this? Or if not, why could a doctor not come out to see David at home if it was necessary that a GP see a patient before calling an ambulance?"

I was treated as if I was out of my mind, patted on the head and simply dismissed without any answer whatsoever to my question.

He simply said, "Go back into the waiting room and wait till the ambulance arrives."

At the hospital I asked the doctor who examined David, "Would the delay in us getting to the hospital have had any affect on my child?" After all by this time it was now over TWO HOURS since David had started his first fit of that day.

"Well in this particular case, the earlier we can stop his fits, then the better it will be long term for the patient," was his reply.

"Well am I allowed to call for an ambulance for him myself if he goes from one fit to the next as he often does on a regular basis?"

"Well not really, an ambulance can only be requested by a doctor AFTER they have seen the patient."

Well none of this made sense to me then, but thankfully we are able to request ambulances or ring the helpline who will do it for us nowadays.

The second thing that made me question doctors was when David was prescribed some medication from the Specialist himself. Usually I simply re-ordered another prescription from our doctor's surgery. However this time I took the prescription that the Specialist had written to the hospital pharmacy and they gave us some medicine.

I must say that David NEVER had a problem in taking his two different lots of medication. He had needed to take these three times a day for a few years, which meant that I spent SIX YEARS and all my lunchtimes during that period, going to his school every single day in order to give him two spoonfuls of

9

medicine as the school would not take responsibility for doing this.

However on the day I started giving him the medicine from the new bottle that had come straight from the hospital, David (aged just five years at that time)) complained that it tasted funny. Stupidly I never listened to him, and gave him a second dose at lunchtime as I usually did. Once more my son complained that it tasted different. This time I did begin to worry a little. I took the bottle to our usual chemist and explained the situation. David had been on this medicine for about three years by this time.

The chemist was a lovely man, "Leave it with me and I'll test it."

An hour later I got a phone call at work from this chemist. "Where is David now he asked?"

I could hear the urgency in his voice. "He is in school," I replied.

"Go and get him immediately and take him to the hospital, call here and collect the medicine and a letter I will write out for you to take with you; his medicine is 100 times too strong for him, and will put him at great risk."

I rang school to say that I was coming for my son explaining why.

His teacher said, "It's a pity he can't have that strength all the time. I have never seen him so bright."

Usually David was half drugged by the medicines and we had a great fight on our hands to even get him into mainstream school. I thought she was well out of order to think that it was okay for David's health to be put at risk, just so that he could be brighter in her class.

The medicine (just two spoonfuls in total) turned my son into an overactive child who could not rest or sleep for **three whole days.** He was admitted, and on the two occasions where I left him in charge of the nursing staff during those three days whilst I went to the toilet, he had two accidents on that ward.

Not only had the Specialist written out the prescription wrongly, giving David a full adult dose, but he had also written his age on the prescription and date of birth, but this had obviously NOT been noticed or queried by the dispensing chemist. David could indeed have died. The medicine looked the same; it smelled the same, but thankfully my son knew far better than I did that it was definitely NOT the same.

After that my faith and trust in doctors and hospital staff were always tinged with suspicion and I checked absolutely everything. Through me doing this many other 'errors' were rectified before any harm could be done.

****

Now I come to the real story in hand '**Upon Deaf Ears**'. Neil's mother Susan instinctively knew that there was something wrong with her son at an early age. However she had so much trouble getting anyone to either listen to her, or diagnose him properly.

Like me, she and her husband Steve trusted doctors and specialists. They were trained, they were respected; they were listened to and treated like demi-Gods after all.

When it comes to PHYSICAL illness, we might have a small inkling whether something is done correctly or not. Susan and Steve had very good doctors following their accident, so they had both recovered extremely well. The doctors had done far more than their best for them, for they had walked that extra mile to ensure that they could BOTH walk again.

After all when all is said and done, if a bone is broken, it soon becomes apparent whether it has healed properly or not, as it did in Steve's case when he had to have another pot put on, then an operation to remove a bone from his own hip, to insert into his leg in order for him to get better. Susan was left with her leg only hanging on at the knee by a small piece of skin. She was sure that she would lose her leg forever. These

11

*two young people were **both** saved to live near-normal lives, by such wonderful and dedicated Specialists due to their extraordinary skills and their great efforts. This was then followed up by a wonderful team consisting of many nurses, physiotherapists, aided naturally by the sheer determination on the parts of the wonderful fighting spirits of the couple themselves.*

****

*However with mental illness, and perhaps also other branches of medicine such as the treatment of the elderly; as ordinary laymen we possess very little knowledge in these fields; we are therefore absolutely **forced to put all our faith and trust in the Specialists.***

*Well there are **good** doctors and there are **bad** doctors, just exactly the same as there are in any other occupation. For most of us we simply have to trust whoever we are referred to for our children, those who are mentally ill, or our elderly loved ones. The patients in these three branches of medicine are most often the most vulnerable in society. They need someone to speak up for them, as often they do NOT have a voice of their own.*

Whilst Susan suspected early on that her son Neil had possible serious health problems, it was all new to her; but she could see that Neil was different than Ryan her first son, but she didn't know at first what it could possibly be.

It took years for Neil to get any diagnosis at all. He was labelled as simply a 'BAD' boy, who was 'SEEKING ATTENTION', then simply ignored.

*Sadly once a label is placed on someone, and is even entered into our medical records, the next doctor often takes this as read and proven. Therefore they see no reason to look any further. Even if they themselves think there just **might** be more to this than is on the patient's file; often their Seniors don't agree with them. If we have an original doctor who is* convinced that he is right, and becomes quite pompous about it, and thinks that he KNOWS EVERYTHING, then sadly no other doctor is allowed to Doctor this patient as relating to change. The patient is NEVER referred elsewhere. The original diagnosis, whether it is wrong or not has now become THE GOSPEL ACCORDING TO THE FIRST SPECIALIST.

So in Neil's case, when he was eventually diagnosed with A.D.H.D, which at that time was a very newly diagnosed condition, which the 'old school' type of specialist did not believe existed, the original specialist refused to take seriously the need for Neil to be prescribed medicine for this condition. He would stop it every time Neil went to see him, just stop it immediately, or prescribe it at the wrong times of day, which served to make Neil's condition deteriorate. Meddling with doses and times or stopping medicines straight off can be absolutely dangerous and should NEVER be done.

Unfortunately Neil did not just suffer from ONE single condition. In his family there were other members who had been diagnosed with mental illness. As this SAME original specialist who Neil was under had also treated a couple of his relatives a few years earlier, Neil **should have been lucky**, as there should have been an immediate connection made between Neil's illness and perhaps an inherited gene.

However his specialist dismissed any chance of this possibility when mentioned by his Junior colleagues, as being complete and utter nonsense; as in his personal opinion MENTAL ILLNESS DID NOT EVER RUN IN FAMILIES. How he came to this conclusion is an absolute mystery to us, as he himself had dealt with at least TWO members of this SAME family and declared them both to be suffering from mental illness.

If he could dismiss this possibility for Neil, then he could ALSO keep others thinking that his original diagnosis that Neil was simply 'BAD and ATTENTION SEEKING' was correct.

13

Worse still this could remain on Neil's records. Naturally the more times he confirmed this, the worse Neil was treated, indeed if he was even treated at all at times.

Neil's label was by now very firmly attached, *and though a few tried to help him, and occasionally someone actually found and declared the truth about Neil, their ideas were always quickly shot down in flames by their Senior Specialist.*

*This same specialist tried to go another step further as Neil got older, by stating his belief to **everyone,** that Neil could NOT possibly have A.D.H.D. now, as it did not continue after childhood. This was yet another way to keep people from listening to Neil and his family. For many people this worked, as they listened to the so called 'GOOD DOCTOR'. No one ever queried at what age this condition stopped. In truth it stopped for **some** children as they simply grew out of it, sadly Neil was NOT one of the fortunate ones.*

*I do not want to spoil this wonderful TRUE story, so I will simply end here by giving you a little known piece of information that should really shock you. **I was under the misconception that if your doctor does not know what is wrong with you, or has made a diagnosis that you believe to be wrong, or at least questionable, then I thought that we were all able to go back to our GP's and ask to be sent for a second opinion.***

This is true, BUT ONLY IF THE FIRST SPECIALIST AGREES TO IT! If he says that he is right then he is <u>under absolutely no obligation</u> either medically or morally to give his permission for you to be sent to someone else.

*Worse still, WITHOUT HIS PERMISSION, you are stuck with the original diagnosis and can **never** move on. I ask you in 2009, is this the way that anyone should really wish to proceed, held hostage by an incorrect diagnosis that blights the rest of your life forever. Even if others argue the point, or do not think that he is right at all, or even beg to take on this patient's case;*

*without the original Specialist's permission **no one is authorized to do so.***

I strongly believe that this loophole in medical law should be permanently, and forever once and for all be closed. *After all none of us are ALWAYS RIGHT, and most doctors will accept that, and be more than willing to pass on their patient to another colleague in order to get the very best treatment that they possibly can for their patient.*

*Shouldn't that ALWAYS be the way? I always thought that **everyone** who ever took the Hippocratic oath as a newly qualified doctor would be obligated to ALWAYS SERVE A CODE OF MEDICAL ETHICS FOR EVERY SINGLE ONE OF HIS PATIENTS, in order to ensure that they always tried to give each and every single person they treated, **the very best that they could offer.** If they weren't able to do this, then perhaps in the jargon of today they would always be able to offer up a fair and SECOND OPINION from a man in the profession who they knew **would** or at least **might,** be able to do so.*

*I don't know if there are **real life doctors** like '**House'** on TV whose job is solely to find out what is wrong with someone who presents with a different, unknown or out of the ordinary condition. <u>However I would like to think that there are!</u>*

*The field of Medicine is not just a job, it is a profession. It requires years of training, and no one person will ever know everything. However in the POOL of medical knowledge, that has been built up and filled with years of experience, there will **always** be someone who comes along who has the competence and skill to find the answer to any problem. BUT WHAT IS THE USE OF THIS, IF THEY ARE NOT AVAILABLE TO EVERYONE AS A LAST RESORT?*

Medicine is an ongoing, ever growing field filled with doctors who have grown wiser on the backs and shoulders of earlier pioneers. There are Scientists who have discovered

15

vaccines and pills which have saved people and have improved lives for so many others.

The **best** people in medicine are usually the **most humble.** They are not looking for glory for themselves; they are NOT desperate to be always right; they are those individuals who care most and keep on trying, those folk who persevere against all the odds to help to make things better for every single one of their patients.

If they cannot find the answer, they will always know a man who can, and they will seek that person out wherever they are, not to take the glory, but to heal the patient.

Sadly for Neil and his family, he was allocated a Specialist who thought that he was <u>above the law</u>. What was even worse though; was that others allowed him to carry on thinking in this way.

When you are involved in a chronic illness, whether it is your own or others around you, either physical or mental in origin; over the years **you** become the expert. This is doubly so if it is your child, or your parent or any other loved one, as **you** know them so well. You understand what is 'their normal' way of life. You have all the inside information. You know of any changes that have occurred. I BEG YOU THEREFORE TO **TRUST IN YOURSELF** AND YOUR OWN INSTINCTS as most of the time you will be correct.

As a parent, doctors accept the information that you give them about your children, hopefully this will be a good guide to help them come to a conclusion as to what is wrong in order to get a true diagnosis to work from for the child in question.

Why then is it that when a child has become an adult according to the law of the land, even if they are elderly and becoming senile, or have a mental illness or take illegal substances which prevent them from knowing or describing accurately how they **really** are, or what their true actions have been, why then do we get told that due to the new laws of

*PRIVACY AND CONFIDENTIALITY we can no longer speak up for them. They have to tell the doctors everything for themselves. We are **excluded** from case meetings, when we have such **relevant information** to offer. So if the patient is **<u>not</u>** able to speak up for themselves rationally for whatever reason**, how is a correct diagnosis ever attained?***

*How on earth do **clever** doctors expect that the information given to them by the patient in any of these listed groups, can in all truth be RELIED upon to give the **full** details that are necessary for a doctor to be given enough truthful and accurate information for them to be able to give a factual and honest diagnosis?*

Please someone tell me what common sense there is in letting the mentally ill patient ONLY, or the elderly early SENILE patient ONLY, or the drug or drink induced patient speak up for themselves?

DOES THIS MAKE ANY MEDICAL SENSE AT ALL?

*It does **not** in my opinion, and it is ALMOST as bad as allowing one doctor to stop another doctor from giving his personal opinion.*

*Neil was robbed time after time of all possible help for his illness. He was NEVER able to speak up for himself, either after a minor crime, self harming or a true suicide attempt. When he was denied **true and much NEEDED medicine,** he was forced to **self medicate** on a combination of drink and drugs in order to try to help himself escape from the voices, and the never ending trials and tribulations of his lonely and desperate life.*

*His problems were beyond the normal scope of help that even loving parents could give him; his downward spiral was forever out of control, a control that a simple, **urgent** and HONEST diagnosis would have given him some immediate relief.*

Why was Neil born with these conditions? Why were other

*family members with similar problems who had been diagnosed with mental illness never connected to Neil? Why were the **few people who did listen to him and his family**, forever placed in the wrong by this ONE Senior Specialist?*

Why are some doctors allowed to NOT doctor a patient? ***More importantly when will this practice stop?*** *No one is perfect. No one is <u>always</u> right! They always say that doctors always bury their mistakes. Why then do we **allow them to get away with this? It has to stop NOW!***

*Occasionally Neil was treated as mentally ill, he was sectioned for several months, he was given psychotic medicines, **promised** that he was going to be treated for his illness, but most importantly he was actually **given some hope**, that at LONG LAST someone was actually listening to him. Help was here and there really was a God.*

Then all his pills were stopped and withdrawn, he was thrown out of his SECURE place in his sectioned ward straight out to either a prison cell, or a cruel world without any help, medication or a place to live.

***These kinds of drugs cannot be played with**, they cannot just be <u>withdrawn,</u> you can't be given psychotic drugs for many months; then be declared fine and the medication simply stopped, full stop. This is enough to send a SANE person crazy or a mentally ill person to his death.*

How many more Neil's are there out there, all alone, in need of proper medicine, skipping in and out of the system, and slipping through the <u>gaping holes</u> in the net of errors that sadly often lead to DEATH.

There are many out there, you will have heard of some of them, for they are the ones jumping off our roof top car parks, the ones hanging themselves, the ones deliberately trying to kill and harm themselves, indeed the ones who were neglected until they could finally take no more.

<u>Every doctor needs to doctor.</u> *Every patient needs an* *accurate* diagnosis. *Those diagnosed with a mental condition are often the LUCKY ones, they get access to drugs, yet still the balance is such that it can all go wrong. For those **without** that diagnosis, **without** the correct medication**, without** a safe place on a section when required, LIFE IS SADLY ALWAYS WRONG for they are accepted by **no one,** taken advantage of by **everyone***, and become the misfits of Society as they are moved on from pillar to post, continually trying to fit into a cruel world, until finally there is **nowhere** left to turn! NO OTHER WAY OUT BUT DEATH ITSELF.*

*Where are our hearts, our consciences, our sympathy and our help for these people? It could be you or I, or a member of our family, <u>**for one in four of us suffers from mental illness**</u> nowadays. Can we learn to listen, to see and learn how to help these people?*

Can we ensure that they are ALWAYS given a SECOND opinion by a doctor who has NOT already been <u>prejudiced</u> by things already written into our medical records?

We all need someone who can accurately judge and diagnose a patient for themselves! A written remark can label any one of us WRONGLY forever!

WE ARE WORTH FAR MORE THAN A SIMPLE LABEL? There is always good and bad in us all, but for most of us there should be a search for truth and complete accuracy.

Neil's life MUST have been for a reason. Perhaps he came here to show us that there is always another way at looking at people.

He cried out for help his whole life, but very few people ever listened. PERHAPS IT IS TIME THAT SOMEONE LISTENS TO HIM <u>NOW</u> – MAYBE IT IS <u>STILL</u> NOT TOO LATE!

If we look ONLY for the BAD, then that is what we will always find! <u>I am begging you to look past the label, and see the person</u>. Not to look the other way or take the easy way out

WE ALL DESERVE TO BE TREATED IN THE BEST WAY POSSIBLE no matter who or what we are!

*When we are sick we should receive treatment, it has already **been promised to us**, from the cradle to the grave!*

Did this promise include every one of us? Of course it did – no matter what race, creed, age or gender. Disregarding completely whether we are rich or poor, we are ALL included from new-born babies to the oldest person in the land – we were promised!

Promises should never ever be broken.

Doctors swore on oath to help us all to the very best of their abilities – so why then can they choose NOT to help when they wish to do so?

This loophole in the medical field needs to be closed with IMMEDIATE effect. After all we ALL without one single exception belong to one family, the family of mankind.

Whatever our gifts, or our jobs, we should always carry them out to the best of our abilities.

Doctors should not be there to judge us – they are there to treat us. Everyone should remember that there is a much higher power who will one day judge us all!

ACKNOWLEDGEMENTS

I would like to start my thank-you's by starting at the very beginning of my book because we had this wonderful surgeon Mr Dennison, who tirelessly put so many long hours into helping to put Steve and I back together.

Without him and his wonderful skill and dedication we would not be here today. My injuries were very serious, which is often the case due to the fact that the pillion passenger usually comes off worse. Staff at our local hospital today are amazed that I am still able to walk on my badly injured legs, as it was thought that I would be in a wheelchair by now. They call me the Bionic Woman due to all the metal in my legs.

So far Steve is still managing to work but with pain. We are both utterly in your debt Mr Dennison. *Please accept our heartfelt thanks.*

For all their hard work in defending Neil in court when he was young, *we would like to thank Mr Cunningham, of Cunningham & Turner Solicitors in Blackburn, and so too Alan Reece. Also for her kindness, understanding and unstinting support as well as her hard work in helping us to take on the Education Authority, Val Shaw, who was also in the same practice.*

To Doctor Pauline Souflas who treated Neil for too short a time at her Marsden Street Clinic in Chesterfield, we would like to say, *that you are a truly amazing doctor and human being. We will be forever in your debt. Please accept our sincere thanks.*

To another amazing doctor, Dr Ian Blake, the psychiatrist we became involved with, again for too short a time at our local hospital before Neil ended up in the hands of the other psychiatrists who succeeded him when he left the hospital to be at The Spinney. *We say that you are the nicest, caring, compassionate and honourable doctor that we have ever become involved with. You Sir are exactly what a doctor should be. We will never forget you.*

We became involved with *Making Space* through a support worker called David Penney, *who was a breath of fresh air. He is warm, friendly and extremely hard working. He tried so hard to help us to get all the 'services' for Neil, starting with medical intervention. He, like Tom Lawman, who stepped into his shoes when he retired, worked tirelessly to help us as a family. Unfortunately neither one of them could make a **doctor, doctor,** or stop the 'services' from following the doctor's lead in ignoring and preventing Neil from getting the treatment and 'services' he should so rightly have received.*
   ***Tom, you did make a difference**. You were always there for me and did all I asked of you and more. Throughout my heartbreak I could always rely on you. You tried so hard Tom with the doctors and the nursing staff. None of this mess was in any way because you didn't do enough. Neil loved you to bits as he too could always rely on you. Although you were sometimes frustrated at him, because he tested you at times, you NEVER turned your back on him. Thank you Tom for being a good friend to Neil, Steve and me. We will always think the world of you. You were our rock. God bless you!*

Sue Barnhurst also worked as a support worker *for Making Space,* and *she looked after Neil while he was living in Preston. It was only over a short period, yet this lovely lady made an immediate impression on us as she identified that Neil was suffering from Schizophrenia and she was the first person to say so. Sue you had insight, and were a great help to us. We wish you well and thank you for all that you did for us. Making Space is an organization that helps Schizophrenia sufferers and their families. It's a truly wonderful organization that helps thousands of sufferers and their families countrywide. We thank you from the bottom of our hearts.*

With a smile on my face I would like to thank *the Marsden Resource Centre in Nelson for the way that they looked after my mum, giving her a reason to get up in the mornings making her so happy. This took some pressure off the madness we had to live with. Thanks to Duncan, and especially to you Pat as you popped out of your office to have a chat and a laugh with Mum. I want you to know how much she loved you as the lovely caring person that you are. So too was Caroline who was also close to Mum's heart, she thought that you were very 'special' and often said that you were the kind of girl that she would have liked as a daughter. Thanks then 'sis'.*

Thanks to Yasmin and Diane too. To be honest most of the staff were warm and friendly. Now onto the drivers who picked Mum up in the morning and returned her back to us in the afternoon. *You were cheeky, funny at times like naughty little schoolboys. My mum adored you all. Terry, Graham, Stuart, Bob, especially you Bob, Mum loved you very much. You bring a smile to my face as I write this as I can still hear your banter and Mum laughing. We are so grateful to you all.*

We remember fondly also all of Mum's friends at the centre who are too numerous to mention, and all the staff. I can still feel the warmth of the centre when I pop in occasionally for my milky coffee. You are all 'special', thank you!

To teachers, staff and especially Hazel, the school's nurse at Eden Grove, who Neil monopolized on many occasions, probably because he cared for her so much, and at that time she became a substitute for me, not because he was suffering from any illness as such, but due to the fact that he needed to spend time with her. As we all knew Neil was clumsy, but he would genuinely need her medical help at times.

I would also like to mention the headmaster Mr Ince who is now retired, but then supported us at Eden Grove School in Appleby in Cumbria. Your school made an unbelievable difference to Neil. He was happy for the first time in a school that nurtured him, and tried their utmost to see past certain parts of Neil's behaviour, to see the good and potential in him. Please carry on making a difference to the children and families under your care. Thank you.

Now to our special Educational Welfare Officer Alan Newbold. *Thanks for your belief in Steve and me for knowing what was right for our son. You supported us through a bad time.*

Moving onto Barbara Worrell, where do I start? *Barbara works tirelessly for her flock of A.D.H.D. sufferers and their families. I turned to you for guidance and you guided me. I turned to you to help to educate the psychiatrists at our local hospital, and you did as I asked, sending information on medication and contacts of people who would be more than willing to help the doctor to help Neil and the staff to work with him.* Alas it all fell **Upon Deaf Ears**, as the Clinical Director and Head of Psychiatric care decided that he was GOD, and even admitting that he knew very little about A.D.H.D. threw your kindness and hard work in your face. He then dug his heels in even more, deciding Neil's fate on his own, quite wrongly willing to listen to no one.

You make such a tremendous difference Barbara to people suffering from A.D.H.D., whether they are children, adults or their families as you really do know your stuff. You hit a brick wall with the so-called doctors who were treating Neil, just as we had done. *You tried your best to help us at that soul-destroying time. Had we still had Doctor Blake, who had worked alongside us and you together, then I'm sure that Neil would still be alive.*

It just shows that one person can help to start the ball rolling towards making a difference. It's understanding the condition, and listening to their families as well as the patient, and being in close contact with organizations such as Barbara's, working alongside them all and gaining help from other doctors who work in a field of expertise that other doctors do not. One doctor alone cannot possibly know **everything**, but he should always be open and willing to gain help and advice off other doctors *Barbara you were, and still are wonderful; thank you!*

*Thank you also Ian Newton the Forensic Psychologist, for your insight into Neil's condition, and for your ability to see as we did that Neil's future looked bleak if we were to continue to see doctors who were **blinkered** in their care. You know the pitfalls in Mental Health and saw no hope for Neil too. We thank you for your candour and honesty. You could be one of those special people who could work alongside doctors like Doctor Blake and organizations like Barbara Worrell's to make an enormous difference in the lives of patients like Neil.*

Many thanks to Councillor Frank Clifford for your help and support. *You tried to change things and make the 'powers that be' listen to you and us. It must have been impossible to have done so because you tried so hard, and you couldn't do it, but at least you did try, and we are very grateful to you for that.*

We went to Farnworths (now called Smith Jones) solicitors in Burnley because we know Richard Farnworth one of the partners. *Richard is a very generous, kind man, who has helped us on occasions in the past, and without charge I might add. We turned to him when Neil was involved with the police, and* *he put us in touch with Dermot Woodhead, another partner at the practice, as Richard didn't work in Criminal Law, but Dermot did. As Richard is, Dermot is. They are **both** so kind and generous, as well as clever and articulate men. Dermot, we spent many hours together didn't we? Neil relied on you such a lot and you **never** let him down. You fought his corner with such passion, and I was thoroughly in awe of you. Alas you turned your back on Criminal Law for personal reasons, and like with Doctor Blake, we lost our unstinting support. Thank you Dermot for the special way that you treated Neil. Again, he tested you, but you came through, and always with flying colours. You deserve everything that is good, as you are a lovely man.*

We would also like to thank another partner at Farnworth's who wrote a letter to the hospital on our behalf, and again without charge for doing so. *To Peter Jones, thank you, we are very grateful. Solicitors like these are few and far between. You are all wonderful.*

The Citizens' Advice Bureau helped Neil through a bad patch with his ever increasing debts. We met Kath Riley and *I would like to thank her on Neil's behalf. Thanks Kath.*

There were few people who stood out as much as Doctor Blake, Barbara Worrell, David Penny, Sue Barnhurst and Tom Lawman, but one *of these was a Drug Support Worker who worked for Inwood House in Colne. His name is Mark Talbot. We will be forever in his debt as we are so grateful to him for how he managed Neil's drug habit, and how he took Neil under his wing in order to help him. What can we say Mark other than thank you, and hope that you are still changing people's lives for the better, as you have a gift for this.*

Through your own bad experiences you managed to turn yourself around into someone who can make a real difference to other people, because you know first-hand just how drugs ruin people's lives and that of their families who have their hands tied when trying to help their loved ones out of their situation. You make a difference, and we thank God for people like you.

Neil was involved with another Drugs Team at Westgate in Burnley, and they too helped Neil and encouraged us to help him. These organizations that make such a difference are under-resourced and bulging at the seams, as sadly the drug scene is rife in all our cities, towns and villages. Yet these people try to make a difference, and they often do, even if it is only to ensure that people use drugs safely. Sometimes this is all they **can** do.

The Support Workers who looked after Neil at Burnley were exceptional, as also were the doctors there who treated him and supplied him with his prescriptions. These people may well be swimming against the tide, because they are always limited as to what they can do, **but they do support these needy people when no one else will.** *Although this service was different to that of Inwood House, as they acted in-house and not in the community with a Drug Support Worker like Mark; they still played their part, and we are grateful for their professionalism. I would like to thank Carol Davies in particular for her help and support.*

I would like to thank the Editor Roy Prenton, and *Nelson Leader* for their permission to allow me to use a couple of cuttings previously published by them.

I would also like to thank Nick Nun, the Editor of *The Lancashire Telegraph* for giving me permission to publish some of their earlier work.

Camilla Sutcliffe was involved in Neil's life before I became aware of her. The first time I met her personally was when she came to my home to report on Neil's death in our local newspaper *The Nelson Leader. Unbeknown to me she was one of the reporters who had sat in court on many of the occasions when Neil was brought before the court and she had reported in the local paper. Also I was completely unaware that she was incensed that nothing was ever done to help Neil, as she always thought of Neil as someone who should **never** have been in court, as all along she knew that Neil was 'different' and not the usual person who she found herself writing about.*

When she wrote her piece about Neil upon his death, it was extremely emotional and very well-written, and I was so proud of her. Her warmth and kind words made a difficult time easier for me, and from that day on she has supported the fact that Neil's very distressing story of his life should be told to the world, and said that the book had to be written by me as she knew that I could do it. She and her partner David Pollard, who is also a journalist, will do their utmost to help me reach as many people as I can as they believe in me. Dave now works as a freelance journalist and a Football Commentator for 2BR Radio. Camilla is the Senior Reporter for the Lancashire Telegraph. I believe that you will do your very best for me as I believe in you both too. Thank you.

The death of one's mother is a very distressing time indeed, and then to lose your son three weeks later is unimaginable. I have written about the wonderful Funeral Directors that we had engaged to care for our loved ones, *and I would now like to thank these lovely people for all they did for us. To Jim Sollis, Emma Carey, Martin Edwards (all Funeral Directors), and Phil Talbot who presided over our 'Celebration of Life' service, and has now taken up his own 'flock' in a lovely part of England. To Carl Taylor, a lovely caring young man who cared for Mum with respect and dignity, when he came to take her away. He was the first on the scene after Mum's death, and it speaks volumes to have him give the first impression of*

Hamer's Funeral Home. Jim Riley was one of the lovely drivers who was as meticulous in his endeavours to keep us at ease.

Do you remember Jim Sollis how we had you open all the curtains and doors and play Neil's favourite music? I couldn't bear for the doors to be shut on him as it is such a lovely place to be. I didn't want Neil shut in behind closed doors. You didn't bat an eyelid Jim; you simply pandered to our every need. Thank you for your kindness and understanding and for the care of Mum (Stella Patricia Robinson) and our son Neil Anthony Green.

Thank you Stella who works at *Open Doors* in Colne for your kindness to Neil and for the lovely letter you sent me. *I will keep my promise to you.*

Many thanks to Badger Books in Burnley for your help and guidance.

We are very lucky to have a lot of wonderful and dear friends that are far too numerous to mention individually. Please forgive me for not doing so, but it would be awful to miss anyone out, but you all know who you are.

Thanks Ann for the lovely flowers you sent me on the completion of my book. *It was a lovely gesture.*

To June, Eric and Margaret, friends and neighbours. *Thank you for your continued support.*

Last but definitely NOT least, our family have been everything to us.

For me, my loving husband Stephen, my rock, my life, whom I would gladly give my life for, and who I will love eternally, I am so glad that you came into my life.

To our son Ryan, whom I hope in time will forgive himself because Neil loved him and wanted to **be** him, so he must have been very special to him. *Ryan, live for yourself and for Neil too! We love you very much. Have a happy life!*

I am so grateful to my parents, Stella and Harold Robinson. I am who I am today because of you and I wouldn't change a single thing. Dad you were the best Granddad to Ryan and Neil. Mum despite the blindness that you contracted in your later years, you soldiered on and enjoyed your life. Steve and I greatly admire you. You truly made us both so very proud of you.

Kathleen our wonderful and brave Mum, you were always there for us. *We love you.*

Barry our 'angel'. You could do no more. *You are not just our brother, you are also our friend. Steve and I BOTH love you dearly.*

Pauline my dear sister in Bolton. *Stay well.*

Thanks to my sister Jean in Australia, for being there for us when we needed you.

To Chris – hope you find what you are looking for, and please be happy.

To my nephew and friend Duncan and your generous brother Alan, *thanks for being in our lives.*

To one last person who has entered our lives and enriched it, and is now a much loved member of our family Nicola – Ryan's pretty girlfriend. *We love you to bits, and because this book is about 'our' Neil, I want you to know that he would have loved you too. Lots of love. X*

How on earth do I describe to you someone who has entered my life and heart; never to leave it because she means so much to me? That person is Madeleine Fish, my editor and friend. *I feel so lucky to have met you Madeleine, but having said that, did luck play a part, or was it destiny for us both to meet?*

I know that no one could have expressed my feelings like you, or would have been as passionate about my book and its contents as you are. You are clever, intuitive, and articulate, but more than that you are genuine, giving, compassionate, loving and one of the kindest and most decent human beings who I have ever been fortunate to meet.

There is no one who could have taken my book to the levels that it has become. You've nurtured and believed in me. All along you've said that this book has to be the best it can be, because it means so much to many thousands of people, as they deserve the issues to be aired for them too!

Madeleine, deeply caring, beautiful and wise, passionate, resourceful, and one of those people (like me) who people run to for us to solve their problems, or to just be there for them. You give of your time so willingly, while dealing with your own health needs, as well as those of your husband Jim, who like you is disabled, and at times in great pain. You are like Mother Earth bringing everyone into your fold to care for them in body and mind.

Thank you for making Steve and I so welcome in your home, and allowing us into your heart where we hope we will stay forever.

I love you very much, and will be eternally grateful to you.

X.

CONTENTS

DEDICATION

I dedicate this book to all the thousands
of Attention Deficit Hyperactive Disorder sufferers
whether they are children or adults,
as well as those who suffer with other mental illnesses,
and I send my love to their families.

Lives are being ripped apart,
and too many of our loved ones are being ignored by
the medical profession and other services
that were actually put into place to help us all.

The mentally ill have rights too.
They have a voice
and they deserve to be heard.

**THIS BOOK WAS WRITTEN
IN LOVING MEMORY
OF OUR SON NEIL ANTHONY GREEN**

BORN 16.12.81

DIED 09.06.06

**His life was too short,
his death was too soon,
but his memory will go on
for he cast a very long shadow.**

**Neil's life left us with many questions
and all too few answers.**

**Perhaps it's never too late
for us to ask WHY?**

CHAPTER ONE
The Beginning

We wanted another child to complete our family. We'd been involved in a terrible motorbike accident when we were both in our teens. Madly in love and engaged for two years already, we were really looking forward to our wedding day in September. Childhood sweethearts we were, soul mates – filled with love and lust, living for today as was our right, when tragedy struck!

Steve and I had met a few years earlier at the Youth Club in Nelson. Steve saw me trying to change a record, but thinking that I shouldn't be doing that, he had pulled my hand away to stop me. The DJ had just left the room for a moment so Steve had decided that he would put on another record for him whilst he was away, but I had beat him to it. He was very surprised when the DJ reappeared and kissed me.

Steve was actually quite jealous, as he had wanted to ask me out himself. However I was completely unaware of this at that time, but as he seemed to be a nice lad I tried to set him up on a date with a couple of my mates. Out of politeness, and wanting to be near me and remain in my circle of friends, he stayed friendly with my mates, but they formed no proper relationship as he only had eyes for me.

Later on we went to the Imperial Night Club in Nelson for the 18's and over, which had another youth part for the 12-16 year olds which was known as the Column. At first we were friends, as I already had a boyfriend at that time who was the DJ at the youth club. I used to go to both parts of the club.

However one evening a guy stopped me going into the junior club saying, "Aren't you are too old to go in there now? Perhaps the adult one is more suitable for you?"

I wasn't really too old for the Column, but perhaps I did look older when dressed up in the latest fashion of the time, and wearing my make-up.

The two mates that I had set Steve up with had both told me that even though they quite fancied Steve themselves, he was more like an older brother to them than a boyfriend.

I went with one of my girlfriends to the Column and rang Steve up to try to get them back together. However Steve never had any intention of getting back with her, as unknown to me I was the only one for him.

I was completely unaware of this until this particular evening, for whilst I was sitting at a table with this girlfriend, Steve reached out and held **my** hand underneath the table.

He told me later, "I had to make a move, as you regarded me as just one of the crowd. I needed to let you know how I feel about you."

The first photo taken of Steve and me,
and yes, the monkey is real!

I realized at that moment that I too felt the same way about him. Perhaps we really were made for each other after all. He walked me home. I found out that he was more outgoing when we were on our own. He sang Alvin Stardust songs which were very popular at that time; he made me laugh such a lot as he wore one glove on his hand imitating Alvin. We got along so easily, and it felt just right! He was a little over a year older than I was, so we had so much in common.

I parted company with the DJ as there was now only room for one man in my life, Steve. In fact it has been that way ever since. We got engaged on my 17th birthday and planned to marry in a year or so. We became inseparable and were so very much in love. Then as now, never one day passed by without Steve telling me how much he loved me. In return I love him just as much.

Photo of Steve and me, taken on our engagement

On that bright day in May, Steve hadn't wanted me to go with him to Accrington; he knew that looking around motorbike shops didn't thrill me; plus he also knew that even though I rode pillion, I wasn't too keen on his motorbike. It was **his** thing! He'd even bought it when we'd split up once, so it was a bone of contention with me, but wherever he went, the bike went and so did I.

'I'll be here long after that bike has gone,' I told myself.

****

He relented, we'd only gone about eight miles when the car came out of the power station and took my knee straight off. The driver didn't even see us. *'Think once, think twice, think bike,'* was the slogan at that time in 1977. It's a shame that man **didn't** think!

Steve was knocked off the bike, but somehow I'd stayed on the machine, then I remember being thrown in the air and bouncing on the road. Steve was screaming; his leg was twisted up his back, but he was a long way away from me. I wanted to reach out to him. There was a row of terraced houses and a man was hiding beside the wall of one of them.

I shouted over to him, "Come and get my helmet off me," I felt stifled. "Please," I pleaded, but he didn't come.

I know it's the **wrong** thing to do, but someone did take my helmet off. It was one of the people in the crowd around me.

"Please someone cover my leg," I begged. It was hanging off from the knee.

Someone covered it with a large white handkerchief. Steve was still screaming, but I couldn't see him. I thought, 'Where do they all come from these people, staring and gasping. I wish they'd leave me alone.'

It felt like forever before the ambulance came. I looked down at my hand, catching sight of my engagement ring. It was all twisted, but thankfully the diamond was still in it. "Where's my shoe? I've ruined my new coat," I said aloud. It was burgundy cord, with a big fur-trimmed hood. I loved that coat!

The crowd dispersed and I could see Steve now. I watched as they gave him something to ease his pain, so that they could move his leg from behind his back. They put us both on stretchers with things on our legs like armbands.

'Did I feel pain? I must have, mustn't I?'

Steve was unconscious, but I told the ambulance men who we were and where we lived. Steve's mum would be at work and his dad, but I didn't have a phone.

"My mum will be so mad that we'd be late for tea. Who's going to tell her that we'd be late for tea?" I whispered.

Endless thoughts circled my brain. 'The nurses don't half move fast around you. They seem to have lots of pairs of hands, touching, cutting clothes off, hanging drips up, checking and yet more checking. I'm completely at their mercy because I can't move.'

"How's Steve?" I managed to ask.

"He's here love; we're looking after him," a voice replied.

****

We were in hospital for many weeks as we both had serious leg injuries. I was black from the neck down and had no skin on my arm and hand, but that leg of mine was under a pot. This bothered me a lot.

'What is really bothering me?' I questioned myself. 'I already believed that I was going to lose my leg. I was so glad that my engagement ring was now tucked up securely in the hospital safe.' That thought really comforted me. I drifted in and out of consciousness, my thoughts alternately racing then resting completely.

I was wrong! I didn't lose my leg.

We were lucky Steve and I. The nurses were brilliant; they delivered love letters back and forth between us. Soon Steve was pushing himself to get to my ward to come and see me. He got told off more than once, but no one could stop him. We were just so much in love. With matching pot legs from hip to toe, what a sight we were!

Steve was so brave, so clever on his crutches, whilst I felt faint with every single footstep. I couldn't go home until I could walk around the ward. I say around, because the ward was in a circle; the beds were placed around the inner and outer circles. It took a while longer for me to master my crutches, but finally I did, so I was allowed home.

Mum and Dad brought my double bed downstairs. Luckily we did have a downstairs loo, but it would be a while before I could manage to go out into the backyard to use that convenience. A surprise was waiting for me when I got home; my mum was so pleased with herself, as she had managed to get a pot bed pan from a lady down the street.

It was so embarrassing at first, but Mum was so good about it that she never made me feel awkward. It made me even more determined to master the stairs and, as the weather was improving I was able to get into the backyard. It's funny how the use of a toilet can make you feel so happy, but after months of using bed pans I thanked God.

Steve visited, at first with his dad bringing him, as they lived about three miles away from us. It was a trial for Steve to manage to get into the pick-up his dad used for his business as a builder. Once inside the vehicle, he had to sit sideways on the seat with his pot leg in whatever position he could muster.

Steve and me sporting our crutches after our accident

I will never forget his dad's face when my mum pulled back the

44

bedclothes and told Steve to pop into the bed next to me.

Steve's dad went home and told Kath, Steve's mum. "You'll never guess what Kathleen, she told our lad to get into bed with her daughter," Ernest told his wife.

My mum was so innocent though. She hadn't mean 'owt' by it, as indeed it just would never have even crossed her mind that she was doing anything untoward; it was quite funny really.

So there we were one afternoon after I'd asked Mum to go down town to get me an L.P. when I wanted to make love. It was difficult with our two pot legs, but as they say, 'Where there's a will, there's a way.' That day we conceived our son Ryan.

It didn't take Steve long to be able to get to my house under his own steam. It was up several long steep hills that he'd to climb with his pot leg and crutches, but he'd also walk his Alsation dog Count with him too. Yes, I certainly knew he loved me dearly.

****

Steve, with his Alsation dog, Count

To this day, I don't know how, but we grew even closer because of that terrible accident we had and the pain we suffered together.

I used a knitting needle to get inside the pot to scratch the itch; I couldn't wait to get the thing off.

Mum came with me to the hospital. She tried to reassure me, but failed miserably. "Don't worry Suey, it won't be as bad as you think it is."

Of course I was petrified, just as anyone would be to see what was under that pot. It had to be awful. I'd no knee cap, so Dr Dennison had made me a new knee joint out of metal, pins, bolts and wires. He'd plated down my leg and used a pivot on my ankle with yet more wires and pins. I was dreading it.

At least my engagement ring had arrived back from Preston's of Bolton, where we had lovingly chosen it together. They had restored it back to its former glory absolutely free of charge.

'Aren't some people kind?' I thought, looking down at the solitaire diamond with the cut outs on either side, feeling so happy to have it back on my finger where it belonged.

Suddenly Mum actually wet herself, and started to fall.

"It's the shock," the nurse explained to me, as she caught her before she landed on the floor.

It certainly took my mind off my leg, 'Well done Mum,' I thought.

Steve had *his* pot off too, but he had to have another one put on. Even when he did have his pot off, he had to wear a calliper on his leg. It was an awful looking thing and he hated it. It rubbed his groin, but he had to put up with it for a long time. If any of you have to wear one you will know how bad it was, you have to have your leg stuck out virtually the whole time. On buses this was always the worst. It stuck out into the aisle and, with his pants covering it up people thought he was ignorant, or trying to purposely trip them up. He certainly got some very funny looks.

Of course I had to learn to walk again without the reassurance of the pot to stop me injuring my leg further. It was all in my head I know; I'd simply lost my confidence. I'd also lost a lot of weight and my periods had stopped. I was on some very strong painkillers, so the doctor had told me not to worry. We had been going to be married in the September, but of course that wasn't possible now.

46

We both had to suffer physiotherapy. I must admit though I did all that I was told to do, even making my own sandbag weight to lift on my ankle, and a blackboard like they had at physio, with markers on to see how far I could bend my leg. Yes I was feeling proud of myself. I'm still proud of Steve; he amazes me so much with his courage.

Steve has a brother called Barry. When Steve and I used to go to his house Barry never spoke to me. I soon became rather wary of him as I am a rather talkative person, and I did try, but Barry just would **not** respond to me at all. However he and Steve always got on well.

****

It wasn't really warm going to Steve's that day, but somehow I felt really faint. I went into the bus station toilets to take off my jumper. I had my coat on and I felt really sick. I caught the bus to Steve's house. It was really odd thinking back that I didn't realize that I was pregnant. I guess with having the accident and sustaining such horrible injuries, being on strong medication and by the way also on the pill, it didn't even cross my mind. I had been on the pill since I was fifteen years old without any problems at all, for as an added bonus, the pills seemed to regulate my heavy periods.

My doctor said, "Don't you worry about your periods stopping, this will just be due to the accident. Perhaps it might be wise at present for you to take a break from the pill. I think it would be a very good idea."

So Steve and I went to the family planning clinic to see about me getting fitted with a coil. What a way this was to find out that I was pregnant.

The nurse examined me. She calmly stated, "I think we are a bit late love." To make sure though, she did a pregnancy test, but really she could already tell, despite the fact that I'd lost weight and was very slim, my stomach was as flat as ever.

You could say though that we were both in shock. I had to go to the hospital for a scan a couple of days later. I'd been with Steve for four years by this time; we were very much in love, he adored me, and was always telling me he loved me; in fact he still does.

I don't know what was wrong with me then, maybe the fact that I had friends who 'had' to get married. I just didn't want to be one of them; although we were engaged, it hit me really hard. I remember asking Steve to just live with me.

He replied, "If you don't want to marry me, I won't live with you. It's all or nothing for me."

We worked through it.

I had the scan which showed that I was already seven months pregnant. Obviously the scan showed a rather big baby, or so it appeared to me. I couldn't get over being so 'far gone'. I just couldn't stop looking at the picture on the way home on the bus.

******

We married in December and it was so beautiful. Steve had to marry me with his calliper still on, whilst I hobbled a bit. We couldn't kneel down, so we had two chairs placed there for us to sit on. However when Steve said his vows to me we stood up and he stared so lovingly into my eyes, that I the coward that I am, couldn't look at him, except to take a secretive glance here and there.

Steve and me during our Wedding Ceremony

I looked out of the church windows. I would have cried and ruined my make-up which had taken me all of fifteen minutes to apply, with dressing myself. I had my three lovely sisters as bridesmaids and I helped them to get ready, but I couldn't have

48

looked or felt more beautiful, because I was so happy.

Steve and me on our Wedding Day

Deep in thought.

Our son Ryan was born on 14th February 1978 by Caesarean section. He wasn't just born on St. Valentine's Day though; he was truly a love child in every way possible.

I had problems near the end of my pregnancy, probably due to the internal injuries sustained in the accident, so the doctor's didn't want me to risk a natural birth. Steve felt cheated at this, as he was so looking forward to being with me at the birth of our baby, which is one of the reasons we wanted another child, (but I'm jumping the gun here a bit).

I remember coming out of the theatre and hearing the nurse telling Steve he had a son.

Steve asked her, "But how's my wife?"

He wouldn't go to see Ryan until he'd made sure that I was alright. I will never forget that, or how, with tears welling up in his eyes, he sat with me holding my hand. Then I was out cold for nearly two days.

Ryan was lovely. I'm not normally a baby person, one of those females who stare into prams and say, "Oh! What a beautiful baby," especially so when they look like wrinkly old men. Also I'm not saying this about Ryan because he is mine, but he really was a beautiful baby. He was weeks overdue and quite scaly, but when he was bathed he was rosy, 8lb 8oz, with lovely blond hair, and he was absolutely gorgeous.

I'd leave my room, but when I returned Ryan was gone. The nurses would pinch him to demonstrate to the other mothers how to bathe their babies and change their nappies. It was because he was so good and, being a big baby, he was easier to handle, so I got used to him disappearing.

There was this young girl on the ward who had given birth on the same day as her cousin. She said that some people from the press were coming to talk to her and take her photo. We were laughing about it.

I said, "I could do one better than that."

She dared me to ring the local paper. Steve and I had already been in the paper with the headline:

'CRASH COUPLE FINALLY MARRY!'

So I thought, 'What the heck, they might as well do a follow up.' This time the headline read:

'SUSAN HAS MIRACLE BABY!'

They ran the story complete with the picture shown below:-

Steve and me with our new-born son Ryan

This was how the hospital staff thought about it, for I had given birth after sustaining terrible injuries, being on strong medication and on the pill. Ryan was indeed a miracle baby, and a survivor.

****

I never touched a dirty nappy. Not many mothers can say that; it's possible that I actually did, but certainly not many if any at all, because Steve wouldn't let me if he could possibly stop me. He washed them with pride then pegged them out on the washing line across the back street. We were living with my mum and dad, (Stella and Harold) in a two bedroom terraced house. It would be a while before we could afford a place of our own. We'd been engaged for two years before we got married, so we'd bought a unit for the living room, a music centre, bedroom furniture and a double bed. We got pleasure in filling our 'bottom drawer' with bits and pieces, saving up and hardly going out because we still needed such a lot.

It wasn't ideal living with mum and dad, and although they had promised not to interfere, inevitably they did.

Steve's leg began to cause him some concern, even though he'd struggled to persevere with the calliper, the bone in his leg was not knitting together as it should have done, so he had to have an operation to take a bone out of his hip to put into his leg.

I watched him walk down the street with the case in his hand and I cried. We had been together 24 hours a day, 7 days a week. I felt abandoned, and also so sorry that my man was dealing with this all on his own. I was still coping myself, but with Ryan to look after, Steve wouldn't allow me to go with him. I felt so lost!

****

Ryan developed asthma as a baby, so he was constantly in and out of hospital. It was also a struggle to get Ryan to hold his solids down; he would be sick by the time I had managed to feed him, so it was never long before he was due for his next meal, which meant that I had to go through all the same process again. We tried all the food brands available; we even pureed our *own* food, but we only found one that did the trick. It was in a box which looked very unexciting, rather like gruel to me, but Ryan liked it, but more importantly, he managed to keep it down as it had no lumps in it at all.

On one of the occasions when Ryan was in hospital I noticed that the nurses were struggling to feed him. It was a good job that I had visited him at meal time and saw what was going on, because the nurse that I spoke to was of the opinion that he'd eat when he was hungry. At this time Ryan would only eat the food **we'd** been giving him as he was used to it; he knew that it wouldn't make him sick. I tried to reason with the staff, but they wouldn't listen to me.

"He should be on solids," they said, and according to them, that was that!

At only twenty years of age they thought that they knew more than I did, but I was already more like twenty going on thirty, as I had three older sisters, so I was having none of it.

I visited Ryan at meal times and fed him myself, bringing my own food for him to eat. It all rectified itself when Ryan got a little older, but we didn't really find out why it happened. It was suggested that it was perhaps a weakened muscle or something like that, but it made no odds to Ryan, he soon came on a treat.

My Mum Stella, with me and baby Ryan

We moved into our semi when Ryan was about fourteen months old. I had Katie my beloved wire-haired terrier dog; she was another love of our lives. We had little in the way of furniture. My sister Pauline kindly gave us her suite. She really didn't need a new one herself, but she had bought one just so that she could give us her old one, which was especially nice of her.

My mum and dad bought us a cooker and a fridge and paid for them weekly for us. We were due to get some compensation from our accident, so in due course we managed to pay them back. We had already bought an automatic washing machine because Mum had a twin-tub. I was mortified when I tried to use it for Ryan's nappies, as it was quite a pain and took ages to use, so we got the washer on 'terms' too. Mum was sorry to see me take it away, but it wasn't long after that before she bought an automatic washer of her own.

Steve's mum and dad (Kathleen and Ernest) had bought us a dryer for our wedding present. Steve's dad was a builder as I mentioned earlier, and he had gone to the Council tip where he saw a carpet that didn't look too bad. He cleaned it and we really were grateful for it. I made all the curtains. Life was a struggle, but we managed. We lived more like servants than gentry, jam butties or beans on toast, but I was a good cook, so when we did get a joint it was like a wonderful feast.

Steve's mum was a love, she'd come around with a chicken, eggs, bacon, butter and other treats on a regular basis. She was always going down town and buying baby clothes. They weren't well off themselves really, but compared to *my* parents they seemed to be.

We never had a car or a phone and only had a black and white T.V. when I lived at home. We had the odd holiday, but my in-laws had a caravan, so when Steve and I were courting they would take it to Morecambe and leave it for us for the weekend, even providing all our food. It was lovely; it also made it inevitable that we could live together after coping in that shoe-box. It was small, very cosy and we loved it; truly we did!

We never had much money when our Ryan was born as neither Steve nor I were able to work for years following our accident.

Mum and Dad bought us a fire surround and an electric fire. This made the room look more homely now; they also bought us a shag-pile living room carpet and an Axminster carpet for the hall, stairs and landing. I was house-proud, so loved making our house into a home with all the little extra knick-knacks we bought too. Steve eventually managed to go back to work, working on the night shift in the mill as a weaver.

My beloved Katie became very ill. Sadly Steve took her to the vets to be put to sleep; he assured me that she died peacefully and he stayed with her until the end. I couldn't go. What a coward I was! I owed her that, she was a wonderful dog and I loved her very much. She was twelve years old.

****

Steve and me pictured with Katie

Ryan was a wonderful child, we didn't have much money, but we were very rich in love. We shared our love with our baby taking him everywhere with us. My mum had bought us a lovely second-hand coach-built, silver cross pram. We proudly pushed Ryan in his pram all round Nelson visiting the parks, teaching and playing with him as much as we possibly could.

We bought a cover for the pram, with big white balls all over it. We'd lovingly tuck Ryan in carefully then we were off. Next we bought a canopy with a fringe on it, which was square and covered the top of the pram. Altogether it looked smashing. The pram would bounce and rock and so would Ryan. We walked everywhere, but mostly to Barrowford Park, usually after calling at Kathleen's first to let her see her lovely grandson.

Steve, holding Ryan in front of his pram.

Once at the park, we'd lay out a rug that we always took with us onto the grass. Steve would lie down, and within minutes Ryan would be crawling all over him as soon as I got him out of the pram. We never did need very much to make us content, as we were always happy just by being together.

We would go to Asda and fill the tray fixed underneath the pram with foodstuff, and hang any extra bags onto the pram. We didn't have a car then, and in those days there weren't any shops on our doorstep. Besides we weren't able to afford corner shop prices as we had to watch our pennies very carefully, so Asda's special offers were very much appreciated.

Earlier I said that when Ryan was born he was such a lovely baby, and you might have thought that every mother would think the same thing about her own child. However Ryan was not only a good baby, he was really bonny. One day we entered him into *'The Bonny Baby Competition'* at Barrowford Show. He won it and received a big red rosette.

Apart from his asthma Ryan was a very happy child. Both sets of grandparents loved and spoiled him just as much as we did.

One day I decided to take Ryan with me and a friend and neighbour to go to look at some puppies. I had no intentions of getting another dog after losing my beloved Katie. However it was a big mistake to take Ryan with us, for as soon as he saw the puppies looking so very sweet together in their wooden box, he picked one up. She had just come up to him and it was sort of love at first sight for them both.

Ryan looked at me with his big eyes wide-open with a pleading kind of look on his face. Naturally I fell for it hook, line and sinker thinking 'Boy would I be in for it with Steve.' But as Steve's full of hot air and as bad as me really, the Afghan puppy simply became a lovely new addition to our family. We called her Purdy, and she and Ryan were almost inseparable as they grew up together.

We enjoyed having Ryan so much, that now we wanted to have another baby, a little brother or sister for him, we didn't mind which, as we didn't want Ryan to be an only child. I so much wanted to have a baby naturally this time just to complete our family.

Ryan with Purdy our puppy.

CHAPTER TWO
Neil

It took a while, and it's not as if we weren't at it like rabbits. We didn't need any excuse at all for our sex life was pretty damn good. I rang my doctors for the result of the pregnancy test and cried with joy when we were told that I was pregnant. We were both literally jumping for joy at the news.

Ryan was now three years old, so there would be a gap of nearly four years by the time our second child was born. We would have liked them closer together, but that wasn't to be.

Steve did love me being pregnant. This time he would have longer to relish that fact as we both knew early on. He still thinks pregnant woman are the most beautiful. Me! Well I hated being pregnant and I didn't bloom at all. I felt fat, ugly and my hair and skin were horrid. I went off sex, whilst Steve was quite the opposite. Well you can't have everything, but I was excited to be having our much wanted second child.

I went to full term and had Neil on Kath's birthday, 16th December. She was so thrilled that her grandson Neil and she now shared a birthday. Steve was with me throughout.

We had arrived at Fernlea General Hospital with a police escort. Steve took me to the hospital when labour started; I guess he panicked a bit for he drove over the speed limit. We turned onto the long avenue where the hospital is situated when Steve noticed the police car with the flashing lights following us. He wasn't going to stop no matter what; he simply put his indicator on to turn right which kept the police car behind us. We turned into the hospital and so did the police, but when they saw me getting out of the car at A&E obviously very pregnant they left us to it.

The birth didn't take long; in fact by the time I had got into the swing of gas and air I'd had him. Steve's eyes were popping out of his head as he was watching me so intently. The midwife was such a

60

spoilsport though, as she unscrewed the mask from the gas and air. By the time I knew what relief it gave me from the pain, I didn't really need it anymore, but I didn't want to give it up just yet. Doctors and midwives had tried to put pressure on me to have another Caesarian, but I flatly refused as both Steve and I wanted a normal delivery, and this time I wanted Steve at the birth.

The midwife asked him, "Would you like to help deliver your child?"

He was there like a shot. He cut the cord. He was so in awe of everything; it was such a joy to see him as he was calm which really helped me. I was so happy that he was there. The midwife was wonderful, but they are all so helpful. I wasn't pleased about one thing though; Steve got the tomato soup and the toast. He said he was exhausted and ravenous to boot. **I ask you?**

I was in hospital for a couple of days. I wanted to get home to my son Ryan to show him his new baby brother, and to make sure that our new Afghan hound puppy Purdy still remembered me.

Steve, with his two sons Ryan and Neil

61

Steve had brought the crib down from our bedroom and placed it in the corner of the living room ready for our new arrival. Steve was still spinning and, when he thought about the delivery he'd cry, as he was so touched. It did bring us together even more if that was possible, after having seen me in such pain. It was a means to a wonderful end though.

Ryan took to his brother so well. He was extremely helpful to me as he would pass me the powder, Neil's bottle or whatever else I needed. He was fascinated by Neil and he watched him very closely. He loved to see him getting bathed. All he wanted to do was cuddle and hold him. If I left the room for a moment, when I returned Ryan would always be cradling Neil on his knee. He was absolutely thrilled to have a new baby brother. He would proudly walk alongside me helping to push the pram. The four of us were so happy together and our family felt so very complete.

We had a lot of visitors, as you do. Neil was such a good baby and he'd sleep the whole night. He weighed 9lb exactly, and again he was a bonny baby. His hair was a little darker than Ryan's was, but then Ryan's hair was nearly white it was so fair. I struggled to tell them apart as babies when we were showing photos, in spite of their hair being slightly different colours, as otherwise they were so alike.

Ryan proudly holding his baby brother Neil

62

You can't help but compare your children, as in one is a good baby or another one cries a lot. One will walk faster, talk sooner and so on, you notice things in your children and mull over and discuss their differences.

Neil couldn't be still. He had a baby bouncer and he loved it; he'd spring up and down laughing all the time. He'd enjoy bouncing and giggle excitedly all the way across the room. He sat up early. He seemed so strong and very aware of what was going on around him. He was just so wide eyed and happy, and he and Ryan would laugh and play together.

My dad was devoted to Neil just as he was with Ryan. He'd always wanted boys, but had had to be content with four girls. However everything did always seem a little more with Neil; more full throttle and definitely more rough and tumble.

Ryan had been a sickly child, which meant that you couldn't throw him up into the air without him getting breathless and coughing or being sick. He was quieter, more thoughtful, and very different to Neil. They were simply chalk and cheese, but little did we know anything at all back then.

I can remember taking Neil out in his pram. It was the same coach-built Silver Cross one that Mum had bought us second-hand when we had Ryan. It was a real joy to push and it still looked great! We left Neil in the pram in the front room at Mum and Dad's as he was fast asleep. We had his reins on him but they didn't save him, for he rocked himself so much, that he fell out of the pram and banged his head on the tiled hearth. He had a bump the size of an egg on his forehead, he was only a few months old, but this was the start of our hospital visits with Neil.

****

For part of the day Ryan would be at nursery, but when I went with Neil in the pram to pick Ryan up he would always be so pleased to be reunited with his little brother. We would all walk home together and Ryan would happily chat away to both Neil and me telling us all about his time at nursery. He would show his paintings or anything he had made proudly to me and Neil. They were so lovely and cheerful together as Ryan was so thoughtful and always included Neil, wanting him to join in and share his life, and enjoy everything with him.

Neil wasn't really any trouble at all, and he hardly ever cried. It was the same with the baby walker; he'd go hell for leather and tip that up, resulting in yet more bruises, lumps and bumps. This was bad enough, but when Neil started to walk, my God I not only had to have eyes in the back of my head but at every single angle. He walked at nine months; he simply got up and walked all on his own one day. Ryan had crawled and shuffled along on his bottom for a while, but Neil didn't bother with either one of these stages; he simply stood up and walked.

****

At this time Neil, as he was very strong even at so young an age, began to scare Ryan a little. Ryan always soon got out of breath due to his asthma, so he had to be a little more careful. He was a gentle soul really, whereas Neil was always full on and NEVER aware of any dangers at all. He would throw all his toys around, usually at Ryan, whereas Ryan would never throw anything back. The reasons for this were that Ryan knew his brother was nearly four years younger than him, and secondly Ryan did not like rough and tumble play at all, as it always made him so breathless and therefore feel the need to sit down and rest for a while afterwards.

This was perhaps the beginning of Ryan starting to move slightly away from Neil. Although Ryan always loved his brother to bits, he probably had a natural kind of instinct that he needed to protect himself from being hurt. It didn't matter how many times we all told Neil to calm down a little, or to play more carefully, or stop throwing things, Neil never seemed to either hear or understand us.

We would take things off him when he threw them, but he would still play rough with something else. We would then remove the second item and so on, but Neil would simply choose another toy; on and on this would continue no matter what was confiscated from him. He did not seem to understand cause and effect, not just as a child, but through into adulthood also.

Neil would never really mean to hurt Ryan or anyone at all, but inevitably he did. Play always started slowly and calmly, but Neil would always take it up to new levels. He always got too excited, too worked up; and he loved to run and move fast. He always tried to do everything at full speed, which occasionally turned out to be dangerous, so he always needed to be carefully watched; after all he was still so very young. He moved quickly on from one plaything to another, as he soon got fed up with that toy, so he'd reach out and grab things out of Ryan's hands. If he saw Ryan with anything, Neil sort of wanted to play either with Ryan's toys or whatever else Ryan had, no matter how many other things there were around.

But Ryan always looked after his toys so carefully, whilst Neil could be quite destructive. Believe me when I say that they **both** had lots of toys. Ryan would share a lot of the time, but not Neil. He always grabbed things off his brother.

Sadly the closeness that the brothers had to begin with when Neil was very small was now beginning to break up and change direction. Ryan was not able to keep up with Neil for very long at all as he was a rather poorly child at that time. The two brothers were somewhat opposite in strength, so Ryan always seemed to come off worst despite the fact that he was a few years older. Perhaps I should say that when Neil got hurt he simply laughed it off, as knocks and bangs never seemed to faze him at all.

Neil could **not** be tired out; he could keep playing furiously all day long. He had such tremendous stamina, whereas Ryan needed to pace himself more, play for a while then rest a little. Neil could never understand why Ryan didn't play with him **all** the time; he did regard him as his pal and playmate, and he always demanded that his brother join him in his very fearless rough and tumble games. So whenever Ryan tried to rest, Neil would be trying to pull him off the chair and back onto the floor to play with him all over again.

If ever Neil did get hurt though, Ryan would always be the first one there comforting him, or helping him up whenever he fell down, but as soon as he knew that his brother was fine, Ryan would move away and play on his own.

****

Ryan loved going to school, as this was one place where he could escape to, relax a little, and simply be himself, playing and learning at his own speed.

The health visitor was still visiting us. "What a live wire he is," she'd say about Neil.

He was that alright. I was so glad that he would at least sleep soundly at night. I could cope during the day, but if Neil hadn't slept at night I would have been exhausted. He was on the go all day which took up such a lot of my time and energy just to keep him amused all the time. We played in the sink a lot as he just adored water. I was always inventing new games to occupy Neil's time, as he couldn't ever be still for a minute.

****

A few years passed by but Neil still remained forever on the go. At least now though we had a garden for him to run off steam in. Poor Purdy our Affy dog, he chased her everywhere. Thankfully she was so wonderfully patient with him. I came into the kitchen one day after going to the loo. It was so difficult leaving Neil even for one single minute on his own as he was extremely active. There was no stopping him; he simply moved quickly on from one thing to the next as he got bored easily and lacked concentration.

I was horrified at what I saw. Neil had tipped a full bottle of tomato ketchup over the dog, but worse still he had a carving knife in his hand. I managed to get the knife from him easily enough, but this incident really frightened me. My heart raced so fast that I thought I was going to have a heart attack.

After that I watched him all the time as he was just too active to be left alone for a second. He did not want me out of his sight anyway, and it got to the stage where he was even following me to the toilet; he wanted me near him and he started becoming so clingy.

****

By now Ryan was at junior school; he had found it very hard coping with Neil. Neil would break all of Ryan's toys. He was years younger than Ryan, but somehow he always had the upper hand. Looking back we did keep pushing Ryan into playing with Neil, as we just wanted them to be brothers and pals, be company and playmates for one another. Ryan didn't like Neil's rough ways, he loved him and he'd cry for him if he hurt himself, but he simply couldn't get on with him. Neil was simply too overpowering for a quiet boy like Ryan. I think that Ryan was actually quite relieved to go to school to get away from his sibling all day.

****

Neil was taking a long time to talk, he was four years old and he was stammering. He seemed to rush his words out, saying things like, "Mummy, mummy, mummy, can I, can I, can I, please mummy, please mummy." It was all very hurried, so we took him to speech therapy.

My mum and dad tried to help, but they were getting on in age now, so found Neil increasingly hard to manage, although Dad would keep him amused by giving him planks of wood, a hammer and nails out in the backyard. He put a chest of drawers out there with old tools in it for Neil. These really suited Neil as he loved them and played happily with everything for a short while on his own. He could concentrate well on things he truly enjoyed.

It really amused my dad to watch him, "A proper lad," he used to say proudly.

My Mum and Dad, Stella and Harold

I found myself relying on Mum and Dad a lot to give me a break from Neil. Ryan was no trouble to them, as he'd just keep his head down hoping Neil didn't try to involve him.

However Neil inevitably did. He wouldn't play by himself for very long; he didn't seem to be able to. When Dad had had enough, Neil soon came looking for someone else to help amuse him, and this person was usually Ryan.

When Ryan was about seven years old he was playing at the front

67

of the house one day. A window cleaner came to one of our next door neighbour's houses to collect his money.

Being a helpful and very thoughtful lad Ryan approached the man telling him, "Mister, they've gone out."

"Thanks lad," the man replied, patting Ryan on his head.

Sadly Purdy our dog (should that be Ryan's dog) misunderstand the man's gesture to his young master. She rushed at the man and at her head level she bit him. Unfortunately this turned out to be the man's groin area.

The same evening the window cleaner came to our door, "I'm afraid that I had to go to hospital for treatment from the dog bite. I know that the dog did not mean anything and was only trying to defend the boy, but the police will be coming round later to see you. I'm sorry about this," he apologized.

I felt very sorry for the man and asked him in an innocent manner, "Oh where did Purdy bite you, can I see your injury?"

The man turned bright red and said, "I'm afraid I cannot show you as I am wearing a truss after my visit to the hospital."

I felt so embarrassed for both the man and myself.

The man had been lovely and took the blame. "It was my fault, I should not have patted the boy's head."

The following day there was a knock on the door. I answered to find our officer on the beat who I knew quite well.

He was laughing as he could not get over being sent to our house regarding my daft and very soft 'Affy' who he knew personally was normally as gentle as a lamb.

He greeted me, "That daft powder puff of yours has bitten someone then?"

Needless to say it didn't go any further, probably due to the poor man's kindness.

****

It was hard for Ryan with Neil as he got older, so Steve would take Ryan on bike rides or to the baths, so that they could spend quality time together as father and son, getting them both away from Neil for a little while. We didn't do this very often however because we were a family, and as such we always preferred to do things for the four of us. We were always going away at weekends, packing up sandwiches or travelling out to a pub for lunch, or to the seaside at

Blackpool or Morecambe. Blackpool Zoo was always a firm family favourite. We could simply go to the park and enjoy the playground or a knock about with a ball.

Sometimes we'd allow Ryan to stay at his Gran's. He was never any trouble, but we did not do this often because we did not want Ryan to feel that he was missing out on being with us, but we did like to give him a break at times.

Occasionally Neil went to stay at his other Gran's whilst we went to the caravan for the weekend or a caravan rally. Afterwards Barry would sometimes bring him back to join us after a day or two, depending of course whereabouts we were in the country.

Usually though they would have had a hectic time with Neil and be rather glad to hand him over. They were very good to help us out like this in the first place to give us a break. However we had never had kids to keep them locked up at home, we always liked to do things with our children, like visiting Flamingo Land or Camelot, and as previously mentioned Zoos were always high on all our lists of priority.

Throughout our life together Steve and I always had our love to help us through. We always tried to add a little magic of our own, the little things that really count like me leaving messages in his butty box, or him putting two teddies with their arms placed around each other in bed ready for me to discover when I went to bed and he had left for work on his nightshift.

Sometimes when I came downstairs in a morning and he has gone to bed after finishing his long tiring nightshift, I find that he had taken the trouble to pick up just one of the many photos we have scattered around the hallway, and beside it he would have left me a love note.

Often these were our pick-me-ups after a particularly bad day, but at other times they are simply lovely loving thoughts that helped to boost us both no end.

I leave him 'Thinking of you' messages all the time, and I keep every single one of his little love notes.

At one time I would come downstairs in the morning to find buckets of flowers from Asda all over the kitchen.

Some of them might have knock down prices still on them, but even these marked down bunches still have loads of life left in them. This little loving thought meant so much more to me than any expensive bouquet of very expensive roses from a rich admirer could ever have meant.

Love is our best blessing, and with it Steve and I have always been rich beyond money, always in abundance, for even today these words of love and little tokens continue to brighten each other's lives. I feel sure that they always will do so.

Neil and a couple of pals at Nursery

We decided to put Neil into the same nursery school as Ryan had attended. We hoped that playing with his peers would be good for him. I'd eventually get Neil ready in his buggy and push it from home up the steep hill, just as I used to a few years earlier with Ryan. I'd take Ryan to school on the way, he really loved it, and it gave him a break from Neil by going there.

Mrs Camdon still ran the nursery the same as she had done when Ryan had been attending there. At first Neil cried and held on to me. I wondered how they would cope with him. He'd had my attention all day playing, and had always been given the one to one attention he craved for.

I wondered, 'Would they be able to give him as much attention at nursery as I had, when they had all the other children to look after? I also worried, would they be able to cope with him?'

I didn't need to wonder for long. They soon found it hard to manage Neil as he was all over the place. He wouldn't sit still for story time. He put sand into the water and water into the sand. He could open the windows and even the door. He would snatch toys off the other kids, then when it was playtime he was overpowering with the bikes and other toys.

Young children sometimes bite, but in those days to show them how wrong this was, Mrs Camden would bite them back. (This was obviously long before the changes came in to practice which meant that children **couldn't** be physically punished). Even though personally Mrs Camden's way of dealing with children who bit others wasn't one that **I** would ever have used it was used in practice by many teachers in those days.

I picked Neil up one day after she had bitten him on his arm. She explained to me that it was Neil's fault as he had bitten another child. Sadly, this was the start of things to come!

After that incident I felt that she was looking down on me and blaming **me** for Neil's behaviour. I would go to pick him up and the staff would hardly speak to me. The other mothers were the same; they'd chat together, but completely ignore me.

I was in my twenties and whilst it did hurt me, I could hold my own. When Neil came running to me with a picture he had painted, all excited, laughing, loving me, that's all I wanted. He was always so sweet and loving and forever giving me cuddles and kisses. They wanted me to doubt myself, to make me think that I was a rubbish mother. I knew that I wasn't!

Steve worked nights. He still does now. He always did his fair share of looking after Neil when he got up in the afternoons. He was shorter tempered than me, but he did a good job all the same. I felt different with Neil, he was too clingy, much more so than normal, but I seemed to know what he would do next, so I always tried to be one step ahead of him; well at least for most of the time, and I took it more and more upon myself to shoulder the burden of him so to speak.

I did ask my doctor about Neil. I told him my worries explaining that I thought that he had a mental illness. I knew even then that there was something wrong with Neil, *something serious*, but the doctors said that he was just hyperactive.

I feel now that I should have persisted more, and maybe insisted that they helped me more. I didn't though, I simply continued struggling on; but it soon became a case that I was the only one who understood Neil and <u>could</u> cope with him. **Maybe then I coped too well**. I should have had a nervous breakdown, but having said that, back then they didn't know of my son's illness or how to treat it or care for it, so I had to carry on doing the best that I could looking for whatever help we could get from our immediate family.

For Neil though, the nursery didn't last long!

****

We had holidays, none of which we would have managed if we didn't have a caravan. We couldn't possibly have taken Neil to a hotel to inflict his rowdiness onto others. We needed to feel secure that he couldn't wander off. We kept him on a tight rein, but it was never easy. We lost him once in a city centre while we were on holiday. It only took a few seconds for him to disappear. He wouldn't cry for his mum, dad or brother, he'd be off on an adventure.

After that incident none of us would ever take our attention off him for a second.

Steve, Ryan and Neil, watched by Purdy whilst on holiday

Neil had an amusing trick of stripping off all his clothes when we walked near to the beach. Suddenly off came a shoe, a sock, followed by his tee shirt, and before we knew it he'd be almost naked. He did make us laugh on these occasions, and being so young we could keep him under control; well for most of the time.

Poor Ryan though, Neil would take all his toys to bits as well as his own. I wouldn't say he was destructive; he just wanted to see how they were put together. Sometimes he *could* even put them back together, though this was not very often.

He still always needed to see how things worked though. I picked up my ship in a bottle one day and the stopper fell out, he'd

73

obviously been fiddling with it. He was so inquisitive.

Steve always worked on his cars, he was self taught and it ran in the family because both his dad and brother Barry were very good at repairing cars too. Apparently Neil had inherited the same bug, and unusually for Neil he would watch intently, squatting quietly next to Steve, while with the car jacked up and with his dad lying on his back, he'd pass him the tools as already he had learned to recognize which tool was which. I can see him now with his duffle coat on, and his scarf and woolly hat. It was a real joy to see. He could be so dead lovable!

Daddy's little helper
Guess who? – Neil of course!

We had little money in those early days, but at long last the compensation we received for the accident had finally come through. It helped us out with our mortgage and bought us a car, but with Steve and me not working for such a long time, it was soon swallowed up. It wasn't like it is today, the Government wasn't

74

throwing money at us, we only got sickness benefit; no one was there to help us claim anything else. We didn't know if we could get, or were even eligible for anything else, so we struggled for a long time; when the compensation finally arrived we were comfortable. At least we had holidays in the caravan which we made sure that we all enjoyed together.

Ryan on the new car bought with our compensation

My mum used to say to me, "You have too many knick-knacks, you shouldn't have a lot of ornaments and expensive one's too when you've got children."

I didn't agree. I always said, "If I have nice things and my kids are always brought up to respect my things, then I will be able to take them to anyone's house and they won't ever touch other people's stuff." This worked out well for they never did touch things at other folks' homes.

******

If I had listened to my family I wouldn't have married Steve, because my dad found out that Steve's father was very volatile. People talked, so quite naturally my dad was worried that Steve would turn out like his father. Steve's dad did have problems with his health, but these weren't addressed then or now, but I'm getting ahead of myself again.

Needless to say I took no notice, when on the eve of my wedding my sister begged me **not** to marry Steve. I ignored her too.

It wasn't because of Steve I hasten to add, but because I was having a baby.

She told me, "You'll never have anything in your life getting married like this, no career, a lovely home or money. Stay with Mum and Dad, they'll look after you and the baby, then you can have a real life."

How shallow and how stupid she was. I knew my own mind. I loved Steve, he loved me and I trusted him. I knew he'd always work hard to provide for me and our children; he wouldn't cheat on me. There are things in this world far more important than money or material things.

I was about to join the police force before we became serious, and yes probably I would have had a good career, and yes at the time it was what I wanted, but perhaps the accident occurred for a reason. I truly believe that no matter what happens to us in life it's destined for us. We can't stop it!

When I had the near death experience in hospital I knew that we are numbered when we are born. I fought to live and, somewhere in my head I was told that it wasn't my time then. Years later my sister learnt how wrong she was.

Steve's mum and dad thought we were too young, but they didn't have much say either, but I noticed a change in Kathleen the very day we married when she came out into the aisle of the church and gave me some beautiful glass slippers to hold. I looked into her eyes and I knew we'd be alright too, and we were. She has been the most wonderful mother-in-law anyone could have ever wished for, and I love her as I do my own Mum. Kathleen always buys me a card for

Mother's Day because she says that she is grateful that I am the mother of her grandchildren. **Thanks Mum. I really love you. Thanks for your unstinting support, you truly are an amazing woman and I greatly admire you.**

****

It took Steve and me ages to get the wardrobe fitment we'd bought put together in Neil's bedroom. It was one of those flat packs where you unpack it only to find less screws than you should have, then find the holes are drilled in the wrong place and suchlike. It was a wardrobe with shelves down the side. We managed it with a few tantrums here and there. I'm sure that you can imagine the chaos, with Steve needing me to help him, whilst at the same time Neil really needing watching over.

It was always hard to do anything while keeping an eye on Neil, for he saw no danger in anything. I could understand those mothers that when they turn their backs on their kids they'd get at pills, bleach and other dangerous items as it is impossible to watch anyone 100% of the time. Usually though I could watch Neil and be one step ahead of him. It wasn't just me who was intuitive to my child's needs, I'm sure that **most** mothers have some kind of instinctive attitude towards their children. I didn't really realize at the time just how 'different' Neil really was.

I just kept the bleach at the back of the cupboard, pills locked away, fireguards on the fires, guards around the cooker, but I also knew that Neil could get around any obstacle if he wanted to, so he always had to be closely watched. I wouldn't let anyone other than our immediate family look after him. I always felt that no one could look after him quite like I could.

So here we were struggling to keep Neil amused while we put up the wardrobe. We were exhausted by the time we had finished, but relieved we'd achieved this amazing feat. Proudly we put Neil to bed that night. However I walked into his bedroom the next morning to be confronted with total disbelief.

"Neil, what have you done?" I asked my son.

We hadn't heard a thing, so we couldn't believe it. There was the wardrobe, completely taken down with all the screws laid out in a neat little pile, next to another equally neat pile of nails. Then there were all the pieces of wood ranging from the largest first to all the

77

others laid out perfectly in order of size, each one very neatly stacked up. His attention to detail was still perfectly intact. He had quite simply been bored.

We had noticed before that he didn't sleep as well at night as he used to, so we always tried extra hard to tire him out in the daytime. We always bought toys that would stimulate him and ensured that he *didn't* have a T.V. in his bedroom. What if we did let him stay up a bit later? We did try this occasionally, but it made no difference, he just didn't seem to **need** very much sleep. We couldn't be mad at him for the wardrobe incident, or the fact that now all our hard work and efforts were for nothing, as we could both see the funny side.

****

Every Christmas was a joy. I've always loved Christmas and I used to decorate the whole house with a lot of help from Steve. In those days we couldn't afford to spend very much money, but we always adored it just the same. Kathleen and Ernest would get two black bin liners and fill them with toys for the boys. Kath would manage to do this by buying a few gifts for them throughout the year, carefully hiding them away until Christmas.

We would always get both our boys the 'in' thing of that particular year. I can remember ringing around all the toy shops to get them what they wanted, and having to stand in line for ages for particularly popular items. One year we bought them both bikes, which we kept at a friend's house, only bringing them home in the early hours of Christmas morning. We fell over them in the kitchen whilst we were trying our hardest not to make a sound.

We'd pile Ryan's presents on one living room chair and Neil's on the other. We always made sure that we always spent exactly the same on each of our sons; we never had a favourite child, we loved them both absolutely equally.

Steve would video them opening their presents. They always showed great excitement, but they also had their good manners and asked who had bought them what, and they would make sure that they thanked them. My mum and dad always gave us some of their presents on Christmas Eve so that we could lay them out ready for the boys on Christmas morning.

However Dad had a ritual of his own. He always came round to our house at 6.00am on Christmas Day just to see his grandsons opening their presents. He got such sheer joy from watching his grandchildren enjoying opening their gifts. Mum would come around later, but they were both always to be found at our house on Christmas Day. It was such a lovely and exciting day for us all to share and spend together.

My Dad (Harold) with Ryan one Christmas

Later on the boys would be off outside with their main gift, which could be bikes, scooters or remote control cars. We'd be outside with them guiding and helping them. They were extra lucky one year, because we bought them a three-wheeled motorbike, which Ryan would drive with Neil sitting behind him.

****

After Christmas we would go to Pilling Sands in Blackpool. We bought a trailer for the bike and Neil would watch intently to ensure that it didn't bounce off. The boys would ride for miles along the sands if we would let them with that bike. It would always start off so well for quite a while, but then Neil would try to take over, even trying to push Ryan off it. He always got over-excited, wanting to ride faster and faster to get a bigger thrill out of it. However the throttle could be adjusted, which we did so the machine would only go at one speed, which eventually caused problems, so we sold it, but while it lasted, it truly was great fun.

Once when we were on Pilling sands I was wearing a short mini skirt. Neil came tearing towards me and ran right through my legs catching me on one leg in the process. He was running so fast and was so very strong that he managed to nip a small piece of skin off my leg. This was so surprising that I just couldn't tell him off, but my leg was surely sore for a while after that. Neil had never meant to hurt me.

Ryan, Neil and me at Pilling Sands

One other source of trouble with Neil was that he knew how to get the locks off the car doors. We had child locks on the back doors, but Neil would open the doors and try to get out which was extremely dangerous. However the child locks didn't really help much when they were on because Neil just knew how to get them off again.

Steve left him in the car once when he was asleep on the back seat. It was only for a matter of minutes, but when he got back to the car Neil was gone. He was only three then, Steve panicked and made sure that it never ever happened again.

Neil was found in a side-street nearby, but we certainly knew what could have happened, and Steve anguished over what he'd done for ages afterwards. Neil could read and write and do basic sums by the time he went to school.

I'd spend hours teaching him; he simply soaked it all up like a sponge, he enjoyed learning things. I drew lots of clocks so that he could learn to tell the time. I've always been able to draw well so I'd draw pictures, simple ones that he could copy or trace, and then after he had coloured them all in, he would carefully help me to place them on his bedroom wall.

****

It was around this time also that I noticed that my jewellery was going missing. When I put Neil to bed one night I found all my precious missing pieces under his pillow. I don't think he intended to steal them as that wouldn't have crossed his mind. He was like a squirrel with its nuts, or a magpie drawn to sparkly things that caught its eye. It was just that he felt close to me in those late hours. I just took them back and hid them away saying nothing to him about them.

CHAPTER THREE
Time for School

"You do look a smart boy," I told him.

Neil was so excited about his first day at school just as Ryan had been a few years earlier. We were lucky that their primary school was just up the road and around the corner from us. Castlecragg was then and still is a neat little school just off the main road a short distance from Meridian Park.

We set out his little uniform the night before. He was already fully dressed in it when I got up in the morning. Steve had helped him to get ready when he came in off the night shift; Neil just couldn't wait to be going to school like his big brother and, with the added bonus of a uniform he was in his glory.

I shed a tear that morning I can tell you. 'Please God let things work out and make the teachers be able to cope with him,' I thought silently, my anxieties creeping in.

I was told at the beginning it was a settling in period, more a matter of play and learning through games. He came home with paintings, and tales of what he had done that day. He seemed to love everything; he couldn't stop talking about different things and showing me what he had done. It was a huge adventure for him.

It was soon very evident though that the school was finding Neil a real handful. It wasn't really surprising of course as he was the same at home. He was never still and, he couldn't concentrate on anything for long periods of time. We felt for the teachers, because if we found it hard ourselves, then how much harder must it be for them with over thirty other children to deal with.

****

I was working part-time at this point; we needed extra money especially before Christmas and I was going 'ga-ga' stuck at home.

When I'd left school I'd trained in an office after school and worked as a receptionist in a car sales garage. I'd been a good scholar at school and thought myself intelligent and I oozed self confidence. When I didn't hit the required standard I was able to bluff my way through it anyway. We had got engaged, so we needed extra money but office work, especially at seventeen years old, was very poorly paid, so I applied at Smith & Nephews in Brierfield as a knitter. I got the job but I didn't tell them I had qualifications. It was a smashing place to work and I really loved it there.

The mill was daunting as there were many departments such as weaving and spinning too. Further down the road was another mill owned by them which concentrated on surgical dressings and other items of that sort. I have very fond memories of the time I spent there, the people I met and the friends I made. In fact I had been working there when I had the accident.

Steve was in another mill in the next town, he was a weaver then. He worked the shift hours of 6-2 and 2-10. Steve would pick me up at 5:30am for the early shift on the 50cc motorbike he'd just bought off his brother Barry. How that bike carried us both for the time we had it was amazing. It gave Steve a 'great longing' for a more powerful bike. He'd pick me up when he finished at 2:00pm. I'd just hang on waiting for him. Sometimes I caught the bus in the afternoon at 1:00pm to get to work for 2:00pm but it wasn't often and Steve certainly wouldn't let me come home at 10:00pm in the dark on my own. I was taken real care of, and I was so grateful for that all those years ago.

****

Now that Neil was at school, I was working at Findels, which soon changed its name to Studio Cards a mail order catalogue company. I'd seen the advertisement for part-time workers in the local jobcentre. They wanted packers for the Christmas period. They hired people to get the orders out for Christmas which covered a period of only three or four months. I knew it would be hard work with Neil being the handful he was, but with him just starting school and Ryan already in school, Steve would stop up later so that he could take them both to school before going to bed, then later on he'd get up to pick them up. He never did get much time in bed; it wasn't ideal, but we needed the money, but more importantly I needed my sanity too, so we bit the bullet and I went to work.

I was terrified on my first day as I stood there on the factory floor with all these people starting at the same time. There was a rail track

83

above eye level all around the factory with big boxes placed on it. They were noisy and fast and it all reminded me of the 'Mouse', one of the fast scary rides at Blackpool Pleasure Beach. I was terrified of that too. I just wanted to run.

"Susan Green," my name was shouted out by a lady with a clipboard. "Stand here, please."

Everyone turned to look at me and I seemed to become frozen to the spot. Many of the other workers were put into groups, whilst some people took them off to the different sections. I wondered what they had in mind for me. I was taken upstairs to work in the offices. I've never been so relieved and glad that this time I'd written down my qualifications on the form that they had given me. I really didn't want to work on the shop floor as it looked so very hectic.

Boy, did I love that job. My boss was such a lovely man. When eventually it came time for me to leave he asked me to stay on. I did so want to do so, but I had only started there knowing it was casual work. He offered me a good position. Was I tempted? You bet I was, but it was impossible. Work for me was a pipe-dream. I wanted the career, I glimpsed what might have been and I felt twisted up inside. I knew I would never be able to have a career with Neil being the way he was.

Steve was counting the days to Christmas before he could have me back home. I was the last of the casual workers to leave and I was given a bag full of 'goodies' by my boss. I used to come home from work, sit down, and fall asleep. I always found head work harder than manual work, but it was so satisfying working no matter what I did. It was great while it lasted!

****

We decorated Neil's bedroom, we let him choose the colours himself. He was fed up with the mural that I had painted on his walls. He was a big boy now and didn't want fields of flowers, lambs and fluffy clouds and borders of alphabet animals. He was into *Knight Rider, 'A Team'* and *'Airwolf'*. He still loved his Wrinkles, which were supposedly dogs that were completely unheard of in this country at that time, but had become very popular in America. They had wrinkled skin and he loved them for years.

They are probably still up there in the loft somewhere even today, because I can't really see any one of us parting with them as Neil just adored them so much that he took them everywhere with him. However when Neil got older, they were relegated to the bedroom; but he still cuddled them to death at night.

*Neil with Wrinkles and Ryan with his skateboard
at Christmas*

Neil's behaviour was now causing us some concern as he was always getting into dangerous situations. He put some metal into the plug socket which threw him onto the bed and burnt up the side of the wall. He was lucky that he wasn't electrocuted, his hair clearly stood on end for a while after that.

He wasn't sleeping much at night and he was up and down going to the toilet, then he'd ask for a drink. I wasn't getting much sleep as

I was always listening out for him. He started going downstairs and raiding the fridge and cupboards. That was bad enough, but then he'd put the dog's lead on and take her out for a walk. It could be the early hours of the morning. I'm ashamed to say that I've no idea how many times he'd done this without me knowing, but I was told by a neighbour that he'd knocked on her door after midnight to ask her if her son was playing out.

I decided to hide the keys to keep him in and safe, but he would climb out of the windows. We couldn't have this as I was exhausted trying to keep awake and listen out for him moving about, and then I would be awakened when I did hear a noise coming from his room. He would go into Ryan's room and take his things, then I'd find them in his room. Naturally this made Ryan very unhappy, so he wanted a lock putting on his door to keep Neil out of his room. We arranged this and for a little while peace reigned.

It wasn't long though before we had to put a lock on Neil's bedroom door **to keep him in**. He'd got out of the house again and was coming home with bags of cement and suchlike. I presume he'd got them from some building site somewhere. He didn't seem to know where he'd been when questioned.

I wondered, 'Was he sleepwalking or what?' I couldn't think straight, I really needed to get some sleep. Steve needed to work without worrying about me or Neil, so we locked Neil in at night; we also took the handle off the bedroom window so that he couldn't open it and climb down the drainpipe as he had done before. The fact that he didn't get much sleep didn't seem to affect Neil at all; it seemed to still be a fact that he didn't need much sleep at all. It had affected me badly though, I needed plenty of sleep as I always felt so shattered.

The school was finding Neil increasingly difficult; he was always in trouble for something. They kept calling me into school. I went there trying to help them with the report cards they were using to monitor his behaviour. Soon I was going in nearly every day just to let Neil know I was working with the school, and that I knew what was going on. The head teacher then was Mr Hatfield and we seemed to get on with him quite well.

The problem was that Neil couldn't sit still for long before he'd get up out of his chair and move about the room, which would naturally disrupt the whole class. Nothing could hold Neil's attention for very long as his mind seemed to constantly wander off track. I'd tell him off for doing something, but he'd do it again just minutes later, making me think that he couldn't keep things in his head. His short term memory seemed to be very poor. Whatever happened just moments ago he would not be able to recall, yet he could remember things from years ago very well indeed. I couldn't fathom it out then, but even now I still feel that it was never done deliberately. Even at that young age I felt there was something wrong with him mentally. The school's opinion was that Neil was just being naughty on purpose.

Mr Hatfield left and Mr Cheesman took over as head teacher. From then on things became intolerable. I still tried to back up the teachers whenever I was called into school, just as I had always done before. The teachers were now becoming increasingly critical. I told them he was punished at home for his wrong doings as we took his toys away, or wouldn't let him watch his favourite programmes on T.V. or play on his Nintendo, or receive treats if he had misbehaved at all. We stopped taking him out for tea.

We told them that his brother Ryan was suffering too because of all of this. All in all we tried everything we could without resorting to hitting him. He got the odd smack on his bottom, but at that time nothing more. He wasn't naughty for naughty's sake, somehow he couldn't stop himself, but no matter what we did to 'punish' him, it actually made no difference at all.

****

Neil was being blamed for everything at school. I know that on many occasions it <u>was</u> him at fault, but by then they had got so used to blaming Neil that more often than not it was automatically deemed as his fault, so he was often blamed for things he **hadn't** done at all.

One case in point was when a lot of kids, classmates of Neil's knocked on my door to tell me that Neil was in trouble again for something he **hadn't** done. In fact the boy who had 'done the deed' was standing in front of me admitting to it. It was something quite minor, but despite the fact that the poor lad had tried to admit to it, Neil was dragged from his seat and made to stand in the corner, whilst the boy himself had been told to shut up and sit down.

On this particular occasion the children had seen the teacher do something they knew was wrong, but how wrong it was I would only know later on when he came home with his dad.

Steve said Neil was late coming out of school as he'd been in trouble again. He was already at the school waiting to pick Neil up when the children had come to our house. I looked at Neil and noticed that his ear was bleeding. It turned out that the teacher had actually torn his ear. She had yanked him out of his chair by his ear.

That was enough for me to hear as I'd had enough. Neil was coming home far too many times with unexplained marks on him. He had friction burns on his neck and a scratch down his face. I'd asked Neil before what had caused these marks, was it the other children? Was he being bullied? He never would say, but this time he told me that the teacher had hurt him. I went to the school and told them I would report them to my doctor, which I did.

Ryan wasn't surprised when he returned home from his secondary school and I asked him if teachers hurt any of the children in class?

He said, "When I went to that school, he would be lined up with other kids who were told to hold his arms down by his side, whilst a teacher would smack him hard across his head. The same kind of thing happened to *other* kids. It's what they do Mum, when you are naughty."

I was shocked to hear all this as Ryan was *never* naughty. He wasn't the handful that Neil was. No one asked us to go up to the school about him, so Ryan thought this was 'normal, acceptable behaviour'. It was all just so unbelievable.

"Why didn't you tell me about any of this before?" I asked Ryan.

"I was so frightened that I'd get into trouble at home too. This was what the teacher told me."

Ryan told me that the teacher had said to him, "It's better that you just accept the punishment from me."

I thought, 'Is this how the teachers got away with it, by blackmailing the children so that they wouldn't tell their parents?'

Anyway Ryan was out of that school now, so it was pointless dragging anything up now. It made me think though. Imagine corporal punishment still being allowed in schools. Neil would be black and blue and, the fact that he was ill and couldn't help it, and didn't know any better, or was unable to stop himself from being the way he was, it doesn't bear thinking about. Still I'm ahead of myself again.

****

An appointment was made for me with my G.P. I told him of my worries about Neil that I thought that he had mental health problems. I also mentioned to him the fact that the school couldn't cope because the teachers were just hurting him. Not intentionally, well so I thought, but I really didn't know one way or the other. The facts were that Neil was getting punished for something that he just could not help. Perhaps also these teachers were not trained enough to cope with a child like Neil.

By now Neil was eight years old and, despite everything else he was enjoying school. He never had a day off and he was never ill. You might think I'm exaggerating, but I'm not, it was perfectly true. At that time and even with his 'little accidents' he would go to school.

I used to laugh with him and say, "You're never still, so the bugs will never catch you or make you poorly."

My doctor informed the Educational Psychological Service and told them to intervene at the school. He also made a referral to the Margaret Bradbury Unit at Fernlea Hospital for a Consultant to see Neil.

Neil's school photo taken at Castlecragg Primary School

In spite of the teachers trying to make us feel inadequate in our upbringing of Neil, telling me off in particular for over stimulating him by having taught him to read and write and do basic sums before he started school, then implying that this had made him unruly, we still went to the parents evenings; in fact we never missed. It was always awful. If only they could just have said one thing that was *positive* about Neil, it would have made us feel a little better about them, but they didn't, so we always came away feeling deflated. We loved our son; he had a lot of good qualities about him too. It did get us down and it was actually quite painful.

I started to see a difference in Neil as regards school when he started feeling persecuted. As he was forever being picked on by the teachers, it didn't take long before the other children began to realize that it was open season. They could actually do anything they wanted to do to Neil, because it would always be him who got the blame. It was hard enough for him to make friends as it was. He always stood out from the crowd as being different. He was the loudest in the group, so soon the other kids found out that they could provide the bullets ready for him to fire the gun, so to speak. He never failed them, as he was such a perfect and easy target as he acted without thought, always on automatic impulse.

I had to watch him like a hawk near roads, hold his hand tightly, in fact very tightly, but no matter how hard I tried to instil the possible dangers into him; he didn't or couldn't take what I was telling him on board. He sets off to cross the roads even now without thinking or looking first. He frightens me now, just like he did when he was a child and he was very clumsy; boy was he clumsy! We still had the problem of him constantly trying to get out of the car before it stopped.

The teachers kept going on about colourings in food. I tried keeping an eye on all of that, keeping a close eye on what he ate, all the E numbers and suchlike. I kept him away from cheap drinks and the orange colouring. I know tomato ketchup and baked beans have colouring added to them, but in fact even oranges had an effect on Neil. I tried avoiding some dairy products, keeping him away from margarine and butter that to this day he won't touch. But still nothing worked! Well yes, I do think that these food restrictions may just have made a *small* impact. Things like the bubble gum drinks he liked so much, and the Smarties, but they didn't **cause** him to be the way he was at all. They just might have slightly exaggerated his condition at times, but I really don't think it was that, in fact I knew deep down that it had little bearing at all, but as they still kept going on about it to me, I kept on trying anything at all I could to help Neil.

****

Ryan had an appointment at the Asthma Clinic at the hospital under Dr Mallard. Ryan himself was always more poorly if he had dairy foods, so I was always extra careful with **both** my boys. I wasn't a mum who ever bought cheap foodstuffs or ready meals. I was brought up to respect food, so I always cooked everything from scratch. We might not have been able to afford all the extras in life, but we all always ate well.

The teachers couldn't push me around and they didn't like that at all. I always managed to stick up for myself. I knew my son. It's always been weird that, with Neil and I, as I understood him, and seemed to know exactly what he was thinking at times, so I could often tell what he'd do next. I didn't know what he was suffering from, but I knew that he couldn't help himself.

Everything around him had to be structured as he didn't like his routine changed. He would set his stall out and it was always the same. He needed prompting all the time to do the most basic of things, even to having to be told to put his coat on. We had to remind him all the time. He would get stuck into doing something, but somehow he would just never finish it.

He had a real fascination for locks, especially those with coded digits. He could crack codes and change them and even remember the new codes well. He'd also enjoyed setting off the alarms. His work was very unevenly divided, with the most effort always being allocated to the *least* important things. He could never estimate time and he always took on far more than he could ever really manage to do. He never has any middle ground, for when he decides to do something, he does it there and then; no matter what else he should really be doing at that moment in time. He is always not only preoccupied, but he gets terribly frustrated, making his life extraordinarily stressful.

****

Mr Cheesman wrote a letter to Lancashire Education Committee on February 20th 1991, in which he said that Neil's behaviour in class was a constant nuisance. Indeed he emphasized that Neil's incessant behaviour wore down his staff, and that in his personal opinion, Neil wasn't in total control of his actions. In fact his view of Neil was almost exactly the same as what I had been trying to tell them all along. Alas this view would continue throughout Neil's later life.

Mr Cheesman also said that Neil was totally incapable of interacting with others, and that this would lead on to dangerous situations, due to the fact that probably Neil needed to dominate every situation at school in the same way that he did at home. However Neil in his opinion again, didn't have the necessary control, and because of this, things led to damage or injury. He said that Neil's attendance was good, but their resources were meagre and limited whilst Neil's behaviour was extreme.

This report would go on to follow Neil throughout his school life. He had now been labelled as having behavioural difficulties, so indeed now he would be treated accordingly in the future.

I am therefore left with a huge fight on my hands to try to get help for my son.

CHAPTER FOUR
Are you the Devil's Child?

I have two sisters who live in Australia. Jean lives in Perth whilst Christine resides in Adelaide. Mum and Dad went to visit them for around three months in October 1986.

I had been working for Clarks shoes in the Arndale Centre in my home town. I'd started off working part-time, but was then asked to work full time with a promotion to Deputy Manageress. It was a really great job and had an added bonus of discounted shoes for my boys. However it was just too good to last, for soon my training days away and weekend stocktaking put paid to me working full time, as it was just too much with Neil to take into consideration as well.

My mum found it very difficult looking after Neil, even though Steve picked him up as soon as he could after he'd had a sleep. Neil was able to run rings around Mum so we knew it wasn't fair to ask so much of her. It was good though while it lasted, and my kids have good feet due to them being able to change their shoes often as they grew. With my training and fitting experience too, I was very good at my job. Parents would wait for absolutely ages with their kids, just for me to personally find the correct shoes to fit their children's feet properly. Saturdays were especially hard, as it seemed that I had to deal with all the 'difficult' kids. I loved it though, and through my own first-hand experience with Neil, I guess I had learnt to be very patient. It was also a job I really enjoyed doing.

*******"

"I'll learn to drive when I'm ready," I told my husband.

Steve had been asking me for years to learn but I didn't want to; we had a Ford Granada automatic. It made that lovely noise that a powerful car makes and it was so comfortable. I liked being a passenger, but driving has almost become a necessity and not a luxury these days. I really did want to learn, but more when I was ready. One of the reasons I decided to learn that particular year was because we thought that the driving instructor who had taught Steve might retire soon. I particularly wanted to learn with him, also Steve had bought me a scooter, and although I gained plenty of road sense it wasn't really very nice on a bike in bad weather. It was handy for nipping about on, but not for going very far.

After just twelve lessons I managed to pass first time. Arthur Peel was a good instructor. I nattered all the way round on my test with the examiner. He said he had to pass me because I was so confident. That's always been the case with me, as exams or tests never seem to faze me at all.

****

My dad had been ill all year on and off. He'd had a double rupture operation and he was never the same after that. He'd had a couple of heart attacks too, so his health was a real worry for us all.

We used to spend a lot of our time at the hospital overall, what with Ryan and his asthma, then Neil thinking he was Superman but instead being a clumsy clot. We also had Mum with her cataracts and then a detached retina, our own medical bits and pieces and now Dad. All in all we were truly sick and tired of visiting hospitals.

It was really sad seeing Dad becoming so debilitated. He was a good worker and never had time off work. He seemed to be struck down all at once and he began to age so quickly. He was always quite a hard man, not really the kind to ever show his feelings; he appeared to be rather cold you might have said. Ours wasn't a loving upbringing; we were forced to grow up quickly. The change in Dad with our boys though was really something else.

Unlike one of my sisters, I didn't blame Dad for the way he was as I understood him. He was changing though because he was ill. He told Mum that he would go to Australia, even though he was far too ill to travel all that way really. They hadn't seen my sisters for about twelve years, so Mum really wanted to go, and he said he would go with her just to please her. It wasn't because he didn't want to see his girls, no far from it, he very much did want to see them, it was simply that he was too ill and I think he knew this himself.

He held my hand the day before they were due to fly out, and he told me he was going for Mum. I saw something in his eyes that I had never seen before.

I said, "Don't you worry Dad, you'll be alright as long as you get

94

over Christmas Day."

I knew he'd miss seeing our boys. He'd visited us early every single Christmas morning since they were babies. My sisters didn't have children so he especially loved our boys. In fact he truly adored them both.

He died of a fatal heart attack on Christmas Day! We didn't have a Christmas and our turkey went straight into the bin. With Australia being ahead of us in time, this meant that when my sister sent her sister-in-law who lived here in Barnoldswick to tell us about my father, it was still very early on Christmas morning.

I asked her later why she had told us so early on Christmas Day.

She answered, "Well my Christmas was ruined, so why shouldn't yours be."

I felt that my children should have been allowed to have had their Christmas Day first. It didn't seem at all fair to the boys. It most certainly wasn't what Dad would have wanted. I couldn't do anything for her because I was too far away, but my thoughts were with her for having to deal with it, but at least she had her husband as well as my other sister and her husband, as well as a whole bunch of friends.

I tried to reach Mum by phone, but being such a special day the lines were constantly busy. We didn't have a telephone of our own then, so I had to keep going next door to use their phone. I felt especially awful with it being Christmas Day, but my neighbours were very good about it.

Mum stayed in Australia only returning home when she and Dad would have normally returned. This meant that Dad was cremated there. It was a bad time for us all, and the fact that I have another sister here in Farnworth and Dad had a lot of brothers and sisters and family here, it was all left to me to explain things. We had a memorial service in Farnworth at their local church for them all, and afterwards we all went back to my sister's. It was really nice to do something to mark Dad's passing.

****

**Photo of my parents Harold and Stella
taken in Australia just before he died.**

Mum had undergone her detached retina operation at Fernlea General a few months before she went to Australia. I'm not saying it was because of that problem that she lost her sight, as we will never really know. All I do know is what my mum told me, which was that she was watching television when her sight went blurred, but instead of ringing 999 for an ambulance straightaway, she rang for her G.P. to come instead. He didn't even come out to see her until late evening, when in fact she had rung first thing that morning. Mum was taken into hospital. We were away at the time, but we went to the hospital as soon as we heard.

The first thing I said to the doctor was, "I want Mum to have a second opinion."

We received an appointment at the eye hospital in Manchester just a couple of days later, but sadly it was too late now the specialist said. They said it was an infection and my mum was now blind at 66 years of age.

****

I was devastated for my mum with this news. It took me back in my mind to my parents' earlier days. My dad was a good looking Royal Marine who had joined up to fight in the Second World War. He was the youngest of nine children born to a domineering mother, and a father who had not been able to find work to feed his large brood. Not being able to provide for his family took a huge toll on my father's father, so much so in fact that he took his own life at a very young age, leaving behind a very bitter woman who had to bring up her children on her own.

Whilst he was serving in Burma, my Dad had become a prisoner of war, and had faced torture, so he had experienced first-hand the terrible atrocities of war. He had received a medal for his bravery, which unfortunately Mum had sold on in later years in order to feed her children.

When Dad came back home from the war he was a broken man, having contracted malaria he was always very thin. His legs were scarred and like matchsticks.

"I was there for the Dunkirk landings," he told me once with pride. However most of what had happened to him he kept inside.

I never learnt what was normal in family life, as coming from a dysfunctional family himself he made many mistakes. He had married Mum whilst he was on a 48-hour pass, having only met her months before whilst he was lodging at her home. I was therefore the result of a loveless marriage, where Dad gambled, so always kept Mum short of money.

I was the youngest of his four daughters. I can remember going to Dad's place of work to ask him for money to feed us as he had left home without giving Mum her house-keeping, and me my spending money of about 50p in those days.

In front of his colleagues Dad would always tip up some money for us. I therefore had to swallow my pride to go to him. He never ever hit me when he got back, but nevertheless I would always keep out of his way.

I used to ask Mum time and time again why she married him, and also why she kept on having children to bring into a family where there was no love?

My belief is that you wanted children to give you love Mum, because you never got any off Dad. But then you weren't able to show any love to your girls in the normal conventional way of kisses and cuddles, or by the giving of your time and attention to play games with us and suchlike. I remember being left to amuse myself most of the time, but I would so love to have had the closeness that I experienced with my own children. As there was a nine year gap between my next elder sister and me, this meant that I felt that I had no one to turn to, so felt alone and left to get on with it by myself. Perhaps Mum, you had enough to contend with trying to cope on your own with Dad's behaviour towards you.

Mum had also been a product of a dysfunctional family; she had brothers yet her father never married her mother, so how hard was that to live with in those days? He was in fact a horrible father who drank, and then not only came home to beat up her mother, but also to sell every stick of furniture in their home simply to buy himself even more drink.

Mum lost her own mother when she was young, and she had been so devoted to her. My parents seem to have been two misfits drawn to one another in a time of war, but they both allowed history to repeat itself. Never did my mother wait for me with the other mothers outside school. I had to come and go alone from a very young age. No one ever came to school to see me being presented with the prizes for my good work, or when I passed my exams.

Mum you even used to even tell me (scare me to death in fact) that you would NOT be home when I got back from school because you would join the nuns and leave me with my dad.

In fact you did leave him a couple of times when I was small, and I remember living off jellies, pop and crisps until you returned. I feel very sad that you and Dad were born to suffer so much. I understood you really as in your own ways you both actually did your best.

I never was a latchkey child though, because Mum you were mostly always there when I came home from school. You cooked simple, but well made broths that I always looked forward to. You only went to work when I was old enough to look after myself.

Dad you were the best Granddad to my sons, they both loved you so much. I am what I am because of both of you. I am good and kind, and not one of your daughters has ever brought any trouble. We have all married well and have turned into decent human beings.

Mum has made up for so much since she lost you Dad; she had the time and energy to become the woman she SHOULD have been without being stifled by the cold man who showed her no love until just before your untimely death. Perhaps your background had turned you into this Dad. Perhaps you could not show her love because no one had ever shown it to you. However you certainly loved both Ryan and Neil and Christmas was always so very special with you both spending it with us as a complete family. I used to love Christmas so much!

Now alas Mum had just been told that she was blind, and she was so lonely. Now she was unable to live the life that we had always wanted for her. In spite of all this, I wouldn't change a single thing, because I was blessed to be the product of this *dysfunctional family,* as my sister keeps telling me that we are. As a result of this background I am strong. I loved you both Mum and Dad, and I always will. God Bless you both.

Your loving daughter, Susan xxx.

****

I was working part-time as a Home Carer then for Social Services; I was also working part-time in the evening at a local chocolate factory. It was fun having a few jokes and a chat with the girls. I'd go to Mum's in the morning, again at dinnertime and after work at tea-time. Sometimes Steve would do the tea-time run and I would look after the kids, but it was hard work running two houses.

I didn't dare think too hard about Mum being blind; she couldn't even tell if it was night or day. If I'd have thought about it too much I know I would have cracked up. My attitude then, as it is now, was to just get on with it. If you can't change things it's no good wallowing in self pity. I'd just lost my Dad, now I was faced with my Mum being blind and I had two sick children to take care of. It made me wonder what would come next. We had to be practical, however it was really difficult.

Mum was given a Home Carer for a few days a week to make her lunch and to do some shopping. It wasn't much, but it was better than nothing. Mum was so frightened of being in the house on her own, that she used to drag a big heavy dressing table in front of her bedroom door every night. This really showed how terrified she was.

We bought her a telephone with great big numbers on it that was meant especially for anyone with bad sight. It was a Godsend. But the best thing of all that she ever had was something that you couldn't ever buy; it was good neighbours.

Mr and Mrs Chew lived across the back street to Mum. No one could have done more than they did for her; they were wonderful, and Mum and I will always be grateful to them for their kindness. Having good neighbours and also having us though, wasn't enough; she couldn't cope, and I don't blame her for giving in to the fears she had.

Mum asked if she could be put into a home; so a home for blind people was found for her in Blackpool. It was a nice home with lovely staff, but obviously it was still a 'home', and although my Mum was blind she still liked a laugh as she was full of fun, very friendly and she never moaned about her blindness or anything else come to that.

It was really awful having to sell all her furniture and her bits and pieces. My mum and dad didn't have a lot of anything really, but most of what they had got was due to Mum, as she'd worked hard to buy things because my dad gambled. He always had, so we grew up with very little in the way of nice things or even food at times. So here I was selling my Mum's hard-earned items. We had an 'open house' advertised in our local paper, then a car boot sale for the things we couldn't sell. I hated it! It's hard enough selling your parents' belongings when they are dead, but having to do this when they are alive, especially so when you are more or less having to give it all away, is heartbreaking, so naturally I was very upset. The whole thing was horrendous!

The old folk in the home didn't suit Mum, some were alright and she had made a couple of good friends, but she was bored. There wasn't enough going on for her there at all. Some 'funny devils' used to tell her to shut up and be quiet and things like that. It got to her; she had a lot going for her, and she was such a lovely person, but with being blind she needed to **talk** to folk as she couldn't do very much else.

We visited her whenever we could, but it was heartbreaking to see her in that home. She never wanted us to go, but it was always so tiring trying to keep Neil entertained. She'd cry when we left her, we used to hear her when we were walking down the long corridors. The kids would cry then and I'd look at Steve seeing the tears in his eyes. Upset and tired we'd make our way home, usually in silence, until Neil started his antics in the back seat tormenting Ryan.

Neil's school made a referral to the Educational Psychologist, Donald Brighton. He came to the school to make classroom observations and discuss Neil with the teachers. Also we were visited at home by a Consultant Psychiatrist from Fernlea General Hospital as this had been arranged by my G.P.

To this day Neil mentions what was said to him by this doctor and he says he will never forget it.

The doctor said to him, "Are you the devil's child, do you think you are the devil?"

Neil was just nine years old at that time. What a thing to say to a child; we were amazed.

An appointment was made for us to visit the Margaret Bradbury Unit at Fernlea General. I wasn't keen after the meeting with the Consultant from there, but I thought it was an opportunity for medical staff to see Neil first-hand, because I had been led to believe that patients were able to be taken into the hospital to be observed and monitored. Even though I was so protective of Neil because I thought that no one else could care for him like I could, we couldn't go on like this as we all knew that there was something wrong with him.

It was nothing at all like we expected; what it was and all it entailed was the examination of parenting skills and using strategies to deal with a child with behavioural problems. I really did not need that at all, as I'd already worked out long ago that Neil needed to be dealt with in a different way, and most certainly **not** in the way this Social Worker was trying to get me to try. We'd already tried everything we could in the past with Neil, so we knew we'd have to look at things in a totally different way. For instance, it was no good jumping on Neil for everything he did that we thought was naughty, because he was *always* doing something naughty. We just did that for the more serious things he did, or the dangerous things he tried out.

If we had taken this item away or that toy from him, then he'd never have things for very long because very soon everything would have had to be taken off him. This woman was telling me to do with Neil what I knew **didn't** work, and also do what I already knew from experience would make him feel that he **couldn't do *anything* right, and that he was *always* bad.** I wouldn't do it!

We did go to the sessions a couple of times, although we knew it wouldn't work for us, but what really put paid to us going there again was that the Social Worker told me, *in front of Neil*, that she was going to report us to Social Services for locking Neil in at night and that he could be taken away from us and put into care. We walked out!

Neil was hysterical all the way home. They had really scared him. I rang my doctor and told him that we weren't going again. I told him what the Social Worker had said.

He replied, "Don't worry; you don't ever need to go there again."

Neil was only sleeping an hour or so at night by now. That night Neil had a nail, and with it he put holes in the wall of his bedroom. We found *thousands* of tiny holes in the wall, and he also used a snooker cue to make a larger hole into the next bedroom which was Ryan's room.

****

We couldn't keep Neil in all the time, as he got older he wanted to play out. We had to let him but it was a nightmare. He would get into all manner of scrapes; then we would have people knocking on the door complaining that he'd done this or that. He was always climbing on roofs and other dangerous places as he had no sense of fear at all. He'd climb into the school grounds. He was always so loud, that we always knew that it was him as he'd stand out in any crowd.

We had a 'beat copper' called Barry. He would see Neil with other lads being taunted into doing something, and he'd very kindly bring him home. He knew all about Neil as he used to come into the shop when I worked at Clarks shoe shop, and I'd talk to him about Neil. We brought both Ryan and Neil up to respect the police and told them they could always go to them for safety and help.

****

Neil was getting quite a reputation in the neighbourhood, especially when the police kept bringing him home. One Sunday afternoon Neil was on a bicycle belonging to another kid, but unbeknown to Neil it didn't have any brakes. As we lived on a long steep hill, Neil was picking up speed as he cycled down the hill. In order to avoid a pedestrian, he swerved and hit the kerb, which caused him to fly off the bike into a pebble dashed house wall.

He was in a terrible state, his poor face. I was out at the time and as I pulled up in the car I saw the ambulance going around the corner. I saw some people standing together in a group; I instinctively knew that Neil was in that ambulance so I just sped after it. He was kept in hospital for a few days and the nurses didn't know what had hit them. They couldn't keep him in bed; he'd go onto the other wards and at night they'd be hunting up and down for him. They were glad when he went home. Poor Neil he had quite a few scars.

****

We visited Mum one day while she was in Victoria Hospital, it isn't there now as it was pulled down years ago. Mum had one of her cataract operations there years ago. There was a park across the road from the hospital and Neil was playing on the swings one minute, the next moment he had suddenly disappeared. Steve found him hiding in some bushes, he'd run into a swing which then caught him on his eye. Steve came running out of the park with Neil covered in blood in his arms. We lay Neil down on the back seat of the car before rushing him across town to Fernlea General Hospital A&E Department. He was bleeding profusely and he was just getting over whooping cough. He still had a cough, but it was nowhere near as bad as it had been. He was on the bed in a cubicle. He coughed and blood shot out of his eye like a hole in a hosepipe, it went all over the nurse and her white uniform. I felt myself going faint and the nurse managed to catch me and sit me on a chair. When Neil had the accident on the bike he had hurt the same eye in the same place.

"Not you again Neil," they would say.

We went to visit Mum at the home at Blackpool. We were quite shocked at how she looked; she seemed to have aged all at once and she had dark rings around her eyes. She reminded me of Neil because he was the same. The teachers used to comment upon the dark circles around his eyes, but what would you expect when he hardly ever slept.

Mum told us about this old fellow who was constantly tormenting her. He had formed a relationship with another resident, so he had pushed mum out of the little sitting room she used to sit in because it was close to her bedroom. He wanted to be alone with his lady friend to 'smooch' as he put it to Mum. This particular room was much easier for her to get to with her being blind, and now she was feeling more isolated than ever.

Without a moment's hesitation Steve said, "She's coming to live with us."

I couldn't have said it, as I would have been too worried about my marriage, but having said that I was also worried about Neil and the mad house we lived in. Mum was just relieved to get out of the home, she did know Neil was hard work, but at that moment in time she didn't care.

Later she was to comment, "My God Sue, I didn't know he was this bad."

****

Things were still the same at Castlecragg. Neil was still being blamed for everything, and the parents' evenings were still a nightmare. We were called into school on one particular day. The teacher said she was severely disturbed by some schoolwork Neil had done in the form of an Essay entitled, *What we did during the summer holidays.*

We had bought a new caravan, a lovely 'Vanroyce'. It was very posh and was supposed to be the Rolls-Royce of caravans. We joined the 'Vanroyce Club' and enjoyed the rallies we went to all over the country. It was better to try and get these rallies in during the holidays when they were far away, also we could travel that bit further then, because with Steve working nights to get off to go to a rally on the Saturday morning when he'd had no sleep was a bit much to ask of him.

Everyone else went on the Friday so they were always well established on site when we got there. I didn't like making an entrance where everyone would look around and watch you setting up. We were forced to do that occasionally, but it wasn't ideal. The caravan was heavy to tow, so we bought our first four wheel drive

104

vehicle which was a short wheelbase Mitsubishi Shogun. On holiday, Steve would get up early to take our Afghan hound out for a walk with Ryan and Neil. They would see the early rabbits in the field and sometimes the odd hare.

Neil had written in his essay that he and his dad would chase rabbits in the Shogun in order to run them over and kill them. Instead of thinking Neil had an active imagination; the teacher told both Neil and Steve off for killing the rabbits for fun. I'm not even going to write anything further about this ridiculous misunderstanding as it's just too daft for words. We were getting so fed up of the attitude of the teachers.

The Educational Psychologist (E.P.) was still having discussions with the school, and the school set up home/school report, school and E. P. to monitor.

The E. P. was Sherry Logan whom Steve and I met. We stated that things had broken down to such a degree that Neil was unhappy, and his morale and self esteem were both extremely low. He was very confused as he couldn't understand just what he'd done wrong most of the time. I saw a happy child who looked forward to school turning into a miserable boy, who simply wondered what he'd be blamed for today.

The school had given up on Neil and was pushing him out, but although we wanted to stand our ground and make the school teach him and treat him like every other child, we knew that they wouldn't. We didn't like the response we'd had from the teachers when I had complained of their assaults upon Neil. They still blamed Neil for getting them worked up to the extent that they hit out. I felt that as teachers they should most certainly be held responsible for not being able to control their **own** tempers.

I went to see my G.P. again, and after we had talked I decided to tell the school that we wanted no more intervention from the Educational Psychologists because they were further alienating Neil away from the other pupils and simply stigmatizing him as being bad.

Neil was transferred to Hill Tutorial Centre. Their file, which I asked to see, stated that I wasn't supportive to Castlecragg. I must admit at that time I wasn't, they'd done too much to Neil and also to us as a family, treating us on occasion with the utmost contempt when we did every single thing that we possibly could do to help them. It was just a fact that Neil's behaviour wasn't down to 'behavioural problems' or bad parenting as they tried to make us believe. They chose to reject Neil; or at least that is how he felt. We had to think of him and try to boost his morale. We felt they were pushing Neil out, we didn't want to make it easy for them, but we had to think of him. After a lot of soul searching Neil went to the Tutorial Centre.

The smaller classes suited Neil; Mrs London his teacher was good with him; she was firm but fair. Through her he regained his confidence, she boosted him when he did good work and things got better. He was there for a little over a year. He was now ten years old and there was a meeting at the school.

At this meeting we were told that is was now time for Neil to go back to 'normal' school which would be better for him for when he was ready for Secondary School next year, that he went there from Primary School.

Oh dear, it made sense as they were saying it, but we doubted that Neil could cope with the freedom of an ordinary school and the large classes. We had tasted the small classes, the one to one attention. He had enjoyed the benefits of teachers who were experienced in caring for 'difficult' children. They said he couldn't stop where he was. It was the right thing to do, they knew best, didn't they?

Neil was accepted at Earl Street Primary School in Colne. We bought another uniform.

CHAPTER FIVE
A Cry For Help

Why on earth did the headmaster at Earl Street School accept Neil into his school? Neil had only been going there for a matter of days before he was ringing me up to go to the school. They obviously couldn't cope, yet they had known *exactly* what they were getting when they accepted him. It was really pathetic and so tragic for Neil.

I was taking Neil to school then rushing back to work after having had very little sleep. Sometimes I was on auto-pilot and I couldn't remember how I got home. Neil was always difficult in the car, touching things, taking his belt off, trying to open the doors and succeeding sometimes. It was very disturbing and you couldn't ever fully concentrate. If you stopped at traffic lights, he'd try to get out. When you had reached your destination and couldn't catch him in time, he'd run across the road. Every single day it was always a manic journey to a school that didn't want him. I was handing him over to teachers whose faces dropped when they saw him, and who treated me with disdain. I hated every minute of it; I wouldn't even dare to think how they were treating Neil.

****

It was about this time that I thought Neil had done something that would lose us our home. He'd gone playing out with some local kids and they'd gone to a building site not too far away from home, where they were building some new houses. Neil had gone for a ride on a mini-bulldozer that someone had **carelessly** left the keys in. He could easily have been killed when he drove it up the embankment and it toppled over. He jumped free of it, but the machine itself was severely damaged, and it had also caused some damage and mayhem on the site. The police brought him back home saying that the damage ran into thousands of pounds. This made us think that we would all lose our home.

As it was though when we went to court, we had to pay costs that

107

did run into a lot of money, well for us anyway, as we could barely afford it, but we had to make high payments every month. The one good thing about it was that we acquired legal representation from a firm of solicitors that dealt in family law, who later on down the line we'd use again to gain medical intervention for Neil to help me to take on the Education Authority

****

It became ridiculous the amount of times the headmaster rang for me to go to the school. He rang my office, where someone would have to find me if they could, but sometimes they couldn't as there were no mobiles then of course.

My boss got mad one day and said, "For God's sake, can't you leave the poor girl alone."

This was said after I had been rung up six times in one week. What was it that he wanted me for anyway? What did he want me to do? He just wanted to sound off at me as to how bad Neil was, and how the teachers *shouldn't* have to deal with such disruption. They had zero tolerance in all respects.

It was always much worse at playtimes, and especially at lunch times as he needed a lot of watching, but I wondered why *they* didn't get more people to watch him instead of keep going on at me. They should have got in touch with the Education Authority and told them that they needed more help. I came out of the school distraught for the fifth time in three days. I talked to the lollipop lady.

She told me, "I help out at dinnertimes watching the kids. I'm so sympathetic to Neil though as he urgently needs one to one help at lunchtime. He **isn't** a bad lad, he's simply into everything. He is all over the place and he needs someone to keep an eye on him all the time."

I was very grateful to her for telling me this and so thankful that someone else knew that it really wasn't Neil's fault. However I was also very worried about my job and it all got on top of me. I wrote a letter to my doctor stating that I felt like killing myself. I'd contemplated taking myself over a cliff top in my car, probably taking Neil with me, as **even way back then** I knew he'd **never** get the help he needed so would be better off dead. I just didn't want him to suffer anymore, because he most certainly was suffering, he was so very unhappy, which in turn made me feel so miserable and helpless to protect my son.

****

At that time Steve and I were arguing about Neil. I said he couldn't help it, but Steve said that I was like a broken record, and that all the teachers, doctors and everyone *but* me, were saying different things and stating that Neil **could** help himself, and that he was just being naughty. I felt so alone at that moment in time!

The doctor's secretary rang me to tell me to make an appointment with the doctor. I told him how hard it was with the school and Neil as a whole. He wanted me to take anti-depressants. To someone who won't even take a headache pill unless I'm absolutely desperate, I couldn't see myself doing that. Onwards and upwards I decided to battle on; and all alone if I had to.

****

Mum was living with us, and everyone knows how hard it is to live with your parents again, or for them to go and live with their children for that matter. It was a trying time to begin with, especially when we insisted that she went to day-care. She wasn't having it and stamped her feet.

"If you don't want me, then get me into another home," she said. "You are **not** driving me out."

I was working most of the day, so I had thought that it would be better for her to have some company. She was going whether she liked it or not I decided and, I was adamant about it. First of all she went for three days a week to settle in. She'd go at 8:30am being picked up by a driver in the Council bus and then she was returned at about 3:00pm.

Thankfully at least one thing worked out well. Now it's her second home and she goes every weekday, but if it were open at the weekends she'd want to go then. She loves it, the staff, the clients, but especially the lovely drivers who she adores because they have her on. She loves a laugh, she is very lucky and so are we to have this facility to give us a break from one another, and also to give her a purpose in life. It's wonderful for her to have something special to wake up for every morning. It keeps her going and they love her to bits too.

We had a hiccup though many years ago when the Disabled Centre was run by a woman who wasn't a nice person at all. I had clients who went to the Centre and they used to tell me horror stories about her, but when she turned on my mum it was truly the last straw.

My mum loves her salt and won't eat food without it. On this particular day she came home and told me that all the clients were banned from using salt and pepper, and that all the condiments had been removed from the tables. Mum had requested that someone put salt and pepper on her dinner but she was told by this woman that she could not have any salt and pepper, because they had already been used in the cooking so that should be sufficient. If she didn't like it she could bring sandwiches. I sent her the next day with a salt and pepper pot. Everyone was asking her for the salt and pepper and the pots were doing the rounds around the dining room. It was becoming awkward and the woman was making it unpleasant for everyone, so Mum decided one day that she wanted to take sandwiches, so I sent her with a sandwich box.

This worked well for a few days, until one day when I came home from work Mum said to me, "You put too much salt and pepper on those sandwiches Sue, I couldn't eat them. I asked one of the girls to throw them away."

I looked at her sandwich box and noticed that it hadn't been washed. It usually was but not this time. Inside, it was full of salt and pepper.

"Mum, I didn't put salt and pepper on your sandwiches, why would I, they were cheese and pickle."

Someone had laced my poor **blind** mother's sandwiches with salt and pepper, and the girls had left it in the sandwich box for me to see. I was fuming. I knew who'd done it, and I wrote a letter of complaint, but knowing how long winded the complaints procedure was, and how long it takes to get to the next level, I was having none of it, because in the meantime this awful woman was still being cruel to the clients in her charge.

I worked for Social Services too, so I contacted Chaddesley House and said I wanted to speak to someone immediately. I did see someone but I was threatened with my job if I made waves and contacted the newspapers as I'd threatened to do.

"Do something now then," I said.

"Remember, you work for us too," he said.

I replied, "Yes I do work for you, which is precisely why I want her out of the job of looking after vulnerable people." I'd made the stand and I would stick by it.

They did get rid of her, but knowing how these things work, they probably paid her off in some way to do so. Anyway as long as she was gone that was all that mattered.

****

The school was still complaining about Neil and trying to make me feel like an idiot. They were ringing me at work for every little thing that he did. It made work very difficult. I was going to work worried all the time and then worrying whilst I was there. What was next on the agenda though was beyond comprehension to me. A taxi was ordered for Neil at dinnertimes, in order for him to be taken to the Tutorial Centre for his lunches. How **insensitive** is that to take him out of one school to another for his dinners. If that didn't make him stand out as different, I don't know what would!

Here we go again at complete loggerheads with the school. But no, it's not me and neither is it Neil. They were wrong for doing what they did.

****

I was rung up on Saturday morning by the taxi firm employed by the Council. They told me that they were sending a driver to pick Neil up on Monday to take him to the Tutorial Centre. He was now out of Earl Street, they'd decided they didn't want him, but *they hadn't even had the decency to talk to us about it,* or to inform us as to what changes they had decided upon. They had set Neil up to fail. Just how bad was it **not** to even tell us about our son?

I couldn't believe this and it made me feel sick. After all they had put us through, we had **never** wanted Neil to go to Earl Street in the first place, but they had all told us that we were wrong and they were right. Poor Neil, they didn't even have the decency to tell us before it was done, so that we could explain what was happening to Neil in order to make it a little easier for him.

We could have taken much of the sting out of this if necessary as to why he had to leave the school. It should have been up to us to safeguard him from feeling a total failure. We could have prepared him. We had bent over backwards to do our bit, and we always went to the school to be ridiculed by the teachers, and especially so by the awful headmaster, but for what?

He had been at the school for just about six months. Neil was back at the Tutorial Centre and he was to stay there for a further six months until he went to Secondary School in August 1993.

We were terrified about Neil going to Prince High School. Ryan was already there and we were worried for him too. He was doing okay there, but he wasn't particularly academic, he was more interested in design and drawing but we thought that perhaps this would be the route he might take when he left school.

The thought of Neil upsetting Ryan at Secondary school by being the nightmare he was at home, and Ryan having to deal with it sent us into a cold sweat. Ryan didn't like to stand out, he preferred to be in the background, and with his asthma still causing him a problem it didn't do for him to get upset and Neil did upset him.

The thought of Ryan having to deal with Neil's mayhem, as we had little doubt that Neil would run to Ryan to fight his battles if he needed any help, worried us both. We had no doubts at all that although Ryan couldn't stand his brother most of the time, he wouldn't ignore his hurt, if he ever needed his help he'd certainly be there for him. I knew that Ryan would **never** turn his back on Neil. We all tried to do our bit knowing in all probability he couldn't help it. It did try our patience though, because it was a day to day never ending problem.

****

Prince is as other Secondary Schools are to the pupil, really quite imposing and somewhat overwhelming. Its corridors run this way, then that way, like a rabbit warren. I can remember the trepidation on my own first day at BIG school. I was really afraid of getting lost. Poor Neil, with the freedom he'd have, he wouldn't stand a chance. All he ever really wanted was to be like his brother.

Neil looked resplendent in his uniform, he was so excited, his bag set out with the same strict attention to detail as with everything else in his life, orderly and not to be touched and moved by anyone else.

'God help them,' I thought, 'and here we go again.' I just wished that we could look forward to things going well for Neil and not have to worry about everything all of the time. That alas I knew would never happen. We did feel different this time though, because we felt that the teachers were trying with Neil. The fact that they had at least showed us some respect, and tried terribly hard to see something positive in Neil went a long way we hoped.

We had the same things happening in that they were structuring Neil with report cards, but at least this time they were getting him a support teacher. He was soon testing them just as he always did, pushing their buttons so to speak, and trying to drive them to their limits. Mr Dalton the headmaster saw Neil on a regular basis, as he was being sent to his office on numerous occasions. Yes, he called us in on a *few* occasions, but on the whole he treated Neil well and judged him fairly, which made us have some respect for him and his staff.

I think the fact that Neil had an overwhelming desire to keep setting the fire alarms off tested the school quite a bit, but unfortunately this problem is set to continue, even today. Another thing Neil felt that he had to do was to abscond on his country runs and then come home. This happened on a regular basis. The fact that the school was so close to home, easily within walking distance didn't help. He walked to school on the purpose-built path beside the railway line. We were very fortunate to be surrounded by schools. There were three Secondary Schools and one Primary School all within walking distance of home, and a Special School whose head teacher was to help me decide on Neil's 'special needs' at a later date.

So here we were in the midst of open fields and lovely walks alongside a golf course and a lovely park. I'm sure Neil couldn't help himself, (a phrase I am to use a lot in describing Neil's lack of restraint) nor could he stop himself. The draw of home and me were far too great for him. He came home and then he was late back to school. The fact was we couldn't trust Neil to even go to the toilet and back again, let alone go on a run with all the freedom that gave him, without straying along the way meant that we were placed in a hopeless situation!

Thinking about what it was like for Neil in such a large school with little constraints; it was all far too much for him and he couldn't cope. Mr Davies was his form teacher and head of year; he was both supportive of Neil and us, and with this being a two way thing we supported him too. He told us how much he appreciated our co-operation. We appreciated going to the parents' evenings without feeling downtrodden on the way home as we had done in the past.

They did try; they even complimented Neil on his good work and the good points about himself. It was always problematic for Neil to start work with such vigour, only to be deflated halfway through after discarding so much work, because he'd gone off the line, made a small mistake or it just wasn't neat enough or reached up to his own high standards of perfection.

I tried to imagine how difficult it was for Neil, for him to even get anything written down on paper was such an achievement, especially so when the fact was taken into account that he remembered very little. I had always been aware that he had to have everything repeated over and over, but still sometimes you'd think he'd completely ignored everything you had just told him. I can therefore imagine that would be the hardest thing for a teacher to think that they had been overlooked on purpose, because someone had 'chosen' not to listen or take any notice of them. After all that is what teachers are there for, to teach.

In Neil's case he was always off on something on his own agenda, such as thinking of that boy in the corner, or wondering why the sky is blue, or would I be cooking him his favourite meal for tea? Perhaps he'd try to understand why the teacher shouted at him for not listening, when he always tried his best.

He'd think, 'Did I bring my shorts for P.E. No, that's tomorrow'; his mind just jumped from point to point like a grasshopper. We could all see things from their viewpoint, but then we always did, but why then could they NOT see Neil's?

We all did our bit to help Neil at Prince High School, but he was just too demanding on people's time and emotions. I must admit for the first time ever I thought that this was one school that had tried really hard. They didn't call us in all the time; they tried to deal with things themselves even when property went missing and Neil was being accused. They didn't come down heavily on Neil all the time; instead they thought things through first. I was grateful, but something happened in his second year at Prince High School that I couldn't ignore, which told me that enough really was enough.

****

We are ALL instilled by the 'system' to want what is in the 'norm' for our children. To be somewhere in the middle is usually

114

the 'norm'. It's thought of as 'bad' to be different. We are pressured to keep our 'different' children in mainstream schools, then told by the education system that it is wrong of us to allow our kids to underachieve. Instead we try to push them on to do the best that they can manage. Just like they told us it was wrong to keep Neil in the Tutorial Centre where he **did** 'fit in', and where he achieved because he got specialist support. No, now they wanted Neil in mainstream but who were we to want different?

If I had known then what I now know I would have really put my foot down and not let them walk all over us. They told us that they knew best, so we had to put our trust in them for the sake of our son. **We shouldn't have!**

Neil's first photo taken at Prince High School

Neil had gone to assembly with everyone else that morning, only in the corridor he was seen to be 'messing' about with a friend who lived around the corner from us. Unbeknown to Mrs Veesey, the

115

Deputy Headmistress, this was a *play* fight with a friend that continued in the assembly hall. She presumed that it was a ***real*** fight and she grabbed Neil and hit him hard across the face in front of the whole school. It was simply a reaction she was to tell me quite honestly later.

Mr Dalton the headmaster was most apologetic, and so too was Mrs Veesey when they called Steve and me into school. Probably they were expecting us to react somewhat differently than we did when being told that a teacher had assaulted our son, who had a red swollen face to prove it. We didn't raise our voices, accuse or threaten, we simply asked Mr Dalton for his help. Help to get our son into a 'Special School' where the teachers are qualified to teach and cope with 'difficult' children.

I felt somewhat sorry for Mrs Veesey, because even though what she did was very wrong, she had 'lost' it with Neil, just like many had done before her, and many others were to do the same with Neil in the future, including police officers who we would expect that they would be trained well enough to be able to control themselves. We were faced with a teacher *completely out of her depth*, who was sorry, who had held her hands up to the mistake she had made, and who would be better able to handle the incident again if it were to re-occur. We **knew** that would have been the case. Her honesty was enough for us. They couldn't cope with Neil, but now let's simply find a school that could.

I have mentioned before about another school whose head was helpful to me. The school was called Gibfield. It was a Special School for children with a disability, whether it was mental or physical in nature they were supposedly able to deal with any children sent to them. I visited the school to ask questions about the 'Statement' procedure, because Mr Dalton had said that in order to progress further we needed to get Neil 'statemented'.

I did think at the time as to why this had never been done *before* now, if what they were now saying was true and there was an obvious need for it. The kids at Gibfield were impaired. Some were slow due to having Down's syndrome as well, although I knew that in all probability some of these kids had slipped through the net so to speak, and **could** have achieved and coped in mainstream school if they'd been given the right opportunity and chances, especially so when offered all the correct help, care and understanding that they personally needed.

I was rather of another view with Neil. He was underachieving because he had different problems. He was diagnosed as having only *borderline impairment* on his I.Q. test for learning difficulties. Perhaps if he was taught in a different way, with a more one to one structured environment, with teachers who understood his complex needs, and in particular could deal with his behavioural problems, then maybe he could actually learn better.

In my opinion though this school wasn't for Neil, as it wouldn't be able to meet his complex needs, but it did give me an insight as to what direction I should be looking in, and the members of staff were all so helpful to us. It was necessary for me to see this school before I could go forward; after all to know what **wasn't** right for Neil, was the next best thing to knowing what **was right** for him.

****

We started the statement procedure. It takes time as it's a very complicated procedure that isn't helped by the people involved being blinkered, and putting Neil into a category in which he just didn't belong. I for one wasn't happy to put him into that bracket at all.

They are a law unto themselves the Education Authority, just like other Authorities that believe that **they** are always right, whilst **you are always wrong**. They believe that they *always know best* and **you don't.** They are qualified but you are not. I could go on (I usually do) but I feel sure that you will have already gathered my drift of this situation. All in all these people are there to put you in your place. So here we go, again.

CHAPTER SIX
Holiday from Hell

Prince High School on the whole tried to do their best. When they did fail it certainly *wasn't* because of their inadequate teaching methods, or the care they gave to their pupils. It was the Education Authority's fault for expecting them to cope with completely inadequate resources, which in turn resulted in them failing to meet Neil's needs, by placing him into a school that wasn't able to cope with his specific needs, as he needed **specialist teaching methods,** which an ordinary school and normal teachers could neither implement or had sufficient training to do so. It was therefore NOT the school's fault at all.

Neil had been sent to Moor Groves Hostel while the statement was being done. It was a large manor in its own grounds which wasn't far away from where we lived. The request had been made by Mr Dalton in April 1994, but he had been told by the Education Authority that this wasn't possible until September because there wasn't a vacant place available until then. In August 1994 Neil set off the fire alarm, he wasn't excluded because this might have jeopardized his place at Moor Groves.

When Neil finally got to Moor Groves it was already the 27th September. In the meantime the school support team was called in to continue working with Neil, and also the Educational Psychologist who provided reports and gave further assessments.

The Educational Psychologist visited our house following contact with the school. We also requested a formal assessment, where we were informed of 'our rights' and requested the same, by writing to the Area Specialist Eductional Needs Officer (ASENO). The Psychologist also requested that Social Service help would be appropriate.

On 5th September, Prince High School urged the Educational Psychologist to complete the statement procedure process as soon as possible. However it was one whole month later on the 5th October before the statutory assessment actually started.

Neil started at Moor Groves. He got on with the majority of the teachers; the only thing was that he was mixing with kids who had been rather aggressive at their previous schools, and had very specific problems. Naturally I was rather worried about Neil being bullied. So far we had NEVER ever previously experienced any aggression off Neil towards us or anyone else. Neil might well be difficult to deal with, but we attributed this to a medical problem, and not that he was choosing to be 'naughty' or difficult on purpose. I really did class Neil as being rather difficult for the teachers to deal with, but not in the *same* manner as was suggested to me that these kids were 'bad' kids. I didn't think for one moment even, that this was the same case with Neil at all.

An interim internal review at Moor Groves Hostel recommended that Neil remained at Moor Groves.

Moor Groves was residential for four days a week, and although Neil hated to be away from home, he did settle in, which gave us our very first taste of freedom at home in so many years. Never had we been able to leave Neil with anyone without worrying, so this gave us all a much needed break from him. We all loved Neil, but we knew that he did get a great deal of pleasure from knowing that we were 'tied' to him.

Even the thought of us being able to go where we pleased without Neil; or the chance for us doing things without him really bothered Neil a lot, I blamed myself for giving him so much attention, but how could I possibly have done anything else? It wasn't because I wanted to be at his beck and call; it was mostly that I was in constant fear if I *wasn't.* It was my duty, he is my son. I took it all upon myself, telling myself that no one else could do it like me, and do you know something this was perfectly true, **for no one could**.

All in all I found the teachers at Moor Groves committed and good at what they did, in fact a lot of what they wrote about Neil I totally agreed with.

Neil had settled in well at the hostel and was used to the routine. His teachers commented on his personal hygiene, and the fact that he paid close attention to his appearance, not only in his uniform but also in his casual wear. His room was so tidy and orderly and his

119

personal possessions carefully placed and looked after. This was due to his rigid attention to detail, which was regarded to be on the verge of having Obsessive Compulsive Disorder.

I thought this very astute of Mr Tempest, as I too had thought this about Neil for a very long time. Neil couldn't sleep at all unless his bedroom was just so, with everything in order and in its place. He had to be totally satisfied to this fact. Neil was said to be a pleasant and a very polite child with extremely good manners. Occasionally he was argumentative, but **never abusive** and, he had never displayed outright defiance towards an adult.

We were told that the same problems that Neil had displayed in mainstream school and at home were evident at the hostel. Neil's general behaviour was said to be hyperactive. He was said to become bored very easily and lacked patience, and always acted without apparent thought, moving quickly away from one activity to another at random. He was seen as restless with poor concentration skills, and had a very short attention span. They had observed that he had difficulty in getting to sleep, yet despite this he still woke up in the morning full of life.

A lot of the teachers had noticed that he was tolerated by only a few of the other pupils, but on the whole he was *disliked* by most of the children, and although he was bullied and openly shown by some that he wasn't liked, it didn't really affect him.

He was very demanding on the staff and expected his needs to be satisfied there and then. He was always interrupting with a speech rate that was high and urgent. It wasn't easy for staff to get Neil's attention though, as his mind quickly wandered off elsewhere, which served to put lots of wear and tear on all the various members of staff. The fact that Neil never seemed to learn by past experiences, and he was poor at reading *non-verbal clues*, plus his response to oral requests from staff was slow, whilst at other times he didn't respond to them at all, which made the staff feel very frustrated with him. They found his social skills complex, fraught with problems, and they were always of the opinion that he didn't understand the impact of his behaviour on others.

In fact his behaviour NEVER differed whatever environment he found himself in, whether it be in the classroom, outside, or whilst travelling to school in the taxi, or in the community at large; it always remained constant.

The staff did manage to contain Neil's excesses and tolerate his disruptive behaviour, because he was now in a highly structured and supervised environment, but his conduct didn't alter, and the hostel's staff members were never optimistic that it ever would change.

They admitted that the hostel provided him with an education that was coping a little but only because he was contained. If he continued to be the same then other services would need to be brought in, in order to give a greater deal of support. This would be especially so if he were to go back into mainstream school. It was generally thought though that this would prove highly **unsuccessful,** and further **stigmatize** Neil, so the majority of the staff became of the opinion that Neil should stay in the hostel for the foreseeable future.

Everything Mr Tempest had said to us, combined with all that he had written about Neil, had made us fully aware of, and led us to believe that he had been thorough. We believed that he had indeed fully grasped Neil's situation.

Neil did settle in well at the beginning, but like everything with Neil it didn't last long. He has honeymoon periods in whatever new situations he finds himself in. He can outwardly display as fitting in, adapting himself, but it never lasts very long, but yet again they would tell me that I have no faith in him and that I must allow him to try.

I always do let Neil try, but I also *know* my son, so it is always the honest truth when I tell them that it **won't work**. It never does, but how many times will they keep setting him up to fail? Many more times yet to come I regret to say.

They tried at Moor Groves, they really did, but Neil wore them down. There was yet another incident involving another teacher who simply 'lost his 'rag' with Neil.

****

Neil was becoming depressed and he was making himself sick. He was feeling very unhappy and always wanting to come home. His teachers weren't sympathetic to him at all. They didn't wish to be seen as failing with him, or so I thought at the time. They said he was attention seeking, but we all knew that this **wasn't** so. Yet again the treatment of Neil by the teachers showed the other kids that it was *open season* on Neil, as they would do anything to wind Neil up so that he always got the blame. This also spilled over into our home life, as *many of these children didn't live very far away*, so he got bullied at home too.

These children would involve other kids who lived near us, so I had a constant stream of complaints from the neighbours. Neil would never run away and hide, so it was so easy for someone to put the bullets in for Neil to fire the gun so to speak, because he didn't ever realize that he was being set up. He couldn't see further than his nose. He didn't plan anything at all, he just ran into everything head on, without any thought whatsoever. It was all so sad, he didn't have friends, he was **never** invited to parties, he was always left out; he stood out as a pathetic soul, dysfunctional and different. We were heartbroken at his plight all the time.

I should have known that they would do the same as they had done at the Tutorial Centre and put Neil back into the school from whence he had come. These placements are only ever *temporary,* so these kids are only given a very **short reprieve** before they are returned back to their previous school. In fact they are sent back to the very same schools *that couldn't previously cope with them*. This never made much sense to us at all; **does it to you?**

Their intention is always to work their magic then reintegrate these kids back into 'normal' school. But as Neil hadn't changed in any way at all, what was the purpose for them putting him back into Prince High School to 'fail again'. I could never see any logic. **Why do these people never learn?**

On 15th December 1994 further Education Psychologist assessment was done as part of the statutory assessment.

On 24th January 1995 a second internal review at Moor Groves recommended that Neil remained at Moor Groves, but consideration should be given to a reintegration programme at Prince High School.

On 27th March 1995 the proposed statement was issued.

On 24th May 1995 I wrote a letter to the Education Authority about the incident at Moor Groves stating that I intended to keep Neil at home.

****

We had holidays away in the caravan, we were in the Caravan Club and we tended to use their certified locations, those that would

122

only allow five caravans on their sites at a time, just so that we could keep a closer eye on Neil. As he grew older he naturally wanted to do things on his own, but we tended to fill the holiday with places to go and visit, and things to do that would serve to keep him occupied, as he got bored so easily. If he wasn't kept under control by us, he'd inevitably stray into trouble.

Years ago, we bought our new 'Vanroyce' caravan and we went to Ilfracombe with friends who also towed their caravan. It was a lovely site with a restaurant. It was good going away with friends because they would help with Neil, and added to the holiday by playing games with the boys, which in turn tended to take a little of the pressure off us. It was also nice for our boys to have somewhere else to go for a chat and be spoilt rotten.

These friends understood Neil a little and knew he was hard work for us, because he was always on the go. We were lucky to know such good people. Things were going well for a few days and we were enjoying ourselves, even giving Neil a little freedom and allowing him to go into the restaurant building after meals had been served and cleared away, to play pool. Unbeknown to me he was playing on the slot machines. We kept change in a tub for the boys to play pool, buy ice-creams and suchlike, so they were always dibbing into it.

On this particular day Ryan came running to the caravan in tears saying, "The lady owner is very cross with Neil and she is screaming and shaking him."

I went running out of the caravan; whilst I was walking very quickly up the path towards the restaurant I could hear her screaming at Neil.

"You horrible little boy, you disgusting child, you are a thief."

My heart sank, I felt sick!

The woman then turned and screamed at me. "Is this **your** son?" she looked at me in disbelief.

I got the impression that because we had a new caravan and car and she was so friendly towards us all the time we'd been on site, that she couldn't believe this 'awful boy' was mine.

Apparently Neil had been putting silver into the slot machine over and over, and even changing what he'd won at the counter to purchase pop and crisps. He'd also been tampering with the machine

123

so that the money would drop somehow. We never did get the chance to get to the bottom of it all, or the fact that he'd seen a teenager doing the same; he'd simply watched him then copied him. She blamed Neil for the loss of hundreds of pounds which according to her had been lost over just a few days by him using the slot machines.

I know **now**, of course I do, that is **totally illegal** for children to be allowed to use slot machines for gambling in the first place, and I should have stood my ground; but at the time I didn't. Instead I just wanted the ground to open up and swallow me up as I felt so ashamed.

Ryan had known what Neil was doing, and another boy off the site was with them, and the woman was holding onto this other boy too. I did know that Neil was capable of this, as he was so clever and mechanically minded. He only needed to watch someone do something with any machine once, before he was able to do it himself. Neil was around eight years old at the time, but he **didn't know** that what he was doing was wrong, as to him it was simply something that he was good at for a change. He would never think that it was wrong or believe that he was actually cheating.

I blamed myself for enjoying the hours of peace that we had without him. It wouldn't happen again! I gave her the hundred pounds that she demanded off me, which was in fact the whole of our holiday money. She then demanded that we left the site, immediately. As we'd paid for the full fortnight, we lost that too, as we'd only been on site for three days, but nevertheless we packed up and left, leaving our friends still there. We felt bad for them as we knew that they would be tarred with the same brush, simply by being our friends. We felt so embarrassed for them.

We were so upset that we cried all the way home. I don't know how Steve managed to drive all those miles back home from down south, so it was a miracle we got home in one piece in the state we were in. Neil knew he had done something wrong because he was quiet on the way home for about an hour, then he was back to his mischief at the back of the car. I looked at Steve crying; it felt like my heart was being ripped out. This was one of the most upsetting times for us. To this day it upsets us to even think about it, as I can still hear that woman shouting abuse at our son.

124

We had many a holiday ruined after that, for no matter how hard we tried to please Neil, and keep him occupied and be with him as much as possible, we weren't able to do this for the *full* twenty-four hours every single day. We were exhausted, so it was never much of a holiday, but it was all we could do, as with all the things we went through, we all truly needed a holiday. We had to try hard for our Ryan's sake too. He deserved so much more, he was such a good son, and was forced to put up with so much due to Neil's illness, and failure to understand that every bad thing caused an unfavourable reaction. Naturally Ryan would be dragged into things just for being Neil's brother, even if he had not been at the scene of the problem. It was just so unfair for us all really!

Once we decided to go onto one of Haven sites for a week and then onto a Caravan Club site another week, so they could have some fun. Sadly that too was hectic, with so much going on there, and the three of us trying to keep an eye on Neil all the time. Looking back I don't know how we managed it, but we were younger then so thankfully we had more energy. There must have been some good times, but they were very few and far between. We lived in constant fear of being thrown off sites after that, so it wasn't nice and we could never truly relax, which defeated the whole point in being there really. A holiday for us was NEVER a time for relaxation!

****

Neil and me
How I would have liked to have kept Neil safe and encircled in love.

We were becoming 'bogged' down with Neil's statement, and the fact that we couldn't get through to the Education Authority that Neil needed a different approach in the way they were teaching him. Previous options had never worked, so a change was required as soon as possible. Yet again our requests fell **upon deaf ears.**

****

We had another disastrous holiday and Neil was arrested for stealing a motorbike.

We had a friend and neighbour who had a scooter that she kept in her house shed. I say *house* shed because the shed is attached to the house and wasn't out in the garden. She had agreed that it was okay for Neil to borrow the scooter occasionally, and to take it along the back field behind her house, on the condition that he always put the scooter back and returned the key to where it was usually kept, as she had very patiently and carefully shown him.

He didn't abuse her hospitality and, he always took very good care of the bike. She allowed him to do this, because she was a *special* person who knew and understood that Neil had problems, so she put some trust in him. In fact she was a very poorly girl on dialysis.

On this particular day in 1995 Neil took the key from where it was kept. He took out the scooter as usual just as he had done many times before. He was riding it merrily away, up and down the field when some bigger lads came and took it off him, only to thoroughly destroy it. Neil wasn't able to do anything about this, so he was absolutely and utterly devastated.

The owner came around to my house in the evening obviously distraught, she didn't want to involve the police but she had no other option really, so I told her to contact them. The scooter was worth a few hundred pounds but we didn't have that sort of money to give her. The boys had ditched the scooter. Neil didn't know any of them well enough to describe to the police, which left her with nothing else to do but to involve the police, and tell them that Neil had taken it *without* her consent.

What we didn't realize at that time when we had agreed that she should inform the police, was that it now meant that he'd stolen the key too, because we couldn't very well say she had left it where she did for him, as to know that he knew this would have given the whole game away. So to top it all, the police charged Neil with burglary as well. It was the only way that she could get the insurance money for the scooter. However the knock on effect of this incident meant that the police now believed that Neil had now moved on up in the world by committing burglary, and they definitely let him know it. We felt bad, and so did she. Neil pleaded guilty. He was given a conditional discharge for twelve months for burglary, having no insurance and driving without consent. Naturally this meant more fines for us to pay.

Neil was also appearing at court at that time as a witness for himself, because he'd been badly beaten up by a local boy who was a real piece of work, and who was always in trouble with the police for fighting. He was found guilty of assault then ordered to pay Neil compensation as it was a severe beating, where Neil had been kicked in the face and had his head stamped on.

At this time Neil was at Brook Bank School in Blackburn. The statement had been finalized so this school had been chosen by the Education Authority as being the best school to fit Neil's needs. We had been taken to the school by an Education Welfare Officer. We had already been introduced to Alan Newbold in this role, but he wasn't available to take us to see the school, so instead we were taken by someone else. I would have much preferred Alan to have taken us, because we trusted him and his judgement. Besides which we didn't know the lady who replaced him.

After all it's not really quite the same when you have already built up a trust and have a rapport with someone. We felt it odd at the time that there were hardly any children at the school, but we'd been told that they were away on a school trip. I didn't realize there was anything wrong at the time. But perhaps I should have!

****

Neil was still causing concern at home. If we went anywhere at the weekend, Blackpool for instance, or wherever else it was, Neil would get it into his head that he could get there himself. Somehow he was like a homing pigeon; he caught trains, buses, or thumbed lifts. He'd have had a wonderful time there, so would just want to re-live it, by going somewhere he felt secure, safe and happy. We'd find ourselves having to go for him, because he had managed to get there under his own steam. This never meant that he could **get back** under his own steam though. In fact he'd not realize what he'd done, or how he'd done it, and then he'd begin to panic.

Usually he'd gone on the train and had not paid his fare. How he got away with that and never got caught was amazing. Please don't get me wrong here; I am not supporting him in this at all, it just wouldn't have entered his head that he was defrauding anybody. He simply didn't think. That's what it was always like; he'd get something into his head and just do it. *It was a Neil thing*, just something he did.

****

I can remember a holiday we had in Coniston on a Caravan Club site, again with friends, but *before* the holiday from hell that I have already written about. We went for a walk up one of the famous hills in those parts, big, big, hills that we decided we couldn't complete the climb before it went dark, so we climbed back down saying that we would do it another day. We awoke the next morning really early. Neil was gone! We ran out of the caravan to see everyone looking up towards the hill in the distance. This hill was so high that it completely dominated the scenery. You could just spot this figure on top of the hill. I knew instantly it was Neil. Steve ran to get his binoculars. Yes it was our Neil indeed! He'd even taken his lime green shorts off and he was waving them above his head. Everyone was gob smacked wondering how a little boy had the courage to do this all on his own in the early hours.

There was no time to stop and chat. We all jumped into the Shogun, and as we passed everyone on the streets looking up towards the hill, we knew what they were thinking, that someone was in distress.

"Hurry up Steve for God's sake," I pleaded.

Steve drove as far up the hill as he could, but we had to walk the rest of the way and Neil met us halfway down. We were just coming away from the hill when a Landrover passed us; it was the Mountain Rescue.

Steve shouted, "Duck Neil!"

Someone had called them to save this poor boy stranded on this hill waving his shorts in the air trying to attract attention. I was the one in distress, my heart was in my mouth; he'd done it again our Neil.

****

I went into the Post Office one day and stupidly left Neil in the car with the keys in the ignition so that he could listen to the radio. My car was still there when I got back, but it wasn't where I had parked it. It was parked in a slightly different spot.

You start to believe you are going mad, thinking that these kinds of things don't happen. I could only presume that Neil had driven it, then returned it to a nearby spot in that short time.

Barry, Steve's brother once left Neil in *his* car when he went to visit a friend. He was standing talking to his friend outside the man's

129

door with one eye on his car watching Neil who was sitting in the front seat, when Barry's car started to move. Neil had taken the handbrake off and it was travelling down the hill. Thankfully somehow Barry just managed to get in before it went into the canal at the bottom of the street.

Oh! He was quick our Neil. Needless to say none of us left Neil in the car alone ever again. We have all learnt our lesson over different periods the hard way.

CHAPTER SEVEN
We Take On the Education

Brook Bank? It was a school for kids with behavioural difficulties. Neil never stood a chance of ever fitting in at this school; so it was totally wrong to send him there.

To this day I can't believe how stupid I was. As I have already said we were introduced to our Education Welfare Officer, Alan Newbold. I have a lot of respect for this *decent* human being. He was fair and honest, and he treated Neil and us with a lot of respect; we trusted him and he never let us down.

On this particular day when being shown around Brook Bank School in Blackburn, he wasn't available to take us. Why didn't alarm bells ring? I could have kicked myself. Had he known and **not agreed** with their decision, especially with knowing our feelings? I would like to think so, because once again we were well and truly stitched up.

"Where are all the kids today?" I asked on seeing no children yet again.

"On a school trip," we were told once more.

There were a few children there, but it soon became obvious that these were the best behaved ones. In these situations you place your trust in these people; you rely on them, like you do with doctors. This was our mistake, **a huge mistake!**

Teachers and the Education Authority, we had put our faith in these people time after time. We were told that they knew more than we did. Sadly this was **not true** at all. It was simply another big error on our part.

If I can get anything ELSE across to you on reading this book before you get to the shocking end, please I beg you always follow your **own instincts**. After all <u>you know your **own** children</u> better than anyone else in the whole world; don't rely on the medical profession or any other so called 'Professionals'. Do question those who 'lord' it over you, by telling you that **you** are **failing your kids**, if you **don't** do as they say, because they *know best* and *you certainly don't.* I therefore implore you **Do NOT** take their word for it. They need to prove themselves to <u>you!</u> They need to do the best for **your child,** to educate them and also fulfil their needs and bring out their full learning potential, as well as keeping them safe!

****

The statement had named Brook Bank School as being the MOST suitable for our son, so Neil was to attend there starting in June. We were hoping for a residential school, but we were told by many that we'd be very lucky if this were to happen, because of the funding.

Neil attended Brook Bank for just two weeks before a problem arose. Never before had it shown up so early on that a school was *totally inappropriate* for Neil. There were a lot of things wrong, starting with the bullying of the kids who were far more aggressive than any other children that he'd ever come across before. Yes he'd been bullied before, but never had he had chairs and furniture thrown at him in the classroom. He was always covered in bruises. I sent him to school **with a neck brace on** after one such incident hurt his neck and back. I was told that I **couldn't** send him to school like that. But really I was extremely worried about a more serious injury occurring if I **didn't** send him *without* some form of protection.

The teachers seemed to turn a blind eye to the most distasteful things the kids did, like when they <u>urinated</u> on Neil, and were also saying the terrible and dirty things that they were going to do to him. I just couldn't believe my ears. These kids were animals! Neil had never heard the like of this from anywhere or anyone before.

We had an appointment with Dr Hussain at the Margaret Bradbury Unit at Fernlea General Hospital a couple of weeks later. We'd had bad experiences there before, but we were becoming really desperate to see a doctor, and because he was new we thought we should at least give him a chance. At this meeting with Dr Hussain, Social Services declined to even attend. Mr Cropper was invited too, he was from Moor Groves Hostel, and someone from Child Welfare and Donald Brighton the Child Psychologist. They were all asked to come but they **didn't**!

Only Mr Brown attended, he was the headmaster from Brook

Bank and as Neil hadn't been there long, he knew him the least. We were really quite disgusted as there was so little commitment from people.

Dr Hussain disputed the findings of the statement as he insisted that Neil needed a residential placement, agreeing with us completely that Neil needed twenty-four hour supervision. He also stated that Neil needed to learn social skills as to how to relate to others, in a social setting that was carefully monitored. After this had been done, we would get prime time to spend with Neil at the weekends, which by now with Neil's behaviour and the constant trouble with the police, together with our continued fight to educate Neil combined, it was doing our heads in.

I rang Robert Hardy after the meeting; he was the Head of Education at Lancashire County Council's Headquarters in County Hall in Preston. Following our conversation he told me to write to Mr Sheffield which I did. I also went to see my M.P. and contacted a solicitor to fight for Neil's right to be in a *residential school*. The evidence was there, and I had vowed to **never** stop writing letters until my hand dropped off. I even actually said this was my very serious intention in one of those letters.

I was incensed after seeing Theresa Riley two days before at the Special Needs Office in Burnley and telling her how bad things had got for Neil at Brook Bank. I felt that I was getting nowhere. I therefore asked Mr Brown to initiate a review as soon as possible, because now I was armed with new information from Dr Hussain, he did as I asked.

We had the meeting with Theresa Riley and Brenda Steele who wrote down the minutes. I was informed that although I had told Mr Sheffield in the letter that I objected to the findings of the Statement, and I wanted to go in front of the Tribunal over a week before the deadline of two months, I could not do so as I was outside of the time limit.

Although I then insisted that I was **not out of time**, it was pointed out to me that because Mr Sheffield didn't send me the correct form to fill in, that I should have gone through the Office of Special Needs anyway, but now I was too late to do this. Sorry, but rightly or wrongly I had written to the Tribunal anyway.

As far as Ms Riley was concerned her decision stood. Neil was at the correct school, **simply because she said he was**. Dr Hussain should have got in touch with her instead of Mr Brighton the Psychologist who dealt with Neil. As far as **she** was concerned, she'd had no *new* information. I got in touch with Mr Brighton to ask him why he didn't recommend a residential school for Neil?

He said he had done so, but Ms Riley always decides for herself what to do, from the information supplied to her.

I personally believed that she had made the **wrong** decision. I wasn't willing to let Neil go down the same road as before and let him stay at Brook Bank only to fail again, and by taking him out ourselves he wouldn't feel as if it was his fault. I knew that Neil needed at least two years at his last school to make any impression; but sadly time was now running out for him.

Dr Hussain had written on the 11th July 1995 both to us and our G.P. Dr Forest saying that he had asked for a formal Case Conference under the Children's Act. He contacted Mr Brighton the Education Psychologist and told him of our concerns regarding Neil's placement, saying that he also thought that he should make arrangements to meet with us as soon as possible.

I wrote a formal letter to the Education Psychologist after my discussion with him. I told him that I was seeking a residential school place for Neil in my letter dated 25th July 1995.

Next I received a letter from the M.P. Gilbert Price, saying that he had also written to the Chief Education Officer pressing him to address the problem.

****

So I contacted Cunningham Turner Solicitors in Blackburn, having previously been informed that Val Shaw dealt in Child Law, and she was willing to take on the Education Authority on our behalf, to push them towards residential placement for Neil. At this time also, we were becoming more concerned about Neil's mental health as his medical condition was changing. I delved into the medical books at the library.

****

Then by simple chance I watched an edition of the television programme on the I.T.V. Granada channel called *Good Morning*, which was fronted by Richard Madeley and Judy Finnigan.

The programme was talking about A.D.H.D. Attention Deficit

Hyperactive Disorder. In those days it was a little known condition, but quite typical of Richard and Judy they were bringing this to people's attention, in order to give this truly life shattering condition the air time it deserved. The condition is far reaching, affecting families and society as a whole.

I would like to say "Well done to everyone on that programme, and to Richard and Judy in particular, as without any doubt whatsoever you helped to change things for us, just as you probably did for many others. In fact I have always thought that it would be wonderful after I have finished writing this book, that it could be Richard and Judy who told the world about my son Neil, and the difficulties and cruelty he has encountered all of his life, and also how the Medical Profession have turned their backs on him. Then also let them relate how much he's been let down by all the 'Services' that are supposed to be put in there to help him, and others like him. Hopefully that could possibly happen in the future, who knows what's in the pipeline for any of us?"

Back to the programme though, where Richard and Judy introduced Dr Christopher Green and told of his book, *Understanding A.D.H.D.* I immediately rang our local bookshop to order this book and for years it was like a bible to me. Everything was beginning to slot into place. **At long last we'd actually found a valid reason for Neil's behaviour.**

****

I asked my solicitor Val Shaw to find me a doctor who treated A.D.H.D. Like I have said previously, this condition was little heard of back then, and most doctors were completely sceptical that the condition even existed, but I really felt like a light had been switched on for us at long last.

We applied for legal aid and were successful. I receive a letter from the Special Needs Tribunal saying that they had received my letter. I then received another letter in August 1995 from the Tribunal together with a booklet entitled, *Special Educational Needs Tribunal: How to Appeal.*

I had to sign the form that came with it then return it with the required documents, being told that I couldn't register an appeal unless I did this. The timescale was that the appeal **must** arrive in the Tribunal Office no later than the first working day two months after

135

the L.E.A. told me in writing that I could appeal. The President of the Tribunal could only extend the time limit in <u>exceptional</u> circumstances. There was more red tape and deadlines, but I was determined not to allow them to tie me up in knots.

Things were becoming intolerable at home with Neil. He was very unhappy at Brook Bank. Never had I had the situation of Neil **not wanting** to go to school; his attendance at school thus far had been exemplary. I had a phone call one day stating that his teacher had taken Neil to hospital after a boy had thrown a chair at him.

There were two separate occasions when I thought that Neil was at school, but unbeknown to me he had been brought home and left with a neighbour. One of the neighbours chosen on one of these occasions was one that I would have said was totally *inappropriate* to look after any child, but especially so a child like Neil with all his problems.

Apparently the heating had packed in at school. I had already complained after the first time for them to always contact me personally for any problem whatsoever to do with Neil; they had a phone number for me and also knew of my daily movements and routine, so there was really no excuse for them to leave Neil with anyone else again. However they overlooked my earlier complaint and instead did what was MOST convenient to them, when I had said that they should NEVER leave him with this particular family again.

This was because we had had some trouble with this family previously, and they had taken it out on Neil in a most inappropriate way for a child, yet here the School Personnel were deliberately going against my strict orders, and leaving my son in a place where we knew that he could be seriously harmed.

****

Some time later we received a letter stating that Neil was to be suspended. He'd mistakenly locked a teacher in a cupboard. He'd been taunted by the same foul mouthed boy he'd been abused by before, and had previously reported to the teacher. He thought that he was locking that boy in the cupboard. This prank lasted a matter of minutes, as the teacher concerned simply rattled the door, and Neil immediately opened it and let her out. However for this couple of minutes of action Neil was to be suspended for a whole week.

I didn't think it warranted such a strong punishment. It was wrong

136

I agree with that, but Neil had misunderstood, then he had apologized immediately completely on his own accord. He had released the teacher after just a couple of minutes.

However there seemed to be one rule for the School and other children, but quite another one for Neil. When it came to Neil's own abuse and assaults from the other boys these liberties and actions were always ignored, so I must confess that I was actually fuming with the unfairness of it all. It all came to a head one afternoon on the way home from school in the taxi.

Neil was pinned between the two boys in the back seat. One of the boys took out the headrest, and with the **steel prongs** actually pinned Neil **around his neck** against the back seat. The other boy physically abused Neil touching *his private parts* like he'd threatened to do before. He also punched him, and **both** boys spat at him. The taxi driver was forced to pull over onto the hard shoulder of the motorway to try and intervene.

Being completely terrified at what was happening to him, Neil managed to get free and got out of the car; he foolishly ran across the three lanes of the motorway into the central reservation, frantically crossing the other three lanes of traffic next, in order to get to the garage beyond. He begged the garage owner to ring me.

The man on the phone told me, "Your son has begged me to ring you. He's in a shocking state. He is bleeding, and his clothes are ripped and he is absolutely covered in spit. He has also been very sick and he is shaking uncontrollably. Now he has run off somewhere."

Neil had become scared again. The man hadn't even got off the phone to me before he ran off. It was really lucky that I was home at the time to receive this kind man's call.

I immediately got into the car and raced on the motorway towards Burnley where the call had come from. Neil was on the embankment of the motorway and he saw me before I saw him and he flagged me down. He knew the direction I would be coming from. I picked him up and kept him off school for nearly one and a half years. **Yes you did indeed read that right!**

****

It is unbelievable to think that these days you are sent to prison if you allow your kids to 'wag' school. I kept Neil off school for well over a year yet no one did anything to me; it seems that there is one law for *some* people but quite a different law for others.

In Neil's case they would have been glad of the peace and quiet whilst he was away. They would not take into consideration that he was *fully entitled* to a proper education just like any *other* child. What he was NOT entitled to though**, but got at school,** was to be **assaulted** every single day.

I kept my son away from a school where he was ill-treated by the kids in it, where the Education Authority knew what was going on but turned a blind eye, but still expected me to continue to send Neil there. We were still seeing Alan Newbold our Child Welfare Officer and he was in full agreement with us that Neil was in the **wrong school**, as in his personal opinion Neil should have been in a Special r*esidential* school with teachers who were trained and capable of looking after kids with specific needs.

So here we are, and what in God's name was going to happen now? For how on earth are we going to cope with Neil twenty-four hours a day? We asked for Neil to go back to Moor Groves Hostel but this was refused because he'd been assaulted by a teacher there. I'd made a complaint therefore he couldn't go back there. All we could do was to push as hard as we could for the residential placement.

I'd been told that it would take months for the Tribunal to get back to me, letters were going backwards and forwards to the Education Authority, M.P.'s and solicitors. I'd even written to the Department for Education and Employment in Westminster, London.

I received a letter **five months later** from them, in which they stated that they had written to the Lancashire Education Authority about the Special Educational Needs of my son and that they would contact me as soon as possible.

****

I received a letter from Val Shaw telling me that she had been in touch with LADDER, the National Learning & Attention Deficit Disorders Association, and that she had spoken with the Chairman of the Association. Details were given to her about various specialists who were knowledgeable in this field. Of the three doctors that Val supplied names for me, she said there was a stronger preference to one particular doctor. Val suggested that we approach my G.P. with a view to seeking a referral to Dr Polly Stevens in Ashton-under-Lyne Hospital.

She had written to my M.P. Gilbert Price to tell him that we had instructed her to act on our behalf following my attempts to have the issue of Neil's education addressed in more detail, as a matter of urgency. She had also written to Dr Hussain and Andrew Cutler, the Chief Education Officer.

By now Neil was fourteen years of age.

In the letter she tells of my disappointment at the Education Neil has received thus far, and of the considerable paperwork available in relation to Neil, and that the Statement of Special Needs was not commissioned at the *earliest* opportunity. Even though Neil had been moved from school to school, none were satisfactory to meet his Special Needs. Even now though, Neil was still down on paper as attending Brook Bank, even though I'd withdrawn him from that school personally a lot earlier.

Val went on to tell Alan Cutler about the concerns I'd voiced about Brook Bank School, stating that I thought it was totally inappropriate for Neil there, and on seeing Theresa Riley at Special Needs I had said I was getting nowhere.

I had told Val that I was finding it extremely hard to control Neil at home, but if he could be placed in a residential school he could be more closely monitored, and being away from his own environment, this would also possibly be a good chance to give Neil a fresh start.

****

At home our neighbour's children were leading Neil astray, as they knew how easily he could be wound up, and found it funny to watch him get into trouble. Although I'd asked Social Services for help, no aid of any kind had so far been forthcoming. They had been invited by a Consultant Doctor to a previous meeting concerning Neil, yet had failed to attend, and actually were showing no interest in him whatsoever. This was indeed just a start in the way they would always continue concerning poor Neil.

****

Dr Hussain had tried to get various bodies to seek assistance. Donald Brighton an Educational Psychologist, was asked to make a formal Case Conference under the Children's Act, but once again nothing further has come of this. Val therefore asked Alan Cutler to

139

give these matters his urgent attention and address the matters in full.

Neil was extremely difficult over this period, and getting into so much trouble that we couldn't cope. In particular this was becoming too much for me and I was starting to get very ill as I was feeling very heavily weighed down with all the endless stress that the whole family was undergoing. It was relentless and very wearing.

Steve, Ryan and Mum, and even Kathleen and Barry who were trying to shoulder some of the strain by taking Neil home themselves for a few days here and there were also struggling. As they only live down the road, they would have Neil while I was at work, and Steve would take over when he got up as he was still working nights. However it was all too much so I got on to Social Services and I told them we'd had enough, as we just couldn't cope on our own any longer, so they would have to take Neil into 'care'. This was our very lowest point, we were so depressed and tired, and I too had been forced to finally admit defeat as I was feeling so unwell.

They took him into a Children's Home in Colne, but this lasted a matter of days before **he simply came home on his own**. As he had been placed only a few miles away from us he could so easily walk back; it was that close. He thought it was so amusing hanging around near his own home, then going back to the 'home' when he felt like it. This meant that he was staying out until the early hours of the morning, yet no one in the home seemed to be concerned in the least where he might be, or what he might be up to.

I asked, "What's the point?"

The police even brought him back to **me** (not the home as they should have done) when he got into trouble. They picked him up in the early hours of the morning, then woke me up and gave me a right telling off for 'allowing' him to wander alone on the streets so late.

It was simply pointless. They police would NOT listen to me at all when I told them that he now lived in a home, as he had been put into care as we were unable to cope with him.

We took him back home with us, and then we continued to lock him in his bedroom. It was tragic and so, so pathetic. Neil was being failed yet again! `

****

I am just thinking how much almost everyone involved in trying to get Neil into a suitable school seemed to fall over themselves to

140

HINDER, rather than help a very vulnerable boy get the education that was his lawful right. It was as if they purposely waged a constant war, littered with huge piles of paperwork and letters that often needed a law degree or a qualified solicitor to understand.

I am just a mother trying to get my son into school, which is the right of every single child. Neil was sent from one **unsuitable school** to another, as if he was a parcel without any addressed destination. If by accident he was let into a school where the staff cared and had the qualifications to help a needy child, they simply moved him out of there as quickly as they could.

Often he was placed in a school that could not cope with his needs, then later removed from that school that was unable to cope with him previously, to simply be returned some **months** later. Urgent letters went unanswered for several months at a time. All the time the only qualifications that Neil was in fact gaining, was how to learn how to fail time after time.

Also he was taught by example that no one cared, and no one really wanted him to be there. Often abuse and neglect directed at Neil were repeatedly overlooked. These lessons were continual and wore us all down as a family.

Whilst I understand only too well that Neil was difficult, I also realize that given a REAL opportunity he might have made so much progress. He needed one on one contact; he needed to be away from home in a residential school in order to flourish. Despite some people realizing and stating these facts, it all as usual fell UPON DEAF EARS.

Occasionally there was a RARE moment when someone actually placed him in a more suitable school. There were caring schools who worked hard for him. However the minute he felt settled and relaxed there he was moved on to somewhere else.

IN THIS WAY, YEARS – yes YEARS of education that had been promised to every child, were lost and wasted. I am just pondering how many other NEIL'S are there out there who have been cheated out of what is rightfully theirs?

Bureaucracy can be a very rigid heartless body to overcome; their administration often grinds slow, and stops and starts as time rushes by. If some person **with an actual face** would take the time to visit the family and really listen to the needs of the child and meet the family, or actually bother to read through the mountains of paperwork that can accumulate with just one case, and read up **all** the reports, (though they are often completely opposite in their nature) then possibly this insanity that says a child is entitled to education on one side, and on the other there are no suitable schools or not enough funding or specialist teachers, could be overcome at an early date. If someone actually sat down and really actually bothered to look into the matter in hand, then probably thousands of pounds of valuable resources in the long run could be SAVED. It would also mean that each child matters, and their rights are therefore safeguarded. EVERY SINGLE CHILD DESERVES THIS. *Looking through at all the letters and paperwork involved just with Neil alone, several trees might well have also been saved.*

This nonsense has to stop – FULL STOP. Our most vulnerable children are being failed and promises are constantly being renegued on.

Meanwhile the paperwork trail grows even bigger!

****

Val wrote again to Andrew Cutler having not received a reply yet from her URGENT letter sent to him the previous month.

I received a letter from Gilbert Price M.P. stating that he'd written to the Chief Education Officer and he'd received a reply telling him that a meeting was arranged for the following month.

Val wrote to Mr Sheffield at Lancashire County Council in Preston asking for the meeting to include Mr Brown, the acting headmaster of Brook Bank School, Doctor Hussain the Child Psychiatrist, a representative from Social Services Department, Donald Brighton the Educational Psychologist, and either Councillor Berry or Derwent.

It was also stated that Neil was to be assessed by Doctor Polly Stevens at Chesterfield Hospital, who was a specialist in Attention Deficit Hyperactive Disorder. Val had written to my G.P. about this and she agreed, as did the other doctors in the practice, to fund this out of their budget.

Val had hoped that we'd have been seen by Doctor Stevens **before** the meeting at Brook Bank, but it would be another five long and difficult months before we even got that appointment. It was remarkably difficult at this time to see anyone who specialized in

A.D.H.D. as in those days they were very few and far between.

Of course Doctor Stevens was already heavily pressurized in her own area, without taking on Neil; so we regarded ourselves as very fortunate to get her expert opinion, and for her to treat Neil afterwards would indeed be an added bonus.

Alas, we could not be seen *prior* to the meeting at Brook Bank, nor had we any report or documentary evidence to show to anyone present there at that meeting.

****

I therefore decided to take the matter into my own hands. I had lost all faith in the Education Authority, and things weren't moving fast enough to help Neil get back into school. Theresa Riley and Brenda Steele had infuriated me at the meeting we'd had at Special Needs in Burnley.

I'd been in touch with a local Councillor who had told me about a family in Barrowford, who had a similar problem trying to get their son into an appropriate residential school. I had been told by her that the family would be willing to talk to me at their home.

To this day I will always be grateful to them for their kindness, consideration and help. They are a lovely family, who like ourselves had fought long and hard to have the appropriate schooling for their son who had specific needs, although they were in fact quite different needs to Neil's.

However I still thought that their approach would be beneficial to him. Neil had borderline learning difficulties, but he couldn't learn because his problems were getting in the way. The approach of the teachers and their teaching methods were aggravating the situation and, just made a mish-mash of his schooling, which meant that neither teachers nor pupil were getting anywhere. This often resulted in a very frustrated teacher, who more often than not, due to their own personal lack of control and training in this particular field, hit out at Neil either physically or verbally.

We talked at length about Eden Grove School in Appleby, Cumbria where their lovely son attended. However the only way for us to be able to tell if it *could* be the right place for Neil was to go and visit the school.

143

CHAPTER EIGHT
Eden Grove

I rang Eden Grove School and spoke to the headmaster Mr Ince. I remember being very guarded in what I said to him over the phone. We wanted to be as any other family in choosing a school for our son, without one single problem raised to cloud the issue by telling them at the start that we were at loggerheads with the Education Authority. We wanted a *brand new* start, in order to wipe the slate clean.

An appointment was made for Steve, Neil and me to visit the school. On the approach to the school we were in complete awe, as the building, like a lot of other residential schools, looked very much like a castle. It had very high walls, towers and extremely imposing architecture. Even on the *inside* it looked like a castle, but it was far from cold and imposing, instead it seemed very warm and inviting. It lived up to our first impressions very well indeed.

Mr Ince met us at the door; I don't know what it was exactly, but somehow we liked him straightaway. We were shown around the school and grounds. Neil was then whisked away by a few other pupils. This then left us free to look around the place leisurely on our own. The teachers were more than willing to talk to us at length. We found Neil on the playing field enjoying a game of football with the other lads. We were invited to lunch, which was very kind of them.

We didn't feel rushed at all, and there wasn't anywhere where we **weren't** allowed to go, or any topic that they didn't want to discuss. Neil felt welcome and so did we. Mr Ince asked for any paperwork we had about Neil and his education thus far, if at a later date we wanted to discuss Neil becoming a pupil at the school. At that moment it wasn't what we wanted to do, as we had to be real sure about this school, obviously due to things in the past we were extremely wary of getting this possibly a last chance for Neil, wrong.

I thought, 'The next time we visit here I won't ring first, and we'll see what sort of reception we get then.'

The next time we visited Eden Grove School there was just Neil and me. Neither one of us encountered any problems at all; just as before we were made very welcome so we stayed all day. We ate with the children this time, which allowed us both to talk to them a little more.

It was extremely favourable, so the next time we visited I asked our Child Welfare Officer Alan Newbold to take us there, just for his personal input. The school passed as being very suitable to him for Neil.

I therefore gave Mr Ince the papers he had requested, and after he looked through them he returned them by post on 25th September 1995 telling us that he hoped all would go well on 10th October at the meeting at Brook Bank.

I had done my homework very thoroughly, so I was convinced that I was ready to face everyone at that meeting. I knew Eden Grove *was* the **right** school placement for Neil, and more importantly so did he!

We were therefore totally shocked and completely unprepared when we were told in no uncertain terms that Eden Grove was **not** the most appropriate school to meet Neil's needs. He would not be allowed to go to that school at all. Instead we were informed that we would have to visit three other schools of the Education Authority's choosing. I was informed of this at the meeting by Theresa Riley of Special Needs.

Once more they thought that **they** knew more than **we did,** about which school would meet Neil's needs. In their opinion Eden Grove just *wasn't for children with Neil's abilities,* so his problems wouldn't be addressed there, and he wouldn't learn there as he was *too bright* for that particular school.

I totally disagreed with their findings, as I just knew that Neil would achieve so much there. They would teach him to learn at his own rate and not expect too much off him. In this way he would have found it much easier to reach his goals, and probably even surpass them, rather than having to always swim against the tide to achieve little, because the powers that be, said he *should do better*, and once again they would teach him the **wrong** way.

It was all so pointless, futile and against all our hopes, dreams and plans for our son Neil's problems simply fell *UPON DEAF EARS*, but we wouldn't be deterred. We did agree to see Underlay School and Witherslack School because we were told that we needed to compare the school of OUR choice, to THEIR choice of school. We certainly couldn't argue with that point, but we all knew that we were all wasting the precious time that Neil had left to get any schooling.

Appointments were made at both of these schools. Steve didn't go to these meetings. I really didn't think he needed to do so, because he'd already lost so many hours/days sleep. It was bad enough for my frustration at these meetings, let alone him having to get worked up and upset after having had so little sleep. Again I tried to put him first as it was all just so unfair.

After all Steve was always being woken up by me when Neil had done something really bad, whenever I couldn't deal with it on my own, or the police were involved, or if there was someone irate, be it a neighbour or someone else who had come knocking hard upon our door.

On top of these episodes were the constant hospital visits, meetings and suchlike. It was inevitable that I tried to cope with some of it on my own. Not that I wouldn't have loved Steve to always be at our side, of course I would have been delighted to always have him with us, but I also tried to cushion a lot of it from him for his *own* sake. Steve worked hard on the night-shift and you can't work without sufficient sleep. God knows he got very little sleep as it was, as there was always some incident or other to contend with. Life was hard enough but the Education Authority was making it a damn sight harder.

My solicitor wrote to Mr Sheffield at the Education Office at County Hall, Preston on 27th October stating that we had seen the two preferred schools of their choice, but I still firmly believed that Eden Grove was the *right* school for Neil. My solicitor also informed Mr Sheffield that my choice of school could educate Neil for a further three years up to the age of nineteen. As the length of education being offered was such an important element, due to the fact that Neil had already missed out on so much schooling, meaning that he was now a very long way behind in his schoolwork, and nowhere near ready yet to take his G.C.S.E's at the standard age of sixteen as would be the case at Witherslack School, my solicitor told the Education Officer that I felt Neil would be able to catch up on his schooling if given the opportunity of a *longer period* of education. She also stated that I preferred the regime offered to Neil at Eden Grove, as I was convinced that this was the right school to meet his needs.

She finished off by saying, "Given the number of school placements that Neil has had, Mrs Green feels that Neil deserves the stability of a permanent school. Mrs Green also feels that she and Neil have been let down by the Education Authority to date, so would welcome your co-operation now. She had hoped that this would be Neil's final placement."

I wasn't able to hold my breath.

On 31st October 1995 I receive a letter from Doctor Polly Stevens saying that she could see us at Marsden Street, Clinic, Chesterfield on Tuesday 5th December 1995 at 2:00pm, and would we kindly bring with us copies of Neil's school reports and assessments and any other relevant information. She also asked for our permission to talk to Neil's last school.

****

Neil was in trouble again with the police for criminal damage. Steve's signature was on the arrest sheet; usually I am the one who has to suffer the indignity of being asked into the Police Station and wait hour upon hour while the police decide how to deal with Neil. It's a process they go through to put you in your place, at least that's how they make you feel, so I won't apologize for saying this. It doesn't go down well with the police that when Neil is brought before the court he is dealt with sympathetically, because they listen to our solicitor and us, who are all stating the **absolute truth** when we tell them that Neil has a medical problem. He therefore always acts without thought or understanding and on impulse.

The police just do their job; they aren't interested in either Neil's problems or ours. I must have put my foot down on this occasion and decided to let Steve wait hours and feel like dirt. It was the same at the hospital during all those times when we had to wait in line to be seen. Don't get me wrong, it wasn't the hospital's fault, **well not then anyway**; it was just that it was always down to me. Sometimes I thought that it would have been nice if Steve had wanted to do it for

147

a change, it wasn't usually happening in the mornings, but late afternoon or at night, so it wasn't as if he was in bed then. By this time Steve was working as a Textile Technician (Tackler). In fact he is still in the same profession at the same place today.

Things were becoming so hard to deal with at this time. I'd missed a lot of sleep inevitably, as by the time Neil had settled in bed and I'd locked him in his bedroom it would already be in the early hours of the morning. I'd be in the living room having my 'quiet time', just trying to unwind, then in all probability writing letters to the various bodies, be it Special Needs, the Education Authority, or Social Services, even to a Tribunal, or the police because they had acted inappropriately towards Neil, or whatever else was needed to be said. It was a constant letter writing exercise, as I was trying to bombard them from all angles to try to get some help, and what was more of a concern to us, to get Neil back into school where he should be.

How I ever managed to work at all at this time is beyond me. Okay I did have some time off, because if I did become ill I couldn't shake it off with being so run down, but I truly loved my job as a 'Home Carer' for Social Services. I was good at my job too and caring for others took my mind off my **own** problems, at least for a short while. I loved my clients and they felt the same about me. Don't get me wrong here, I certainly didn't take my problems to work, but sometimes my problems came to me whilst I was working, usually in the form of Neil or rarely his dad, when something really bad had happened with Neil or about him. It was a constant pressure so I was worried all of the time.

A friend of Neil's came to our assistance at this frustrating time; she owned a local corner shop. She felt sorry for Neil and was very understanding of his problems and knew that keeping him busy was the answer, so she let Neil help her in the shop. She took him to the 'Cash & Carry' with her as Neil was a tall, strong boy with a lot of energy. She was a life saver to us at that time; we were all so very grateful to her. At that time she was a single lady. We liked her because she was bubbly and intelligent; she had a knack for winning competitions because her winning slogans were so clever. It was really no wonder that she won so many times. She even won a car once, and she was such a lovely outgoing person.

148

****

On 10th November 1995 I receive a letter from the Special Educational Needs Tribunal. They were telling me that they had written to me on 25th September about my appeal against Lancashire Education Authority's decision about Anthony's (they had used Neil's second name) Special Education Needs. Lancashire Education Authority had **not** met the deadline for opposing my appeal, therefore it was to be referred to a Tribunal to decide whether there needed to be a 'Hearing' at which the L.E.A. would **not** be represented, or whether the case could be decided on the basis of my notice of appeal and the other documents I had sent them.

If it was decided by the Tribunal that a hearing must be held, then they would be in touch with me about the arrangements. If not, a copy of the Tribunal's decision on the appeal would be sent to me as soon as possible.

A week later I receive a letter from L.E.A.

In it they said that they received my letter of 9th November 1995 that I had sent to the Chief Education Officer, and had noted my concerns regarding Neil's ongoing education. The management of a person's individual Special Needs lay with someone called Mr P. McGregor. A copy of my letter had therefore been sent to him and my complaints were the responsibility of the Chairman of Governors and would be delegated to him.

The Annual Review papers were complete and an application was being made to Wellington Hall School for a residential placement. He knew that I was in favour of Eden Grove, and he said that the Authority's initial response to the Tribunal was that this school was not appropriate for a pupil with Neil's level of cognitive ability.

I could not believe that they had sent Neil's papers to Wellington Hall for their consideration, which meant even more wasted time for them to look over the papers, and then to contact me to go and see the school with Neil. All of this was going on before the start of the new term which was January 1996. Robert Hardy was to handle communications.

On 18th January I received a letter from the Special Educational Needs Tribunal. I had rung the Tribunal's Clerk because time was moving on, and I felt that everyone concerned was just dragging their feet. I knew that Eden Grove had been approved by the Secretary of

State for the education of boys aged between eight and sixteen with moderate learning difficulties. I didn't need for her to tell me the *same,* but what she was telling me was that the Tribunal had the power to order L.E.A. to name the school of *my choice* in his statement, but in order to do this I would have to demonstrate that there was a place available for Neil at that school. I knew that I would really have to push the fact that I knew that Neil needed to be taught at a lower level in order for him to achieve his goals. The L.E.A. wanted him to be taught at a higher level, but I knew from all my previous experiences with him that this **wasn't** the way to teach Neil.

On 16th February 1996 I received yet another letter from the Educational Needs Tribunal. The Tribunal had had a Preliminary Hearing and had decided that a full hearing was necessary, but the L.E.A. would not be represented. They weren't satisfied that my choice of school was appropriate for Neil, or that I had satisfied them that there was a place for him there. I had to send more documentation to the Tribunal which had to arrive by the 18th March.

The Hearing was arranged for Wednesday 10th April at 10.00am in Burnley.

So we were about to go to the wire on this one with the L.E.A. I wouldn't let them make any more mistakes with Neil if I could possibly help it, as he deserved better than this. Although I was very nervous, as I imagined this would be like being a witness at court, there was such a lot at stake. In fact there was the whole of Neil's future happiness. I therefore MUST do my very best to make the Tribunal not only *listen* to me, but more importantly *believe* everything I said.

We had our appointment to see Dr Stevens at the Marsden Street Clinic in Chesterfield. I remember quite vividly my conversation with Steve in the car on the way to see her.

He said, "What if she doesn't agree that Neil has A.D.H.D.? What will we do then, and where would we be able to go to for help from there? The doctors don't know what they are doing with him, so where would we be able to turn?"

I felt a little out of my depth hearing Steve speaking his thoughts out loud. It was me and only me, who was actually saying that Neil had this condition. Not one other person had said that it could be even be a possibility. I was telling Steve and the rest of the family it was so, trying to convince them. They didn't deny it *could* be true, but I felt that they were just going along with me and allowing me to get on with it.

I replied to Steve's questions, "She will say that he **has** got the condition, because he **truly has**." I was determined not to doubt myself now.

Dr Stevens was very thorough, she already had a lot of information about Neil, and she'd talked to the teachers and doctors about him. Although she talked at length to Steve and me too, it was always Neil that she was most interested in talking to. She used to take him away to talk to him for hours at a time. I got the impression that she was in demand and had a very large workload. I also felt that she was hard pushed, very generous of her time, and completely dedicated and committed to the children and families in her care.

We had started off really early to see Dr Stevens as Chesterfield was a long way from our home. We arrived there hours before our appointment to ensure that we had plenty of time to find the Clinic. We parked the car in the car park then we went to have a look around Chesterfield which is famous for its crooked spire. After a while we then went back to the car to eat the sandwiches that I'd made very early that morning. We had butterflies in our stomachs as this was an important day. It was also a very long awaited day, especially so for me. I knew I was right about Neil, but at the same time I felt there was *also something more.*

He was a very extreme case if it was just A.D.H.D. I had my doubts that it was just that. Perhaps you could call it a mother's intuition or what you will, but I knew somehow that there was something **else** wrong.

****

There we were sitting in the car talking about Tess the new addition to our family. Tess was our Border Collie puppy that we'd been given by a friend and neighbour called Reg. He'd had a heart attack shortly after he got her, so he wasn't able to cope with her himself. I'd seen her in his arms one day. He was standing at his front door, and wasn't able to put her down on the floor because she hadn't had her injections. She was so alert with pointy pricked up ears. I just completely fell in love with her.

We had lost our Afghan Hound Purdy as we had to have her put to sleep because the lumps she had developed were cancerous. After a final holiday in the caravan we had her put to sleep when we got home, and didn't tell Ryan until afterwards as he was so upset and heartbroken.

When Reg became ill he asked me to take his dog in, as he knew we would give her a good home. I rang Steve at work as soon as he asked me.

Steve said, "We'll talk about it when I come home."

Tess was behind the door in her basket when he came home the following morning as Reg had said that he was too ill to cope with her, and if I didn't take her he'd have to put a note in the pet shop window the next day. I couldn't let him do that. I knew Steve wouldn't mind. He soon loved her to bits too, our beautiful Tess.

We had arranged for Steve's mum Kath to call at our house and let her out and feed her whilst we were out. We were beginning to worry now about Tess as well as Dr Stevens.

Dr Stevens came back with Neil; we were in the waiting room surrounded by toys. We went into her room and she invited us to sit down.

"Yes, I agree with you, Neil is suffering from A.D.H.D." she told us.

(If I revert back to A.D.D. instead of A.D.H.D. forgive me because at that time it was only called A.D.D. and that is what we knew it as. The hyperactive bit in its description seemed to come about later but it was always the same condition).

I will never forget her saying it in those exact words. She knew that saying it that way gave me a tremendous feeling. I simply started crying.

It was the start, she wanted to put Neil on Ritalin straightaway, as she explained to us that he was a particular bad case, saying that it was like the rungs of a ladder and Neil was at the top. She agreed to take Neil on as her patient, and she said that she would contact my doctor, the hospital and my solicitor. This was all a great deal of work for her at the beginning, but she was wonderful; we were so very grateful. We both felt such elation.

We felt now that at last we could move on, we had a diagnosis, so people would **have** to listen to us now. Oh! How very important it is to have a diagnosis, as we were to find out later, especially regarding mental illness. Our high spirits however would be short lived, but at that time we felt that we had enough leverage to push Fernlea Hospital and the Education Authority into providing for Neil.

On 5th March 1996 we received a letter off my solicitor Val Shaw. She informed us that confirmation had been received, and that we **would** be getting legal aid, but we would still have to pay a contribution towards the costs. Although it was tough to keep forking out, we always did this readily.

Advice had been received by Counsel and she asked as a matter of urgency the following:

a)   Confirmation in writing from the Educational Psychologist Mr Brighton and psychiatrist Dr Hussain that their view is now that a residential school is the best option for Neil.

b)   She would write and endeavour to obtain such written confirmation.

There was already a report from Mr Brighton, which was dated the 27th September 1994. Of course this was somewhat out of date now and it did not specifically recommend residential schooling.

Counsel referred to the Statement of Special Needs of which he was supplied with a copy. Of course this did not state that a residential placement was necessary. Counsel asked for sight of the Notice of Appeal that I had submitted to the Education Needs Tribunal.

Counsel also stated that we required a report from Dr Stevens confirming that Neil was being treated for A.D.H.D. That was received and Val had sent me a copy.

In order that we were successful, we knew that we would have to give fuller information, and if possible documentary evidence to show why we felt that Eden Grove School would be a more appropriate school than either Witherslack or Wennington Hall Schools.

Legal aid wasn't available for representation at the Special Needs Tribunal. As such Val wasn't able to attend at the Tribunal, despite the fact that she would assist me as much as possible before the hearing date, she could not go with me.

Counsel said that at the Tribunal it would be stated that the L.E.A.

are only obliged to maintain such Special Education provision as is set out in the Statement, but of course the Statement we had at that time did not **insist** that a residential placement was necessary. We therefore had to appeal against the content of the Statement by first persuading the Tribunal that a residential placement was necessary, together with a report to back that up. Secondly we had the more difficult hurdle of persuading the Tribunal that a *particular* school was really necessary.

Counsel had suggested that we wrote to the Education Authority to see in the first instance if they would confirm that they now conceded that a residential placement was appropriate, so that this would then narrow the issues that needed to be dealt with on the Appeal Hearing.

In the meantime of course we needed to be obtaining the appropriate information. Our legal aid in relation to judicial review had at this stage been refused, as of course the Legal Aid Board wished that all alternative options should be pursued first. Counsel stated however, that if the Statement were amended, and it did satisfy Eden Grove and the Local Authority, then failed to follow the amended Statement, they would then leave themselves open to a Judicial Review for which legal aid would then be available.

We had at this stage been granted to make representations under Section 17 of the Children's Act 1989, which states that *it is the duty of the Local Authority to provide for children in need*. Counsel stated that any complaint would have to be brought through the representations procedure set out in the presentations procedure (Children's Regulations).

Counsel seemed to suggest that the best approach was to deal with the Special Education Needs Tribunal first, because if this was successful, then of course the issues would be resolved. He didn't think that we would be successful in forcing the arm of the L.E.A. to provide a specific placement like Eden Grove School.

Counsel gave us some advice as to the conduct of the Appeal. He stated that witnesses could be summoned, and it might be useful therefore if Dr Stevens and either Mr Brighton or Dr Hussain were to attend.

Mr Ince the headmaster had written to my solicitor after having had a phone conversation with her. He told her that I had visited his school Eden Grove on three occasions. I was pleased with my visits and Neil was enthusiastic at being placed there, and we were all as a family strongly of the opinion that this school could help Neil with his behavioural difficulties. He did state that the school was usually asked to take pupils with *less* academic abilities than Neil had, but he was sure that the school could address his problems.

He further said that he was not against considering Neil for placement at Eden Grove as he had much sympathy with our predicament, but he was unable to respond to a request by us for a placement unless the referral was made by the relevant Education Authority.

CHAPTER NINE
Attention Deficit Hyperactive Disorder

At this point in my book I think I should talk about this far reaching condition. Today this condition is more recognized than it was in 1996. Having said that, it is in fact often *still* misunderstood, ignored and mistreated. There are very few doctors specializing in the condition, so to even find a doctor or psychiatrist to treat it is near impossible. The condition is ongoing, and it is certainly capable of following our children into adulthood. I was told that the condition could possibly diminish as Neil got older, but to be aware that it could also follow him into adult life.

There are different degrees of this condition. Some children can be *very aggressive*, although in Neil's case he was **not.** We regarded this at least as a blessing. Dr Stevens said there was also O.D.D. Oppositional Defiant Disorder, within the condition which made the child defiant and happy to the fact that he'd hurt someone physically or verbally, whereas Neil **didn't intend** to do so intentionally, so he was always sorry afterwards, but he simply couldn't help himself.

Obviously I can only talk about **Neil's condition** and how it affected him and us also. I am aware that it can be *different* for other children and their families. I'm no expert, but I do pride myself in the way I handled Neil often on my own, even before we were given the diagnosis of A.D.H.D. for him.

Often it's down to common sense and being in tune with your child. You need to ignore *some* bad behaviour, as you simply cannot be going on at your child every single minute. So unless it was something extreme; or of course dangerous behaviour; we usually allowed Neil a little leeway.

I do also think, but this is purely my own personal opinion, that there are too many parents too eager to **label** their children as having this condition, and then jumping on the band wagon so to speak. There truly are badly behaved kids, just as there are also some uncaring adults who have never learnt good parenting skills.

Neil's condition was in the extreme, but not all A.D.H.D. sufferers are as bad as Neil, nor would they feel the need to turn to substance abuse as Neil did later on to tend to his needs. But that too could equally be put down to the fact that the doctors (psychiatrists) and the 'Services' turned their backs on him and ignored Neil's cries for help. But once more I'm getting ahead of myself.

****

Now I'm getting back to back to March 1996 and the medical report from Dr Stevens.

Dr Polly Stevens had prepared a medical report for my solicitors as they wanted a diagnosis of Attention Deficit Hyperactive Disorder, and what type of residential establishment she thought would be most suitable for him. The doctor talked about his constant, restless, unproductive over activity, saying that he couldn't settle down to tasks, and was always seeking stimulation. Neil was always fiddling with things which would inevitably get broken or damaged. He was irritating to others and didn't make friends easily. He did endear himself to some people either adults or children occasionally. However once some children knew that they could easily egg him on to do things, because he wasn't able to anticipate the consequences of his actions, they would take advantage of him which in turn often lead Neil into trouble, which they thought was funny. So a lot of what he did led to deviant activity often through no real fault of his own.

He had always been bullied and he was very easily distracted in the school setting. His memory was poor, so he couldn't remember things or follow instructions, plus he was always fidgety no matter where he was.

Dr Stevens thought that Neil had some development immaturity and a conduct problem. We had conveyed to her that Neil had shown some improvement in residential school and she had noted this, but overall even though many different approaches had been made, there was no success of any substantial nature. We had tried enrolling Neil in clubs, but after a short term settling in period, he was always asked to leave as he was too disruptive. This sense of failure carried on throughout his life.

Dr Stevens realized the stress that we were under as a family, and how difficult it had been for us to teach Neil from a young age even to dress himself properly, because his learning was slow and tainted. He was a clumsy child and indeed is still clumsy. Dr Stevens could see how close he was to me, but had also noticed that he wasn't the same with Ryan. This was most probably due to the fact that Ryan couldn't relate to, or understand Neil's behaviour.

When Dr Stevens tested his I.Q. levels she said that the W.I.S.C. Test gave Neil a global I.Q. score of 75, however this was artificially inflated by an unusually high score on one of the tests. Overall he was tested and given a low-average level, putting him three years below his peer group.

We then talked about his offending; it was agreed by Dr Stevens and the police that they were relatively minor impulsive property offences, but it was regarded as quite a different matter when it came to the bulldozer incident as this was far more costly. Even though Neil's own account was of 'messing about' with some local lads, it was obviously much more of a worry because of the possible dangers involved.

Dr Stevens said it was Neil being impulsive in driving the bulldozer up the steep embankment, then simply losing control of it and fortunately escaping it as it overturned. Dr Stevens did say though that the participation here was impulsivity, without any thought whatsoever to the possible consequences, which was a strong characteristic of Neil's condition, rather than any criminal intent.

Neil's interview with Dr Stevens showed him to be a pleasant slim young man, who was both highly fidgety and talkative, but as usual moving from one subject to another in rapid and not usually logical succession. He was always willing to co-operate, so at this time would have made quite good eye contact.

This changed and became different as he grew older, as his willingness to talk about himself or his difficulties would show little capacity to reflect on his behaviour, as he didn't have any insight into his situation, or the means to be able to make the situation better. Like a child he was always preoccupied with the silly day to day events, and he lacked a great deal of abstract thought.

He was able to discuss ideas about the future, but he really didn't understand what would be necessary to change things. He lacked confidence in his abilities and he showed *extreme sadness* about his situation. Dr Stevens noted that Neil was clearly much closer to me than any other family member, and the fact that our interaction as a family reflected the tension we were all under, and had been so for a long time.

Dr Stevens told Val that she had no doubt that Neil suffered from Attention Deficit Hyperactive Disorder, and that having been given the drug Methylphenidate Neil had shown a good response. Her comments on his schooling were that children with Neil's condition often do badly in mainstream school, so Neil was in great need of an education placement which could offer stability and consistency over a long period of time.

This placement would need to be able to offer education which she believed needed to be pitched at a *lower level* than his superficial I.Q. figure, in order to allow him a baseline of achievements upon which to gradually build. His teachers would need to accept that Neil had limited ability to link cause and effect, and to understand that he didn't understand the impact of his behaviour on others, because he was really well below his chronological age.

Dr Stevens also said that because Neil had an extremely close relationship with me, it was necessary that any placement was fully supported by both Neil's father and me, so that we had the necessary collaboration between our contact with the school and home. Neil also needed ongoing child mental health monitoring and his medication needed stricter reviews and control. She also said that our family would benefit from supportive sessions, especially given the enormous stress that we were all under.

******

I will comment about this report now, but also at a later date, because this mental health problem that is *stated as so,* was most definitely **denied as being so** by the psychiatrists and the Mental Health Team at Fernlea General Hospital, who have to this day **still denied** that Neil **ever** had an enduring mental illness, even though on top of this he was seen as psychotic by a number of people, including doctors and health workers.

On top of this, there was **known documented evidence on file of family members suffering from manic depression, schizophrenia and also suicides of members of the family.** When all of this is taken into account, treating Neil, AND knowing these facts is not only disgraceful and totally irresponsible; it is in *my opinion* **also criminal**.

This was also coupled by the fact that the Head of Psychiatry Dr Leister, had himself treated two of these family members before treating Neil, so he was privy to, and knowledgeable of these facts, but as mentioned I will say more later on about Dr Steven's report.

****

To you Dr Stevens, I would like to say a deep and heartfelt thank you for the little time we had with you. We will be forever in your debt as you have so much insight into this condition, and I have no doubt that your dedication has helped numerous families. Our contact with you was short-lived, because you had to finish due to ill health. It wasn't your fault that we had to fend for ourselves, as I lay that very firmly at Fernlea General's door.

In the report Dr Stevens stated that I finished work to look after Neil. I actually didn't! I did cut my hours down drastically though, with the help of my employers, because then it was totally unheard of to work as few hours as I did, yet still have the benefits that I kept for working for Lancashire County Council. I was very fortunate, and it showed in what high esteem they held me and the work I was doing. I was also looking after my mum, so it became impossible keeping up with my full work load. I had to weigh it up, but I really didn't want to give a job up that I enjoyed. I couldn't go for a better job, because you had to at least work full time. I couldn't be career minded while looking after two disabled family members. Although working got me out of the mad house I called home, I was becoming physically unfit, due to my 'bad legs' after the accident we'd had, my mobility had become more painful. Stress too was a major factor, and although I had a high pain threshold, mentally I was flagging.

Regarding school and mentioning Neil's attendance, Neil never had any days off school so his attendance was exemplary as I've stated before, but when he attended Brook Bank this wasn't so. He was bullied, abused and attacked by other pupils, he was badly hurt at times, and even though he was *still actually on the books at Brook Bank,* I'd taken him out of school.

****

Neil's petty crimes continued, but when he reached an age when the police and the Criminal System could criminalize him, they did so with a vengeance. I was told by numerous police officers that it wouldn't be the same when he was seventeen as then they could deal with him without my interference.

They did, but they were *wrong* to do so. All I'm saying now is that Neil suffered from the same illness at the age of seventeen and eighteen as he had as a young child, so why then given this fact, the knowledge that he was ill and by then suffering from a more serious mental illness such as psychosis, schizophrenia and only God knows what else, was he treated as a bad person, a criminal when he was just impulsive and acted without thought to the consequences, which was just an unfortunate but very real characteristic of Neil's condition, rather than criminal intent as had been carefully pointed out and stated to be so by Dr Stevens.

Clearly too Neil's age was of little importance, because as Dr Stevens had also stated Neil was acting at a much younger age.

I have often said that the Criminal Justice system didn't work for Neil. I said this on many occasions that he couldn't help or stop himself. You could cut off his toes, fingers, arms and everything else really, **but he still wouldn't be able to stop doing the things that got him into police hands.**

So please can ANYONE at all out there, tell me why or how the law and the scales of justice itself, could possibly be right to punish someone like that? How could you stop him? You couldn't, but you still did criminalize him. You made him suffer when he couldn't help it. How much and how far did you go in doing this? Well everyone reading this book will see towards the end.

Dr Stevens also stated how responsive and co-operative Neil was in interview. This was always a trait he continued to display, even with the police and their interviews, which were so sad at times. He was so vulnerable and such an easy target.

These people *weren't* his friends, they were there to ridicule, to punish him and then pass him onto someone else to do the same. **Poor Neil, he didn't stand a chance**!

In Dr Steven's report, she mentions Methylphenidate (Ritalin). Neil was on a larger dose of this medication than most other children because he was a very tall and well-built for a child. He had been given medication before, but he had always to be given a larger dose in order for it to have any affect on him. At that time, and going off

161

his acute condition, I deemed it to be the correct dose. This was to continue for a while under Dr Blake, but after he left Fernlea General Hospital, boy did they make a mess of it, as for years they completely **denied him his medication**, despite the fact that he was still suffering from this *same* condition.

Neil as is stated couldn't plan ahead or understand situations. Still he was treated as if he could by all those around him.

Dr Steven's says about Neil, "He has disarming fluency."

I know it's hard to see this good looking boy, then man, and see that there was **anything** at all wrong with him. He was so clever at covering up that he had anything wrong with him mentally. If you were a little more patient and stayed around for a little longer, it always did show up eventually.

No one ever does stay for long enough, whether it was doctors, friends, or even girlfriends; they all only saw him over a short period of time. We were often left swimming alone against the tide, telling people that he was ill, and therefore could not help his actions. As usual though whatever we said, almost always fell *Upon Deaf Ears*. **So this is a really good and apt title for this book, don't you think?**

My God, life was hard, and Neil my love you made it a whole lot harder for us all, yet you also made it so much easier for the Medical Profession to ignore us, as they listened to you covering up, wanting so badly to be simply 'normal'. So often we were told by the psychiatrists that they didn't need to listen to us. Of course they didn't want to.

"We listen to the patient, and what *they* want," was said so often.

This statement, repeated so frequently to us made absolutely no sense whatsoever to me. After all we have all these mentally ill patients *mostly denying* that they have any mental illness problems at all, as we were told they all do. So in this way the doctors *have no actual requirement* to treat *any one* of them; instead they can simply **overlook** all their problems, because the patients themselves think that there is nothing wrong with them. Doctors are therefore given a reason to completely *ignore* their illnesses. **What a huge cop-out!**

Still, it saves them money doesn't it? "Neil cannot link cause and effect or understand the impact of his behaviour on others," so says Dr Stevens. "There also needs to be ongoing child *mental health* monitoring of Neil and his medication," she states.

Think of these remarks throughout this book, because it doesn't get any better, and as his mental health becomes worse, they still NEVER ever got his medication right, as Dr Stevens, friends, family and everyone who has ever been in contact with Neil already knows.

Why is it that I understand what it was that my son needed, and that I was always right where he was concerned?

My son thought that I could move mountains to help him, and I did try to do whatever I possibly could do for him. **However I could not make a doctor, doctor.** I'm so sorry Neil, I really did try!

CHAPTER TEN
The Fight Is On - But No One Wins

The points we made to the Special Needs Tribunal were as follows:

1) Neil has had numerous educational placements, none of which have been successful.

2) It is now acknowledged by the Education Authorities that Neil requires a residential placement.

3) I am concerned to find a residential placement that will address not only Neil's Educational needs, but also his social needs.

4) Two schools have been offered to Neil, but I do not feel that either one of these schools will be able to meet Neil's needs. These schools are specifically geared towards improving Neil educationally, but are **not** specifically concerned with also addressing his social needs.

5) Eden Grove would be a better placement in this regard. It can provide placement up to the age of 19 whereas the other two schools will only provide placement up to the age of 16. A placement that is offered up to the age of 19, also teaches the children to be able to fend for themselves in their adult lives, by teaching them practical skills. I feel very strongly therefore that this would be much more suited to Neil's needs.

6) I had to provide the report from Dr Polly Stevens the psychiatrist, confirming that Neil suffered from Attention Deficit Hyperactive Disorder (A.D.H.D.) and that he was

approximately three years behind his peers. He required an Educational placement that could provide much needed stability for him. Dr Stevens also said that in order for the placement to work, it was necessary that I as his mother approved of that placement.

7) I stated that I would be attending the hearing myself. Val my solicitor wrote to the hearing saying that I was an intelligent and caring mother, who had supported Neil throughout his troubled Educational career, and was clearly aware that her son was suffering from some sort of medical condition, as opposed to being a naughty child.

8) We also quoted Dr Hussain's recommendations that Neil needed a highly structured environment, with the facility for small groups, and one to one supervision and teaching. Sensitive teaching methods were required and the curriculum needed to be flexible. Close and mutual rewarding school/parent liaison, on an ongoing basis were also needed in order to ensure consistency.

Teachers were required who had the relevant skills, training and experience in dealing with children with emotional and behavioural problems were imperative. Neil needed time to develop positive attachments with his peers, carers and teachers. It would give Neil a chance to break away from his delinquent peer group in his neighbourhood, and it would also help to bring down the high level of anxiety in Neil and his parents. There also needed to be a 24 hour curriculum.

Dr Hussain ended up by saying he believed in the choice of school we had chosen, and that it would meet Neil's needs on all fronts.

Dr Hussain came up trumps for us, and I noted a more willing response from him to us after he'd heard about Neil's diagnosis by Dr Stevens, but nonetheless we thought that he worked hard to get us what we wanted. He went to **all** of the meetings we asked him to, and he was always *more than willing* to speak out on our behalf, so we could not fault him. He was a good doctor!

****

It's March 1996 now and we are still paying to the court at the amount of £8.00 per week for the damage to the bulldozer. It will be many weeks before we settle this debt that ran into hundreds of pounds.

I received a letter dated 26th March from the Special Educational Needs Tribunal that the Tribunal Hearing would be held at 10:00am on 10th April at the Oaks Hotel in Burnley. The L.E.A. will **not** be attending. Included with the letter were a map and further summary information and guidance.

This was laid out as follows:-

Case Reference number 95-01106, Neil Anthony Green. Tribunal Hearing Wednesday 10 April 1996 at 10am.

Flag A - Notice of Appeal and Accompanying Documents
AiNotice of Appeal 18.9.95 with accompanying letters 17.8.95 and 29.8.95
Aii Decision letter from Lancashire L.E.A. 25.5.95
Aiii Statement of Special Educational Needs with appendices 25.5.95
Letters. Standard letter from SEN Tribunal to Mrs Green 25.09.95
Letters. Standard letter from SEN Tribunal to Mr Sheffield 25.09.95
Standard letter from SEN Tribunal to Mr & Mrs Green regarding full hearing 16.3.96
Flag B - Correspondence relating to named school
Bi Tribunal letter to Mr & Mrs Green informing terms of Secretary of State's approval of Eden Grove School. 18.1.96
Flag C - Further evidence from Mrs Green.
Ci Letter from Mrs Green to SEN Tribunal 18.1.96
Cii Letter from Mrs Green 10.8.95
Ciii Letters from Cunningham Turner Solicitors to SEN Tribunal 13.3.96 and 18.3.96 plus enclosures on possible school placements.
Civ Letter from Cunningham Turner Solicitors to SEN Tribunal 22.3.96 plus Psychiatric Report.

I'm pondering now on whether or not to write down everything as is written to us in the summary information and guidance, but if I don't, you will **not** get the same feelings as I did on reading it, and I want you to at *least understand,* that to a lay person, this is very

166

daunting indeed. I am trying to give everyone as much information as I can, so that as you read my book it will truly be a true and fair (real) account so please read on:-

Coming to the Tribunal.

We aim to begin hearing your case promptly. You should therefore be in good time, arriving at least ten minutes in advance of the starting time.

Conduct of your case.

You have the right to conduct your case yourself, and you can have one person to help you if you wish. Or, whether or not you come yourself, you may choose to be represented by someone else, who may be legally qualified, but need not be. If the President has given you permission before the hearing, or if the tribunal gives permission at the hearing, you may be helped by or represented by more than one person.

Witnesses.

You are responsible for ensuring that your witnesses know when and where the hearing will take place, and for their attendance.

Interpreters.

If in advance, you asked the Tribunal to have an interpreter at the hearing, we shall make the arrangements for them to come.

Documents.

You should bring with you all the documents which are relevant to you and your case. The tribunal members will have a copy of all those documents you sent to the Tribunal office, and all of those submitted by the local education authority. An index showing the order in which the members received the documents is enclosed. It would be helpful to the tribunal members if you could bring your papers arranged in the same order. You are entitled to bring other documents which have a bearing on the case, although it is more convenient for the Tribunal to have them beforehand.

Result of your appeal.

The tribunal will decide the appeal after the hearing finishes. The result will not be announced on the day of the hearing, but will be sent to you (or your nominated representative) by post later, normally within the next two weeks.

If you cannot attend.

If for any unexpected reason beyond your control you are unable to attend the hearing, you should notify the Tribunal office in London immediately, giving the reason. The tribunal may decide to postpone the case. When ordering a postponement, the tribunal has the power to order you to pay costs and expenses. This would normally only be done where you were responsible for the delay, and it could have been avoided.

In other circumstances, the tribunal may hear and decide the case in your absence. In that case, it will take into account the papers which the parties to the appeal submitted in advance. You, or your nominated representative, will be sent written notification of the result of your appeal.

Payment of expenses.

You and your two main witnesses can claim travel expenses. Public transport should be used wherever possible. You can claim Standard Class rail fares and bus fares. Taxi fares can only be reimbursed where public transport is not available or where there are particular needs which merit exceptional circumstances. Tickets and receipts must be submitted with all claims. You can also claim mileage if you travel by car. Mileage will be paid at a rate of 23p per mile. Other costs such as car parking or tolls, however, cannot normally be claimed. Witnesses can also claim a fixed amount for lost earnings comparable to the amount paid by the Lord Chancellor's Department for jury service. You will not be able to claim any expenses on behalf of your representative.

The tribunal clerk will give you forms at the hearing for you to claim expenses for yourself and for your witnesses. Please attach any tickets and receipts to the forms. If possible, please complete the forms and hand them in to the clerk before you go. If this is not possible, please send them to the Tribunal office as soon as possible after the hearing. This will help the Tribunal Secretariat to arrange for you to receive payment promptly. You should normally expect to receive your expenses within ten working days. If waiting for the money will cause you financial difficulty, please let us know as soon as possible, and at least a week before the hearing, and we will give you some of the expenses on the day.

Phew!!

I don't know about you but I found it all a bit overwhelming. It's no wonder that people don't go to this length. It's not easy to carry all this through, and they make it this way to deter you I'm sure. We'd done it once before (first stage) this was the *final* hurdle, but again they are long winded and it's been months since the last tribunal hearing, and again we'd be looking at many more months before a decision, then a place has to be found if we were lucky enough to win, all of which takes time, but of course the L.E.A. know all this and they have nothing to lose, the longer they keep Neil out of residential school the more money they save. It's a win, win, situation for them. Ruthless aren't they? Callous and cruel too in my personal opinion.

****

Val wrote to the Special Needs Tribunal asking for a copy of L.E.A.'s reply to our Appeal, but this couldn't be complied with because the L.E.A.'s reply was not submitted to the Tribunal by 25th October, which meant that the Authority forfeited any right to make representations on our Appeal.

The L.E.A.'s letter and enclosure dated 13th November were therefore struck from the record, and would not be included as evidence to be considered by the Tribunal. What fun! The L.E.A. weren't that clever after all!

I'd written to the Department for Education and Employment in Westminster, London complaining about the L.E.A. in that they hadn't provided an *appropriate school* which could cater for Neil's Special Needs and that he needed a residential placement. They said that I had agreed with the final statement naming Brook Bank.

It is true that I had, because I had been told in no uncertain terms that this was it as far as the L.E.A. was concerned; so we'd run out of options. My argument was that the L.E.A. knew *themselves* that Brook Bank **wouldn't** meet Neil's needs, so they had us look around the school when most of the pupils **weren't there.** Why did they do this unless they were in fact trying to hoodwink us?

Residential placement had never been offered to us, in fact when I mentioned it I was told that it wasn't an option, not one that I could either ask/or fight for.

I simply wasn't given any information, or told what our rights were. We were kept in the dark about the whole process. Indeed, I was told about the *Children with Special Needs, Advice For Parents,* booklet and where to get it from, **only** from the very same family who had helped us before, who hadn't been given this advice themselves either, but who had given it to us after the Statement had named Brook Bank. We'd been given no information like this from Special Needs, which we should have been given. **How can you possibly fight for your rights if you don't know that you have any? Or if there are any other options available to you.**

If you are kept in the dark like a mushroom, they hope that you will simply accept their decisions. I've never been one for keeping quiet, I always have asked questions, especially when I know that I know more about my son than these so called experts do. I really do hope that this helps anyone else who is reading this book, as we never ever want even **one more single family** to ever have to go through all these same heartbreaking processes that we've had to.

Surely **everyone** has a right to have an education, or is that only something offered to those who are classed as 'normal', whilst the rest of us have to settle for what is left, but still they are NOT allowed to rock the boat, or we (the almighty powers that be) will ensure that you are kept out of school. Yeh! That sounds about right, that way they will win anyway.

The Appeal Hearing at The Oaks in Burnley went ahead and all that came out of it was that they agreed that Neil needed residential placement, and that the Statement of Special Needs would be changed stating that fact. The appeal had now been registered and they have written to L.E.A. to ask them if they wished to oppose it, giving them time to do so.

The appeal will be heard during the fortnight starting 2nd December. So there we went again with even **more delays**, and more time for them to respond. This was so silly and even more unfair. Nothing was ever cut and dried at all. There were still more stages to get through, which in turn meant even more lost education for Neil.

170

Everything gave us more frustration. Neil had already been away from school for well over a year at this point alone.

To add insult to injury, I received a letter from Theresa Riley at Special Needs and she says that although I have asked for a specific school, the Education Authority doesn't consider that the school that I have chosen is suitable to meet Neil's special educational needs and she is asking me to consider yet another school that is much the same as the two they have already had me see; she will give me two weeks to consider the school.

Wasn't this yet another smoke-screen, another delay tactic? I felt like a puppet, what are they trying to do to us. I was sure that this school would be the same as the other two that they approved of. **I was right**. The school in fact would have been the *least favoured* of the three. We all felt straightaway that this school was totally inappropriate for Neil. Where Wennington Hall School pushed for the academic and educational needs, we felt that this school did the opposite. O.K. it would educate, but the expectations were lower. We couldn't get it through to them that we wanted Neil to get a good education, but also gain social skills and be taught at Neil's rate which would have been good provided that the other aspects were defined and worked upon. We were banging our heads against a brick wall.

My complaint was justified because Special Needs and the Lancashire Education Authority were treating us with contempt, and emotionally and physically they were dragging us through the mine-field of the education system. They tired us out and wore us down. It worked but we continued to fight them because they were wrong. They continued to drag their feet and tie us up in red tape.

I had already received a letter from the Special Needs Tribunal telling me that they had received my notice of Appeal on 31st July 1996 against L.E.A.'s decision about my son's Special Educational Needs and that they were sorry to inform me that they couldn't register my Appeal as there was no indices attached to the statement. Could I please send these documents to reach the Tribunal by 21st August when they would consider the registration of my Appeal?

I did send them what they asked for, but it was an oversight on my part and a serious one that nearly cost us the Appeal, but all this stuff was new to me and Neil being out of school and causing

171

mayhem and trying to work and look after Neil, Mum and everything else was taking its toll on me. Little sleep too, no doubt. I'd have to be better than this, lift myself up and try to keep my eye on the ball. It was hard. No excuses but I'd have to do better.

****

Neil was involved in an incident at our local swimming pool. He and another lad had stolen some money that a gentleman had left wrapped in his clothes.

Neil came home with all these food stuffs from our local supermarket; two carrier bags full of pop, crisps, sweets, ice-cream, angel delight and other such goodies. This is precisely why I tell you that Neil cannot cover up his theft, he'd immediately spend the money and like a child buy all these items, not thinking about the fact that he would be caught out, he wouldn't try to hide them. I rang the police. In those days I was a believer in our criminal system and the police. I'm not now, but you will read about that later.

Neil had done wrong and I wanted the police to get involved to give him a short, sharp shock. Also too, I wanted to pay back the money stolen from this gentleman. I never condoned Neil's misdemeanours and I would be totally honest with Neil and the police. The other boy was as much to blame; he knew it was wrong what Neil had done but he intended to benefit from the theft. I ignored that fact, he was somebody else's problem and I had to deal with Neil.

The police spoke to the gentleman concerned, he rang me to say that he blamed himself for leaving his money on show and not in a locker, and that he thought the temptation would be too much for Neil; the policeman had obviously told him that Neil had problems. I thought the gentleman was amazing. He didn't even want the money back off me, which was really kind of him. Neil was lucky about that, but the policeman really went to town on Neil to try and make him think twice the next time. I knew it wouldn't, if it happened again minutes later and having just talked to the policeman he'd still do it again. He wouldn't be able to stop himself.

****

I had to request a witness summons from the Tribunal for Mr Ince, headmaster of Eden Grove to have him attend the hearing on 4th December. I would also have to serve him with it and provide expenses for him to attend.

It was all a bit cloak and dagger and quite daunting, but I did it probably with an 'air of confidence' whilst shaking like a jelly inside.

At least if Mr Ince was made to go to the Hearing he could say to L.E.A. he had no choice, so wasn't taking sides. He could be honest and they couldn't blame him or accuse him of taking sides, not that he would. I trusted him as being professional and honest.

I asked Mr Ince to give me an indication of what I would expect from Neil educationally if he was to go to Eden Grove. I asked him to pick out his brightest pupil and tell me what he had achieved. He wrote this down for me:

A.E.B. Associated Exam Board.
Achievements tests in Literacy Level 3   85%
Achievements tests in Numeracy Level 3   95%
A.E.B. Basic tests in Communication Skills. Pass with Merit.
Basic test in Numerical Skills. Pass with merit. 90% Basic test in Health, Hygiene and Safety 85%
Also (Cadets)
Work experience Open/Sheltered
Youth Award Scheme.
Bronze/Silver level (ASDEN)
YAS-Summary of Structure
Award , Ages, Core Skills Assessed.
Working Towards Independence, 14-16, Familiarisation only.
Towards Independence, 16+. With Core Skills.
Bronze, 14-25, in particular, improving own learning,
working with others, communication and problem solving.
Silver, 14-25, NCVQ Level 1, 4 Units.
Gold, 14-25, NCVQ Level 2
Platinum, 14-25, NCVQ Level 3

Neil was very interested in the Youth Award Scheme. He listened with enthusiasm to Mr Ince talking about this with excitement. It was nice to see him like that, they'd made a connection. He talked of work experience in the local garage and bakery.

All was favourable.

****

173

We had been to see Dr Stevens on a number of occasions but we received a letter telling us that she was on indefinite sick leave.

I received a letter from Mr P McGregor dated 24th October 1996. He was the Special Education Officer I had complained about Brook Bank back in December 1995. The complaint was about the times that Neil had been brought home and left with neighbours without my knowledge.

He said, "Unfortunately, due to an error on my part, the letter was filed rather than followed up, and it has only just come to light recently that your complaints were still outstanding."

Nearly a year later plus he'd only asked Mrs Moorehead (acting head) her opinion, but a year later she couldn't recall the incident. What a waste of time that was, still I'd learned to expect very little and to ask the Education to be professional and do their job properly was a lot to ask.

I received a letter from Mr Sheffield, Special Educational Needs Officer; it was a copy letter that had been sent to the Special Educational Needs Tribunal, London, dated 29th November 1996.

The letter was about the Appeal which was to be heard on 4th December 1996. The Appeal against the Authority's refusal to name Eden Grove on Neil's statement. It said that they had received new information from Eden Grove about the provision which would be available to Neil and having considered that information and reviewed the papers they were now ready to amend Neil's statement and name Eden Grove in Part 4.

We withdrew the Appeal.

They took it right to the wire didn't they? The Hearing was just days away and we'd built ourselves up for it. We eventually got what we wanted.

Here's a summary of how we got there.
Starting at Brook Bank.
05.06.95 Neil attends Brook Bank.
25.07.95 Letter from Educational Psychiatrist, discussion with Mrs Green she is seeking residential school placement for Neil.
08.08.95 Meeting-parents and Area Special Educational Needs Officer (ARSENO)
10.10.95 Review meeting held at Brook Bank School.

174

18.10.95 Mrs Green and Neil visit Witherslack School.

09.11.95 Letter of complaint from Mrs Green to Chief Educational Officer

17.11.95 Case papers sent to Wennington Hall School.

20.11.95 C.E.O. response-advice that application to be made to Wennington Hall for residential placement.

Dec 1995 Mrs Green and Neil visit Wennington Hall- express desire to return at a later date. This was totally UNTRUE.

17.01.96 Phone call from Mrs Green to County Hall-didn't intend to visit Wennington Hall again.

18.01.96 Letter from L.E.A. to Mrs Green seeking confirmation of current situation.

10.04.96 S.E.N. Tribunal.

30.04.96 Tribunal decision-statement to be amended to provide for residential placement.

16.05.96 L.E.A. Letter to Tribunal seeking clarification of Tribunal Order.

27.05.96 'Holding' reply from Tribunal.

13.06.96 Letter to Mrs Green from Burnley Office with amended statement, following Tribunal decision and review report from 10.

10. Review-statement recommends residential placement.

17.07.96 Letter from Burnley Office with final statement naming Wennington Hall.

24.07.96 Further amended (corrected) statement.

26.07.96 Further Appeal to Tribunal, for Eden Grove to be named on statement.

26.09.96 L.E.A. submission to Tribunal.

27.09.96 L.E.A. write to Mrs Green proposing Underley Hall School and suggesting Mrs Green and Neil visit school.

07.10.96 Letter to L.E.A. from Mrs Green-decided against looking at other schools pending the Tribunal Hearing.

18.10.96 Parental response to L.E.A.'s Tribunal submission received.

11.11.96 L.E.A. letter to Eden Grove seeking view on whether the school could meet Neil's needs.

20.11.96 Letter to L.E.A. from Headmaster Eden Grove School.

29.11.96 Tribunal pre-hearing (hearing set for 04.12.96) agreed that on basis of further evidence, agreement could be given to a place at Eden Grove.

Letter and amended statement naming Eden Grove sent to Mrs Green.
Neil started at Eden Grove January 1997.

CHAPTER ELEVEN
Family

I don't intend to delve too much into the past or into the privacy of Steve's family, because this book is about Neil and 'our' family, but it wouldn't be an honest, accurate account of this problem of mental illness if I didn't explain to you why I think we've got to the point of knowing that **not only with Neil**, but also with **other members of the family,** the doctors didn't listen, care or treat people suffering from any kind of mental illness or disorder of the mind properly, or any of their families, to the degree, or with the dignity that they should always bear in mind. After all they are dealing with human beings with an illness which every single one of us might be born with, or get later on in our lives.

Kathleen, Barry and Stephen have lived with mental illness for many years long before Neil was even thought of. They have lived *in fear* of the symptoms of their husband/father Ernest. I have to be very careful here as I have to respect Kathleen and Barry's privacy. Kathleen is a very proud lady, 'with 'lady' being mentioned in the truest sense of the word.

All those years ago when I was courting Steve, I knew very little of what went on at his home; inevitably things happened that they couldn't hide. It only dawned on me much later on, some of what they did hide, cover up, try to keep from me, as after all it didn't involve me. I was the outsider.

Steve's dad Ernest was volatile. I'd heard the rumours about him, as people *always* talk. Steve talked little of his dad, but was obviously very close to his mother. I wouldn't say he was guarded against telling me what went on, but he must have thought at the time that it might just frighten me off. Honestly though, his family were at the time *no different* than what I'd expected. His dad worked very hard, if Ernest wasn't doing his building work he was in one of their many garages, with Barry doing whatever was needed with their cars or motorbikes. I got on with Ernest, he'd joke with me, but I thought he was in **awe** of me; being very confident as I was, I didn't think that he was used to dealing with a young, strong willed girl, who was extremely verbal as I was back then.

Barry though was very different, he *didn't* speak to me. You might find that odd, but he didn't. I tried, and yes, I'd get the odd word back, but that was all. I thought him introverted, shy and quiet.

'I wasn't everyone's taste,' I thought, and was perhaps too much for him, a silly, girlie girl. He was shy, wasn't he?

His dad was strict. Steve had to be in on time, but we foolishly tested things on occasion. **Cracks emerged.**

One day I noticed that Steve had a footprint on his back. His dad had kicked him down the stairs; he had been wearing heavy boots at the time which had made the tread mark on Steve's back. I cried! I had now glimpsed for myself the other side of his dad.

At times when we'd all go on holiday together; they would be in their caravan and Steve and I in a tent. I couldn't understand at the time why it was that Kathleen would insist on taking 'Aunty' or anyone. Why didn't she want to be with her husband and sons?

Steve's dad Ernest with Ryan

I worked it out that she didn't want it to be just the three of them,

178

as with someone else being there it might put enough *controlling influence* on him. Maybe they could stop him, or make him think, before he blew up. I really think that was the reason.

On this particular occasion, he was in one of his moods and pulled out the pegs of our tent. We'd neither said nor done anything wrong. You never actually *needed to* as Kathleen and Barry were used to it, living in fear of saying the *wrong thing* and never ever knowing when the table would fly up in the air. They were always forced to walk on proverbial egg shells.

Ernest was on tablets to calm him down, sometimes they worked, but at other times they didn't. There would be times when he'd take his pills, and other occasions when he wouldn't. He'd cry like a baby when he'd gone too far. There were many times when I felt sorry for him as he didn't seem to understand how or why he got like this.

He wasn't a *bad* man; he was generous and kind a lot of the time. Kath didn't know how to deal with him; she stuck up for him, took it off him, she really loved him, so she'd stand by her man. This was all well and good but what about her children; her sweet and innocent children. Why should they have to suffer? He'd often go through them to get to her; but sometimes he never got to her at all. It makes me so mad now, just thinking about it. Her children were being used as a shield. My God! Was this really how I saw it?

Steve was mine. I'd look after him, I'd shoulder his pain. Barry his brother was still then the sweet, caring, loving angel as I now know him to be. What must you have gone through Barry, especially when I took your brother away from you? I know now, but I didn't understand at all then. We left you with no one with whom you could share your pain.

Barry isn't like Stephen. It's hard to have to put this down on paper, for it is something I know, but I really don't want to even talk about, because then that sort of makes it all seem so real. It's something you know but you never speak about; it's simply something that's just there. Is it why things got so bad when I took Steve away from you?

The preferred son, the son that was 'normal'. There I've said it! You are *touched a little* by it Baz my love, but you are **not the same** as your father, nor are you as severe as our boy Neil was. You were simply a little bit slower than your brother Steve. However

179

knowledge is power, and NOW you have the knowledge and the power, the power to be different and to reflect. You are **very strong,** and you can hold down a job, drive and do lots of other things, so being academic isn't everything. We are simply **all** different and we all have to live life at our *own pace.* In the future you tell me that you are 'bad' because you saw a trait in yourself like that of your father. No Barry, you are **good,** thoughtful and kind, you have nothing at all to blame yourself for. You have taken the *best* from your father **not** the worst. There are a lot of things that happened, some of which did involve us, but I'm not even going to write about them.

I had met Alan, Steve's Uncle. He has schizophrenia; he was then living with his Aunty, who was a lovely lady who was getting on in years. She looked thoroughly worn out, and in retrospect it was obvious as to why. Alan would sleep on the floor; he would go out and paint the grates with yellow paint all up and down the streets. He didn't speak to me; he was wary and uninterested, dealing only with things inside his mind. Well that's what I thought at the time.

Steve recalled vivid memories of visiting Alan in the Secure Unit he used to be in. Steve said, "It was horrible." Then in the next breath he would say, "It was a Sunday afternoon outing for us visiting him."

'What a place to take children,' I thought.

It's a memory that Steve tries hard **not** to remember, but nevertheless it will rear its ugly head in the future with our Neil.

****

Ernest used to break his own windows. Time after time doors were left open throughout the house. We'd close them then tidy up the mess, but no one ever spoke about it.

Yes, Kathleen did involve several doctors. "They were useless," she'd say. "They would ONLY listen to my husband; he wasn't an intelligent man, and he didn't understand what was happening to him. He couldn't, or certainly didn't get across to the doctor what he was doing to himself, his wife, his sons, or his environment. People avoided him! He didn't have the capacity to insist that they helped him, but he knew he *needed* help. Sometimes he'd take the pills they gave him, but often he blamed me his wife for his trouble and for his life in general. It was never deemed as his fault though. Something or someone else was constantly making him like this; he was not responsible for anything he did. It was NEVER his fault!"

This was a lot of the trouble, for as Kathleen said she was made to feel inadequate, and to blame. He wasn't like *she* was saying, or *Barry* was saying according to the doctors. Kathleen and Barry asked for very little. **They got even less!** They were proud people getting absolutely nowhere.

"They listen to **him**, when he **covers things up**. They won't *ever* listen to me. I felt dirty with the personal questions they were asking me." Kathleen was talking about Fernlea General Hospital and the psychiatrists who were treating her husband.

I was told years down the line that he was diagnosed with manic depression.

The two of them, his wife and son, shouldered the whole burden themselves, well as much as they could; until they could stand it no longer.

"This time she has to stay away and **not** go back to him, she has to think of Barry," I told Steve.

We had him arrested when he broke our window, and we told him that we would do it again. We'd been married nearly four years and I was seven months pregnant carrying Neil at that time. It had happened before; even when we kept away for years as we could NOT stand it any longer, we still had our property damaged.

Battery acid was poured all over our new car. When Steve's beloved dog Count his Alsation, that he left at his home when we got married, because it was a guard dog and lived outside was poisoned, we didn't want to think Ernest was capable of doing that terrible, terrible thing. But he was indeed quite capable of doing this. When I saw the look on his face when he told us, I just knew that he **had** done this to his son's dog.

Kathleen had left Ernest before, when she with her son felt that things had become just too intolerable. They had been frightened, shaking, having nothing at all except what they stood up in. The last time this happened they were in their nightclothes having tried to sleep in the car, so as not to put on us again.

I didn't mind, we were family, "But this time it's for good," I told them, but they couldn't stay with us for long as he'd always come after her.

I didn't want the damage that always occurred at such times, or being shown up again. How Kathleen stood it I don't know, he got physical with her, but worst of all was all the mental abuse. She was tortured and so too was Barry. This went far beyond anything you can think of, but I only learned more of this much later on.

We put our caravan on a site that was not much more than a field. We got her and Barry's clothes from their house and other things they needed. Ernest was quiet for a while after that, but he tried looking everywhere but thankfully he couldn't find them.

We were lucky enough to get them a council flat just down the road from us, which is where they are now. They did not possess one thing from their house other than their clothes and Barry's car, and even that was vandalised on more than one occasion.

It took a long time for them to be able to save up to buy furniture, but eventually through their own tremendous efforts and sheer determination on both their parts, they ended up **owning** their own flat. It's still theirs, it is their castle, and it is kept in wonderful order. Never having things broken or taken away from them brings them both such peace of mind. It is somewhere they can keep their photos, where no one ever rips them up, as always used to happen in the past.

Peace! Their own safe haven, it's all they have ever wanted, and us, one tight family unit. We come together us Green's, no matter what life throws at any of us; we will always deal with it together. Alas though this means that we don't see Steve's Dad. We had to make a conscious decision to do that, more to safeguard ourselves.

I did go to see him though when he heard about Neil being in hospital and all the publicity that surrounded that. After he saw it in the paper, he appeared at the hospital to visit Neil.

Neil couldn't remember him so well, but he still knew who he was. The last time Neil had seen him before that was when Ryan, who was then nearly fourteen years old, took Neil who was just ten years of age to his house in Barrowford after Kathleen had left him.

He said to his two grandsons, "Get lost, neither one of you means anything to me."

I'm really glad that Neil couldn't remember that, but sadly Ryan does remember it, and it has emotionally cut him quite deeply.

As I said I went to see him. He was living with a lady friend in Brierfield. I could tell that she *didn't* want me there. I don't know why she felt the way she did, she knew nothing about me or my family, and I never wished her any harm. In fact I was happy that he had found someone, somebody it seemed to me who was quieter than Kathleen.

People like Steve's dad are better with *quiete*r people, someone who didn't raise their voice or take him on, or even fight back; it would help the situation if people around him kept calm. Though not everyone can do that; I know I couldn't. I could manage to do this with a child yes, but **not** with an abusive husband or partner.

Kathleen was quite fiery herself, so she gave as good as she got sometimes. It was like oil and water; they just didn't mix.

This new woman in Steve's dad's life looked totally the opposite of that. It was only a first impression I admit, but I wished them well. He told me he was sorry; he also told me about other members of his family going back generations who had severe mental illnesses. Because of their problems, he also remembered that there were some suicides.

Ernest told me, "You have to remember that in those days people hid such things, even away from their own family members." It was easier to do this, especially so in his family, as they lived on farms in the middle of nowhere. He could recall a relative of his hanging himself in the shipham.

"My father was overly strict," he told me, "he gave my brother such a hard time."

I imagined terrible beatings there too. His upbringing wasn't good, and he was left with his dad because his mum had died young. He used to stammer a lot. So I could see that history was now repeating itself.

He looked happy enough though with his new lady friend. Yes he looked fine. I wish him well, but I know he'd slipped through the net and wasn't being cared for as he should be by the medical profession. He might not even be aware of trying to get himself some help, as he's always been left to deal with things in the best way he possibly could. I worried a lot about that. He didn't see Neil or Ryan again, nor have we seen him since.

****

My parents knew of *some* of the things that went on, but we didn't tell them much, because it would have put a strain on us when we were courting, and even more so when we were married. We did try to ignore it. Steve spent more of his time at my house, and my parents wanted it that way. Dad used to have me on about us being all over one another, you could say that we were demonstrative, but he *really* didn't mind. He was very fond of Steve and he knew how much he loved me and that would do for my dad.

Things got worse though after I knew that Steve was getting hurt, but even before I asked Mum she said, "He's coming to live with us."

Years down the line Steve returned the favour for my dear Mum, 'our Mum' as he thought of her.

It wasn't long before we got married anyway, and true to tradition Steve went back to his Barrowford home the night before our wedding.

Kathleen and Barry said it was then that things got really bad for them, when Steve left home for good and married me. She didn't tell me this though till years later after we got close, when she'd finally *talk* to me, telling me what they'd all been through. To hell and back is probably the best way to describe it.

****

Before Neil started at Eden Grove there was a matter to sort out which involved Neil, his friend who owns the shop he'd been helping out in, her boyfriend, her previous helper and then friend (once a friend to her), the police, court and a gun license.

This isn't something I find easy to talk about at all, and it was a disturbing time for *everyone* concerned. It also showed the extent that some people will go, and also shows you that confrontation **isn't** the best way to deal with Neil, especially when it concerned pure aggression directed toward him.

It had surprised us all the fact that Neil was behaving himself working at the corner shop, and that the owner could cope with him as he'd be a handful and get into everything, and always needed watching. It wasn't as if he'd be with her all day, every day, he wasn't, but when he was with her it was for a few hours. She was good with him, and kept him busy. She had a way about her which he respected; in fact he thought the world of her. He was so proud of her, so he always tried to do his best for her because he wanted to please her.

I knew he was fond of her. I would pop into the shop now and again because I would be shopping for clients. I prayed he wouldn't let her down by doing something stupid, as he was so impulsive. I was so grateful to her for what she was doing for him. She had a couple of part time ladies in the shop who were also as caring in their ways for Neil and they were 'fun'.

The atmosphere in that shop was lovely until an old boyfriend came on the scene. He didn't like Neil and neither did Neil like him. The boyfriend didn't like the attention that she gave Neil, or Neil gave to her. Neil was in the way as far as the boyfriend was concerned, and he made Neil very much aware of the way that he disliked him. He'd been nasty with Neil when he got him on his own, and he was extremely threatening towards Neil. Obviously Neil was frightened of him, but he did try to stick up for himself a little against this man.

I went to visit a client one morning and called into the local newsagents, the owner asked me if I'd seen the note in the van used by this man for his building business. "It mentions Neil", she said.

I went outside to look at the van, and where the tax disc should have been, he'd written that, 'the reason there isn't a tax disc is that Neil Green has stolen it.'

I was later asked by my solicitor to photograph the note, which I did. I did believe that Neil could have done it as a prank, but he denied it at the time. He continued to help in the shop and all was fine until the boyfriend came in from work. Neil thought he was jealous because he was close to his girlfriend. Things got really nasty when some money went missing out of the shop, a few hundred pounds. They blamed Neil, but he denied it.

I believed Neil because he couldn't have hidden that sort of money from me or from anyone else as it just wasn't in his nature to be deceitful. He would have gone out and spent the lot on rubbish or a pair of trainers maybe, and sweets more than likely, you name it, but he *couldn't* have hidden it. It wasn't in him to be able to cover it up, he never did; he never thought in that way; it wasn't in his nature.

No, this was different, there was something not right here. The boyfriend went to see one of the part time workers to try to get her to blame Neil for the tax disc, but she wouldn't do it. She told me later that she felt threatened by him and didn't like him. She wasn't on her own in that. I didn't meet anyone who **did** like the boyfriend.

I found him menacing too, although he didn't face me and threaten me in person, but in the early hours of the morning some red paint was thrown all over my front door and that very morning I saw him painting the floor with red paint on a house he was working on.

Neil was hanging around the shop and tormenting him, provoking him and if you think about it, if he was blamed for something he *hadn't* done it was no wonder that he reacted in this way. I couldn't reason with Neil as he seemed to hate the man.

We involved the solicitor. It was just a continuance of everything else that was going on.

****

On the way to work one morning I heard a screech of brakes. Neil accused this man of trying to run him off the road while he was on his bicycle. There were other disturbing incidents, and I saw the man's van parked up the street from my home. Neil's expensive mountain bike was damaged outside the bakery, and Neil said that one of the girls working in the shop had seen his girlfriend jump up and down on it.

She wouldn't admit that to me when I asked her, nor would she tell the same to the police, but the police arrested the girlfriend all the same. You see the police knew as my solicitor did, that all this had happened before with a previous lad who had also helped out in the shop like Neil did. I'd met the boy; he was a lovely lad and he had worked there a long time.

I'd not heard anything about any of this before the solicitor told me. All I could think of now though was Neil's safety, as I realized that all these horrible things that Neil was telling me had happened to him at the hands of this man, could indeed be true.

The boy who had worked there previously had also been accused of theft then had been attacked, chased along the road then onto the grass verge, then into a field, all the time being chased by this man. The boy really thought that he would be run over and killed. He was so terrified of the man that he left home and has never been back there since, because he was told that if he did the man would kill him.

All this was verified to me by the boy's lovely mum who had also informed my solicitor. So now I knew why my solicitor was so worried about Neil, had believed him immediately, and had also started injunction proceedings against the couple, even though he didn't want to tell me all the facts; he'd told me that the man had a gun license and had guns in his house.

I had a nasty letter dropped through my letter box by the girlfriend, banning me and all my family from going into her shop.

It was awful, as I had to tell my clients who lived near her shop that I couldn't get their shopping from her shop. People were taking sides; she had been well respected, but they didn't know what I'd been told.

****

Neil, as I've said before, started at Eden Grove in January 1997. He'd settled down there very well, but there were times when things were going on at home that caused Neil to have to stay at school for the weekend in order to protect him. This naturally didn't go down well with Neil as he thought it was a punishment; it really wasn't of course.

He didn't like being away from home as it was, and he was becoming sick of it. The school was in Cumbria, so a taxi would pick him up and bring him home at the weekend. In the taxi he would have an 'escort' and one day it was my neighbour who was with the taxi driver taking Neil back to school. She was employed by the Council to be an 'escort' to these 'special' kids.

She still talks about that day when she took Neil back to school, only for him to arrive back home under his own steam even before she did. He'd get back by whatever means he could. We presumed that he'd thumbed lifts, but on another occasion he'd got into the boot of the taxi at the school and got out when the taxi arrived back. He loved the school when he was there; he just didn't want to go back after he'd been home at the weekend. He loved his home, he loved us, being so close to me he never wanted to leave me, so it broke his heart; but it had to be this way, *we needed* some normality in *our* lives, and some much needed peace.

I got on well with the teachers, but they were still trying to tell me that Neil should be trusted to come home by train and said, "We instil independence in our pupils."

I told them that Neil couldn't be trusted, he'd not get home, and he certainly wouldn't get back to the school if I was to put him on a train. They did try it for themselves, but then they reverted back to the taxi service which in itself could also be a hit and miss affair. It must have been a headache for them; it was for us too having to get Neil back to school ourselves, as the school was a long way away, and Steve's brother Barry would lend us his car on occasion, or sometimes he would take him back for us or pick him up when he would have taken off and become stranded somewhere.

Neil was taking his Ritalin and he was good at taking it, he knew he was 'different' when he took it, more 'normal' and that is why we had no trouble at getting him to take it. He still wandered at night though both at home and at school. The drug was fast acting and it had to be given at *precise times* just so that he could concentrate and learn, but it wore off quickly. There was another boy at the school taking Ritalin but not as big a dose as Neil. The local doctor that they used for the boys at the school knew a lot about A.D.H.D. and he was very helpful, especially in helping us to claim disability benefit for Neil.

It was coming up to the holidays and we were told to apply to Social Services for funding to pay for extra time spent at the school. We were told that they would have to fund it, because the Education Authority was doing its bit. I knew it would be long-winded, they *wouldn't* just stump up the money. The thought of Neil being at home all those weeks spurred me on I can tell you. They did fund for Neil to stay at the school, not for as many weeks as we would have liked, but they gave us an extra six weeks, which was better than nothing. We would work it out with the school.

Mr Ince retired from Eden Grove as headmaster on 31st March 1997. The new headmaster was as dedicated as Mr Ince so we saw virtually no difference in his commitment to the school or to us. We couldn't foresee any problems, and we continued to work alongside the school.

We received a letter from Special Education Needs stating it was time to arrange a review of Neil's statement, dated 6th June 1997. We were told that the headmaster would be in touch to let us know of the arrangements for the review and we would be able to give our views on Neil's progress.

****

On 14th July 1997 I received a letter from the Planning and

188

Community Services Division, Area Education Office in Burnley, concerning Neil's transport to and from Eden Grove.

It said that because there had been some problems in the past in relation to Neil absconding during journeys to and from Eden Grove, and on occasion being unwilling to use the transport provided, that they would be using a different operator and this would be starting on Neil's next journey home on 25th July 1997.

They were always willing to listen to those people who organized Neil's transport and this was a case in point. They tried very hard to accommodate him.

Neil was given the opportunity of attending an external work placement for two weeks. This involved working from 9.00am to 4.00pm in a *real* place of work. Neil was ever so excited about this. The very fact that he was capable of work, doing 'normal' things meant the whole world to him. All Neil ever wanted to be was the same as his brother, who at this time had been working in a factory making suites for a good few years, and earning good money, and with that being able to afford to run a car. Ryan was helped on his way with his first car by our family, so the same would happen for Neil when he'd learnt to drive and passed his test. One of the reasons we wanted to do this for them both, was that we wanted neither of them to get a motorbike for obvious reasons.

This was one important step further for Neil and he was so excited about the prospect of work placement; he was so looking forward to it. Do you know what? He worked really well, and was given a lot of praise from his employer who said he thought Neil had the capacity of going on to do better things than what he'd done on the work experience. I think Neil had surprised him.

We knew Neil had it in him in to do better for himself that this man had learnt in the short while he was with him; it's just that he wasn't able to put it into practice over a longer period of time. He could pick things up easily as we already knew, and with a lot of bravado on his part, he appeared to be accomplishing much more, but sadly this was short lived and would be very little by the time he'd finished.

We'd learn more later on about Neil and how he was changing, and also how his illnesses were starting to take over his life. Up to this point however, Neil was simply getting by.

CHAPTER TWELVE
The Right School

Neil said years later that his schooldays at Eden Grove were amongst the happiest and most rewarding times of his life.

It had its ups and downs, but a lot of it was down to Neil's behaviour and the changes he was obviously undergoing in his mental health. He managed to cover up a lot of what was going on within him, and to be truthful we were so relieved that he was in a residential school and giving us much needed peace for a little of the time, but we weren't actually seeing the changes as soon as we should have.

Neil's illnesses were always complex, but it would be years from now before we got a handle on them, having not been told what to look out for by the medical profession, but left to have to work everything out for ourselves.

We aren't medical people in any way at all, so we didn't know what this is or that actually meant. We knew Neil's odd behaviour wasn't intentional a lot of the time; he didn't know what he was doing. He was certainly a lot better on his Ritalin though, as he could think better for longer while he was taking it, but it didn't prevent him from doing things he shouldn't. He was still impulsive, acting without thought, still walked into the road without looking, as these things would always be the same, so it was still quite a nightmare for us all.

His mind was racing a lot of the time; he needed to be kept occupied, but while everyone else was asleep he was still going. This fact always caused problems for the school and particularly so at night time. Neil needed attention, someone to keep an eye on him. I'm sure he got up to allsorts that the teachers were quite often unaware of.

The school nurse was a particular favourite of Neil's as she was kind to him and had a lot of patience. A lot of the teachers were good with him, so it isn't *really fair* to single any one person out, as there were a lot of helpful teachers there for him. However Neil did inevitably have a problem with one teacher who lost control with him and Neil accused him of hitting him.

I say inevitably, because this has happened so many times, and I do believe Neil was never usually willing to point a finger, because he knew he provoked people into behaving like this. However he couldn't help it, in fact, he **expected** people to go for him. The thing is though, these people were *supposed* to be *professionals*, so as such and they ought **not** to lose control as we have to protect our kids. But when being told and seeing your son with bruises on him, you just couldn't ignore it.

Yes, I felt sorry that my son provoked such behaviour from adults, as I too lost it on occasion with Neil, but not all the other kids had concerned parents, so how far would they go with them if they had no one to stick up for them? I talked to another member of staff about the incident.

She said, "You should make a complaint about this individual," she implied that she'd seen things herself that weren't right. "I believe what Neil says in this matter quite categorically."

So I complained and the L.E.A. passed my complaint onto Cumbria Authorities (Social Services). I made the complaint at the beginning of October 1997 and I received a letter dated 11th May 1988 saying they were sorry for the delay, but this was due to Local Government Reorganisation within Lancashire (I thought that they were going to say that they had filed it again). They still said the child protection investigations rested with Cumbria Social Services.

It had all taken too long, the outcome had we carried on with it, would have been different if things had been put in place straightaway. Nothing would be achieved by it now; it would have been a waste of time. It took ages after that for someone to get in touch with us from Cumbria Social Services, so we just left it on the understanding that as long as there were no more problems with that particular teacher, we'd leave things as they were.

They dealt with it in house so to speak. They certainly didn't make Neil feel awkward in any way. It died a death, and it wasn't mentioned again. Neil was happy, he was achieving. He was doing the Duke of Edinburgh Award and he was so proud of himself. He'd already been on work experience in the factory, packing biscuits.

His employer wrote, "Neil is a very able young man, who has potential for work more taxing than packing biscuits."

He had learnt to make a three course meal from scratch and was really into baking, and on occasion made his Grandma some really lovely Parkin, and believe me; it was good! He was being taught life skills as well as doing well in Numeracy Level 2, he received 95% and in Literacy Level 2, he received 90%. He had the basic test in Health, Hygiene and Safety and passed with merit 85%. He went on to Level 3 and did as well. He was given a burgundy folder to keep his certificates in, and no matter what happened to him in life he kept them safe. I'm looking through them now with tears in my eyes because he was so proud of them. He had his Bronze and Silver Awards, Certificate of Achievements, Team Building Certificates for being a Team Player, Certificates for Cross Country Running, Relay Race, running against rivals Underley School and Wennington Hall in the Wennington Challenge, which they won that year if I can remember rightly. He was also rewarded with a medal. He entered a swimming challenge too and got Bronze. All in all he did well and we went to Parent's Days and it was so good, as for a change we felt happy and welcomed, but most of all so proud of our son.

Neil with his Youth Award and the medals he won at Eden Grove

We had the meeting with L.E.A. and Special Education Needs for a Review of Neil's Statement and Mr Hardy from L.E.A. who was the man who had the say when it boiled down to it to put Neil into Eden Grove. He was also the one that I locked horns with who denied us this precious school for so long. Guess what he did?

He put his arms around me and said, **"You were right!** "Neil is in the best and most suitable school for him and, THE KID'S DONE GOOD."

I know my son!

However it was at least something for Mr Hardy to admit to a fault at long last. Better late than never!

Christmas cake made for us by Neil at Eden Grove,
He was so proud of his baking skills,
Especially when he came 2nd in the
Icing Competition for this cake.

Time went by so quickly, Neil needed longer to be in school, he was in Eden Grove for only one year, which was nowhere near long enough. We saw him achieving, actually *learning*. At last he had confidence in himself, his self esteem had risen, but he wasn't ready to go on to the next stage, which was either College or work.

We tried our utmost to convince him to stay at Eden Grove, as he could have stayed there until he was nineteen years old, and it would have been so different for him in the New Unit, having more freedom to bring his life skills to the fore. However he was having none of it. The teachers kept telling him his 'rights' but I wished that they'd shut up. I knew him like no other, so I also knew he **couldn't** cope with the options that they were giving him. He was still so immature and confused.

The outcome was that we lost and Neil won. He got his own way and chose to leave Eden Grove and enrol at College on a Public Service Course. He wanted to be a fireman.

****

Thinking back, but I didn't know this at the time, Neil must have been under extreme pressure. He was looking forward to a time when he would be leaving the security of Eden Grove. The false expectations of people telling him he was *capable* of going to College and forging a career and living an independent life, had boosted Neil's ego into actually **believing** that all this was a possibility for him; when in actual fact he was truly in denial. He had been given a view of himself that was both fictional and fantasy. His whole outlook on life was unrestricted by reality. It was completely irrational, and would be proven to be so as time went by.

He was also having conflicting thoughts himself, which led to him panicking. I noticed that he was talking to himself, and this always became even more so in times of stress.

****

There had already been times when we had involved the police perhaps when he hadn't come home, usually because he'd set off on one of his jaunts, where he'd gone somewhere to re-live an experience, or visited someone and forgot the time, or gone too far and couldn't get back for whatever reason. Maybe there'd been no trains or buses available in the early hours. I've lost quite a few photographs that I had to give to the police so that they could find him. The police helicopter was often sent up to look for him.

His memory was poor, so we bought him a mobile phone in order to remind him to take his Ritalin. He always carried some just in case. He kept a diary, in which he wrote down the simplest of things in order to remind him to get home for meals, or whatever else. At this time the police were very good with Neil and always trusted my judgement about him, believing me when I said he was mentally ill.

****

Neil had done a 'runner' from Eden Grove and come home. There seemed to be nothing any different about that day, or so I thought at the time. He came home and took away with him all of his Ritalin tablets. He had his mobile phone and I rang him in a panic when I realized not only had he run away from school, but had come home and taken his pills.

He sounded strange on the phone so I became more worried and I rang the police. They went out looking for him. He rang the police himself and told them he was going to take the pills and he needed help. They rang me saying they were on the way to where he said he was in Barrowford, but he wasn't there. I got into my car and raced towards Barrowford. I couldn't find him and I was returning home when I saw him on the bridge that crossed the motorway.

I had to get his attention to stop him from doing what he was about to do and bring him back. I mounted the grass verge blaring my horn. Other people must have thought I'd gone mad; it did the trick but Neil ran off. I'd lost him again. He eventually came home himself, then bombarded himself in his bedroom. He'd taken some of the pills, but I managed to snatch others out of his hands, but he snatched them back so quickly, then he ran up the stairs. I called the police who came straightaway and asked me who was in the bedroom with him?

"No one," I answered them; "he is talking to himself."

They rang for an ambulance then busted the bedroom door down to get him out.

We went to the hospital with him where they gave him charcoal to drink to absorb the medication. I told the doctor that if they did do that, then they'd have to be prepared for what he'd be like when it absorbed the medication, because he'd be a handful.

They had problems alright; they rang for me to return to the hospital to help them. It was late in the evening, a time he'd be wound up anyway after coming down off his Ritalin. How did they think I had coped all these years? He needed a different approach to four security guards pinning him down. He *wasn't a wild animal*; he was frightened, worried and scared witless.

They had tried to sedate him, the doctor telling me she was surprised that she'd given him a very large dose of the injection but it wasn't touching him. It was always the same.

"If I give him any more medication he'll end up in Intensive Care," she said, but that's what she did.

So naturally he did end up in Intensive Care just as she had forecasted.

He came round the next morning and jumped out of the toilet window with nothing on but a hospital gown. I went to visit him, without knowing what had happened, and I was confronted by Dr Mallard, who'd treated Ryan for years for his asthma.

He told me, "My nurses shouldn't have to deal with people like him."

He was both uncaring and nasty and I will never forget it.

At this time Neil was only sixteen years of age and still at school, so in the eyes of the law he was actually still a child.

To this *'so called doctor'* it didn't matter one iota about Neil, who at that moment in time was a very confused and sick individual who needed <u>careful</u> handling. He'd been given an enormous amount of medication, which the doctor herself predicted would land him in intensive care, then when he jumped out of the window, no one even thought to go and check if he was alright or not. IS THAT WHAT WE CALL CARE IN OUR HOSPITALS?

Nor did it matter about me just arriving and finding out that my son had jumped out of a window and **the people supposed to be looking after him** didn't know or care where he was. They were just pleased that he had gone. Wherever he had gone to in that frame of mind should have been an **urgent police matter,** as he could be hurt, panicking and in great danger.

Dr Mallard acted completely illogically; his thoughts should have been for the patient. Neil should have been his <u>number one priority</u>. This was followed by **not** informing us that Neil had jumped out of the window and **might be hurt,** and then **not** followed up BY ANYTHING FURTHER. These were certainly NOT the actions of a TRUE AND CARING DOCTOR for a sick sixteen year old child who had been placed in intensive care.

Once Neil jumped out of the window Dr Mallard forgot about him completely and turned and vented his anger on me, who at the time was still trying to grasp the facts as to what exactly had happened to my son?

196

I was totally disgusted by this episode, but I'd long been getting used to people like him turning their backs on us. They didn't even contact the police. This was the start of the way we were to be treated at Fernlea General Hospital, and became typical of the doctors and the staff there.

I say 'staff' because it was right across the board, and even continued up to the board, because later on it involved the Trust, the Executives, Directors, not only the psychiatrists, management, through the nursing staff to seemingly everyone.

For eight long distressing years they would deny that Neil had an enduring mental illness. If 'they' didn't diagnose him as suffering from such an illness, then in their personal opinion 'they' didn't have to 'treat' him; and boy did they go to extreme lengths **not** to 'treat' him. Please read on.

****

Neil had run away, no one rang me when it happened. I've always had an answering machine; they wouldn't have known that I had set off for the hospital, but there was no message left. They didn't care that I was panicking. I didn't know what was happening with Neil, he could have gone to the motorway bridge again for all I knew. What state was he in? He had no medication. I knew I'd have to go home and ring the police then wait.

I was at home by the time Kathleen rang me to tell me that Neil was with her, and would I bring him some clothes. He'd eventually managed to get someone to stop in their car. What a sight he must have been with a hospital gown on and nothing else. I don't know if I'd risk picking up such a person and drive them anywhere. He has his faults Neil, but he was (and I realize what I've written, so will you) a very caring, well mannered, loving person who endeared himself to many folk, and on this occasion, must have done the same. He was taken home by this kind person. **Thank you, whoever you are.**

We were so relieved. Of course we told him of the risks. He'd listen but the risks would be forgotten and vanish from his mind in a flash. I contacted Social Services, things were getting worse and we urgently needed help.

****

Neil had started on his 1st Diploma, Public Service Course. He'd

197

started with vigour, head high, loving the idea of going to Nelson & Colne College, being a student, mixing with his own peer age group and meeting girls. He was a good looking physical young man outwardly, but he really wasn't quite as he appeared. He was also a very immature young man, and especially so with girls.

Of course he wanted a girlfriend, but the girls who were drawn to him were much younger, probably in effect of a similar age to his own maturity age rather than his *actual* age. This meant that they were usually under sixteen, which naturally made us worry all the time. I was waiting for an irate parent to accuse Neil of rape. It was a nightmare and was another reason why we needed help from Social Services.

He started well at College. I was always accused of not believing in him and being negative, but as I've said so many times before I know my own son very well indeed.

He couldn't get anything down on paper. We bought him a little tape recorder to use in class and at home, so he could hear the teacher repeating over and over what he needed to remember. The teachers already realized that they had a problem. They got help from the Adult Learning Services Team but they couldn't have a person sit with Neil all day.

His honeymoon period was over; he was again disrupting the class, and wandering. They tried but they couldn't help him. I had to make them realize he was serious about the course, but sadly it was just beyond him. The freedom within the College didn't help either him or his teachers. He managed to get RLSS Life Support 1 Certificate and a Notification of Performance Certificate Module. Value Level Grade Pass, Public Service Skills, Pass, The Individual & Society. It stated that this student had completed the above modules but is not yet qualified for the above award.

Again these certificates are in the same burgundy folder as the other certificates he gained at school, and he was so proud of them.

****

Neil had to leave the course and we were left to pick up the pieces, which meant that things were bad for him once more. He had failed again. He wanted to be the *same* as the girls and boys he'd met, but this had brought it home to him that he wasn't. We felt really sorry for him but we were at a loss as to where we could go from there. Social Services and the Lancashire Education Authority had given up on him, he was told to go to the Careers Office and The Jobcentre.

We couldn't see him ever holding down a job of work. He was on benefits but he had all this time on his hands. I contacted the D.H.S.S. who told me that Neil could work and still claim his benefits as long as he only earned a certain amount of money. I was told to get my G.P. to write to them.

Our doctor did write; he told them that Neil had Attention Deficit Hyperactive Disorder which was reasonably controlled, but that he had episodes of acute disturbance and some very recently. He benefited by having his time occupied, and that he thought it would be therapeutically beneficial for him to find some light occupation but he wasn't fit to work full time.

Neil was always willing. He would start a task with such vigour; he'd paint my fence panels in the garden, taking them all out, all 6ft 6ins of them. He'd paint a few, then his mind would take him somewhere else, then we would be left to replace the panels and paint them ourselves. He would go around other people's houses to ask to do odd jobs, and as long as they didn't take long he'd succeed and do a good job, and then be rewarded with a little money in his pocket.

He was of an age where his friends were going out drinking, going to pubs and nightclubs. We had our caravan on a caravan site and we'd go every weekend as it kept him away from that scene to an extent anyway. The site had a club house where on an evening we would go with Neil to socialize, to play pool, bingo and other games.

There was a really lovely atmosphere and we had a lot of friends who took Neil under their wing which helped to keep him out of trouble; he looked forward to going, and with all of his energy he'd help people on site doing little jobs, like helping the owners to mow and strim the lawn edges of the site.

It was a close knit community where Neil felt safe, secure and happy. He was more at home in this caring, nurturing type of life than being with his so-called friends. He yearned for friends and tried to 'fit in' but he never did. He'd think Ryan's friends were his friends too. Ryan had a lot of friends, and being older they understood about Neil and his problems and tended to look out for him. They'd try to steer him away from trouble or people who were out to use him, or get him into situations that he didn't have the maturity to look out for himself.

It was a worry for everyone as Neil was strong willed at the best of times. We just had to tie him to us as much as we could, but that made **us** prisoners as well as Neil, but letting him do as he pleased would have made it a lot worse for us.

Neil found a job himself. He kept asking in shops if they needed any help? Having helped out in a shop before, he was given a chance of working in a local mini-market which didn't last long and in a local chip shop which went the same way.

I'd written to Social Services and I received a letter from a Case Assessment Manager who said that he needed an updated assessment to be undertaken on the needs of my son, but when he had received a more recent account of his identified needs he would be in touch with me again.

I also asked my G.P to find us another specialist in A.D.H.D.

While at Eden Grove Neil had seen Dr Burbury from a hospital in Cumbria; it wasn't a continued thing while he was at that school, but as we were told that his condition should be monitored especially with him taking Ritalin, which was still a controversial drug.

In fact there was a doctor at my own practice who categorically refused to prescribe the drug. I had to avoid seeing him. I can remember having a very heated discussion with him in the foyer of the surgery. I was nearly screaming out that this drug was the only thing that was keeping me from going insane, as while Neil was taking it both he and I had at least a chance of a life, and it stopped me from murdering him too. It truly was that bad. You could have taken anything away from me, but if you took that drug away I would have fought to the death. This really is no exaggeration!

Dr Fleashman relented but only this once; all the other doctors prescribed it. Anyway, because he needed to be monitored by a specialist the school did get Dr Burbury involved with Neil, he saw her once. My G.P. tried to get her to see Neil, and in desperation because he didn't get a reply he contacted Fernlea General Hospital and asked Dr Ian Blake to see him. He worked in a clinic at the hospital in the Mental Health Clinic. He was one of the psychiatrists there. An appointment was made for 14th December 1999.

Neil had sent off for his Provisional Driving License. I wasn't happy about it. The thought of him driving when he couldn't even cross the road without being pipped at by other drivers, because he'd set off without thinking was just too much. Steve too was in dread of this.

The thing was though that no one could prevent him from learning to learn to drive. His illness didn't stop him. A.D.H.D. would not normally stop anyone from driving, but as far as I was concerned he didn't only have A.D.H.D. There was no way that this was all he had in my opinion.

Once again though, everyone was telling me that I had to let him learn to drive; he wanted to be like anyone of his age. It would give him something to look forward to. Stop tying him to your apron strings, let him have a life. No my heart told me! No my head told me! It wasn't right at all! Anyway it was all to no avail as Neil learnt to drive.

"He picked it up really quickly," the driving instructor said.

I'd had no doubt of that. He was quick alright.

"Soon he'll be going in for his test," said the instructor.

We were lulled into a false sense of security. Neil was happy and looking forward to his lessons. He seemed to have a purpose in life. Was he growing up a little? Should we back down and let Barry buy him the little car he'd seen at a good price? We had promised to treat him the same as Ryan, and we had bought Ryan his first car.

Neil was like an elephant. He never forgot a promise. He'd be so good, learn how to do the mechanics, and this would keep him out of trouble.

"Dad and Barry will help me," he told us.

He knew how good they were at tinkering with cars. No one could deny Neil anything if he was enthusiastic, they would take this snippet of enthusiasm and push him towards doing anything for himself. Neil got his wish. We rented him a garage. Then Steve and his brother went to look at a car.

CHAPTER THIRTEEN
Good Intentions

A sky blue coloured Ford Fiesta with sporty wheels was chosen. I would have been proud to drive that car myself. This was no rust bucket for Neil; in fact it was an absolute belter, and something of value. Would he look after it? It was a very clean car indeed.

Neil was told in no uncertain terms that the car would be locked up in the garage. He could get it out when one of us was with him, only then could he tinker away with it, and drive it when someone was with him. Otherwise he'd have to leave it where it was. It wasn't long before he would be taking his test, so we insured the car. I had no doubt that he would pass his test first time. He sailed through the theory test. He could drive the car as he'd picked that up amazingly quickly, as with everything else mechanical in his life.

He couldn't leave it alone. He thought of nothing but the car; he was relentless, pushing all the time to go to the garage, just to back it out. That wasn't enough though for Neil. It was too much of a temptation. It was madness. What had we done?

It was a Saturday, and we couldn't do a thing with Neil. He was abusive; he was smashing things in the house. Barry was trying to control him, he came to help, but he ended up fighting with Neil as he was uncontrollable. He damaged my front door. Barry was doing his best to try to calm him down, to contain him. I told him to let Neil go. He'd taken the car keys, the garage key and the steering lock key. He could get into the garage and drive off in the car. If he got it into his head to do something no one could stop him; it was better to let him go. It wasn't often that it would become physical; usually it was more a case of verbal abuse, but with trying to calm him or contain him until he calmed down, we could get hurt and things did get damaged. I could take it no longer. My health was already suffering and I was a wreck.

Neil ran off. We could do nothing but inform the police and tell them that he had the car keys and give them information about the car. He had also taken my house keys. None of us slept that night. Neil hadn't had any medication for days. He told me later that he slept in the car that night. The night after Steve went to the garage but the car was gone.

I rang the police and told them Neil had taken the car. He had only a provisional license. The same night he crashed into a van not far from home and was arrested by the police. The driver of the van had given details to the police about the car that had hit him. Neil had already garaged the car when the police apprehended him and they asked Neil to take them to the car. That is when they formally arrested him.

We knew we couldn't control him as we were thoroughly worn out and needed to have our wits about us to handle Neil. So Barry said that he and his mum would look after him for a few days to give us a break. Neil went on his own accord to Social Services on the Monday. He told them he was homeless as we had thrown him out of his home. They just turned him away.

Once more we were left to pick up the pieces. I had a severe chest infection that would **not** get better. I'd passed out twice and my legs were like jelly. I cried all the time and I was having panic attacks and felt scared to go out. Social Services didn't want to know and they wouldn't get involved.

In desperation I rang a disabled charity D.I.S.C. who in turn put me on to the Advocate Council who put me in touch with Daniel Pounder, a care worker for *Making Space.*

My G.P's readily admitted that they knew nothing of Neil's condition and continued to try and refer Neil to Dr Burbury in Cumbria. They asked her to take Neil on as a patient, but she didn't get back to them. I noted that I had rung the hospital she worked in six times just to try to get an appointment, talking to her secretary on a number of occasions. Everywhere we turned no one would help us and we received another blow as the D.H.S.S. wanted to stop Neil's D.L.A. The future was looking very bleak. We were living a nightmare and we could see no way out.

I was noticing a change in Neil; he'd started to become really paranoid, accusing people of watching him, staring at him, following him, talking about him. No matter where we went in the country certain people were there, they were after him, there was little doubt that he got people's backs up, but were they really out to get him? It wasn't happening all the time, but as we didn't know at the time and he was so believable, because it was real to him, we *did* think people were really after him as we believed him.

In fact it would be years down the line before we would realize that this was all in Neil's head, and not real at all. He'd talk on his mobile phone to people who weren't there, and the phone wouldn't even be turned on. He'd have such elaborate conversations of meeting places, picking up people, money and cars. He was in a dream world. It was a fantasy with made up friends, yet to him it was all real, and also appeared to us to be so for a time.

He started to drink *Wicked* and other Alcopop drinks. He'd hide them around the house and in the bin space outside, and even down at his Grandma's. At this stage it hadn't become a problem to the extent that it did later on, but I didn't like it and tried to put my foot down, but as always he ran circles around me.

****

We saw Dr Blake in December 1999. We all liked him instantly. For the first time in such a long time we had a psychiatrist who actually *listened.* He fully admitted that he knew very little about A.D.H.D. but what he didn't know he found out about.

He contacted the Marsden Street Clinic in Chesterfield where we had seen Dr Stevens, and he asked to talk to someone who had taken her place. He got in touch with Barbara Worrell who ran an organization that helped A.D.H.D. sufferers and their families. We'd been in touch with her on many occasions and she was wonderful, so helpful; she knew about the drugs to treat the condition. She told us about the use of Clonidine in the evening and also St. John's Wort to help with Neil's depression. I had told Dr Blake about her and he contacted her. She sent him information too.

Neil was taking 120 micrograms of Ritalin plus Clonidine in the evening to help him to relax and sleep, but it still wasn't easy for him to get any rest. It helped a little, but it wasn't a miracle cure and he had to have regular check ups, because Clonidine can make your heart race, but luckily Neil was always okay with it.

I'll say this for Neil, he was always willing to take medication when it was given to him. He still needed to be prompted, but this was because he had a poor memory, and was never able to take it on time by himself. The Ritalin was fast acting but needed to be given at *precise* times. We had it off to perfection. Dr Blake noticed that Neil was depressed and he left it to me to decide if he did become worse and the St. John's Wort wasn't enough, that we'd tackle this too with medication, but I thought Neil was taking enough medication as it was. I never gave him Ritalin lightly, but Neil was a case in the extreme and even though he was no angel, he could be the 'devil incarnate' without it. He didn't like himself without it either. He was intelligent enough to realize that Ritalin helped him a lot and improved his life greatly.

Dr Blake said we were a partnership and he'd listen to both Neil and us as his parents. He was a wonderful doctor and a very nice man. He was so generous with his time, overworked as he seemed to be; he was always doing more for his patients and staying on at the hospital to finish things. He must have had a very lovely wife and family who thoughtfully and most generously understood his dedication. He stayed on at the hospital on one occasion for us that we knew about simply to write to the D.H.S.S.

He wrote that Neil had well documented Attention Deficit Hyperactive Disorder and that he was eighteen years old. He said that intensive treatment was required for him over a long period of time. His illness was severe, needing frequent medication, and his *abnormal mental state* severely affected his level of functioning. He required constant supervision and support from his caring mother both during the day and at night, and this had been confirmed by their GP. He went on to say that without support he had no doubt that his mental illness, and in particular his inability to attend and concentrate, would put Neil's health and safety at risk.

The reason Neil had been declined his higher rate of mobility component was that it was considered that Neil did not need help with getting around. Dr Blake said he **strongly disagreed** with that, and he told them that our G.P. was of the same opinion too. He said that he believed that Neil's attention and concentration weren't sufficient for him to be aware of common dangers. He also said that he was aware that without supervision at night, Neil had a tendency to wander and behave in such a manner that put his health and safety and sometimes that of others at risk as he possessed no real road sense whatsoever.

He went on to tell the D.H.S.S. that he could always be contacted if they wanted more information about Neil. He also wrote to me giving me the name of someone in the Welfare Rights Service who would be willing to help us.

****

Neil had started work in a very busy Fish & Chip shop and I was waiting for it to all fall apart.

I was getting frightened of Neil involving me at times like this, because I couldn't very well support Neil and believe in him, because it always went pear shaped. I have always told the truth, so therefore if I was ever asked about Neil I wouldn't stick up for him or lie for him. I didn't trust him now; in fact I wouldn't even go into town with him if I could help it, because he was always walking out of shops with stuff he hadn't paid for since he first could walk more or less. The latest fad of his were colourful bicycle chains, and he was told by his solicitor to leave them all near the tills of the store he had got them from. I would have been mortified if I'd been stopped by a store detective. He'd pick up the most useless items. Sometimes, if I knew about it I would take it back to the shop. I did feel ashamed even though I knew he couldn't help it.

He was enjoying himself working in the Fish & Chip shop, he was kept very busy, and tested the owner at times but she put up with him for a long time. They were lovely girls in the shop and Neil felt good in their company.

I did something around this time that I *wasn't* proud of, and I knew in all probability that Neil would hate me for. I did it anyway, because I knew if I didn't, I wouldn't be able to live with myself and it was the right thing to do. I was so honourable back then, and fully believed in justice, and right and wrong. The police were there to protect and honour the criminal justice system, *our justice system*. Prisons are for criminals; doctors care for you and treat you. **Everyone matters**.

Sadly I didn't know then what I know now, that all of that *isn't true,* and that people with mental illness *don't have a voice* and are **ignored** and treated as the lowest of the low, as if they don't matter and they are just nobodies to most people!

I had my G.P. write to D.V.L.A. and tell them that Neil was unfit to drive because of his mental illness and have his license revoked. He wasn't for doing it believe me, but I convinced him by telling him it would be his fault if Neil killed someone or himself. Again he listened, I could make people listen; well I *thought* that I could.

Why then couldn't I make the psychiatrists listen who took over Neil's care after Dr Blake? Why did they do the terrible things they did to Neil? Poor Neil, you don't know it yet, and neither do we. We are in 2000 and the D.V.L.A. did do as my G.P. asked.

The Licensing Authority asked a Medical Advisor about Neil's inability to drive and he wrote a letter to Neil explaining why it was considered necessary to withdraw his license.

The reasons were given that his severe Attention Deficit Hyperactive Disorder was of the extent that it would affect his ability to drive safely. He could re-apply for his license at a later date, but he would need to be supported by his doctor who would have to say that Neil had recovered from his illness. He informed Neil that medical standards required for licensing are determined by expert medical panels. Neil was told that he could not satisfy those standards as he had a relevant disability, and the Secretary of state must therefore remove his entitlement to drive.

I opened the letter and I kept it from Neil because of how it was worded, but I did let him read the one that came the day after. This one said how sorry the Medical Advisor was that he had to recommend that Neil should not drive because of his illness and that he had to revoke his license and asked that Neil send back his provisional license.

I don't think he ever did send the license back; it was like a trophy to him. I doubt he'd have parted with it.

****

There was always a deep closeness between Neil and me. Although he didn't like what I'd done, he knew I'd done it with the 'Best Intentions' and with his safety in mind. He knew that I was honest, and when I meant business, I really meant business. He knew he couldn't win with something like this because he knew deep down that I was right. I was always right where he was concerned. We had a bond, a real deep understanding. I talked him through it; he accepted it. He honestly knew deep within his heart that I was right. He always did. No matter what Neil did and how bad things got, we

207

never gave up on him. Never!

****

I think I should clear something up here quickly before everyone suffering with A.D.H.D. panics about Neil losing his driving license in this way, and they think this could happen to them. Please don't worry. I knew at the time that if Neil contested this decision we would have been on a sticky wicket, because we had no actual diagnosis of serious mental illness, but everyone knew I was right in saying Neil had little control of himself, and that he was therefore a danger to himself and to others. I quoted what the D.H.S.S. had written in order to give Neil his D.L.A.

Help with getting around:

You are entitled to the lower rate because you need someone to guide and supervise you when you are out walking on routes that are unfamiliar.

Help with personal care:

You are entitled to the higher rate because you need to be constantly supervised, with or without short breaks throughout the day, so that you do not cause substantial danger to yourself or others. You also need someone to be awake to watch over you at night often, or once for a prolonged period, so that you do not cause substantial danger to yourself or others.

Also, talking about Ritalin:

Ritalin is a short acting amphetamine medication, hence the need for it to be taken several times daily.

One would expect that if this medication was omitted it would lead to a rapid deterioration in attention and concentration leading to behavioural disturbances and forgetfulness.

To me a car is a missile and can maim and kill. I couldn't allow Neil to have this at his hands; it was like giving a child a loaded gun. I wasn't one to say on the one hand Neil was so ill he needed money to be given to him because he was unable to work, because in order to be given money by the State I had to say that Neil was mentally ill and prove the point, which I did. It was therefore very hard to admit this about my son but it was true so I stand by this and the D.H.S.S. for having the wisdom to warrant payment because he was as I'd said. This was more down to me than the doctors.

I couldn't turn around because Neil wanted something so badly, and then agree with him to please him and prevent the inevitable problems he'd give me when I refused him. No, I tell the truth and the truth is he should *not be able to drive* he was suffering from more than A.D.H.D. and that was the point of denying him, because I again believed something was different about Neil, and although Dr Blake hadn't seen it yet, with time he would.

The thing was that at this time we hadn't found out about all the family members who had suffered with mental illness, but if we had known this at the time we would have been better prepared to look out for it and question Neil's behaviour, at this moment in time we were still very much in the dark.

I did ring the Marsden Street Clinic in Chesterfield and spoke to Dr Lowry in order to prepare myself if Neil did contest the decision to revoke his driving license. I needed all the facts.

Dr Lowry told me that he had found a copy of, *'For Medical Practitioners - At A Glance Guide To The Current Medical Standards of Fitness to Drive'* issued by the Driver's Medical Unit, D.V.L.A Swansea, July 1999 and that he could find no reference within this document about Neil's condition, nor the medication that he was taking, so he thought that there was no justification for the precipitous withdrawal of his driving license.

He continued to give advice on how to obtain useful information about A.D.H.D. and he gave me www. addresses saying that he hoped that I would find these useful.

****

Neil was drinking we knew that, but he always stated that he could control it. I doubted that he could, because he wasn't able to control anything else in his life. We had always been told and also read it in books, that adults with A.D.H.D. more than children are given to unstable moods. They have tendencies towards addictive behaviour. The addiction may be a substance such as alcohol or cocaine.

There is a mention of dopamine levels in the brain and A.D.H.D. sufferings having low dopamine levels to begin with; then if alcohol was added it would exasperate the condition. We were worried, but at that time we were seeing Neil only on occasion drinking the Alcopops he was keen on. We didn't know for definite; we were always being told to believe Neil and give him the benefit of the doubt, but we knew better really.

****

Neil was arrested for burglary, for breaking into the very Fish & Chip shop that he worked in. We know a lot more now than we did back then, at the time we couldn't piece together Neil's state of mind. I will give my opinion after I have given you the facts as the police record shows, and the report made by Dr Blake for David Woodman at Faulkeners solicitors.

As far as I am concerned, I regard this as the turning point of Neil's deterioration, in fact the start of his Psychosis and Schizophrenia. I didn't know up to that moment that Neil suffered from delusions, was psychotic and yes suffered from Schizophrenia; only time would show that to be so. I just believe that this was the start.

On being asked by the police officer as to why he was covered in blood?

Neil replied, "Because I've been beaten up." He had a bleeding hand and blood coming from his mouth; his clothes were blood stained and ripped.

The same Officer who had arrested him on this day came to see my son Ryan years later, to take a statement off him when he'd been assaulted outside a night club.

He told me, "I felt so sorry for Neil, because it isn't normal for anyone to wait in the state that Neil was in on that night to be arrested." He too learnt more about Neil after more dealings with him after that.

It was true, why would you stand there waiting to be arrested? Why wouldn't you run away? Why wouldn't you try to clean yourself up, or at least try to cover up the fact that you were covered in blood, hide or something?

The answer was really obvious. *Because he hadn't done it.*

Yes, of course he **had** actually done it; however Neil *didn't know* that he had. He had been there, actually looking on, but it *wasn't* him. He'd thought that **he'd** been beaten up. He'd said that probably because he thought that the people who were after him, had actually caught up with him and beaten him up. In fact he was paranoid.

210

I already knew that he was like a homing pigeon, drawn to a place of safety and security like when he travelled up to Cumbria to Eden Grove. He was getting worse in his health then, he'd gone back to where he felt happy and safe. His former nurse rang us that night as she had taken him back to her house.

We went to get him. I understood. I felt so sad for Neil. He was in a house trying to cope and failing miserably. We all cried that night.

He told the Officer he couldn't recall the full events, he must have broken the window and stole the petty cash. Daniel Pounder from *Making Space* acted as the Appropriate Adult. He told the Officer that if Neil drank with his medication he would suffer memory loss.

If Neil had only consumed a small amount of alcohol which he said he had, then that didn't account for him not being able to remember. He certainly wasn't drunk.

My solicitor and I insisted that the police only question Neil with an Appropriate Adult present, because this was his right being that he was mentally ill. But there were many times in the future when this request was totally disregarded. They were absolutely wrong in doing so at the times when Neil was obviously in a dreadful state.

It states too on the arrest sheet that Neil knew the difference between right and wrong. Of course he did, **but he couldn't think at the time, that is the whole point!** I've always said that the criminal Justice System doesn't work for Neil, he acted without thought. He didn't *choose* to do the things he did at times, in fact on some of these times he did do them, he believed, **truly believed** that they were done by someone else. I don't understand it, but I saw Neil struggle to remember, he'd swear that he hadn't done it, someone else had. He was not actually lying as he believed this to be the actual WHOLE TRUTH at these times.

****

Dr Blake wrote a detailed report for Neil's solicitors. Remember that Dr Blake at the time thought that we were only dealing with A.D.H.D. although in the extreme, as neither he nor we knew at the time what we were dealing with as regards Neil's illness.

He told David Woodman that Neil had well documented Attention Deficit Hyperactive Disorder, and although he had only been diagnosed with this condition at the age of thirteen, he was sure that the account that was given by Steve and me that Neil had been suffering from this condition from at least Primary school age was correct.

He went on to say that the condition leads to poor attention and concentration with memory impairment. Neil had behavioural disturbances too. The condition is partially treated with Ritalin medication.

Dr Blake stated, "That in his considered opinion Neil would **not have been capable of forming intent** at the time of the offence, and was clearly *unable* to perform quite complex mental and physical tasks at the time. At the time of the offence his attention, concentration, restlessness and agitation would have been quite marked and this is why Neil had no memory of the events.

I do believe that Dr Blake made an accurate account of Neil at the time.

****

We knew that around this time Neil started to show signs of other illnesses, psychosis, paranoia, delusions but also he was good at covering things up, he denied that he was mentally ill for years, so when he finally did say he was suffering from voices and admitting lots of things to the way he was feeling and begging for help, the doctors and Mental Health Team who were involved in treating him at Fernlea General Hospital **ignored** him, and even more importantly they **denied him a SECOND OPINION** and turned their backs on him. Instead they pushed him into the Criminal System, but worst of all they completely denied that he had mental illness. This was after dear Dr Blake left Fernlea General.

****

Neil pleaded guilty to the burglary. Dr Blake had seen him twice and admittedly whether we'd not picked up on enough of Neil's mental health problems, or whether it was that he wasn't as bad then, or was better at covering up I don't know. I can't answer that, but what I do know is that Neil was **never** capable of forming appropriate intent. Which SHOULD HAVE MEANT to the C.P.S. that he was wholly incapable of controlling his criminal behaviour. Why then did they never take this on board?

With my last breath I will still say that Neil was **never** fully in control. He could **not** decide what to do or not to do, he just **did**

212

things on impulse.

I said to David, Neil's solicitor that they might as well blame me, let me go to prison because I was as much to blame for the crime and I hadn't done anything at all in my life to warrant as much as a parking ticket. I don't have a dishonest bone in my body, but that's the point. I'd do his time because I *knew my son* and I truly believe he could not control his actions and isn't that a worry? How do you punish a lad who breaks the law but he can't help it? I've said it before, you can take away his possessions, his liberty, his limbs but it wouldn't stop him. It couldn't stop him, because he couldn't stop himself.

So you punish my son, and punish him again and then keep on **continuing** to punish him. It may well satisfy the criminal justice system but it is against anything I believe in. **The law is there to punish a criminal, not a mentally ill person**.

The *criminal* in this story is the Medical Profession and NOT our son. All Neil did was to commit PETTY CRIME because he was left to treat himself because the Medical Profession mistreated him and denied him.

Due to how he was treated it's a wonder that he was such a likeable decent human being. He was too; he was loving and caring towards his family. He was respectful to us and to others even when he thought that they were treating him badly, it was still very typical of Neil to step in and help someone else who was in trouble.

Neil was NEVER abusive verbally or aggressively to anyone in authority or otherwise. I know that these people might well have been acting in that way towards Neil, as this was obvious in the way that he was treated. He was a big well-built adult and child, and others had been misinformed that Neil was a 'bad one', especially after there had been so many previous arrests. When tackled and told that he had done something that he had not done, Neil's reaction was to become stubborn in retaliation for the harsh way that he was often treated, this situation meant that this led to a stand off, where the loser was ALWAYS Neil.

When he did anything wrong himself, as in the case where the Officer's spectacles were broken, Neil always apologized and admitted that he had done wrong.

213

CHAPTER FOURTEEN
From Bad to Worse

Neil started seeing a young girl. I liked her, but was aware that she had had a troubled upbringing. They were drawn together probably because they *both* had problems; different problems it was true, but I knew that Neil was both fond and protective of her. She was fifteen years old and he was eighteen at this time. I knew that they had been to the family planning clinic, and I was pleased that they were being responsible. Although Neil was the older of the two, I would say that his girlfriend was more grown up.

Being a responsible parent I made the first move to go and see her parents. I saw her mother first and then she and her husband both came to our house. Neil wasn't pleased about this because his girlfriend was frightened of the response by her family, especially her brother and father.

Things weren't right! I knew that; the girl was introverted, scared at times and far too quiet. I was worried about her; not just for them as a couple, but for the girl herself as she seemed to be very troubled indeed.

Neil told me some very disturbing things about the family being into witchcraft and the occult. I questioned friends and colleagues at work. Social Services were involved with the family, and I guess because of my involvement and the questions I was asking, it didn't go down well with the family. I met her brother and realized that he had issues himself with his own family. I was *doubly* worried.

Neil, being the caring lad he always was, was worried about her. I could see why as I was fond of her too. He didn't like what was happening at her home, and he was showing her parents that he was on hand to look after her. She felt the same about him, but her family wanted to split them up.

I told Neil that there was little that he could do to help as she was under age. Trouble was brewing though and I knew it. I didn't like her brother; I felt instinctively that he was trouble.

We had a disastrous holiday in Weston-Super-Mare. We were on a caravan site and Neil was with us. My neighbour rang me to tell me that someone had pulled out all the plants that I'd lovingly planted in my borders and hanging baskets at home. My neighbours and Barry had cleaned up the mess. Neil was in constant touch on his mobile phone to his girlfriend; she said it would have been her brother as he lived very close to us. It was hard for Neil being away from her, he was worrying about her so much and wondering what was happening to her at home.

It was fast becoming a waste of our holiday. Neil was agitated and he kept disappearing. He didn't come back one evening and we couldn't contact him on his mobile as it was turned off. It was unusual for Neil to have his phone turned off. We had no choice, so we contacted the police.

They were wonderful and sent someone straightaway. It was about 2.00am and they searched the site because there was a lot of land and deep ditches surrounding the fields, and the compound with caravans that had been left in storage. They brought dogs and woke up our fellow caravanners and searched their awnings. They got the police helicopter up to search the surrounding area. I was so sorry for disrupting the site like this and felt so embarrassed.

We were up all night but there was still no sign of Neil. We decided to go home the next day. It had happened before and it would happen again, so we were used to being upset on holiday for one reason or another, usually down to Neil. We were always torn or pulled this way, and always worried. I don't know why we even attempted to have holidays sometimes. I guess it was trying to keep some sort of normality in our lives, but sadly we weren't like other people, we were living on a knife edge.

****

We had to book Mum into a residential home a year in advance, and we tried ever so hard to try and keep her out of the problems we had with Neil. We tried, but it didn't work out that way most of the time. We were the same with Kathleen but she was uncanny, she could always *feel* it when things weren't right with us. She is still very much the same, picking up that either one of us is a bit down or depressed. Mum was at a lovely home in St. Annes near Blackpool.

We had tried to get her near the seaside. You might think that as she was blind this was daft thing to do, especially so as she didn't venture out herself. Because Mum could feel the sea's breeze on her cheeks and hear the seagulls, we thought that it was like she was having a holiday too. We always went to see the homes she went to beforehand, because we couldn't put her in anywhere that we weren't happy with. If I liked it for myself, this was always the best way of judging it.

Naturally Mum would always have much preferred to be at home. She wasn't selfish, she knew that we needed a break, and would never put her own happiness before ours, which made it harder for us knowing all this, because our holidays were often ruined by Neil.

****

On this occasion Neil had managed to get home from Weston-Super-Mare, he'd hitchhiked. He wouldn't have thought about the dangers, or about us, or where he would be sleeping. He was blinkered. His girlfriend was in trouble at home and she needed him; so he simply took it upon himself to be there for her.

We were upset and depressed by the time we got back and very tired. We had come off the previous caravan site that we had left the caravan on all year. We'd been very happy on that site; we'd been on there for around ten years, but the lovely couple who had owned it had sold it to a farming family, and as soon as they took over we tried to find another site.

The new managers were horrible and treated us and others badly, breaking rules and regulations that had been put into place to keep us all safe, but their changes now made it dangerous and unpleasant for everyone. It used to be such a *happy* place. I was disgusted by them treating people so badly, and I couldn't keep my mouth shut, so they asked us to leave, which we were doing anyway as soon as we could find somewhere decent to go to.

We had tried to get on this particular site for years and we were lucky that year as they had a vacancy. We are still on that same site, and have been there now for eleven years. Everyone there is treated well and the site is happy and friendly with lovely people who run it well, so the atmosphere is warm and caring, and consideration is given to everyone. We had to be near home to be able to go back and forth to look after Mum and be on hand for Neil.

****

We had found a lovely psychiatrist in Dr Blake, but it was short lived. He left Fernlea General Hospital to take up a post at a private hospital. He wasn't happy at Fernlea General and who could blame him? Sadly though, we lost our wonderful doctor.

We tried to shoulder Neil's problems as well as we could, but he was becoming worse in his mental health and he was admitted to hospital by Dr Kumar.

I do realize that when anyone is admitted to hospital, especially if they have mental health problems, they might be taken off certain drugs in order to see what they are like without them. I presume Neil was taken off his Ritalin, but it was *just stopped immediately.*

I was always told that you cannot do this with amphetamines. You should be weaned off them gently. I cannot understand though why they would even want to do this at all with Neil, when he had been diagnosed and had well documented Attention Deficit Hyperactive Disorder for some time.

Naturally **without** his Ritalin Neil became anxious; he was all over the place. They couldn't cope with him and they wouldn't listen to me.

In fact they said, "If I didn't like it, I could take him home."

He was bouncing off the walls but I took him home. Dr Kumar **wasn't** interested, and after his total lack of consideration towards Neil and us, *we weren't interested in him either.* Things went from bad to worse after that, and we found Neil really difficult as his behaviour was causing us great concern. It was a case of what, or who, gave in first.

We had to stand our ground, but at eighteen years of age Neil thought he could do what he wanted, because boys of his age were going out drinking, so he thought he should be doing the same, but it was always a case of fitting in, which he never did.

Actually there was a more sinister reason for him turning to drink. He used it to *block out the voices in his head.* Not only was he **hearing** voices in his head, but he was also **responding** to them, and he was extremely suspicious, agitated and pressured. The trouble was at this time, that it wasn't as bad as it got, but also we weren't as aware then as we grew to be later on.

Daniel Pounder saw a different Neil opening up to him. He

217

believed us, but when he started to see the changes in Neil for himself, he wrote to Keith Deighton at the Community Health Team asking for help for us. He told him that Neil was seeing Dr Blake on a regular basis and he was also receiving intensive treatment for A.D.H.D. and that because of Neil's difficulties, and supervising and managing his illness, we, his family were requesting assistance. We needed a Social Worker to assess his support and accommodation needs. Also Neil required a C.P.N. to monitor his medication and treatment.

Daniel Pounder said, "I hope that the Team will consider this request at their next referral meeting."

We saw Keith Deighton and Sarah Connors from Social Services at a meeting in Lowmount Clinic at Fernlea General Hospital, and they said that there was little that they could, or would do, because Neil **didn't have** an *enduring mental illness.*

I knew what Dr Blake had said, and Dr Stevens and everyone that knew anything about A.D.H.D. were saying that A.D.H.D. **was a mental illness in itself,** but as far as him suffering from anything else such as enduring mental illness he was not, and A.D.H.D. is not a form of mental illness as far as they are concerned.

They were so smug and horrible and treated us like idiots, ridiculing everything we said, and then they dismissed us. I will remember those two people as **two of the worst human beings** that we have ever encountered.

Yet another build up of our hopes had turned to disappointment.

****

Neil was in trouble again. This is a statement that was used by David Woodman at court:-

I am 19 years of age having been born on 16th December 1981.

I am charged with offences of Assaulting a Police Officer in the execution of his duty, and of causing Criminal Damage to the spectacles belonging to that Officer, both offences to have occurred on 28th June 2000.

I have presently pleaded Not Guilty to both charges, but confirm that it would be my intention on the trial date to enter a plea of *Guilty* to the Criminal Damage.

I also confirm that I have instructed my Solicitors to put forward certain proposals to the Crown Prosecution Service with a view to avoiding a trial. In particular I have indicated that I would be prepared to plead Guilty to an allegation of Obstructing a Police Officer in the execution of his duty, in place of the current Police Assault Charge.

I am a single man residing in my own accommodation.

I am unemployed and in receipt of Disability Living Allowance.

I suffer from Attention Deficit Hyperactive Disorder and have done so for a number of years. I receive regular medication for that, and have recently been admitted to hospital for investigation/treatment of complications arising from this condition.

I also confirm that I have a number of previous conditions recorded against me.

I am subject to a Conditional Discharge imposed in June of last year for an offence of burglary, and have appeared before the court twice earlier this year in connection with allegations of theft, police obstruction and possession of an air rifle, and on both occasions I was fined.

The circumstances of the current offences are as follows:-

At the time I was engaged in a relationship with a girl. It is fair to say that relations between myself and her family were somewhat strained at the relevant time, and indeed her parents have made it clear that they did not want her to continue seeing me. She however made it clear that she did in fact want to continue seeing me, which has led to a number of arguments and disagreements between me and her parents.

On one such argument on the evening of the 28th June near to her home, during the course of that argument I was assaulted by her father. I therefore rang the police on my mobile phone to ask them to make some arrangements to attend, and speak to him with regard to the assault.

Officers did attend, but made **no attempt** to speak to him and appeared to take the view, without any justification whatsoever, that I was inevitably responsible for the trouble that had occurred. As a result of this there was an argument between me and the police which resulted in me being arrested, in order to prevent a breach of the peace.

I can confirm that I had consumed some drink during the course

219

of the evening and was extremely agitated and upset by what had happened, and the fact that whilst **I was the person** who had been assaulted, I was also the *only one* that the police arrested.

Unfortunately, that rather coloured my view of matters when I was in detention at the Police Station.

I do not recall asking to see the Police Surgeon, but did advise the police of the difficulties that I suffered from, and indeed the Custody Officer was well aware of these difficulties having dealt with me previously.

To the best of my recollection, the Police Surgeon in fact happened to be at the Police Station at the time dealing with somebody else, and was asked to examine me in order to ensure that I was fit for detention.

As indicated above, I was already in drink and somewhat agitated, upset and distressed at the manner in which I had been treated, and I fully accept that as a consequence of that I was *not* entirely co-operative with the police.

Sergeant Hill was escorting me to the Police Surgeon's room and, as indicated above, I accept that I was not being entirely co-operative, and as a result of that he was behaving towards me in a manner that I did not consider to be either necessary or appropriate.

As we got into the Police Surgeon's room, he was effectively pushing me along, and kept insisting that I sit down on a couch in that room. I refused to do so, and he effectively pushed me backwards on a number of occasions towards the couch.

Indeed the Officer accepts in his statement that he pushed me in the chest causing me to fall backwards onto the couch. I stood up immediately afterwards and again Hill pushed me backwards, this time with his right hand on my throat.

I considered that I was being treated with a complete lack of courtesy or respect, and consequently concede that I was shouting at the Officer and conceivably waving my arms about. I am not aware of having come into contact with the Officer whilst doing so, although I readily concede I *might* have done so. If I did then, whilst my behaviour was *not intentional*, it was perhaps reckless.

The incident continued as set out above and as a reaction to what had occurred I removed the Officers glasses from his face and snapped them in half. I fully accept that I was not legally justified in doing so, and am consequently **guilty** of the offence of Criminal Damage.

Immediately that had occurred the Officer then punched me violently in my left eye, causing me to fall backwards on the couch, notwithstanding the fact that I was *not* displaying any violence towards the Officer at that stage.

I was effectively lying on my side on the couch and fearing for my safety. I lifted up my arms in order to cover my face and head. I felt a number of further blows to my body, I could not say from how many people, or whether any form of weapon or other implement was used, but they certainly did **not** appear to be blows from a fist.

At no stage during that part of the incident did I offer any violence towards the Officers concerned, and indeed was not even in a position to properly to defend myself.

I was then effectively dragged to the ground and handcuffed to the rear being thrown back into my cell.

I was then subsequently examined by the Police Surgeon who clearly recorded the injuries to my face. I cannot recall whether I told him about the injuries to my body, although I suspect I may perhaps **not** have done so.

I was detained until the following morning when I was produced at court and bound over in connection with the allegation of breach of the peace, and made immediate arrangements upon my release to make a formal complaint to the police about the conduct of Sergeant Hill. I also made arrangements to have photographs taken by the police of the injuries I sustained.

In the circumstances, whilst I fully accept I am guilty of Criminal Damage, and may conceivably have obstructed the Officer in the execution of his duty, I deny that I am in fact Guilty of Police Assault.

****

To read this again is very upsetting and Steve happened to pick up this Statement as I am sitting here writing this book. Tears well up in his eyes and he leaves the room.

I can remember vividly seeing Neil in front of the Custody Desk on this occasion with his swollen and bruised face, not knowing of the terrible bruising beneath his T-Shirt until he lifted it up to show me. The feeling of despair and sickness I felt at that moment I can't possibly convey to you. I brought my kids up to *respect* the police and to turn to them for help, and by giving them respect they would in turn be given it back by the police.

Sadly I have a *different* view of the police now. They lie, and can assault a person and get away with it. I have experienced the presence of the police, and been in their company for a lot longer than anyone would probably ever see for themselves. The future will see Neil being arrested *every* week, maybe up to three or four times in one week. I therefore feel that I have the necessary experience to be able to comment on the police.

Steve and I have come across police officers who threaten and tell lies about **us**, so it's not just with Neil. We have seen it first-hand, and will tell you about that as it happens in this story of my son's sad short life.

****

Neil accepted that the Officer would 'lay into him'. "I broke his glasses because he treated me like dirt."

I believe Neil's account of this arrest and what happened after. He was severely beaten, and he believed it was with a truncheon that the bruises were made. His injuries really were quite horrendous.

I asked the question. *"Would the police treat Neil with such contempt if he had had the backing of having a serious mental illness diagnosis, together with a psychiatrist who understood his needs, and were to tell the police so?"*

I think that Fernlea General's failure to diagnose Neil's condition accurately, and give him the necessary medicine and treatment for this illness, plus the help that would follow on from such a diagnosis, led to so much heartache and pain for my son and us as a family. Ignorance is one thing, but to totally ignore him having treated two members of our family previously with mental illness is absolutely disgraceful. It also has no place whatsoever in modern society.

Doctors should be MADE to doctor! They should also be qualified enough to be able to do their job properly. If someone keeps trying to kill him/herself by jumping off bridges or trying to hang him/herself, or keeps coming through their doors, jumps out of windows straight after coming out of intensive care, and self-harms to the distressing levels that Neil did, then he/she is DEFINITELY ILL and in need of help. He is NOT SEEKING ATTENTION – he is definitely way beyond that! If a psychiatrist is unable to diagnose a patient properly, then that **said patient** MUST be allowed to go elsewhere – to see another medical person, not be placed into the penal system.

No one should be allowed to act as God, for every single one of us is fallible, no one is perfect. Those doctors who blindly follow others are letting their patients down, and certainly not doing their jobs correctly. Bosses are **not** always right! It might save time, but ultimately it might also lead to loss of lives for those who are allowed deliberately, or through ignorance, or fear of losing their jobs, to allow mentally ill people NOT to be diagnosed as such. One in four suffer from mental illness at some time in our lives, is this how you would like to be treated?

As the doctors, and especially Bob Gardner, Manager/Administrator denied Neil's mental illness, and told the police so on many occasions even down the line after numerous incidents. However the police themselves believed Neil **had mental illness,** after seeing him displaying the same characteristics so many times.

They would often even take Neil to the hospital for his own safety, hoping that he would be admitted. Then when Bob Gardner was contacted, this resulted only in the psychiatric staff being told to show Neil the door. This was the same routine that continued even after Neil had seriously attempted suicide.

Do I blame myself for bringing Neil up to expect people in authority to treat him with compassion, civility and respect, and being proud of my son for the manners he showed these people only to have it thrown back in his trusting face?

I knew as I told Neil's solicitor David at the time that keep taking him through the Court's Criminal System and having offence after offence documented, would make the police and courts treat him as a hardened criminal, a bad person. It would only show up after *hundreds of arrests*, when someone would actually begin to think for themselves. "Hey wait a minute, what is going on here with this lad?" Then it would happen. "There's something not right here." If this didn't happen, then it **certainly should** have done.

David said, "We needed the help of the police and the courts, and the only way to make someone sit up and listen was to put Neil through the Criminal System."

The thing was though, that is just what Fernlea General wanted, Bob Gardner and the psychiatrists; they wanted to off-load Neil, because if he was in custody or in prison **they didn't** have to treat him.

It is the truth! They pushed Neil into the Criminal System for their own sakes, and the worst of it was, that they were *allowed* to do it. It is a **disgrace** that a *mentally ill man can be sent to prison* **instead of being treated in a hospital,** which in effect is *exactly* what did happen.

****

The police officers always said to me that they were **not Social Workers** and they are *right* it was **never truly down** *to them* to look after Neil in such a way, but it's because the Hospital and staff therein turned their backs on Neil, that the police were left to pick up the pieces, just like us, but they have to do their job, which meant that Neil was put in danger because they *weren't given the correct information about Neil's illness,* or how he would react and demonstrate such illness. They weren't prepared for him, and neither did they understand him; but they had no one else to turn to.

Police Surgeons are only GP's, so they never understood Neil, or gave the proper advice. Neil's 'front' never told them what he was really suffering in his head. He drank alcohol **to blot out his pain and the voices in his head,** but in doing this it did something else.

He couldn't remember half of the time what he'd done, where he'd been or what he'd said. It changed him extensively later on when he drank excessively. He wasn't Neil, but when later he drank to excess he was a monster, and no one including me, could bring our lost Neil back. He was a frightened trusting 'child' but he was 6ft 4ins tall, muscular, with an 'air of cockiness' that wouldn't endear him to people when he was that 'way out'. **I pitied him.**

I wanted Neil to make a complaint. He was given advice from his solicitor **not** to go ahead with the complaint, because as he said we needed them on our side. **I wasn't happy.**

When the police are free to police themselves, it doesn't give me much hope of achieving anything out of it anyway, so I had to let it go. It wasn't my call. Neil in the main looked to me to help him and 'do the right thing'.

Did I let you down Neil? I'm so sorry Neil if I did for it was never ever my intention.

CHAPTER FIFTEEN
Trying It Alone

Neil did move out of home into a rented property in the next town. We couldn't carry on living the way we were doing; life was a nightmare. I was always ill because of the stress, and so was Ryan with his asthma. My mum was getting older and needed me to tend to her needs a lot more.

I guess when Neil asked me to help him to move out I was taking into consideration what I had to do for Mum, Ryan and my husband, and weighing up Neil's needs I gave in to look after the many, rather than just Neil.

It wasn't an easy decision, but don't think I was pushing Neil out or anything like that, as it was his decision. We couldn't carry on the way we were doing. With Neil pulling to do what he wanted to do all of the time, and making it a house full of arguments and stress; he was really fighting for his independence. It was the only way out. I did think that the pressure would have been off us all. I had to let him go, but again I was torn. I expected some trouble, but what I expected wasn't as bad as what I got, that was surpassed tenfold.

I always knew that Neil *shouldn't* live on his own, as he needed to feel secure. He couldn't handle money at all; he'd spend the lot the day he got it, on nothing of real value or necessary items. You could ask him what he had spent his money on but he couldn't tell you. I'm sure he didn't know what he was doing half of the time. He couldn't budget; he couldn't remember to take his medication. What was I doing? He wanted it this way though, to leave home and be independent.

As we didn't get any help from the Mental Health Team or Social Services, we were left to find accommodation for him ourselves, as they thought that it **wasn't their job** to do that. They would say it was up to Neil to do it for himself, to fill his forms in and all the rest. They were useless and knew nothing at all, if they thought that he was *even capable enough* of doing any of these things for himself. We went to a housing rental company. I didn't want to do it because being the person that I am, I didn't think it right to ask for a property for a severely mentally impaired man, especially as I knew that he **wasn't capable** of looking after himself, or taking care of a house. I knew it was wrong, but what else could I do?

People kept telling me, "Let him try," thinking that he was able.

I have always been right about Neil, about his health, his capabilities, the police involvement and knowing he wasn't accountable for his actions. Over and over he was put into positions that he couldn't control, and this was one of them. The other major one being relationships. How could he form relationships with anyone else in the state he was in; it wasn't fair to him or the people he became involved with.

I am sitting here thinking that he would have been better off if he'd been born *physically* disabled. He would get the help then, as people would **see** his disability and help him. This is **not** so when you are *mentally ill*, no one wants to know, you are shunned by society, as an outcast, and if, as what happened to us, the medical profession then turn their backs on you too, what do you have left? We've been told that one in four (a quarter of the population as a whole) gets some form of mental illness at some time in their lives. **All I can say to that is God help us all!**

I went with Neil to the housing agency and took along his benefit book. He was given a property to rent. It was a neat little terraced house. There was already a cooker in the property, so we bought a second-hand fridge and applied to a local charity that provided furniture for people who had little money, or were on benefits like Neil. They provided him with a suite, a lovely wall unit, and we let him take his own bedroom furniture. We gave him other bits and pieces and we bought the rest. He had a lovely place by the time we had finished which looked very comfortable.

The next step was to make sure that he had a telephone; that was always a priority for Neil, as he would need to keep in constant touch with us.

For the first couple of weeks before the D.H.S.S. had given Neil control of his money, I was taking him for his shopping and suchlike. He received housing benefit so that took care of the rent. He hadn't

227

had any bills as yet, and I knew that would be a testing time for him, but we would help him with that. The trouble was when Neil did get his own money, he wanted control of everything. We knew that he would get into a mess this way, but we couldn't **do** anything about it. He got what he wanted.

It wasn't long before people realized he was vulnerable and an easy touch. There was always a house full of people in his home, usually more girls than boys. They realized he had money, so they used his house as a 'doss house' and they'd often be drinking there.

He got involved with a girl who was still at school. It didn't go down well with her parents and who could blame them? Her father was threatening her and Neil, and once again there was trouble.

****

Neil rang us from hospital; he'd been rescued out of the house by firemen after the house had caught fire. They said it was a chip pan that had caused the fire. Neil knew nothing about it, a passer by had raised the alarm, and Neil was rescued out of the bedroom window in just his underpants. He blamed the people who were after him. The doors were often left open.

We'd already had our kitchen window broken by someone who threw a brick through it, and I had rung Neil straightaway because I thought it could have been him. He wandered at night, and I'd often see him, or I would be aware that he was hanging about the house in the early hours. I shouldn't be thinking that my *own son* would do such a thing, especially to me the one person that he loved so much, and told me so up to twenty times a day when he'd ring me for reassurance all the time, but I knew he wouldn't have *known* he'd done it, even if he had, so I rang to make sure he was in the house. He was on this occasion which meant that it definitely <u>wasn't</u> him, but it was probably to do with something relating in some way to him. So there you go, he had enemies, and his problems and his enemies rebounded on to us. Would it ever be any different? No I'm afraid not.

Whenever Neil rang me, even when it was up to twenty times a day, he never hung up until he had told me that he loved me. Also when he came round to our home he never went until he had kissed both me and his Dad and told us both that he loved us. It was exactly the same with his Grandma; he would kiss her on the top of her head telling her that he loved her too. He was a totally loving person was Neil.

We never got to the bottom of the chip pan fire, but Neil was now homeless again. Barry, bless him, made many trips to Neil's house to bring out as much furniture and other items that he could. A lot stunk of smoke, but he was able to rescue some stuff which he stored in his garage for Neil. Once again Barry came to our aid to help shoulder some of the chaos in our lives with Neil.

Neil again stayed at his Grandma's until he was given a Council House to rent near our home at the time. More stressed than ever, my incapable son was out there all on his own again. We went through the same, moved him in; sorted out his furniture and everything else as we had done before.

'Here we go again,' I thought. 'How long would it be before something happens this time? God help us and forgive us.'

****

On 19th January 2001, I received a copy letter that Daniel Pounder (Care worker, of *Making Space*) wrote to Dr Leister, the Clinical Director/Consultant Psychiatrist, of Lowmount Clinic, Fernlea General Hospital.

He wrote to Dr Leister on our behalf to ask for the help of Fernlea Health Care Trust Mental Health Services, telling him that he ought to be aware that Neil had previously been accepted for treatment by Dr Blake, and he knew that Neil's GP. Dr Spercer, had already written to him requesting that Neil's situation and needs be considered by the Trust. In the meantime it was his GP who was prescribing medication in an attempt to control Neil's condition.

He told him that Neil's family members were in desperate circumstances. It was still a nightmare trying to manage Neil's illness, and we urgently needed to access local mental health services. He told him of the history of Psychosis in the family and mentioned that he knew that two of Neil's family already suffered from Schizophrenia, one of whom had spent most of his life in a mental institution.

He went on to tell him that he had observed Neil first-hand and that he was of the firm belief that Neil suffered from **more than** A.D.H.D. and that we as a family had confirmed that Neil experiences paranoid delusions, and indeed believed that people

229

were out to get him. He drank alcohol to try and mask or blot out his fears and stress. Police records showed that he has threatened suicide by jumping off the top of the multi-storey car park.

In fact Neil talked of ending it all and was self harming to an alarming degree. Daniel Pounder told Dr Leister that he'd acted as Neil's 'Appropriate Adult' at the Police Station, and Neil had broken down in tears and in great distress, due to his fear of being locked up.

Daniel had a good insight into Neil's behavioural problems; he thought that his personal development had been damaged by his disturbed and confused mental state. Also, he was of the opinion that Neil's insight was impaired, in that he was unaware of the connection between cause and consequences of his actions.

This was just the same conclusion that many other like-minded 'Professionals' who had been involved with Neil before had presented to us.

Daniel Pounder went on to tell Dr Leister of the many times Neil had been attacked, which he said showed how vulnerable and at risk Neil was due to his incapacity to realize common dangers. He knew first-hand that Neil's concentration and memory were very poor. He said that we, Neil's family, didn't know who to turn to for help, and that these were *critical* circumstances as the prognosis wasn't good. We were all extremely worried for Neil's safety and well being. **Daniel asked Dr Leister for help and advice on this as a matter of urgency.**

****

On the mention of Neil attempting suicide by jumping off the multi-storey car park, I must tell you that when we received the letter from Daniel Pounder, this was the first time we had <u>even heard</u> of this. On the night in question, Neil had turned up at his Dad's place of work covered in blood. It was in the early hours of the morning, so Neil went to the rear of the mill where he knew his Dad would be. Neil pounded on the door, which was opened by one of Steve's co-workers who was greatly upset on seeing Neil.

She went for Steve and told him to bring Neil in while she attended to his wounds and cleaned him up. He told them that he had been beaten up by the people he'd kept telling us were after him. They believed him as they had no reason not to. Neil believed it to be true, so why should they not believe it also?

230

Neil had been dragged back from over the multi-storey by the police, who'd noted his injuries, yet had never informed us. Poor Steve it was bad enough for him when he knew he was leaving me with all my troubles when Neil was small, and the times when it was too much, as only in dire need did I ring him at work to return to help, but still he suffered, having to work when his loyalty lay with me and our children. He worried and stressed out just as I did. Then Neil would go to his place of work on more than one occasion, often in pain, hurt and confused, sometimes in drink. He felt useless in most situations. He didn't like Neil being in the papers because he was a **proud** man, who knew that many people just wouldn't understand.

There were many times when I saw him broken!

****

On 29th January 2001 I received a letter off Gilbert Price M.P. He'd been in touch with Social Services on my behalf and they had written to him stating that Neil was an adult now, so they said that they wouldn't be able to provide practical assistance for Neil, and so we should approach medical services. He was sorry that Social Services were not more helpful.

Dr Spercer received a letter from Dr Leister saying that he would be happy to see Neil along with Steve and me. He knew that we had been let down and neglected by the Service, but that the Service remained open to us, but he knew that Neil was unwilling to go into hospital. He knew that Neil was out of control, and that he was often arrested by the police, and he believed that Neil would end up in some sort of institution. He knew of Neil's **strong family history** which he found very interesting, and that he'd treated Neil's Granddad and Great Uncle who were Schizophrenic, and someone in the generation before, who also had suffered from Schizophrenia.

He said, "*It* is therefore clear that Neil has strong family evidence of psychosis."

We thought at this time that Dr Leister had a reasonable insight into Neil's medical condition and seemed willing to try and help him. He knew that it would be difficult, as Neil was intent on staying out of hospital, but Dr Leister knew that it was just a matter of time before he was brought in by the police on a Section 136, because he'd become so chaotic that he'd have to be sectioned in the

231

community and brought into hospital.

He also knew, and had said, that Neil had a propensity for running off, and we were clearly distraught at his situation and he had firmly agreed with us. He was *not sectionable as yet,* so there was very little Dr Leister could do to help either Neil or us.

He said that he wanted to make it clear to Neil and us though, that it would be open to him at any time should he wish to be admitted, or if he became sectionable due to outside influences, or if the courts requested it. He did not feel that the answer was probation and outpatient care, but for him to be admitted.

****

I was told about East Lancs Advocacy based in Accrington. I rang the Advocacy Service in March 2001. I was put in touch with Stacy Brambles, the Mental Health Team Leader and she wrote to Neil telling him that she had spoken to me, and that I thought that he would benefit from the support of an Independent Advocate. I had told her that Neil was being threatened with eviction from the Council, and of his trouble with the police and issues regarding his treatment and diagnosis by Dr Leister, and previously Dr Kumar.

An appointment would be necessary for her to meet Neil so that she could explain in detail her role as an Advocate, and how she could support Neil. In the letter she enclosed some leaflets about this service and what she was able to provide for him.

Stacy in fact suggested that I get in touch with Keith Deighton at Community Mental Health. I had done this before and so had Daniel Pounder even having a disastrous meeting with him at Lowmount Clinic at Fernlea General Hospital, with that awful Social Services woman Sarah Connor when they both said that the service *wouldn't* help Neil.

I did as she asked though, in a letter dated 8th March 2001. I stated in the letter that I knew Neil needed secure and supportive accommodation and that he needed this to happen as a matter of urgency, because he was under threat of being evicted by the Council. I said that things were **desperate,** and we were in need of a great deal of help. I asked for a Mental Health Social Worker to be allocated to Neil, and all this to be brought up at their next meeting, which I was told was on 12th March. I was sure that as before he would ignore my plea for help, in fact I **wasn't** disappointed.

I also wrote this letter to Dr Leister at the same time:

Dear Dr Leister,

Firstly I would like to thank you for taking us seriously regarding Neil's A.D.H.D. and the fact that we have always thought Neil had an underlying mental problem and not just A.D.H.D.

*Daniel Pounder as you know was in agreement with us. When we came to see you with Neil you were of the opinion that Neil should have a Mental Health Social Worker. I have written to Mr Deighton to request this with the help of Stacy Brambles from East Lancs Advocacy who has helped us before, putting us in touch with Daniel Pounder. Neil is in 'dire straits' as he is facing homelessness due to the fact that the Council want to evict him from his home. He was blamed for his windows being broken by a **third party,** noise nuisance, and the fact that he goes out in the early hours and the neighbours hear him. Of course this is down to his illness, and the fact that he wanders at night because he can't sleep, also the neighbour is bitter towards Neil knowing he is mentally ill.*

He says, and here I quote, "We shouldn't have to live next door to people like that."

While there may be faults on both sides I feel very strongly, that with help Neil should be given the chance to live on his own and it would be far better for him to be away from the neighbourhood he was brought up in, which is prejudiced against him. If he'd had a Social Worker I think things would not have got so out of hand. Daniel has tried to intervene with the Council but without success.

I did as you said and complained to the police about not using Section 136 to get Neil into hospital when he tried to commit suicide.

*Inspector Howes said, "The Police Surgeon saw Neil covered in blood and with his injuries had deemed him well enough to be released. He also went on to say that this would **always** happen."*

Neil was arrested a couple of weeks ago for taking his girlfriend's car without consent. He was taken back to Colne Custody by P.C. Howes and having known Neil for a long time he was very offhand with him, poking fun and disbelief of there being anything wrong with him.

He bent Neil's fingers back so hard that it made him cry and then said, "We understand one another, don't we Neil?"

233

This was done in front of the arresting officer, and I have brought it to the attention of Inspector Howes, although as with the other officer who seriously assaulted Neil, I expect little to be done.

I rang P.C. Howett after Neil was arrested and asked if he'd seen a solicitor?

He said. "No, he didn't want one."

I said, "He's in no fit state to decide one way or the other."

He said, "Come on Mrs Green, I'm not going to argue with you, you know there's nothing wrong with him."

He was sarcastic and nasty and to be quite honest no different that I'm beginning to expect. The police are always harassing Neil, there isn't a week that goes by without him being stopped by the police and searched. They seem to get great pleasure in radioing in Neil's name, and Neil hearing that he's suicidal and listing his misdemeanours.

They have told his friends, "Why do you bother with a nutter like him?"

Tonight, Neil has come home to tell me he's rung his girlfriend up to be told that her parents have been into Colne Police Station and they have been told that Neil is a 'looney toon' prone to suicide bids and sectionable.

*He was in tears. The police disgust me, they treat Neil terribly; they laugh at me when I try to get him his rights, such as an Appropriate Adult and suchlike. I know that they ill-treat him. I don't trust them, and when last week he tried to commit suicide, threatening to jump off the motorway bridge, and the police were trying to get him into hospital on Section 136, but being told that because he'd been drinking he was not suffering from a mental health problem. He was therefore turned away, further making the police believe that he **isn't** mentally ill. I couldn't then ask for help from them when a neighbour came with pills that he'd had on him, but had dropped and knowing that he had a knife. I was more worried about what the police would do to him, rather than what he would do to himself.*

*I know Neil missed his appointment with you. He's confused and feels **everyone** is against him. I will bring him to see you if you will give him another appointment. He'll come if I do. Please continue to be supportive, we need you.*

I also sent copies to Dr Spercer and Daniel Pounder.

I wrote this letter before Dr Leister even treated Neil. He did not consider fully Neil's A.D.H.D. It was a letter of hope that I wrote to a fellow human being, who also happened to be a doctor. I did not realize at that time that he was an uncaring, unfeeling excuse of a doctor. I was only to realize this fully some time later.

CHAPTER SIXTEEN
Admitted To Hospital

The day Neil moved into the Council house, the next door neighbour came out and said to my husband. "Why is a young lad living in a three-bed-roomed house with a large garden? We don't want lads living on their own; we've had enough with the last lot on drugs; we got them evicted you know."

It was always the Council knowing how bad the feeling was in this neighbourhood that was at fault, for putting Neil there to begin with; but having said that, we also knew trouble would always follow Neil.

Neil believed that he was being followed. On a couple of occasions a neighbour of mine walked him home and made sure that he got into his house safely.

He came out of his house one evening to come to mine and he was hit on his back by someone with a lump of wood, which broke a rib. The police were informed and he had hospital attention.

He was sent a letter by the housing officer as if he'd broken his **own** windows. Further letters came saying he was causing a nuisance. The neighbour we'd seen made complaint after complaint; some of it I dare say *had a shred of truth* in it. One letter was because he had banged on the other next door neighbour's door, but Neil was in fear of his safety, and frightened.

"They'd come back," he explained to them but they ignored him.

A lad befriended him, he lived down the street, and he offered to wash Neil's clothes to save him going to the launderette. Neil had expensive designer clothes and trainers that we had bought him, but the lad didn't give them back. So Neil refused to give him back the drill he borrowed off him, until he returned his clothes, so he had broke one of Neil's windows. He then continued to harass Neil, throwing beer bottles at him whenever he passed his house.

Neil had a friend to stop one night, and someone wearing a

balaclava entered the house brandishing a piece of wood. Neil was beaten about the head and ended up with severe bruising and a black eye, the other lad ran for help and the police were called.

Neil then retaliated, because he believed the lad who'd kept his clothes was the *same* one who had attacked him. Neil put a brick through his window. The next thing that happened was someone put a paving stone through **our** new car's windscreen causing £2,500 worth of damage. The trouble was relentless!

I went to Neil's as I was quite worried about him. Knowing that he'd lost his mobile phone. I took him a new one. I was assaulted by his neighbour, and was both verbally and physically abused. I had to retire from work due to ill health, and as I already wore a knee brace and walked with a limp I couldn't run away. I was terrified but I managed to ring the police. The woman across from Neil's house was hanging out of her window egging the men on. They all had cans of beer in their hands.

Neil's Grandma Kathleen had her windows put through, and she and Barry live in an *upstairs flat,* yet someone threw bricks through them. Neil also had his windows broken and once again OUR window was broken. We didn't know who had done it. It seemed feasible that it was someone who was somehow involved around Neil. It was certainly worse than ever believing people were after him. We saw the animosity that surrounded him wherever he went.

On more than one occasion he came to my house frightened and disturbed; they always blamed Neil for everything that happened because he was so chaotic, but I saw first-hand what he had to put up with.

These were thugs, and the old lady shouting out of her window was a disgrace. They'd gang up on Neil and torment him, and made him in fear to the point that he hardly dare set foot out of the door. The police *couldn't* understand how it was that every time Neil did set foot out of his house, he was set upon. After what had happened to me, they realized it wasn't all one sided, and that these people were picking on Neil, and reporting to one another.

P.C. Greaves came to my aid that night and he took care of Neil too because he was so upset. I didn't realize it at the time but I was affected by the incident very badly. My doctor said I was suffering from a trauma exasperated by the fact that with my disability I was

237

vulnerable, as I couldn't run away from the danger. I was prescribed medication and for a while I became too frightened to go out on my own.

****

I received a letter from Sarah Connor, Senior Social Worker based at Fernlea General Hospital dated 16th March 2001. In the letter she says that the only way forward is for Neil to have a period of inpatient admission, in order for them to make an assessment to establish whether Neil had any underlying psychotic illness.

This meant that as a mental health service, the only way that they could offer support was if Neil had a *clinically diagnosed mental illness*. Then, and only then, could they offer him a community care plan and if eligible, Home Care Support.

I made a note on the letter from Sarah Connor. I have written;

This is the reason why they have **never** given Neil a diagnosis, because if they *don't do this,* they *don't have to treat and fund anything*, this is why we needed to go out of the area and see another Consultant but they wouldn't let us.

For around five long years we asked for a referral to another Consultant; we were prepared to go **anywhere in the country,** but they would **not refer Neil** and we never knew why.

Sarah mentioned Home Care Support, and we knew what a joke that is, and five years on as I write this book I know that to be true.

****

Back now to 2001.

On 2nd April 2001, police called at my address; they were worried about Neil as he had rung them sounding distressed and frightened; they therefore asked me to go up to Neil's house with them. I was still suffering from the previous incident, and I was feeling quite ill.

I rang Steve at work and he met the police at Neil's address. They couldn't get in as Neil had barricaded the door, and they didn't have the key to his other door. Steve didn't want to linger and draw too much attention, so he decided to go back to work, on his return to work he was told to make his way quickly to the motorway bridge as Neil was hanging off it. After running a red light Steve hit the central reservation causing extensive damage to the car. The police had called negotiators from Liverpool.

I attended to hear my son screaming his head off for three and a half gruelling hours. I hope no one ever has to hear such blood curdling screams from anyone *they* love. He was in such pain, yet we couldn't do anything. I wanted to be the one to go to him but they wouldn't let me near him. We were crying, as we both felt useless.

They did manage to get Neil down off the bridge. He was taken to the ambulance that was waiting, and then taken to Fernlea General Hospital. Steve and I were clinging together both shaking. I went with Neil to the hospital and Steve went back to work, picking me up in the early hours of the morning from the hospital.

Neil was given a Social Worker, **at long last!** Donna talked to him at length and on 3rd April 2001 she organized a Section 2.

A couple of days later Neil left the ward and went back to the motorway bridge after falling down the stairs at the hospital, and dislocating his arm. He was brought back by the police only to run away again, and after police chased him, he jumped into the river.

I remember Neil ringing me upset, and telling me that the police were throwing stones at him. I could hear them shouting at him, and calling him names. And yes, I heard the splashes in the river. I couldn't believe this myself, so I passed the phone to Steve. He wasn't surprised anymore by what the police did; he doesn't like them through all the experiences of how we and Neil have been treated by them. **Not all of them** I wish to emphasize that, but enough to have a *tainted* view.

Neil had the insight to go to Steve's cousins in Barrowford. She made him take a bath and gave him some clean clothes.

****

Neil went back to Ward 20 and we had a ward meeting a couple of days later. Kathleen came to give us some support, and try to get across to the doctor how bad Neil was in his mental health.

Ben Law was at the meeting having taken over from Daniel Pounder when he retired. We will be forever grateful to Daniel though as he was a blessing and did so much for us; he really was the breakthrough for us. He tried ever so hard to get the doctors and services in to help Neil, but he couldn't, and as Ben would say also, **you can't make a doctor, doctor** *or the services do the job they are employed to do,* because they hide behind what the doctors say too, and then they can blame the doctor and think that they are *innocent* of any blame.

I say, **"No you are <u>not innocent</u> at all. You are just as much to blame as the doctor is."** I can say that *because I have a voice. I'm <u>not</u> mentally ill.*

****

Ward 20 was a locked ward, but on the day that Neil was admitted a lad came over to tell him that all you have to do is kick the door, it's easy, and it was.

It was always a bone of contention to me the fact that Neil was on a Section yet it was so easy for him to get out. **Where's the logic in that?**

It didn't take long for me to realize that the staff members were *unprofessional* in the way they spoke to Neil and us. It wasn't just the way they talked either, it was also the way in which they showed Neil that he was a nuisance, and that they couldn't be bothered with him. They didn't have time for him; he was too much trouble, and took up too much of their time.

Because of his illness Neil was hyperactive; he talked extremely fast and needed to be reassured all the time. He needed to talk and to be kept occupied. He was like a caged animal. They were totally unprepared for him, and then when Dr Leister started messing about with his Ritalin, first of all stopping it completely then replacing it with other drugs, after all this happened Neil was uncontrollable, so the staff were kicking off that they **couldn't cope.** Ben and I asked Dr Leister to put Neil back on his Ritalin. He wasn't for doing it, as he said Ritalin could bring on a psychosis.

I was in constant touch with Barbara Worrell, Chairman of A.D.H.D. North West Region Association. I told her Dr Leister wouldn't listen to us. She wrote him a letter to try to help not only Neil and us, but Dr Leister too.

In the letter she tells of how she supported us, and was now aware that Neil had deteriorated and was in hospital. She tells of how Ritalin works, the dosage, and that the drug **should <u>not</u> be given at night,** as late afternoon should always be the *last dose of the day.* One of the reasons she wanted to write to Dr Leister was to tell him about a new slow release Ritalin SR drug, and also another drug Equasym. A further release version of methylphenidate, which is available in the U.S.A. called Concerta and she informed Dr Leister that it would be available here in England in about a year.

240

Barbara has a daughter with A.D.H.D. and she tells of how other drugs are needed such as Prozac to help treat her A.D.H.D. and her moods. Barbara had told me about Risperidone and Olanzapine, antipsychotic drugs that may be useful, and could maybe help Neil. Most people affected benefit greatly from other forms of therapy, and she did say that when Neil was to become more stable, that he should have the opportunity to access services to provide for his needs, and cognitive behavioural therapy which would be a large plus.

With the letter Barbara enclosed her information booklet and other articles for his information, and also stated that if he wished to discuss any pharmacological problems, that she knew of a doctor who in addition to being a Consultant Psychiatrist was also a qualified psychopharmacologist and also a Specialist in A.D.H.D. Added to this she also gave the name of another person, a Professor who is based in London and is very well informed.

She went on to say how grateful she was for his support and understanding, and that we felt the same.

Dr Leister chose to <u>ignore</u> everything in the letter, and was *insulted* at being asked if he would contact anyone else about one of HIS patients.

<u>This was the HEART OF THE PROBLEM REALLY, which is more important – the doctor's ego or the Patient in their care?</u>
There SHOULD really only be one answer to this!
****

I was in constant touch with Ben Law, (care worker at *Making Space*). He came to the ward meetings and when Dr Kay put Neil on Section 3 we were both relieved.

We were told by Dr Leister that Neil was **psychotic;** so he put him on antipsychotic drugs.

However Stacey, one of the staff on the ward, frequently said that they **didn't** think that Neil's **psychotic** just *badly behaved.* He had behavioural problems and Ben Law was told the same. This was very early into Neil's Section 3.

Although I didn't agree with Neil's cocktail of drugs, I knew that he would be taken off the Ritalin. I was afraid of the Haloperidol, especially so after I'd heard about Neil being prescribed the maximum dose, very often, and that drug being prescribed *together*

241

with Lorazepam.

We took Neil to Blackburn one afternoon to buy him some new clothes, and we went to McDonalds for our Big Mac Meals that we all enjoyed. To write about this is very upsetting for me as both Steve and I were horribly disturbed to watch our much loved son with his tongue hanging out so much, that he could hardly eat or drink. He was like a Zombie, and the thought of it will stay with us forever.

Never before had we felt so sorry for Neil; *up to that point*, as our poor son is to suffer a lot more in the future. They started Neil on the Ritalin as the effects that he was showing were because he **needed** the Ritalin. However they started him on it without a proper consultation. They were prescribing it and giving it to him at 10.30pm **which is unheard of** as it's a stimulant, that **MUST NEVER** be taken at night.

Dr Leister hated the fact that he'd had to put Neil back on Ritalin, as he had said all along that Ritalin brought on psychosis. Even after he'd had the letter off Barbara Worrell, explaining Ritalin *in great detail*, and giving the name of 'experts' to help him. He told me he knew little of A.D.H.D. We all thought we were helping, but he didn't want us **telling him anything** or asking him to get in touch with <u>other doctors.</u>

However I got in touch with one of the doctors myself; he told me that he was more than happy to talk to Dr Leister, but it would have to be Dr Leister who rang him. This was another lost opportunity for Neil as I knew that Dr Leister would <u>never </u>do that.

Neil's health was deteriorating. The staff was mishandling him, and making him worse. A partner of David's at Farnworths solicitors kindly wrote to Dr Leister saying that we had instructed him to write because of Neil's rapid deterioration while on the mental health ward at Fernlea. He told of our desperation to obtain appropriate treatment as soon as possible, and that I had been in touch with a leading Specialist whom Barbara Worrell had told us about, and also to Dr Leister when she had written to him. This doctor was willing to assist in the treatment of Neil.

He finished the letter by saying that we appreciated the care given to Neil, but for his welfare and that of the staff we were requesting that Dr Leister urgently sought the assistance of this doctor. Once again this fell "UPON DEAF EARS".

****

Eventually they realized that Neil needed to go back on his Ritalin, as you have to treat the *underlying* illness first, and this would have to be with Ritalin. The whole thing was a complete shambles, as the timings have to be *precise as* it wears off quickly.

Over five years we'd tried all the different times and combinations of other drugs, herbal and otherwise, this trial and error took a long time to master. Up to Neil leaving home we'd felt that we had cracked it during the day with medication, but he needed something else at either late tea time, or *early* evening.

They started Neil on a low dose of Ritalin, but *often forgot* to give it to him. We were told at one of the ward meetings that **Neil should** remind the staff to give it to him. **This was ludicrous**, **as Neil's memory was shocking.** I went to visit Neil around 'med' time one day, just to see if he got his medication on time. **He didn't!**

Sometimes, he was going five hours, having to wait until they'd finished doing all the other medications for everyone else, as Ritalin was always kept in a locked cupboard. We complained, but still it took a long time for it to get through to them. It was only when Dr Kay was standing in for Dr Leister that she insisted that the staff gave Neil his medication **at the times stated**, but it was still chaotic.

Dr Kay tried to get an 'Agency Nurse' to come and take Neil out for a walk around the grounds; she tried, but she was always overruled by Dr Leister. Instead, they even stopped taking Neil out on the limited times that the staff usually did take him out, until gradually he wasn't allowed out at all. He was cooped up in that awful environment without leave until **we** took him out for short periods, but for a super active lad it must have been dreadful. He was like I have said before, a caged animal.

****

We went to visit one day when Stacey was sitting in a chair just inside the door. Steve and I walked in and she immediately shouted. "I'm sat here because of your son."

He'd been kicking his way out. We didn't know where to look or put ourselves, we felt like 'lepers'.

As I've said before, the staff members were *unprofessional.* I had

243

a call from a member of staff stating that when Neil was out with me I'd allowed him to get some headache pills and take them back to the ward. Neil hadn't told them this by the way, they had simply *presumed*, and jumped to their **own** conclusions as they always did. In fact we'd delivered him back to the ward, then afterwards one of the staff had let him go out on his own, which is what they said he *couldn't* do. He went for a walk around the grounds, and what he *actually* did do was to go off the grounds to the nearby shop. At this time *he shouldn't have even been allowed out on his own.*

I was then accused of buying alcohol, or allowing him to buy it while he was out with me.

I had given an amount of money for Neil's use to be kept in the safe. I **expressly** told the staff **not** to give him more than £1.00 a day for the telephone; however they gave it **all** to him and he went out and bought drink. So once again I was forced to make a complaint.

****

We were going to purchase a new caravan, so we couldn't make it for just **one** Monday afternoon ward meeting. I gave our apologies to the staff, but as Steve works nights and the caravan place was quite a way off, we could only go there on a Monday.

Sue, a member of staff said to Neil, "What's more important, **you** or a caravan?"

Again, I complained. I asked for the staff *to keep their comments to themselves.*

****

Neil was getting out often, and Darren Hall the Ward Manager told Neil that, "They are sending you to a **Secure Unit** in Cheadle."

Obviously Neil got really upset and worked up on hearing this. Again I complained.

****

Neil would go to a member of staff to talk if he felt stressed, but they would tell him to go away, as they were too busy. They **would not** say this nicely though as in, 'I'm sorry Neil but I'm a little busy at the moment, but I will make time to talk to you shortly, or something on those lines.'

This is what we and his care worker would have expected them to say. No one there seemed to ever *talk* to the patients. Whenever I went on the ward; the patients always talked to me and told me **their**

244

problems.

Neil used to say, "Have you come in to see **me** Mum," he didn't really mind as he used to do the same.

He'd talk so nicely to the other patients. They were a nice bunch; most of them didn't ask for much. Neil made a couple of close friends. He liked Sherry, she was a lovely girl, but very thin, if I remember rightly she had anorexia or something like that. She always carried a bottle of water around with her; she and Neil got on well. She was a lovely bright considerate girl, who was pretty too. There were a lot of lovely people on the ward when Neil was in, and most of them needed to talk and be reassured, just like Neil did. They could all have similar problems, and they are ALL special, needy people who just need that little bit more help at their times of chaos and stress. It doesn't take much to talk sensitively to the patients; well it seemed that way to me anyway. They tend to look after one another as comrades. The qualified members of staff are the worst as the others seem to be more giving.

****

We were taking Neil out for the day, and we had planned it well in advance. On the Wednesday it was put in the patients 'log' that we had eight hours leave on Friday as we were taking Neil with us to pick up the new caravan. We needed to be away from the hospital at 8:00am prompt, so we asked for Neil's medication to be ready at that time.

Late on Thursday afternoon Neil **also** mentioned it to a member of staff, but he was told that he couldn't go as they hadn't got a doctor to sign a 'script' for his medication.

Neil rang me in a terribly distressed state. I told him, "Don't worry, they've made a mistake, and he was going."

I rang for the on-duty doctor to sort out Neil's 'script' and he did, so they'd simply got Neil all worked up for *nothing*. There was another occasion before this, when they hadn't got Neil's Ritalin ready for me to take him out for a short while. I said that I had some Ritalin, so Darren Hall the Ward Manager said that it was okay.

On another occasion we took Neil to the hairdressers, but as it took longer than we expected, meaning that I wouldn't be able to get him back for the specified time, I rang the hospital.

I said, "I would get him back an hour later, and I'd give him his

245

Ritalin."

I was told, "You'd better not!"

This was despite the fact that Neil needed to have his Ritalin at *precise* times, and I'd already explained to them that what they were doing by giving it to Neil **every four hours or more,** as it was *too long a gap* and I wasn't prepared for him to go **five hours or more.**

I rang Dr Kay just to tell her what I'd done, "She replied I can understand why you've given it to him, but really the staff *should* give it to him."

There was one member of staff who none of us liked; she could sour milk, and it was usually her who loved any excuse to try to ridicule us, as she'd bark at us at every opportunity.

The staff would ring me at midnight or even later, to tell me that Neil was being a pain.

I told them, "If you had Neil on the correct doses of Ritalin and always gave it to him on time; and CERTAINLY NOT at **10:30pm,** then he wouldn't be like this.

They were finding him increasingly difficult, and he was always getting out and sometimes buying alcohol. Why then didn't they do something about THAT DOOR?

****

We had a meeting with Dr Leister, Mr Makin (Director, Trust), Bob Gardner (Nursing Manager, Administrator), Ben Law (Care worker at *Making Space),* Fred Clough from Community Health Council, Steve and me.

We were told that they were looking for a more appropriate hospital for Neil; that was more secure. I had asked for Cognitive Behavioural Therapy for Neil, but was 'scoffed' at by Dr Leister. But now **he** was saying that the hospital they were looking at had that.

The hospital in question was St. Andrews in Northampton. I'd mentioned St. Andrews before to Ben and Fred. I'd first met Fred when I contacted the Community Health Council for help when I thought that we were getting nowhere with the hospital.

I mentioned the drink, and the fact that Neil had also started smoking like a chimney to Dr Leister, and he told me that Neil was **self medicating**. He said Neil had a lot of problems and Fernlea General wasn't the right place for him. *You could say that again.* This was all said at the meeting. Ben brought it up about the staff on

246

the ward seeing fit to take all of Neil's belongings off him as a 'punishment'. Only **we** were told that, it **wasn't** a punishment.

"RUBBISH!" we **all** said together. He was getting out and buying drink, so they took his clothes off him, which **wouldn't** stop him. I could work out their logic though. They put his mattress on the floor, took away his 'Walkman' and all of his belongings. Cooped up, not allowed out, with no music to listen to or videos to watch, you could imagine how boring it was for Neil. They just seem to mismanage him, and always did the *exact opposite* of what is recommended. I'd written out pages and pages about A.D.H.D. about what is recommended and how to cope and handle it, in order to try to help the staff, but they weren't interested. They always believed that they knew best.

Neil used alcohol to blot out his fears and stress, and to self medicate, but he was punished for it.

We asked them, "Why then do you take Neil's 'stuff' off him?"

Bob the Nursing Manager said, "It was a staff judgement call; but he'd make sure that he got his 'stuff' back."

None of the patients in Fernlea as far as we were aware were ever told why they did it. We could perhaps understand their clothes being confiscated in order to possibly keep them on the ward, but not their other personal items. Bob went to the ward after the meeting to tell his staff to return Neil's property, but the staff **didn't** do this, so Ben Law complained.

The members of Staff were a law to themselves; they seemed to *overrule* Dr Leister and do what they liked.

Neil arrived at our house one evening. He told us that he wasn't allowed back on to the ward. We looked at one another, here was Neil causing no problem at all, very calm and not drunk. He had been told that if he went out again he wouldn't be allowed back on to the ward. We told him that he was going back, he was on a Section, so they **couldn't refuse him**; he had come home in a mate's car.

He went back then he rang me, as they wouldn't allow him in. I told him to ring the police, and to tell them that they wouldn't let him in. I used to do this, because the police told me to, because whenever they got involved, a record was made as they always logged it.

The same applied to Ben, Neil's Care Worker, I made copies of *everything* that went on, both on the ward and off it. I also noted things down in my diaries so that NO ONE can **ever say** that this account of what happened to my son isn't the truth. It is a very honest and accurate account because it is true. ALL OF IT!

Neil did as I asked, he rang the police and they came promptly. It caused some merriment to the police officers. They said that they were used to taking people **back** to the hospital when they **didn't want to go back** but *never before* had they been asked by a patient to get them in.

The police argued with the staff; then they told the staff what they thought of them. I heard all this because Neil had given one of the Officers his mobile phone, and they let me hear what they were telling the staff, that Neil was **not drunk** *and neither was he causing a problem,* so what was their concern? The police did get *some* things right. Neil was well known to them, and most of them were glad that finally something was being done for him. The staff members were forced into letting Neil back onto the ward.

****

One day we were taking Neil out and we needed medication. He'd had so many changes we were lost with it all. Val more or less threw them at me. I looked at her; then at the bag of pills just all mixed up in a see through bag. I had to go to another member of staff to get them to document and write down what pills should be given to Neil, and at what times.

Once again we had come across their unprofessional and uncaring manner. It was completely and utterly out of order.

****

When we had the meeting and talked about Neil going to St. Andrew's in Northampton; he got into the office and read it in his notes. Neil could master the digits on the locked doors. He'd only have to see it done once, before he could remember the code. He was a devil with that.

The staff had to change the codes so many times because of Neil, that they were always forgetting the numbers. He'd be looking over their shoulders telling them the new numbers.

Sometimes though, they left the office door unlocked, so **if it was because of this or not** I don't know, but Neil got into the office and read his notes. *I wasn't pleased.* It was something we wouldn't have told him until it was finalized, it wasn't worth getting him all worked up over, especially so if it didn't materialize.

We went on holiday for three weeks. We badly needed to spend some time away. Neil had been in hospital for many months. We were torn; in fact we were always torn. Would it ever be any different?

Kathleen, Barry, Ryan and Ben were visiting Neil regularly and taking him out. We kept in constant touch with everyone, including Neil. All seemed fine for a while. Neil was still getting out and still buying some alcohol, but he wasn't getting drunk or causing many problems.

They decided to move Neil to Rossendale Hospital on Ward 10. If we had been at home we would **never** have allowed it. Ben couldn't understand it either.

Dr Leister said afterwards, "I don't know anything about it," and he wasn't pleased either.

The way it was put across to Neil, was that there were two brothers on the same ward, and they wanted to split them up by sending one of them to Fernlea General. So they asked Neil if he would like to go, and he had said yes.

So they took him and all of his belongings to Rossendale. It lasted a matter of days, because they couldn't keep an eye on Neil there at all, as he was all over the place and he was going out drinking. It was a totally inappropriate place for Neil and he went back to Fernlea under a cloud.

Ben Law from *Making Space*, as I say kept an eye on Neil, and even when there were a few hiccups with Neil, the staff told him that even though he was having a drink he wasn't causing trouble, and seemed a lot more stable. Obviously Neil didn't always help his own situation at all.

Here was I telling the doctors and staff that Neil was hearing voices talking on his phone, when there was no one there, and how paranoid he was, but all the time Neil was denying it. He wasn't on the ward as much as he should have been, and also his drinking didn't help. Further to this, Neil was a complete and utter pain to them, so they didn't want to be in his company for long; so all this didn't stand him in good stead, especially so when they were supposed to be monitoring him. I found the staff in the main to be rather useless, so they wouldn't really have been capable of making a

249

proper judgement anyway.

I was often told by them that they didn't have to listen to *me* or anyone else, (including Ben Law) ***because Neil was the patient.***

Wasn't there enough evidence without it? Of course there was. Did they want there to be? NO, they did not!

Most importantly how can a serious mentally ill man ever be able to tell them the true facts? This was especially so with Neil as his condition deteriorated so often. At more rational times Neil would always tend to hide his problems or deny that he even had any.

After all shouldn't doctors and staff in this particular profession be well aware of these matters-, and therefore know to monitor their patients better?

CHAPTER SEVENTEEN
One of the Worst Times of Our Lives

We came back from our holidays late on Sunday 29th July 2001. We went to the ward meeting as usual at 2.00pm on Monday 30th July. While we were standing outside the locked door we were seen through the glass in the door.

A member of staff shouted out, "It's Neil Green's Mum."

I felt uneasy. Where was Neil? **He wasn't there!**

Three patients came towards me to tell me that Neil had been locked up by the police for stealing.

A very irate patient screamed obscenities at me, "That little bastard is very bad."

Steve and I were met further down the corridor by Ben Law, who explained to us. "Neil isn't here, he's been arrested. He was caught red-handed stealing from another patient, so I'm told."

This had happened in the morning, yet no one had thought to ring us. I went into the office as no member of staff even bothered to come to tell us what had happened.

Suzanne, the one who could sour milk, stood facing me saying nothing.

I asked, "Is there going to be a ward meeting today?"

She snapped back, "Oh yes!"

Then another member of staff came to Ben to tell him that they were ready for the meeting. We went into the meeting room, there were Dr Leister, Dr Kay, Donna Castle Calder, Andrea Robbins (both Social Workers), and two other people who we didn't know.

Dr Leister stated that Neil had been caught stealing and so he'd been discharged from his Section, and also from the hospital. He continued, "There would be no chance of him coming back onto the ward, as the person he stole off was on the ward, and he doesn't want Neil on the ward with him.

Dr Kay asked, "Could Neil go onto another ward?" She tried

251

really hard to get her point across.

Dr Leister talked her down saying, "Certainly not!"

When I'd calmed down I asked, "What will happen to Neil now then?"

Dr Leister replied, "Neil's GP will have to take over his medication."

Donna said, "Neil **isn't** mentally ill, so we have no responsibility to lend support, but I will give you a list of bed and breakfast places for him."

Ben said, "I cannot believe my ears at what I'm hearing here!" He also said, "You can't do *tha*t as **YOU DO** have a responsibility of care to Neil."

They all denied it.

Donna said, "I'll have a word with someone, but as far as *after-care support,* they **don't need** to supply it."

That was that, we walked out of the ward into Jordan Whaite's office. (He acted as Neil's Advocate). We caught Darren Hall the Ward Manager who told us that he **wasn't at the meeting** but would go and find out what was going on, as he said that he knew nothing.

We stayed there for another three hours before Darren Hall came back to us, and more or less repeated the same to us as Donna had said earlier.

I asked, "What will happen when Neil is brought back by the police?"

He said, "Nothing, because the police have already been told **not** to bring him back. Anyway, he'll only be given a list of bed and breakfast places."

Steve, Ben, Jordan and I were all in the office.

Darren Hall then went on to say, "The trouble is we have difficulty on this ward to make out whether people are MAD or just BAD."

I rang the police who were very helpful, they did **not want** to press charges; they insisted that it was a *terrible state of affairs* and had made comments to that effect on the charge sheet.

Dr Leister faxed a letter to them saying Neil was **not mentally ill**, so he was fit to be charged. Discharged of his Section and discharged from the hospital.

Neil's solicitor was there and read the fax. The police tried really hard to change things, but it was all to no avail. However Neil's solicitor insisted on Neil getting an Appropriate Adult, so Social Services were called and Donna Castle Calder attended the Police Station.

Neil was **not** discharged off his Section until the afternoon, because that was when the paperwork was done. In fact Dr. Leister had been **totally wrong** to fax the Police Station that morning saying that Neil had *already been discharged off Section*.

He had purposely lied. It was exactly the same regarding the discharge from hospital. *The paperwork for this **wasn't done** until the day after.* The police were appalled, and so too was the court when these facts were put before it.

It was all beyond comprehension. **How did Neil come to this?**

He was living on his own, couldn't cope at all, having set fire to one house, or so we believed, then he ended up in hospital having been rescued by firemen. He left hospital, was given a Council rented property, he was living in a terrible state, was vulnerable and people were taunting and tormenting him. He'd been attacked, he was led on to drink; people were using him, eating all his food and 'dossing' at his house. They were also stealing his medication.

When he did have any left to take, **he didn't take it!** He wasn't compliant and he *forgot* to take it. All his windows were boarded up. He was stressed and frightened, due to him having delusional thoughts; he was also paranoid, psychotic and moving headlong into schizophrenia.

Ben and I both felt that when Neil became stressed (and he was always stressed to some point) that this was when he had psychotic episodes that were sometimes particularly acute. If he did level out in hospital (and we very much doubt that he did) it was because he was in a safe environment, so he wasn't as stressed as he would be when trying to cope on his own outside. This had never altered in the past so why or how did they mean it had now?

Dr Leister and his staff, in my opinion, had engineered Neil's demise. Then they had realized that they couldn't cope with or treat Neil. But instead of referring him to someone who could, perhaps in a different hospital, they had tossed him out like rubbish, and thrown him to the wolves. What happened to St. Andrews in Northampton?

They just got rid of Neil with no planned aftercare that they

253

should have provided after he'd been released off a Section. Disgusting wasn't a strong enough word to use. I'll use the word again, but it's nothing to say that I was disgusted by Dr Leister, I was more than that. I was **sickened** by the hospital and the Trust, and I truly do personally believe with all my heart that Ward 20 and the other mental wards at that hospital should be **closed down**, and the useless members of staff choose careers to which they are more suited. But definitely NOT in a caring or nursing profession I might add.

This is what I had written then and also copied for Ben and he stated it was a true and factual account. I filed it away with the rest of the papers relating to Neil. I have many files and diaries that I am trawling through to give a true and factual account of Neil's life. Why did I save them all and write a diary just after Neil was born? I must have known that I would need them one day, to tell the world how little our mentally ill loved ones are thought of and how cruelly they are treated on OUR mental health wards in OUR hospitals.

In order to work in these very specialized environments, the first quality that ALL THE STAFF really MUST have in order to do this heartbreaking work is to CARE enough, to LISTEN to their patients, give them a voice, and then have the patience required to help these very needy patients. SADLY WE ALWAYS FOUND 90% OF THE STAFF VERY LACKING IN THESE QUALITIES. They found the patients too demanding, and they ridiculed, rather than helped them. **The doctor refused to doctor! And instead of speaking up for their patients, the staff followed his lead.**

****

On the 1st August 2001, Neil rang me at tea-time from Lancaster Farms, A Young Offenders Institution. Neil was crying, and he sounded terrible. He asked me what they were doing to him, and told me that he'd cut his wrists.

"I can't cope here Mum; I want to die."

He was hearing voices telling him that he was no good. "I can't think straight, and I'm getting all worked up. I swear to you Mum that I didn't take anyone's money. Simon takes my hangers and I was simply taking them back. I got into a confrontation with him when he caught me getting **my** hangers back from his wardrobe. I broke the wardrobe door in the struggle but I didn't mean to. It was

254

only the hinge that had come off the door, and the staff caught me just putting the **door back on."**

So there you go. Neil was actually sent to Lancaster Farms for kicking a wardrobe door off its hinge. The other offence that they said he had done? Well there wasn't even any money on him; this could not be proven so the charge was dropped. Apparently the police were already on the ward, so the staff saw their chance to get rid of Neil with a *false accusati*on, a trumped up charge. The wardrobe door wasn't even broken at all, as Neil had managed to put it back on himself immediately. So how did they get away with this?

Neil said he'd not had any Ritalin on the day he rang me, but they'd ordered it. He did actually get one tablet given to him whilst he was still on the phone to me at 6.30pm, 10mg. He was told that after the doctor had spoken to Dr Leister at Fernlea Hospital they'd decided to cut his medication down. So he'd to be punished this way too eh! Dr Leister you make me sick!

This was truly one of the worst times of our lives. We could not believe it had come to this. How can a doctor do this to a sick and vulnerable human being, who'd done **nothing** except be born with mental illness that was running throughout his family. It was a terrible, terrible time for all the family, to say we were devastated isn't enough; it was our **worst nightmare** (well at that time it was) and I was terrified for my son. To hear him now, upset me so much. I hated Dr Leister at that moment. Not thinking things could get much worse than this. I was **wrong**, they got much worse; in fact as bad as they could possibly get.

****

Neil had been given a Barclays Connect Card. It was like putting a chocoholic into a chocolate making factory.

Not knowing very much about such things, I would have thought that a Debit Card would be refused by a shop if the purchaser didn't have enough funds in his account. *This was not so*!

Neil would go into a shop and buy a few items, and the check out assistant would say, "Cash back Sir."

Naturally Neil would answer, "Yes please." Then he'd be given the cash.

By the time we'd found out about it Neil had racked up over £2,000-00 worth of debt. Yes, I couldn't believe it either. I contacted the bank after I had seen the numerous letters, then threats of Court Proceedings. It was only when Neil got into such a mess, which was very distressing for him, which was another reason why he was messed up, and became extremely depressed due to his mounting problems, that we found out.

How could this have even happened in the first place? Why would they keep allowing him to withdraw money when he had none? It was quite beyond me. I took Neil to the Citizens' Advice Bureau.

Kath Riley was wonderful and she took up Neil's case. Luckily the bank *wrote off* the extensive debt, after they were informed of Neil's lack of control and mental illness.

Neil couldn't possibly have dealt with this alone, like a long list of other things that happened to him. He would ALWAYS believe that there was no way out, and he'd have to die to get away from it; which was very much like the time he took his girlfriend's car. She knew he had no license herself, but she still allowed him to drive her car. But when he lost control of it, he came around to where he always did in his times of crisis - our house, his home, as was always the case and would always continue to be.

There we were Steve and I huddled together in the dark early hours of the morning, after hearing the screech of brakes up and down our street, we looked out of the landing window to see this car narrowly missing parked cars. Neil panicked, as he was just overwhelmed.

"I'm bad and I'll just end it all," he said to us as we were rushing out in our nightclothes to stop him.

We needed to bring him back to reality, to the here and now.

"I'll have to fire it; I'll have to kill myself. What have I done Mum? What have I done?" he cried out.

Neil couldn't cope with the enormity of what he had done. He was a childlike man who couldn't deal with things. He would always blow things up out of all proportion, and escalate things out of control.

All three of us took in a deep breath as none of us could stop shaking. We understood Neil, but I doubt my neighbours would have done so if he'd bumped their cars. It was a miracle that he hadn't, and another one that no one else was out seeing us at this moment. I

256

handed him over to police. They always knew he'd turn up at home eventually; he was always a homing pigeon as I have told you. They never had to look very far for him.

We had just sorted one problem out with the bank, now on to the rest. I must have rung all the banks and building societies in the area, and they all told me the same. I couldn't do anything about Neil being given Debit or Credit Cards, he was eighteen years old, and unless he was classed as incompetent, and I had power of attorney, I couldn't do a thing. We didn't doubt then that we would have to go through the same process again in time.

I'm telling you all this now, because we were dealing with this while Neil was in hospital, and we received the letter of confirmation off the C.A.B. and Barclays Bank to say that they had called off the Debt Collectors. This affected OUR Credit Rating for a long time, because even though Neil was **not** living at our address, he did so in between, therefore our address was the one that the demands came to a lot of the time, which meant that it took ages for us to change things.

****

Ben and others told us about Fernlea General Mental Health being allocated tens of thousands of pounds, but only using this cash to get their waiting lists down for operations. **Tell me NO more!**

I'm not surprised at this, as we all know what these people think about the mentally ill. They think that they are *worthless*, *have no voice* and are *not worthy of anything being spent on them at all,* so if they can ***avoid diagnosing as many of them as possible*** *as having any mental illness,* they can get away with it completely.

The Trust is contemptible to allow this. We were always being told that they had **little resources** in Mental Health. Money isn't handed out to them, as they are always the last on the list. It was just the same as I was told that by another local hospital, that was £100,000's in the red, but had paid tens of thousands of pounds to an acting group to teach the Managers how to be patients.

I call this absolutely irresponsible madness. It was many years before a Secure Unit was even built at Fernlea General. What a waste of money that is though, as the hospital still have the **same staff** working in the service. Things won't change until a clean sweep is made, but that won't happen, because they **never learn by their**

257

mistakes. There are many people *still* being ill-treated now which will more than likely continue in the future. They don't learn because they don't care! They are not fit to look after the mentally ill, and if I had my way the mental health wards at Fernlea General would be closed down and I wouldn't allow the same staff to work at other hospitals, like they are doing now, because they are ruining those hospitals' mental health wards too.

People working in mental health need to be re-trained, not moved on to bring <u>chaos elsewhere</u>. Where do you put the mentally ill who do still need to be institutionalized, as the powers that be have closed all those places down? Oh yes! So sorry I forgot there for a minute, you put them in prisons instead!

****

On 1st August 2001 David sent Neil a letter while he was in Lancaster Farms. He'd been in court with Neil on 31st July. Neil told him that he *wasn't responsible* for the offence of theft, and while he inadvertently had caused some damage to the wardrobe door, he didn't accept that it was deliberate or indeed reckless, so he wasn't guilty of the offence.

He told Neil of his options, but as there was no accommodation available to him of any description, it was reluctantly accepted that there was no point in making applications for bail at court, and there was no other option but to remand him in custody.

David has always described Neil's position in great detail in court so that there was no misunderstanding of his predicament, and the court of course expressed a considerable degree of concern for the manner in which he had been treated by the Health Authorities generally. It amazed me how David talked in court, and how well he got on with Neil.

He understood Neil to a point, but had to take everything that Neil told him at face value, and even we at the time didn't know what was going on inside Neil's head.

Neil felt secure with David, he trusted and liked him. We were filled with admiration for the way he talked about Neil in court, hardly taking a breath, and wondered how he remembered what he did for so long. He was totally amazing, and we were in awe. David also got the court to wipe out all of Neil's outstanding fines.

I went to see my M.P. Gilbert Price with Councillor Fred Clough, and after our meeting Gilbert wrote to the Chief Executive of Fernlea General Health Care Trust D.J. Cue. This was on the 3rd August 2001.

He wrote of his concerns about Neil who was still languishing in Lancaster Farms. He told Mr Cue that the police had been misinformed at the time of Neil's arrest at the hospital, because they had been told that Neil *had <u>already</u> been discharged from the hospital before the incident with the wardrobe door.*

Neil was NOT in fact discharged until the following day. Gilbert went on to say that it was my opinion that Dr Leister wanted to wash his hands of Neil, and wanted him out of the hospital because he was too much trouble, and that Dr Leister wanted to highlight the lack of secure beds at Fernlea. Gilbert further mentioned that he was concerned at what was happening to Neil, and that an agreed care plan should be set up, as this needed to be fully investigated in a secure hospital setting. He then said that I was fearful that if Neil was to remain at Lancaster Farms, that he would be likely to harm himself.

David wrote to Fred Clough on 9th August 2001. He had in actual fact faxed the letter to him in order to save time. He told me a little of the Court Procedure. The court has various powers available to them when dealing with mentally disturbed offenders. Firstly, if a court considers that a Defendant is suffering from a mental disorder, such that he does not have the capacity to understand or participate in the Court Poceedings, then they must obtain a Psychiatric Report. If that report confirms that the Defendant is not fit to plead, then a Hospital Order can, and indeed **should** be made, provided the Defendant has been convicted of a relevant offence, or proved to have committed such an offence.

This presents two difficulties with regard to Neil's present position. Neil was able at the time (or so was thought) to understand the proceedings, and to provide David with instructions. Furthermore, David had already obtained a Psychiatric Report which stipulated that Neil **was not suffering** from a mental illness even after he'd been sectioned in hospital, and had a hospital stay; there was the ridiculous situation where Dr Leister had stated both to David and the police that in his considered opinion Neil was **not** suffering from a mental illness.

The second difficulty was of a practical nature, in that even if we felt that Neil was now suffering from a mental illness of the type referred to, the power to make a Hospital Order is in with the sentencing exercise, and it obviously requires a Hospital placement to be available. In essence what would happen is that the case would be adjourned for a report to be prepared. If the court then decided that they were going to make a Hospital Order, then the case would be further adjourned in order to ensure that a vacancy in a Mental Hospital had definitely been arranged.

Neil would then be detained in Hospital under the provisions of that Order, and would be discharged as and when the Mental Health Authorities considered that to be appropriate. The Order would normally last for six months on the recommendations of the Mental Specialist in charge of him. Thereafter the Order could be renewed for periods of one year.

Neil or someone like me acting on his behalf, would have the right to apply for his discharge from hospital at any time after the first six months of the Order, or whenever it was proposed to extend it.

Whilst this provision would obviously put the Authorities under some pressure to find a suitable placement, and in the event of them failing or refusing to do so the court would no doubt direct that someone from the Health Authority attend at court to explain the position, it did not deal with the short term problem of getting Neil into hospital. It is a form of sentence, and not something that can be ordered as part of the Remand process before sentence.

As far as the Remand process is concerned the court can express concern, as they have already done so on **two** previous occasions, and may ask for members of the Health Authority to appear at court and explain themselves. This does not however give the court power to order the Health Authority to make a bed available for someone in Neil's position, however desirable that may be.

Neil had already been seen by a doctor at Lancaster Farms, and a more detailed assessment was to be done the following week. David said that the psychiatrist doing this would be Dr McKewen from a large mental hospital in Preston.

David and Councillor Clough were writing to one another and keeping each other informed about discussions within the hospital that Fred was dealing with, and Court Proceedings which David was dealing with. David gave a brief description of Neil's predicament, although he knew that Councillor Clough already knew; he still did everything in writing so that there was no possible misunderstanding.

He detailed how Neil was arrested on the ward at Fernlea Hospital on Monday 30th July while Neil was in hospital under the provisions of a Mental Health Act Section. Neil was ultimately charged by the police with relatively minor offences of theft and criminal damage, and that he was present at the Police Station when the Custody Officer was advised that the Mental Health Section had been cancelled at approximately 2.25pm on 30th July, and was further present when the Social Worker, Donna Castle Calder was advised by the Hospital Authorities that Neil had been discharged fully from hospital, and in effect the Hospital Authorities had washed their hands of him.

As a result of this there was no suitable accommodation available for Neil, and he therefore appeared in custody before Burnley Magistrates Court on 31st July when the position was explained to the Bench, and that David was not in a position to make an application for bail due to the lack of accommodation. The proceedings were adjourned until 7th August and Neil was remanded in custody to Lancaster Farms.

During that seven day period endeavours were to be made to obtain a Hospital placement for Neil, as it appeared to have been accepted that he was in need of treatment, and that a secure bed was perhaps required, and that he ought **not** to have been discharged from hospital without some follow up care plan being prepared and agreed.

Endeavours were not made as I'd been told would be, and Neil came to court and was further remanded back to Lancaster Farms until 14th August.

It was accepted by all concerned that **under no circumstances** ought Neil to be detained at Lancaster Farms, as the establishment was *entirely unsuitable* for somebody with Neil's specific problems and requirements.

As David said there was an element of 'buck passing' as regards responsibility for finding a suitable bed/placement, so David needed to clarify the current position for when he returned to court on the

261

following Tuesday, so that arrangements could be made for Neil to be released from Lancaster Farms.

David told Fred that Neil was in the invidious position that the court had no current power to insist that a Hospital placement was made available for Neil, and in effect all they could do was remand Neil on bail in custody, and he is presently remanded in custody on the basis that it is necessary for his own protection.

David told Fred as I did that the concern was that unless some progress was made fairly swiftly, major problems were likely to arise, as there was indeed a real risk that Neil might ultimately do himself some real harm.

David asked for Fred's assistance to let him know what present efforts were being made to secure a Hospital placement for Neil, and what short term prospects of success are in relation to those endeavours.

Ben Law was good enough to fetch all of Neil's belongings from Ward 20. We were used to having to store Neil's stuff, as this happened all the time for one reason or another, and this would be set to continue into the future. The only trouble was that there was a lot of his stuff missing, including his videos and speakers. You would have thought that they would have put his belongings into safe keeping. I was told to write to John Duggan. I did so, but I didn't get a reply, so Neil was left missing a lot of his belongings.

I was in constant touch with Lancaster Farms, and I was asked to send some information I had about Neil to help them to understand him, in order for them to pass it on to Dr McKewen. They had put Neil on antipsychotic drugs.

Neil appeared yet again at court just to be once more returned to Lancaster Farms, after being told there was no bed to be found for him in hospital.

David had been to see him and he said he was unusually calm, which was a sign to me that things were about to change.

****

I can remember one time at Fernlea General Hospital when two police officers had taken Neil on Section 136 to try to get him Sectioned for his own safety. They asked me to meet them at the hospital. They were so worried about how Neil was acting with me that they wouldn't even leave me alone with him. We were awaiting

262

three 'Professionals' to Section him.

Neil suddenly changed and said, "Watch this!" and he talked calmly and said everything they wanted to hear.

Then he laughed uncontrollably when they refused to Section him. He is clever, but he can't fool me, and he knows it. His mood changes so fast, he can be down to rock bottom one minute and up the next. It was very frustrating for us to get people in to look beyond his facade. Appearing and acting calmly doesn't mean he really **is** calm; it's usually just the lull before the storm.

****

I think it's time that I make a few things clear at this time in my book. I will shatter everyone's illusions, as what I am about to convey to you is something I've only touched upon before, but it will rear its head throughout my book.

<u>You or I cannot see another Consultant unless the Consultant that you are under, (and it's usually at your local hospital,) will let you</u>. In other words, *they* have to make a referral. We tried for years to see another Consultant in A.D.H.D. and in Mental Health. Indeed both mine and Neil's GP also tried. (We were both under the same doctor) Dr Parsons, who tried in vain to get us a second opinion with another Consultant only to be told and here I quote below:

"This isn't the way these things are done."

The Consultant she tried to get to see us said, "My hands are tied. Protocol, dictates that I can ONLY see a patient by the Consultant referring the patient to me, a G.P. **cannot** refer to a Consultant Psychiatrist like me, or to any other Consultant."

Sadly this is the truth, yet we all wrongly believe that we are entitled to a second opinion. **You are most definitely not**. If you don't like the Consultant that you are under, and you feel that the feeling is mutual, or you don't like the treatment, or God forbid you think he or she has missed something. **Tough!**

You are at their mercy whether you like it or not. Even if it was like in our case when Dr Blake broke the said 'protocol' and asked Bob Gardner to allow him to take Neil on as a patient at our request, he was told **No, definitely not!** This was when Dr Blake was at the 'Spinney'.

****

In the future we see Brian Newscombe, Forensic Psychologist at

263

Chorley Hospital, and he tells us that under Dr Blake at the Spinney Neil would have Cognitive Therapies, and the treatment that he could provide would be just what Neil needed.

We had talked at length and Brian Newscombe did not know we had previous knowledge of Dr Blake, or had been under his wing when he was at Fernlea. We told Brian that we held Dr Blake in high esteem.

Brian answered, "Yes I quite understand that, he's a very good doctor."

It all made sense and I wrote to Dr Blake and put him in an awkward position, but even if I did he still tried for Neil and for us as a family that he worked so closely with.

I had a heated argument with one of the new doctors in our practice Dr Brown. I told him that we couldn't get a second opinion when he asked me if I knew any psychiatrist that we'd prefer Neil to be treated by.

"Yes, in fact anyone who is NOT from Fernlea General," was my reply and also Neil's. But we can't see anyone because the psychiatrists at Fernlea General will **not refer** Neil, or even seek advice from an A.D.H.D Specialist.

"Everyone is entitled to a second opinion," he said.

"NO, you are not Dr Brown," I informed him. "You get us one then I said."

He tried but even he couldn't do so!

I had another heated conversation with the same doctor in 2006.

He said, "Neil's discharged himself from hospital."

I said, "Yes, he has."

He then said, "He shouldn't have if he wants treatment," implying that it was his own fault, and no doubt getting the SAME biased view from Fernlea General doctors and Mental Health Team.

I then informed him, "Neil discharged himself because the ward he was on was rife with drugs, hard drugs, and he was not going to be seduced into that, because he would be the one caught with it and blamed."

The doctor put the phone down on me, he must have thought I was making up excuses, but I wasn't, I was telling the truth.

This happened a few weeks before the significant end to my book. That date in June 2006.

264

Now back to 2001, and my son is languishing in Lancaster Farms Young Offenders.

We were sick to the pit of our stomachs the day we visited Neil at Lancaster Farms in Lancaster. Neither one of us could eat before we set off to Lancaster after going through the process of getting a 'Visiting Order'. We couldn't believe this was happening to us. We were decent people, honourable, law-abiding folk. We had brought our children up 'right'. We felt degraded, but what made it even worse than ever, was that if we had gone against what his solicitor David told us, and given Neil a Bail Address, our address, Neil still wouldn't be here.

I couldn't have coped with Neil, with the severity of his mental illness, and the numerous suicide bids. It was a fact that quite legitimately he now did need to be in hospital receiving treatment. He was very ill, severely ill. We all knew that, and so did David, and he advised us **not to allow** Neil back home, because if we did, then that would be it, we would never get any help for him.

I know we were battling with Fernlea General Hospital because they were cruel and incompetent, but the truth was that Neil needed treatment and we were stuck with them, but this was a hard pill to swallow. We had to let things take their course, but it was sheer hell for all the family. We were wracked with pain and guilt. I can write no more. I'll continue tomorrow. This is so hard for me to write.

****

We parked up in the large car park. We were early as usual. There was a smaller building where we parked and another building not far away but much larger. Both looked quite new buildings and were very modern.

We sort of sat there watching the comings and goings. We saw a lot of young kids carrying babies and toddlers tagging alongside them, as they kind of grouped together. You'd think they were on an ordinary day out with their families, not visiting a prison. You could tell it was something that they were used to, as they looked at home with it all.

What about us? Well we felt ashamed, degraded. No one tells you what to do or where to go. We look around for signs or some instructions, but saw nothing. We followed people into the smaller building. While waiting we see a group of people being escorted from the other building.

Just the way the receptionist asked us to give her the name of the person we'd come to see, upset me. It wasn't **her** fault though. I wanted to scream that my son *shouldn't* be here. We were all treated the same, as a criminal's family, and we were all left to sit around waiting.

Did the others feel like me? I guess not many. I felt awkward. Steve looked the same as I did. I realized something that day. We **were** like these others waiting to see their loved ones. We were *exactly* the same.

They were warm and friendly and they kindly took us into their fold. They talked us through what would happen. They didn't care what our son had done, we were one of them. When they did find out off us why our son was there, they couldn't believe it, and they felt sorry for both him and us.

They said it was disgusting, and shocking. Throughout my life I will be a *better person* because of this experience. I will learn not to judge people, as they didn't judge us. I <u>won't</u> think that I am <u>better than them.</u> I really don't think I was like that anyway before. I am a very caring person, and I would help anyone, and go out of my way to do so. Steve said that I was too good to others.

"No one will be there for you," he'd tell me, and it was true. We have had to deal with so much on our own.

So here we are about to visit our son. He tried so hard not to upset us. He didn't want to worry us that he was suffering. He was though and we could easily see that. We were able to buy pop, crisps, chocolate and suchlike. It soon got to the time to leave. We tried to hold the feelings back; we did to a point and then let go when we got away from Lancaster Farms. We both cried buckets uncontrollably in the car on the country road.

We had told Neil that we would bring his Grandma Robinson to see him the next time. We didn't want to leave him at all; we were torn from him quite literally. We loved our poor sick child. He didn't deserve this. **Was this hell?** It really felt like it!

****

Mum was happy to go the next time we visited; she loved Neil, he was such a loving lad, full of cuddles and kisses.

It was totally genuine when he said," I love you, Grandma." He wasn't frightened to show his feelings, or to tell anyone around him.

God love him, and take care of him!

It was a terrifying experience for my Mum though, with her being blind and having to go through the many procedures you have to get through when seeing someone in the prison system. She did it though. She did it for her 'special' grandson.

God love her, and take care of her too.

It made Neil happy just to see his Gran; he adored her anyway but even more so for doing this for him. He said he was so proud of her. He knew how hard it was for her.

My Mum taken at the Marsden Resource Centre for the Disabled.
She's the one holding up her striped knitting.
This photo was featured in the Nelson Leader to show that people were knitting little tops for babies in the Third World Countries, even my Mum who was totally blind.

Every time we visited Neil, a piece would be chipped away from our hearts.

Neil showed me the letter he got off David.

Bless you David. We couldn't want for a better solicitor. I know I didn't like a lot of things that went on in the 'battle' with the criminal system, such as when Neil had to plead guilty to something, in order for it to be dealt with quickly. It was all politics. The criminal system amazes me. I believe in right and wrong.

We used to have David 'on' because he was Neil's solicitor for years. We used to kid him that Neil alone would have bought his new Private Number Plate for his car.

He'd laugh and say, "Number Plate, he's bought the whole car."

We did like and respect David and he did do a wonderful job, but he too was tied to what he could do, as he had to go through the process of the so called 'Criminal System'. He saw the injustice with Neil, so it wasn't ever easy for him either.

He was so eloquent how he talked about Neil and his problems in court. We were all grateful to this warm and caring man. He was so good with Neil, and I would recommend him to anyone. Neil was especially hard to deal with, and David got mad with him at times, but he knew that in the main Neil *couldn't* and *wouldn't* stop himself.

He felt he had to just be there for him. He always was, and the same goes for me when he always rang me back after I'd rung, even if he had been in with a client. His secretary was lovely and so thoughtful and the receptionist too. They always knew my voice and answered me by name, and put me straight through; we felt like Royalty.

Our contact with David during this time helped us through such a terribly distressing time, but neither he nor us were fully aware at the time that Neil was suffering from psychosis and paranoia to such a degree, that he was accusing people of wrong doings, when a lot of it was just in Neil's head. He was running circles around David and us when we believed all that he told us. He was so believable, he'd fooled us all. Poor Neil his thoughts and fears were worse than we knew.

CHAPTER EIGHTEEN
Brought Back From Death

Neil had been brought back to court twice at this time. I don't know if you know the process Neil would have to go through each time he was produced at court. He would have to pack all of his possessions into a see through plastic bag, just in case he was to be released at court, but if he wasn't, then he'd have to unpack it again when he got back. How disheartening and heartbreaking this must always have been for someone like Neil.

Each time he came to court he was told that a bed in hospital **hadn't** been found for him, and he'd have to go back to Lancaster Farms. His health was getting worse, and he'd already started his regime of antipsychotic drugs, but while this had *some* impact on his mental illness, they were still worried about him. In order to control him they put him on the punishment block, thus treating him as if he was being punished. We had hit this before, and were to again in the future, as because he was causing staff a problem just because he was ill, they would put him where they could keep an eye on him better, but then he was treated like anyone else who had warranted exclusion.

Here he was on remand, but was only there because he'd been thrown out of hospital, as they'd found him difficult to cope with. He hadn't been in a secure unit where he <u>couldn't get out</u> to buy alcohol and cause mayhem. **Is it right that they can do this?** *Should the hospital staff have the right to place mentally ill patients into the hands of the police, and then trawl them through the courts and dump them into the Criminal System?*

Would it not be fairer and better to treat these people properly, either with correct medication and show them the kindness they deserve by diagnosing them properly in the first instance, then treating them as they so rightly deserve in a humane manner?

It makes it look better for the N.H.S. Service **not** to have all these patients 'clogging' up hospital beds; it is really down to money, lack of beds, and uncaring hospital staff from the Specialists down. As before I say NOT ALL of them, but many are not fit to be in this profession. They take advantage of these poor people because they have no voice. If they can complain no one listens to them anyway, as long ago they were simply labelled as BAD. Sadly labels stick!

If they can move them on out of hospital and put them into the Criminal System where they end up out of their depths, with the poor Prison Officers completely and utterly untrained for such people, no wonder they are left frightened and worried, and so many of them end up harming themselves, as other prisoners soon learn to take advantage of them as they are so lost and vulnerable and feel so alone.

They do this easily and are **allowed** to do so, and it's not just Neil we are talking about, as there are thousands of people in Prison when they really should be in hospital. The Prison Service knows this to be true, as I've personally been told this by their staff on a number of occasions. We are then told that the prisons are overcrowded.

Naturally they will be, because a lot of the people in them **shouldn't** be in there in the first place. It is a crime of Society to allow this to happen, and it's one of the reasons why I have no faith in the Criminal Justice System anymore.

By putting mentally ill patients like Neil into an environment that is dangerous, with people who don't understand them and treat them as criminals, when in truth they are simply ill, you are putting their lives at risk.

Prison officers were being told off for being too lenient with Neil whenever they felt sorry for him, knowing that he shouldn't be there; but unfortunately this placed Neil into the crossfire, because other officers said he should be treated like everyone else. If the *hospital doctors and staff* didn't know what they were doing with Neil, how do you think the police and Prison officers would know? He was put in danger so many times it was absolutely ridiculous.

****

Councillor Fred Clough had again written to David, and had said that whilst he recognized the difficulties that existed at Fernlea General Hospital, with regard to managing patients without having appropriate staffing levels and secure beds, it was clear that at the time of the alleged incident Neil was indeed receiving treatment, and that no planned discharge was in hand, nor was there a clear pathway for his continued care thereafter. He said that going off the information, the alleged incident was the final straw, and the subsequent discharge took place not wholly based upon the patient's clinical needs. Why else after his intervention, would the medical directorate be seeking a secure hospital bed, if as alleged there is no underlying mental health problem? He said that it appeared to be a frustrating knee jerk reaction to the incident, and the lack of adequate facilities in terms of beds and staff to cope with the complexities of the patients who presented at Fernlea General Hospital.

Desmond Peters the Chief Executive of East Lancashire Health Authority, is the named proper officer responsible in law for seeing that secure beds are available to patients in East Lancashire.

The last letter I received from Fernlea Health Care Trust denied *everything* that Fred had said in his letter to David, and that Neil **never had** an enduring mental illness.

****

Five years later, after I was begging for help for Neil, they said this, and it was like a kick in the teeth after everything we had been through, especially so after all the Sections, all the different drugs, secure unit and finally Out Reach being involved, even if it was only for a couple of weeks.

Why are they allowed to keep changing their minds over something and someone like they do? Why can they always overrule the people who really know the truth of these matters?

****

Week after week we were in court while Neil got the devastating news that **no** hospital bed had been found anywhere in the country for him. Our hearts were being ripped out on every single occasion. I saw Neil deteriorate. I cannot find the words to tell you how we felt, as it was agonizing.

I wanted to scream at the people on the Bench to get the doctors here; they should be the ones in the dock, they are the criminals along with everyone else at that hospital. It was easy to acquire a bed in the hospital, just kick someone out of one like we'd seen happen when *they* wanted to, but I forget, it's Neil we are talking about. They **never** wanted him.

271

You may think I sound cruel, and as heartless as these people running the hospital, when I say kick someone out of a bed, but through experience we had learnt that it *was easy* for some of the patients to pull the wool over the eyes of the psychiatrists and nursing staff. They knew how to play the system. They had learned to tell them exactly what the doctors and staff wanted to hear, in order for them to get labelled as being mentally ill.

God only knows why, but it was true, some patients went in hospital when they wanted to save up money, because they were still in receipt of certain benefits that would accumulate for them when they left hospital.

Darren Hall had said they didn't know whether the patients were mad or bad, and none of the staff could tell the difference. Neil could always tell though, he knew who was faking and who was *really* ill. There he was denying his **own** illness, yet being seriously mentally ill, whilst many others were feigning it, and being believed. This was all so crazy! Yes, they could have found Neil a bed if they had wanted to, but I always found it **<u>very odd</u>** that they wanted to keep Neil to themselves, especially when we were always pushing for Neil to be seen outside of the area, so that Fernlea **wouldn't** be involved, at possibly some other hospital with a neutral doctor, Neil could then be truly diagnosed and all his mental illnesses could then be treated accordingly, and perhaps Neil could be finally helped.

****

Dr McKewen saw Neil at Lancaster Farms. Neil told me he was distrustful of him. I think he felt that way about a lot of people at that time. I know how he felt. I know the prison officers were worried about Neil, as on visiting Neil and the phone calls I received off them showed me that. I have no complaint of how they treated Neil; it was just that he *shouldn't* have been there; he was ill and in a bad environment with people who *didn't understand*, including the other inmates. Our boy was vulnerable and at risk, and our hearts ached for him.

A prison officer rang me after Neil had been seen by Dr McKewen. I believe the officer and what he told me about Dr McKewen seeing Neil hearing voices, and responding to them also. He said, that the doctor said that **<u>Neil should be in hospital</u>**, and that was what the general consensus was at the prison.

272

To listen to Fernlea General's Bob Gardner this was untrue; he said that Dr McKewen had said that Neil was **not suffering** from any form of mental illness. I didn't believe him, and asked for him to show us the report as we all wanted to see it for ourselves, but he wouldn't show it to us. I really cannot believe this coming from one of the psychiatrists from The Guild. They are Forensic Psychiatrists, so shouldn't have had an axe to grind as Fernlea General's Psychiatrists did, and I'd put the likes of Bob Gardner and John Duggan in that bracket too. They intended to follow the same path as they'd made their mistakes with Neil, so they stuck to their story. I doubt very much that Dr McKewen and later Dr Samuel Plackett would want to be labelled as being in the same classification as them.

****

On 24th August 2001 David again writes to The Chief Executive, East Lancashire Health Authority.

At the end of the letter he stated that Neil had been in Lancaster Farms for five weeks, and that it was a wholly inappropriate and unacceptable state of affairs. He was asking him to clarify for him in some detail the endeavours that had been made by the Health Authority to find a secure hospital bed for Neil since his initial court appearance.

****

The *Lancashire Telegraph* ran the story of Neil on 25th August 2001. It made the front page headlines.

I had got in touch with them because I was afraid the Neil would kill himself, and I told them that hospital bosses said that he was too dangerous for the psychiatric wards at Fernlea General Hospital. The reporter had been in touch with a health watchdog spokesman who said that he was horrified by the situation, and accused the hospital of dumping Neil into the prison system.

Fred said that he was horrified that Neil, who has had mental illness throughout all of his life, was in Lancaster Farms, which at that time had a poor report from the Inspector of Prisons. He said that he believed that the Trust took the opportunity to dump this lad there, and that he truly believed that to be true, as to get him off their ward was an urgent priority for them because he needed so much support and help.

Trust Executive D. J. Cue said patients who were so disruptive

273

needed particular health care needs, which could not be delivered in Fernlea. Local units are not geared up for dealing with that level of disruption, and they were still trying to find appropriate accommodation for Neil. There was a national shortage for secure beds for patients with needs very similar to Neil's.

A week later after this Neil was again produced at court, and once more the local newspapers ran the story of no hospital bed for youth in jail.

Below is the article that was printed in the *Lancashire Telegraph* on the 30th August 2001, with a photo of Neil.

■ Ordeal may soon end for mentally ill teenager

No hospital bed for youth in jail

By WENDY BARLOW
Court Reporter

A MENTALLY ill teenager who is in jail because no bed can be found in a secure hospital unit may soon see an end to his ordeal.

Neil Anthony Green's solicitor Dermot Woodhead, told Burnley Magistrates the defendant was due to see a psychiatrist at Lancaster Farms next Tuesday and the outcome may well be that he would not be at the young offenders' institution much longer.

Neil Green, 19, has spent three weeks in jail at Lancaster Farms young offenders institution after hospital bosses said he was too dangerous for the psychiatric ward at Burnley General Hospital.

He was a sectioned patient under the Mental Health Act in a psychiatric ward at Burnley General Hospital when he damaged a wardrobe door last month.

He was arrested and taken to the police station and charged with causing criminal damage.

The next day he was discharged from hospital. He appeared at Burnley magistrates court, pleaded guilty and was sent to Lancaster Farms pending completion of a psychiatric assessment and a hospital bed being made available.

Three times he has appeared in court and been returned to Lancaster Farms.

Frank Clifford, chairman of the health watchdog Community Health Council, said the case highlighted a lack of secure hospital accommodation for people with problems like Neil.

Trust chief executive David Chew, said patients who were so disruptive needed particular health care needs, which could not be delivered in Burnley.

He said local units were simply not geared up for dealing with that level of disruption and they were still trying to find appropriate accommodation for Neil.

There was a national shortage of secure beds for patients with needs very similar to Neil Green's.

Green, of no fixed address, was remanded in custody until September 13 for reports. He had earlier been convicted of aggravated taking of a vehicle, driving with excess alcohol, not having a licence, no insurance and damage.

He has written to his mother, Susan, ★★★★★★★★★★★ ★★★★★ saying he could not stand it any longer at Lancaster Farms and she fears he may kill himself.

She and her husband, Stephen, have made a formal complaint to the Community Health Council and intend to sue the Health Trust.

After yesterday's court hearing, Mrs Green said: "It still all depends on them finding a suitable bed outside of the prison system.

"In the meantime, he is still languishing in the prison system and I am getting more and more worried. he is not getting the specialised treatment he needs. He is mentally ill and getting into more trouble while he is in there."

ORDEAL: Neil Green, who's mentally ill

274

Gilbert Price M.P. wrote to the Prison's Minister, Beverley Hughes M.P. about Neil's case.

I received a copy of the Pre-Sentence Report prepared by the lovely Rosemary Powers, who had been so generous in giving me information in the past, and who continued to be professional and understanding towards Neil's needs. I had seen her on numerous occasions at court and I found her very sympathetic and warm.

She wrote:

When I interviewed the defendant at H.M. Y01 Lancaster Farms he seemed to be agitated, although co-operative, he said he was experiencing problems in custody. He could not stay on "normal location" due to his behaviour - which he described as "hyper." The hospital wing or the "Punishment Block" was his main accommodation. He seemed a combination of exasperation, agitation, depression and anger, which he saw arising out of the lack of a service from the local health service. He told me that from the age of just seven years, he had behavioural problems, which were diagnosed as Attention Deficit Hyperactive Disorder later.

He was moved between schools due to his behaviour, as they could not cope with his needs. In his words, "It has always been a struggle." In his teens he was sent to a boarding school in Cumbria until he was sixteen years old. He said he was literate, numerate and had the potential to learn.

Mr Green was prescribed the drug Ritalin, which controls the worst aspect of his Attention Deficit Hyperactive Disorder. However the defendant stated that in recent years other problems had emerged - in particular psychotic symptoms, hearing voices and feeling persecuted. Alongside these have been the misuse of alcohol which Mr Green firmly believes helps to blot out how he feels.

Mr Green's family have been through a great deal and are "at the end of their tether." They have absorbed much of his behaviour and have sought out medical opinions and services for their son. They have been very disappointed by the local National Health Service provision, and have approached newspapers about their son's situation. It is their view that Mr Green requires specialized accommodation, which is therapeutic and secure. This is, in their view, for their son's welfare, but also to prevent the risk of harm to the public. They have been concerned about the escalation in his behaviour, and the fact that he has no concept about the harm he poses. It is not just a hospital bed that is required, but also an aftercare plan is needed urgently. There have been a series of meetings involving medical personnel, and his legal representative might have more information.

Conclusion.

When the court adjourned for this report it indicated that "all options were being considered." Mr Green has now been in custody for nearly two months and he has found it a distressing experience. His family told me that they thought it was "the wrong place for Neil."

In terms of community based penalties, I cannot offer a proposal due to Mr Green's mental health, and the Probation Service does not have the necessary skills or resources to deal with Mr Green's problems. It was Mr Green's and his family's hope that a bed may be available at Preston Hospital, where he can be re-sectioned under the Mental Health Act 1983. The family of Mr Green have been making enquiries of their own, and a facility exists in the private sector at St. Andrews Hospital in Northampton. However the stumbling block is always the question of funding, either for the treatment at Preston or St. Andrews.

Gilbert Price M.P. has written to the local Health Care Trust and is still awaiting a reply, and because he knew ultimately that they were dragging their feet he spoke to John Duggan, Divisional Manager for Mental Health at the Health Care Trust, he said that he had been faxed the medical report from Dr McKewen which outlined his assessment of Neil and his suggestions for his future management.

The information was shared out with the appropriate sector Consultant Psychiatrist, the Community Health Team and the East Lancashire Health Authority. This had enabled the Health Care Trust to begin contingency planning to manage Neil's care should he be released from Lancaster Farms. Their aim was to co-ordinate a complex package of care around Neil, supported by funding from the East Lancashire Health Authority in the hope of maintaining Neil in his local community.

Mr Duggan had mentioned to Gilbert that he was awaiting Neil's Probation Officer to let him have her view; and he had also spoken to Ben Law of Making Space.

Gilbert did think at the time that things were moving in the right direction, and that he hoped that it wouldn't take long for Neil to be released from Lancaster Farms and that the care package planned will ensure that Neil receives all the help he clearly needs.

Neil's story is again in *The Lancashire Telegraph* after he appeared at court for the fifth time, and then was sent back to Lancaster Farms. This was 19th September, 2001.

We received a phone call from Lancaster Farms.
NEIL HAD HUNG HIMSELF IN HIS CELL.

He was resuscitated.
Prison Officers said it was a **serious** attempt to take his own life, because he would not have known anyone would check his cell when they did.
Where do we turn?
I even wrote to Lambeth Palace, Church of England to the Archbishop of Canterbury.
All that was said, and it was probably from an 'aide' was that "all those that are caught up in the criminal justice system are regularly included in our prayers."
It just shows the extent I would go to, to get help for Neil, but this didn't help, we needed **more than prayers.**
****
Neil was in the papers again on Saturday 22nd September because he had been sent back to the ward from which he came at Fernlea General Hospital. It was said that nobody at the Health Care Trust would comment on the apparent about turn, which had allowed Neil to be sent back to the hospital.
I told the press on leaving the court that day he was released to the hospital, that I hoped it wouldn't be long before they found him *somewhere else to go* as I didn't want him on a ward at Fernlea for long after all they had done to him previously.
I had asked for a secure hospital environment and I hoped it

277

wouldn't be long before he was moved.

Neil's solicitor had said at court that arrangements had been made for Neil to see a Psychiatrist, and he had been assured that there was now a bed at Fernlea available for him. He will now either be admitted to that bed today, or if appropriate the hospital has a special duty to provide him with proper residence placement and care. He applied for a three week adjournment pending the assessment.

Asked if he wanted the case to proceed yesterday, he told the court, "I am exceedingly skeptical that the Health Authority will do what they say if Neil is no longer in the Court Process."

The case was adjourned until October 12th.

Bail was granted on condition that Neil resided at the hospital or in accommodation provided by the Health Authority.

A spokesperson for M.I.N.D. (National Association for Mental Health) said, "This is a very unhappy story. We feel that inhuman or degrading treatment such as being held in prison when a person

278

apparently needs mental healthcare is a violation of their rights under the European Convention.

No one was ever brought to task for what they did to Neil.

Nor would they be in the future…

CHAPTER NINETEEN
Into the Lion's Den

We didn't want Neil to go back to Fernlea General Hospital, of course we didn't, but again my thoughts return to why? Why do they think they can cope any differently with him there now, than they had before, especially so when nothing of any significance had been done at all? Also is it right to do so with all the bad feeling they had for Neil? It was like sending your child to school, knowing that he/she would be viciously bullied every day. I knew they would make him suffer, especially when we'd got Dr Leister denying that Neil had mental illness, and Bob Gardner wanting to 'win one over on us'; it seemed to me that was what he was doing, but at whose cost? Neil's of course! All we were doing as every one of you would have done, was fighting for our son to get treatment.

So here we were taking him into the 'Lions Den' to staff who knew he was there only under sufferance.

We **never did** say that we were going to sue the hospital. I was **never** told that we **could**, but I did want to get proper medical attention for Neil, so we did contact a solicitor to try to seek out that help, but none of the solicitors we got did anything to help us get that help. We were left completely in the dark.

I rang the Mental Health Charities and they gave me some names of solicitors that dealt in Mental Health Law, but what could they do to help when the Psychiatrists themselves are GODS who believe that they are *always* right. I can't tell the doctor, *you can't*, **they tell you**. I say it again; you cannot make a doctor, doctor. You can get a second opinion. I forgot, Neil couldn't, as **they** simply wouldn't allow him to do so.

Ben used to say to me, "Don't complain; don't do this, or that, because if you get their backs up, and question, they won't want to do anything for Neil."

Excuse me, it's because they weren't doing anything for him in the first place. They are the ones who have made the mistakes, lied, neglected, and treated Neil cruelly. Should I have stood back and let them ignore Neil's pain and suffering, and toss him aside to fend for himself?

Well, *they* did that anyway, so obviously I didn't fight hard enough for him, or they are getting away with MURDER. If the former was true I wouldn't have entitled my *book "Upon Deaf Ears, A Mother's Fight for Her Son."*

Sorry Ben, I quite understand your predicament, because you have to go into hospital, and sit beside these contemptible people to 'help' your other clients. You know yourself that Neil's was a difficult case, even for you, he wasn't straightforward, his problems were complex but he deserved better, don't you think?

I couldn't EVER do your job, because I couldn't sit on the fence and beg for a crumb here and there. The psychiatrists are doctors, the same as the rest who take the Hippocratic oath, to care and do their utmost for their patients, yet for Neil they never did, but then they covered up their crime with the help of managers and executives from the Health Authority, it was always swept under the carpet. However I **won't let** there be a cover up, because it should NEVER happen again to any other poor souls or their families.

What happened to Neil, the way they got him into police hands, had happened before, and probably will again until someone stands up to stop them. I know of one young girl who was sent to Styal Prison after she had set fire to her bed at Fernlea General, and they had her arrested. Neil told me that she had attempted suicide, and he thought that she had succeeded, but I'm not totally sure about that, but I was told about others too. It seems so logical that if they were getting away with doing this to Neil, they had done it all before. They did in fact try it on two other occasions to Neil, but I was one step ahead of them on these occasions, because I asked the other patients to keep an eye on Neil, and to ring me and note down things that they thought were untoward. They were all in the same boat and clung together, because **they all knew it was wrong** what was happening on the wards.

****

Neil was obviously happy to be out. We had an appointment with Dr Janger as soon as we were released from court. David wasn't daft,

281

and he made sure that Neil was kept in the 'Court System' to safeguard him a little, so that Fernlea General's psychiatrist's couldn't continue trying to offload him. Ben came to the meeting. It used to really annoy me going to these meetings because you had an appointment and all the people, be it, psychiatrists, social workers and other staff were in a room discussing Neil, and then they make their decisions and call you in up to an hour later. I'll tell you about one of those times at the end of my book when Steve, as mild mannered as he is, flipped.

We wanted Dr Janger to Section Neil and he wouldn't. Neil had just hung himself at Lancaster Farms, *and he was still voicing a tendency towards killing himself.* He was also severely depressed, but Dr Janger said that he **wasn't Sectionable.** Neil had a deep red mark around his neck, yet they were to take Neil on the ward without a Section? So here we go again.

Another reason why we wanted him Sectioned was that we wanted him in a Secure Hospital. A Secure Hospital that would actually treat him I might add, not one that they used as a 'Holding Centre' whilst they still had the entire control over him from the day he went in. No not one of those, but more on that later. Everything I remind myself of in writing this book just frustrates and maddens me. Try unbelievable, that's it. *It was truly unbelievable.*

The conditions of Neil's bail were that he lived and slept at Fernlea General Hospital or as directed by the local Health Authority.

******

Saturday 22ⁿᵈ September 2001

Neil rang his Grandma Green and Grandma Robinson stating that he was going to kill himself. We were in our caravan which was on a site just a few miles away. Kathleen was so upset that Neil would either carry out his threat, or come to the caravan, that she and Barry came to the caravan themselves.

I rang the ward and spoke to Angela. She said that Neil was not displaying any suicidal tendencies, and they hadn't heard him ring anyone stating the same. Kathleen knew Neil as I did, and she wasn't *easily spooked*, so for her to come to us like this was very unusual, because she would normally try to keep everything away from us, especially if she thought he didn't mean it.

282

She was worried I could see that. Later Neil rang us from his mobile phone saying that he wasn't allowed back onto the ward because he'd been drinking. He told me that the staff had called the police and that the police were there with him.

I told him to pass his phone to the police officer; (I'd been here before).

I asked the policeman specifically if Neil was causing any trouble?

The police officer said, "No, it's just that the staff on the ward had stated that they don't have to let anyone onto the ward if they'd been drinking."

I told the officer that, "Neil's Bail Conditions stated that he has to reside on the ward at the hospital."

He asked me. "Can you have Neil at home?"

I said, "Definitely not, tell the staff in no uncertain terms that Neil has to be on the ward."

He held the phone open so that I could hear him telling the staff what I'd said. Neil was let back onto the ward.

****

Sunday 23rd September 2001

Neil rang me on and off all day, sounding more depressed and more unbalanced as the day went on. He said Jeff Maroney who had been on Ward 20 when he'd been on before (he's now on Ward 18), a staff nurse, had been upsetting him, winding him up, calling Neil an 'Arse Wipe'.

I believed Neil straightaway, (anyway Neil didn't intentionally lie to me so I shouldn't say that). I had heard this man saying that before about another patient when he was on Ward 20, and Neil *didn't* know this. He told Neil that he was there under false pretences, and that he should still be at Lancaster Farms as it was the best place for him.

Neil rang me later at tea-time, a blurred message; this was on my answering machine because I was making tea at the time. Neil said that he loved me and Dad but he'd had enough. As soon as I heard the message I rang direct to Ward 18 and Jeff answered (I always asked the names of the staff).

I said, "I don't want to talk to you, will you please put someone in charge of the ward on the phone."

283

He just put the phone down on me. I rang again and he put the phone down on me AGAIN. I rang the main hospital number and got the receptionist on the switchboard. I told her that a member of staff had *deliberately* put the phone down on me.

She rang the ward and then got back to me to tell me that no one on the ward would talk to me. I'd have to talk to Bob Gardner, and she'd get him to ring me as she would have to ring him at home. I waited panicking for what seemed like ages.

I couldn't understand why anyone on the ward wouldn't talk to me. I didn't say anything wrong, if asking for the person in charge was wrong, then I was guilty of that, but that is all I said. It made me think that something bad had happened to Neil. Had he harmed himself? It was taking forever for Bob Gardner to ring me.

I rang the police, asking if Neil was with them?

"No," they said.

"Have you been called to the Hospital? Is Neil involved?" I continued questioning them.

"No," they said.

A full half an hour later Bob rang me, and we argued. He said that he would tell the ward if I rang again that they *have* to talk to me. He'd mentioned that he was in the room when Dr Leister rang St. Andrews and he was told that Neil **wasn't suitable** for St. Andrews. I found this hard to believe and made a note to tell David.

We went to the hospital and rang Neil to meet us outside, and we managed to calm him down. They had really worked him up.

30th September 2001

We arrived home from the caravan and were coming up the hill towards our home when Neil came out from nowhere and jumped into the middle of the road in front of the car. Steve braked hard. Neil was in an agitated state and argumentative, we couldn't get through to him. Steve took him and the lad he was with back to the hospital. I expected trouble.

We went to Kathleen's, came back and there was a message left on my answering machine. Neil said he was going to kill himself. I rang the ward to have the phone put down on me AGAIN.

Neil rang a little later, with a jumbled message saying he'd cut his arms with a razorblade. I rang the switchboard operator and asked for

284

the on duty Mental Health Doctor. The switchboard operator kept me hanging on for ages, only to tell me that the doctor wouldn't talk to me; she asked if the Ward Sister would do?

I knew what would happen but I said, "Okay."

The operator came back to me on the phone to state that the Ward Sister wouldn't talk to me, and she'd get John Duggan to ring me.

They never did ring me off the ward to tell me what harm Neil had done. They said later that it was just a scratch. There were eight **deep cuts** above Neil's wrists, but NO SCRATCHES WHATSOEVER!

1st October 2001

We went to see Neil on the ward after Ben had left at 5:00pm. Ben voiced his opinion on the ward as to how I was treated, and the fact that he had seen Neil's arms and they were **not scratches** but deep cuts.

Annie came to see Neil from Harrogate. She's such a lovely girl. Neil had met her on the ward and she'd been discharged and they'd formed a friendship.

Neil had been drinking; he said that he'd shared a bottle of vodka with another patient. I went into the lounge and watched with amazement when a few of the patients came back from the shop with bottles of coke and a bottle of vodka, and tipped coke out to top up with vodka. I also watched as money changed hands around the room.

Another patient asked Neil to go to the shop for her some alcohol, and told him that if he did she'd treat him to a bottle of *Wicked*. Cannabis was being smoked by some of the other patients.

I was told by a patient that a member of staff told her, "Why hide it; you might as well do it in front of us, as we know you are doing it."

I was told that they turn a blind eye, and because I could plainly see the staff simply going about their duties and completely overlooking what was happening on the ward in front of them, I personally know this to be true. I was told by a patient that Neil was caught with his pants down quite literally. He was having oral sex with a female patient.

"If they hand it to him on a plate, a good looking lad like that, he's bound to take it, be daft not to," she said.

I was told much later by staff something else that I found astonishing, and if they knew it to be true why did they let it carry on? It was the fact that their medication made the patients highly sexed. Surely if this is true, it is a good reason NOT to have mixed sex wards isn't it? Surely the women need to be protected?

"They are the worst ones," I was told.

I still found this notion absolutely unacceptable. Mind you, I found it all totally inappropriate.

There was a drug dealer who actually parked his car at the entrance to the Mental Health wards, which was situated well within the hospital grounds, in order to supply and sell his drugs. I had been told this by Neil, but now the other patients were relating the same tale to me.

Good God, call me naïve, but I thought the idea of being in hospital was to get **better.** The only difference about Ward 18 to a 'Bordello/Brothel' is that money wasn't changing hands (well except for shots of alcohol or drugs. Neil didn't smoke or drink alcohol every day BEFORE he went into hospital, at least NOT as he was doing now. He didn't usually sleep around either.

'He'll be a drug addict, alcoholic, get cancer and a sexually transmitted disease too at this rate,' I thought.

Tuesday 2nd October 2001

I took Neil back to the hospital at 4:00pm his Granddad had dropped him off at my house after he had taken him out for a meal. We saw Dr Janger because he had asked to see me. He talked of Neil going to A.A. I couldn't believe what he was saying to me. It's the situation that he is in that's making him turn to drink. In my opinion the hospital ward was perpetuating Neil's demise. He was self medicating. Neil had drink and drugs there on tap whilst he was in the hospital.

If I had to live like he was having to, maybe I'd be the same. We didn't see a way out while he was at that hospital. He wasn't getting **any treatment**; obviously they were just waiting for Neil to do something daft and pushing him at the same time towards doing so. I always thought that it was the Trust that made the decisions, **not** the psychiatrists.

A member of staff was sitting with us and Neil came in, he'd been told by a patient that the ward had called the police on him, and they'd been in while he had been out. I looked at Dr Janger.

"Not again, what for this time? You'd better not have, not again."

He shrugged.

I came out of the room to talk to Bridget, who shouts to me, "It's about this morning, Neil and I were the only ones in the lounge, and Neil did a daft thing when lighting his cigarette, he lit the empty cigarette packet. It was nothing really! I took it off him and put it in the ashtray; it wasn't flaring up or anything, there was no danger; in fact nothing was even burnt. They are always picking on Neil over the smallest of things. When Christine attacked a member of staff, they didn't call the police on her, or when chairs have been thrown and things have got broken, and how many times have the TV's got broken too," she said.

Two members of staff came towards me and ushered me into a room. They told me that Neil had tried to set fire to the hospital.

"You were there, were you, at the time, you saw it did you. Who called the police?" I asked. Bridget's just told me *exactly* what happened."

The member of staff looked at me and said, "But she is mentally ill."

"So is Neil," I said.

"Take your hands off the door," I said, as she was holding it shut to prevent me from leaving. I went to the police who were in the office having just arrived.

I told them, "If you want to talk to Neil then do so in front of his solicitor."

I went to ring David. I was fuming. The police officer came towards me and said, "Don't worry, we're not going to see Neil, we're going now."

Neil was shaking, partly with temper, but he was scared too. How dare they do this to him again, threaten him and make out that they were going to get him arrested again. I felt so sorry for him.

A member of staff told Neil the reason they wouldn't talk to his mum was that I was suing the hospital, and it was Bob Gardner who had told them not to talk to me. (Bob was the Nursing Manager/Administrator). Now we know. The two faced bleep, bleep.

287

Can you imagine what all this did to us? Our hands were tied, we were banging our heads against a brick wall; they were playing games with Neil's life. How cruel were they? It's unbelievable, isn't it? **It's all true, every word**. I kept a diary because I knew that they were victimizing Neil, and I couldn't do a damn thing about it. Just thinking that all these disgusting people are <u>still</u> working in the Health Service makes me feel sick. It's no wonder that people are begging me to write this book. It couldn't get any worse I thought; but sadly it could.

3rd October 2001

We had another awful meeting, with everyone sitting in a circle, too many people all having a dig. Neil had slashed his arms again, to ribbons this time, much worse even than before. He felt so tormented, unhappy and ridiculed; all the staff members were making his life a misery. I know he was hard to deal with, but he was very ill. They just kept trying to prove a point. It was personal, it had to be personal. These aren't professionals, they are rubbish. These are not caring staff, they are thoroughly heartless. They are the kind of people who get great satisfaction in mocking the afflicted not helping them in any way whatsoever.

They were saying that they were looking at care in the community. Neil was getting wound up because he knew he'd not cope. We argued. I argued with everyone. Dr Janger for not Sectioning Neil, as he was deeply depressed, and was self harming to an alarming degree. I accused him of listening to management and the Trust must be pulling his strings, as he wasn't making *clinical* decisions. I called all the staff for treating Neil so badly and picking on him, making him suffer and for being nasty towards us too.

It was just pointless calling anyone else really, the 'buck' stopped with the psychiatrist, as it's always on his say why the staff were treating Neil like this. We left Neil distraught. I asked the patients to look out for him.

Neil rang me three times up to and around 8:00pm, saying that he couldn't cope with living on his own. The last time he rang me he told me that Janet was kicking off. I heard her screaming.

Kristina rang me at 8:25pm telling me that they'd got Neil down on the floor. I heard him screaming and shouting. She told me that they had accused him of assaulting a member of staff, and they'd called the police. She told me that Neil had gone towards Janet's room as the staff members were searching it, and Janet became upset. Neil had gone to her to try to talk to her and calm her down. (They were all like this with one another, the patients, looking out for one another, and they needed to be, with those God damn awful staff).

One of staff told Neil to "Eff Off" and pushed him away.

Neil had shouted, "Keep your hands off me."

Then a member of staff grabbed Neil's legs and pinned him to the floor. They were quick at restraining patients; they kind of got pleasure out of it, a sort of real adrenalin rush.

They had done the same thing to a patient on Ward 20 when Neil was on there, and that time they had broken the patient's leg.

The long haired member of staff had said that Neil had tried to head-butt him, which Neil denied. They had actually told the police that Neil HAD assaulted a member of staff. They told me that they would never have come to the hospital in the first place, if they hadn't said that.

Kristina said they were injecting Neil. I told Kristina I was on my way there, and asked her to tell Neil. She again assured me that Neil had done nothing, and that the other patients would tell me the same. I told her to write it all down what they said and she did. Bless her, not only did she do this, but she signed it too.

8:25pm –   They had Neil pinned down on the floor.
9:40pm –   The police arrived.

She wrote that down and by the time I got to the hospital after getting the car out of the garage it was around 10.00pm. They'd had Neil pinned down to the floor for over one and a half hours.

I arrived to see SIX members of staff holding Neil face down on the floor. They were hurting him as his face was red and swollen. He'd been crying. I saw two police officers. There was also a deep red mark around Neil's neck.

Kristina came towards me and she told me that they had been winding Neil up, and laughing at him. I had heard them laughing when she rang me, and Neil was shouting can you hear Jeff Maroney laughing. That creep was involved again! He's the one that calls

289

patients 'Arse Wipes'.

Robert (a patient), took me to one side and told me that he had helped Neil down, but it was a struggle because Neil was so big and heavy.

Neil was found by Robert hanging in his room again, just as he had done before in prison with his laces. The staff **didn't mention this**, nor did they bother to <u>tell</u> the police. Instead they had just abused Neil on top of him just trying to hang himself. They do not even share ONE heart between them these people. They are a TOTAL disgrace to their profession.

The police officer told me that they had asked the staff to let Neil get to his feet, but the staff refused and kept him pinned down to the ground.

I insisted in no uncertain terms to the staff that they got off him and allowed him to stand.

The police said, "Do it, I'm not asking you, I'm **telling** you."

The staff didn't like me talking to the patients, as they were all sticking up for Neil, and telling the police too. The staff tried to remove me from the ward.

I refused to go, so they got one of the police officers to escort me off the ward, but they just took me into the corridor.

They took Neil away after arresting him. Meanwhile on the ward they had sent for Bob Gardner and he arrived at the ward at 10:20pm.

Kristina was still writing it down, what he was saying to the staff, she was listening to everything he was saying. She wrote that he was telling the staff that he wanted Neil to do something so that they would be able to send him back, and that they were only having to keep him on the ward because of his bail conditions.

He said that he didn't care about Neil's Mum as he could sort that. He moaned that he'd spent two hours with Neil at the meeting and this after last Sunday.

Bob Gardner was at the meeting earlier on and he was talking about last Sunday, when the staff kept putting the phone down on me, but he'd had to ring me after the switchboard operator had rung him at home. Kristina didn't know a thing about all this, and I hadn't even told Neil about last Sunday. It would have upset Neil to know that the staff were treating me with contempt; he was upset enough as it was. I knew Kristina had heard correctly, and that everything that she had written down was perfectly true.

The police at Burnley were kindness itself from the moment that we were off the ward. One officer in particular was brilliant with Neil. They let me go everywhere with Neil, and they didn't put him in a cell, instead they actually let him go into the 'yard' for a smoke. This was more like it. This was really how to treat someone with a mental illness, with patience, kindness and understanding.

The doctor was already at the Police Station and he saw Neil pretty quickly. He asked Neil and me lots of questions.

Neil was hearing voices and he was talking to himself. I hadn't seen him acting like this before. He'd changed facially too. I felt funny looking at Neil as it was all new and very strange for me, as if it wasn't our Neil, but then suddenly he was back from wherever his head had taken him.

I can't explain it very well. It hurt me though, I know that. The officer put his arm around me, sat me down and got me a drink. I didn't know it but I was shaking.

A really pretty police officer was talking to me, she said, "I know Neil, and I like him, and I'm so sorry that he has deteriorated so much."

The doctor was sympathetic. He went to the Custody Desk and he asked me to sit with Neil in the office. He came back a little later and told me that he'd been on the phone to the Administrator at the hospital and Neil was going back to Ward 18. I had known all along that Neil hadn't done anything, and that this was all yet another ploy to get rid of him. I went back to the ward with Neil and Bob Gardner was there with a face like thunder.

Sergeant Simpson told me not to worry; if the staff on the ward hadn't lied to them, the police officers would not have gone to the hospital in the first place. I asked him to instill into his officers what the hospital staff members were trying to do, and in future would they question it if it ever involved Neil again?

As far as I was concerned, Neil was not fit to be in the community, and if I could do anything to stop that happening I would do so. So at the meeting that day when they said they wanted Neil to have care in the community, this was a non-starter as far as BOTH Neil and I were concerned.

Sergeant Simpson told me to tell David to bring it up at court the

291

following week that drink and drugs were freely available on the ward, and Neil should not be allowed **out** of hospital until he'd had Specialist Treatment, which could **not** be provided at Fernlea General as Neil was a danger to himself and also to others.

Friday 5th October 2001

Dr Janger rang me to say, "They've found Neil a place at Healey House."

I said, "Neil is not ready to go anywhere yet, after another attempt on his life, his self harming and how bad he was displaying at the Police Station on Wednesday."

I told him that the police said that he shouldn't be in the community like this. He'd seen officers who he had known for ages, and they were quite astounded at his level of deterioration. I felt he needed specialized treatment, and he hadn't had any. He isn't ready; I asked for a second opinion from a doctor who had no connection whatsoever with Fernlea General or the East Lancs Health Authority.

We went to look at the house that Mary Healey ran on Ormerod Road in Burnley. I had no intention of Neil going there, but we went to see it with Ben. Neil would have his own room, but share the other facilities with other people. It was similar to a place that I would have loved for Neil in the future, when he had gotten proper treatment off an honest and fully competent doctor, and was stable on a regime of medication, and wasn't trying to commit suicide or self harming any longer. Both Ben and I were honest with her and told her of Neil's drinking and everything else.

She said that she could probably cope with the drinking, but not with the self harming and the other things. "What are the hospital thinking of?" she asked.

They didn't care who they offloaded Neil to, did they? All the good work this lady was doing would have been put at risk had Neil gone to her. It doesn't bear thinking about!

Saturday 6th October 2001

We brought Neil home for tea, he said he wasn't ready to go and live at Mary Healey's house, but he would if I wanted him to.

I said, "No Neil, I agree with you." He was telling me that he hadn't had a drink for a couple of days. He didn't seem as if he'd been drinking. He was a bit on edge, but he seemed better in himself.

Monday 8th October 2001

Neil arrived at my home at 5:15pm with a friend. Neil seemed fine, but they had both been drinking. I told him to get back to the hospital and not to have any more to drink. Neil ordered a taxi, and he rang me after he had arrived back at the hospital like I had asked him to do.

I heard a member of staff shouting at him about the bottle of *Wicked* he had in his hand.

9th October 2001

I went to see Ben, as he said that he would copy some papers for me. He was always there for us. I felt sorry though that he was so frustrated that he couldn't do more for Neil, and that he too couldn't get through to anyone at Fernlea, as he was hitting brick walls and speaking to deaf and closed ears.

It wasn't Ben's fault. He did speak up. He told them that he didn't like what they doing to Neil; it was so wrong, but like us there was nothing he could do. They could do as they wished and there was nowhere we could go to change things. It would have been much harder for us if we hadn't had Ben to turn to. I know how you are feeling Ben, this day 8th September 2006. Don't you think that you **didn't** try your best for Neil; none of it was **ever** your fault. I don't blame you for not doing enough. I blame all those at Fernlea General and the Trust and Health Authority, but *never* you. We know Neil thought the world of you. Thank you. Thanks for trying.

I went to see Neil at 10:55am. He looked awful. He seemed so downtrodden, and really depressed. He said that they had stopped his P.R.N. medication, and if he wanted anything it was to be done by injection. *Alarm bells started ringing.*

I took him to Kwik Save for some bits, and then we went to the chippy then back to the ward. I spoke to Judy one of the patients.

She said that she thought that Neil was a bit quiet, and that she knew that he'd had a drink that morning.

Marjorie (another patient) shouted to Neil, "Go to the shop for me Neil I'll treat you, do you want a bottle or some cigs?"

I decided to follow him. My legs were very painful, but I wanted to watch Neil go to the shop, so I waited as close to the shop as I could without Neil actually seeing me. He came out of the shop and he had a bottle in one hand, and one in the other. I was worried about him he seemed seriously withdrawn.

Later on Neil rang me and left a message saying that he was out with three other patients. Steve had heard the message and was worried about him, so he rang him. He told me later that he had told him to get back to the hospital; he thought that he had sounded like he was 'stoned'.

Steve also rang the hospital at 8:00pm to make sure that Neil had got back. He was told that Neil was in with the doctor.

10th October 2001

We went to a Ward Meeting. Neil's arm was bandaged and he said that he had cut himself the night before. Neil seemed to be under the influence of something. I don't know how many times we had asked at those meetings that we wanted them to **not** involve so many people, as there was always a room full. A lot of people always served to wind Neil up. He was sick of all these people talking down to him. It was always about bad stuff, never ever anything positive was mentioned. Talking all the time about Neil's drinking, Bob Gardner was the worst. He knew just what buttons to press to wind Neil up; he knew what he was doing alright. Now he was going on about all the reasons why they would **not section** Neil.

Neil's Advocate Jordan Whaite asked him to please tell then what constitutes a Section then? Not serious self harm or attempted suicide apparently.

Bob said, "There are four psychiatrists who have said that Neil was not sectionable."

Ben, Steve and I all said more or less at the same time. "Are all of them from this hospital?"

He said, "No, not all, because Dr McKewen had said the same when he'd visited him at Lancaster Farms."

I complained to Bob in front of everybody about holding Neil pinned down to the floor for nearly two hours, and the staff lying to the police again.

Neil was getting agitated and he said, "If you lot are not going to help me, then I might as well stop taking the medication." He insulted Dr Janger.

Dr Janger snapped back at Neil, but this was rightly so I thought.

I didn't like the way Neil had spoken to Dr Janger. When we met Dr Janger after Dr Leister we thought that we'd be treated better. I liked him first off. I thought he was a gentleman. He talked really nicely. Now I was putting him in the same bracket as Dr Leister.

I really didn't like Bob Gardner at all; he was smarmy, full of his own importance. He reminded us all of the Fat Controller *on Thomas the Tank Engine*. He was clever enough, but I didn't trust him. I never had trusted him. I was right about him, as he was a proper two faced man.

I expected more though from Dr Janger, but he let us down. I still didn't like Neil insulting him though. I told Neil that we don't have to stoop down to their level, but it was at least to his face and not behind his back. Ben also spoke out and the meeting became very heated.

I thought, 'If that Donna Castle Calder calls me Maureen once more I think I might swing for her.' I snap at her, "My name's Susan." She was getting on my nerves, and now she was talking about referring Neil to Calderstones.

I wasn't too enthusiastic about that. We didn't want to go anywhere until Neil has been seen by someone at Northampton. The meeting became more heated than ever, and when we had finished I went home with a terrible headache. I felt really down, demoralized, shell shocked, frustrated at getting nowhere, furious and so very down. I wrote in my diary, 'Worst day, worst meeting.'

Neil rang me to top it all off and he was threatening. I threw the phone across the room in temper. I'd had enough.

Thursday 11ᵗʰ October 2001

I rang Dr Janger. I told him that I would be getting my solicitor to write to him so that he can state in writing the reasons why he won't section Neil, what he feels is wrong with Neil, and what his prognosis is for the future?

He told me that Neil had made another attempt to hang himself last night.

"What is wrong with you? Neil has to be Sectioned but St. Andrews won't accept him if he's not."

He said that he would ring me back. He rang later stating that he was going to Section Neil, saying, "I'll ring you back later with the time. I'll get Dr Wells (your G.P.) to come with the Social Worker."

Neil arrives back onto the ward having walked out of the hospital. We thought it best to be at the hospital, so as soon as Dr Janger had rung the second time we set off there.

Neil was agitated and we tried to calm him down and keep him more tranquil. I rang David to tell him Neil's to be Sectioned. They were to Section him around 7:00pm which was still hours away. They had to wait for Dr Wells to finish his surgery. We stayed until after the Section until 9:00pm After Neil's initial shock he soon settled down knowing that he was now Sectioned. He still managed to get drink though, as this had been brought in, but we had a relatively quiet weekend.

Monday 15th October 2001

Dr Janger came to see Neil on the ward in the afternoon, and on leaving Neil walked him to the door and Neil stayed at the door. He left the hospital with Sam (another patient) and they went drinking as Sam gave Neil some money. Neil bought some razor blades and he cut himself really badly, and he needed stitches.

Steve had been to see Neil on the ward before this; he told me that they had had a good afternoon. He took Neil for a walk and took him for a haircut. Neil liked the time spent alone with his Dad, but then he went and did this afterwards, and his Dad was so upset by this after spending time with Neil and leaving him happy.

Tuesday 16th October 2001

Staff rang me at 1:30am, "Neil's got out of a window on the ward, and we've informed the police."

A police officer rang me fifteen minutes later saying, "We've picked him up in the grounds of the hospital."

Wednesday 17th October 2001

I'd asked Dr Janger before the Ward Meeting not to have all those people at the next meeting. He had listened and we went into the meeting with just six of us.

He looked at me and said, "You like it better?"

I said, "Yes, I like it better this way."

Things improved. Dr Janger mentions that he's trying to get Neil into Chorley Hospital.

Thursday 18th October 2001

Kate (staff) rang to say that they had a bed at Chorley Hospital for Neil, and he's to be moved in the afternoon.

I said, "Not until I have spoken to Dr Janger." So she put me through to him and he told me that we can go with him.

We arrived at the ward and Steve's got a suitcase in his hand.

Neil asks, "What's that for?" **They hadn't told him**.

Good, within half an hour the ambulance comes to take Neil to Chorley, and we follow by car.

First impressions? Small ward, a bit claustrophobic, locked doors, nice bedroom, four other patients, plenty of staff.

Neil's upset, "Where have you put me now?"

We are extremely upset going home. What have we done? What a place! Everything is checked before Neil can have it, that's good. We've been invited to a Ward Round with Dr Chaucer.

Friday 19th October 2001

Arrive for the meeting for 10:00a.m. Dr Chaucer seems very nice, but admits to knowing nothing about A.D.H.D. None of the staff knew anything about this condition either. He asked us to explain Neil's condition as he hadn't had time to read through Neil's notes. He says that as Dr Janger wanted to continue treating Neil, he had no problem with that. He was quite happy to have a supporting role.

What? We were so shocked? We asked if we could take Neil out for short breaks. He speaks to staff after we had left the room and it was thought best not to allow this yet, until they have had time to assess Neil. We would talk again next week. Neil said that he understood.

Saturday 20th October 2001

Barry and Kathleen go to see Neil.

Sunday 21st October 2001

We went to see Neil in the afternoon. He seemed to have settled in well, as usual though he's bored, but apart from that the staff are nice. He seemed so much calmer. We came away feeling better.

Monday 22nd October 2001

Ben came to see us. He said that he was told that Neil seems to be a lot better. I asked Ben if he would like to speak to Neil? He said he would so I rang the ward and asked if I could speak to Neil. Neil was upset, he started crying. Ben gave me the phone.

Neil was telling me that he was fed up; he needed something to do, and said he wanted to sleep all the time, to sleep his life away. I made a note to ring Dr Janger. Barry called and said that he would take me to see Neil at 7:00pm. We went and I was so glad that we did.

Tuesday 23rd November 2001

I rang Dr Janger, he said that he has had a letter from St. Andrews thanking him for the referral. I tell him that I feel that Neil is better at Chorley, and would he ask Dr Chaucer to let us take Neil out, if only for a walk around the grounds. Neil was so bored. He assured me that he would. He said he was to visit Neil himself on Friday. Jordan Whaite (Advocate) rang to ask me if it was alright for him to continue to see Neil until he moved again in his job.

I rang to talk to Neil. He rang me later too and he sounded a lot chirpier.

CHAPTER TWENTY
Neil to Appeal against His Section

We felt better knowing Neil was out of the hands of Fernlea General's staff. The Chorley Hospital members of staff were a lot nicer, and seemed to be more professional, more hands on, and watchful. The patient ratio to staff was also better. We saw a problem though straightaway, how would Neil cope with the boredom? The staff talked to him, played games with him and other things, but this wouldn't be enough. Neil had already said that he would like to sleep his life away.

The biggest issue was the fact that they *weren't treating* Neil at Chorley, as Fernlea General still had 'control' of that. Chorley Hospital was simply 'holding' Neil, because Fernlea General didn't have any secure beds.

Dr Chaucer told us that he would have nothing to do with Neil's medication, as that would be dictated by Dr Janger, and they still had Neil on very low doses of Ritalin given at four and a half hourly intervals, and also at the *wrong* times. By this point even, Neil had given up arguing about it, and just took it whenever it was offered.

I knew that they would be assessing Neil, but that they were taking all their cues from Fernlea General. I knew that they would therefore be saying the *same* things, and coming up with the *same* views, as in this overruled way of doing things, nothing would ever change.

David went to court on 9th November to plead, instead of Neil having to go, because we all thought it best because we wanted him to settle in at Chorley Hospital. David said that he would invite the court to conclude the proceedings at this stage, by giving Neil an Absolute Discharge in relation to all the offences to which Guilty pleas had been previously entered. That was effectively the *only* *sentence* that the court could impose in Neil's absence.

The court did exactly what David thought they would do by

giving Neil an Absolute Discharge. The C.P.S. had already dropped the charge of theft. Neil was banned from driving for a period of twelve months.

****

On 19th November 2001 I received this letter:-

Dear Mr Green, Re: Application to Appeal - Mr Neil Green.

I am writing to inform you that I am processing an Appeal against Mr Green's detention under Section 3 of the Mental Health Act to the Mental Health Review Tribunal.

As the nearest relative, you have the right to either attend the hearing, or alternatively you can write to them to make your views known. If you choose to write, please address any correspondence to me and I will ensure that this information is passed on.

I do not yet have the date and time of the hearing, but I will write to you as soon as it has been confirmed

If you have any queries, or require any further information, please do not hesitate to contact me.

This was from the Appeals Coordinator.

On 22nd November 2001 I receive a letter from Gilbert Price M.P.

He asked that I recall a letter that he wrote to the Home Office Minister, Beverley Hughes. He says that she passed his letter on to the Minister responsible for Social Care, Long Term Care, Disability and Mental Health, Jacqui Smith M.P.

Gilbert sent me a copy of the letter that Jacqui Smith wrote to Gilbert, and rather than taking bits out of that letter, because I am not allowed a word for word copy of that letter, I will copy the letter that I sent to her to reply to her letter, and then you will quite understand how mad I was, as I always am when these so-called 'professionals' believe other so called 'professionals'.

God forbid a doctor to be wrong. God forbid a hospital would cover up the incompetence of their doctors and the cruelty dished out by nursing staff.

Please read on:-

I will now reply to Jacqui Smith M.P.

I know you know not of what happened to Neil at the hands of those so-called experts. How he was treated by psychiatrists and staff on the wards. How, after numerous attempts to kill himself, and he'd also self harmed to an alarming degree, that he was ignored and ridiculed and left to deal with it himself.

How after years of pleading, I was the one who diagnosed his condition as A.D.H.D. but at the same time said it was only one of the conditions he had. Remember at that time I knew little of the serious hereditary mental illnesses going back generations in my husband's family.

How I found a specialist in A.D.H.D. all by myself. How is it then also, that one of your so-called experts, indeed the Head of Mental Health at Fernlea General Hospital Dr Leister, stated to us and Ben Law that Neil should be in prison?

*He would get better treatment there, when you state in your letter and I quote, "He was **subject to a number of expert opinions**. These included treatment in secure accommodation, with its structured and controlled environment, would **not** have been appropriate in Neil's case at that particular time," unquote.*

*I put it to you, as I have to others Ms Smith, that is **exactly** what Neil needed, but **not** a prison I might add, although that is all they wanted at Fernlea General, for Neil to be locked away and forgotten about. What did that man from the charity M.I.N.D. have to say about locking mentally ill people in prison? **That it was a violation of their human rights!** Remember this Ms Smith when the end of my book is written.*

Diagnosis Ms Smith

*Neil has **never** been diagnosed by psychiatrists at Fernlea General, so how can I possibly be disappointed with something I have **never** had. Neil was **never** treated for the residual symptoms of A.D.H.D. because Fernlea General ignored the correct and careful doses and timings of the medication needed to treat this condition, and by doing this they did in fact make his condition worse. **Well controlled you say**. Rubbish I say!*

301

Social Difficulties

*What's this then? The fact he's paranoid, psychotic, hears voices, talks to people who aren't there. Sees crimes having been committed, but does **not know** that it was him who carried out these crimes. He is schizophrenic, suffers from delusions, lives in a fantasy world, can't cope in society; he also is unable to make people listen to him or provide him with care and treatment.*

Those Social Difficulties.

Alcohol?

I guess he found more help in the bottle than he did at Fernlea General Hospital.

*Neil's condition **didn't** deteriorate on 11th October, but I guess Dr Janger couldn't hold back the Section any longer. **He did try though!***

*Do you know the <u>worst thing of all</u> Ms Smith? There was **never** any intention of sending Neil to St. Andrews in Northampton. The referral was NEVER made. I've written in this book that numerous people, including yourself, were told this lie. I contacted St. Andrews myself after Neil got so fed up of waiting on the ward at Chorley. He'd coped well with the confinement, prepared himself for long term care, because finally he would get 'treatment'. Not being just 'held', but actually going to get the proper medical attention and cognitive treatments that he was promised, those that we were also promised that he would get.*

CAN YOU IMAGINE ALL OUR HOPES BEING RAISED – THEN DASHED TO THE FLOOR?

I spoke to the very person who the referrals would be dealt with, and she stated that NO referral was made by Fernlea General. She actually checked, then double-checked for me. They had <u>never heard of Neil Green,</u> and as assessment would have been done properly at the hospital, not at all like Dr Janger said in February, after the Tribunal that he'd had a letter at Christmas stating that Neil wasn't suitable for St. Andrews, and that they'd wrote and told him and he hadn't said anything to us, saying this without anyone from St. Andrews actually seeing or assessing Neil.

THE STAFF AT FERNLEA GENERAL WERE FILLED WITH MORE FANTASY AND MAKE-BELIEVE THAN NEIL WAS!

I had in fact been told by Bob Gardner that the referral had been made by Dr Leister over the phone, which the lady told me was **nonsense,** as it **isn't** done this way.

Yes I did make a complaint about Neil's treatment, a formal letter of complaint, which was replied to **over a year later** which I will write about later.

No, I didn't instigate proceedings against the hospital or try to 'sue' them, as you will appreciate that I was trying to get treatment for my son, which was my ONLY priority at that time, so you were **lied to** about that also.

So we are now put in the position of knowing Neil wants 'out' he's not going to St. Andrews, **he never was,** so he's not going to get any help or treatment, so he does what anyone in his position would do he **_Appeals against his Section._**

Neil did settle in well at the beginning at Chorley but he became depressed. He said he heard voices but no one believed him. He'd been so good at hiding it, and then he'd say it was because I wanted him to say it, or it was because he wanted to 'get off' in court, when in fact **none** of this was true. He'd set off the alarms on the ward. He managed to pinch the keys off a member of staff and got off the ward. He was 'fraternizing' with the female patients. He pinched the office phone and used it in his bedroom to ring everyone he knew. This was due to not enough medication to call anything, and the **wrong dose** of Ritalin and simply being bored he was pretty disruptive.

The staff tried to label him with personality disorder. I was waiting for this one and I was ready with a reply.

I had kept a paper by a specialist in Neil's file, which states that Adult A.D.H.D. patients are not only often depressed, but also anxious. (I know Neil. I know when he's depressed, but time and time again this was denied by staff, then Neil exhibited 'bad behaviour' as they say which has stemmed from his A.D.H.D. and the lack of treatment for it).

Clinical experience of Ritalin or dexamphetamine is that they are good anxiolytics. Personality Disorder (if I'm told by Paul Harper, charge nurse, one more time that this is **Neil's problem** I'll scream) in this I include psychopathic personality, it's considered by psychiatrists to be untreatable, in spite of the enthusiasm of a small minority. Although any associated depression, anxiety, psychosis or *drug abuse, alcohol abuse is managed or treated, the core diagnosis of personality disorder is viewed as chronic, untreatable and ameliorated only by AGE.*

*A significant number of adults, LABELLED as suffering from personality disorder, are MISDIAGNOSED, and are in fact unrecognized adult A.D.H.D. sufferers. (I had to do the medical professionals' job for them by diagnosing Neil's illness, which is still only a **part** of his illness, and I had to take him to the relevant doctor in Chesterfield to treat him for it).*

In a seminal study of 91 men followed up from their hyperactive childhood to a mean age of 26 years, Mannuzzo et al found that antisocial personality disorder (known as psychopathic personality disorder in Britain) was TEN times more likely to occur in the group of individuals who had been hyperactive since childhood, than a control group also followed up from childhood. In other words, psychopathic personality disorder was hugely common in these patients with a diagnosis of A.D.H.D. in their primary school years. Adult psychiatrists should NEVER make a diagnosis of personality disorder without first checking that hyperactivity, poor concentration, impulsiveness and poor motivation were not present from young childhood. A diagnosis of personality disorder or 'psychopathology' is a painful label for many patients to bear, and it is usually a diagnosis of therapeutic <u>nihilism</u> and <u>clinical rejection.</u>

*Why do they label people? Because giving a diagnosis of personality disorder is giving the medical profession a **way out** of treating a patient. There is no cure for personality disorder, which is precisely why they are so eager to diagnose these poor people with that disorder. How many patients have they done this to? How many A.D.H.D. sufferers have they done this to? We had the diagnosis of A.D.H.D. (thankfully) but they still tried this on with us. Neil was a terrible case of an A.D.H.D. sufferer, because as we know it wasn't just that he had this condition, because his tortured mind was changing as he got older, and he was becoming psychotic, schizophrenic and the rest. **<u>I know my son</u>**.*

I wouldn't let them label Neil as having a personality disorder to diminish his mental illness. It was one of the hardest things that I have ever had to do in life, to label my own son with a severe mental illness, but I was doing just that. At first it was so hard because even

304

though he was exhibiting what we will say is A.D.H.D., but I also knew that there was more. No one in the medical profession believed me until I pushed and pushed, then he displayed other mental illnesses, and in all probability being as useless in their diagnosis, they clearly shut off to the rest, but I still think it was personal, and a way of not having to do anything for Neil, because they thought they were GODS, (something that the Hippocratic oath warns NEW DOCTORS ABOUT BECOMING) and they didn't want anyone else to take him on and treat him, OR TOPPLE THEM OFF THEIR THRONES, AS BEING WRONG! Or perhaps even have to spend any money on him. They would dig their heels in, and all the time Neil was becoming terribly ill. He was so very poorly, and this was absolutely so unnecessary and extremely cruel.

*This was the time, time to get the **proper** help. I'd sent for all the literature about St. Andrews in Northampton, so I could see what they offered. It was the **right place at that time** to give him the much needed help that he so rightly deserved. Neil was compliant, he wanted it so badly. He wasn't the mess he became, or under the influences he became involved with. This chance was ripped away from us though.*

****

I write this letter in response letter to the Appeals Co-Ordinator. Dated 10th January 2002.

The medical profession is not going to do this as they are trying to. Neil is not suffering from a personality disorder. They will not diminish his mental illness by keep saying this, or stop trying to dictate these feelings to me, as it doesn't hold water. **If you don't know what you are talking about, find a doctor who does.**

I know Dr Caldwell from the Priory Hospital is willing to give input on Neil's case if requested. I will **not allow** *people who know nothing of Neil's condition,* to keep commenting on it. Chorley Hospital is now obligated to keep Neil safe if nothing else. If you **can't** treat him, find someone who **can,** as the emphasis is on **you,** and if he wants to come off his Section, he can try to do so.

1. Make damn sure that you can find a doctor who knows his stuff about A.D.H.D. at least.

2. Look back at Neil's life thus far, and **don't listen to Neil** when he denies all that has been well documented ie, hallucinations,

psychosis, depression, self harm, suicide attempts and suchlike.

Ok he has rights, **but he also has rights to be kept safe,** and treated for what his illness is. Neil's outlook is fantasy.

3. I also state that we have rights too as parents of a mentally ill man. People who Neil will come into contact with have rights too. Ok, take him off his Section, but you will have to put him on an open ward first. **I insist on it**, the staff on Charnock Ward have already stated *they won't allow it,* but **I insist** on it, if you contemplate on letting him off his Section. I will look upon this with interest, if you won't listen to me and the experts; then do your worst; all I have to do is to wait then tell you, I told you so.

****

I state again about the history of family members who have been labelled probably wrongly, as Neil displays all their illnesses, such as manic depression, schizophrenia, psychosis, numerous suicide attempts where two members succeeded in killing themselves. It is a fact too in A.D.H.D. that it is strongly hereditary. Show me another member of the family going back generations where A.D.H.D. has been diagnosed. **There is none!** I see Neil's illness in their lives, as traits of Neil show up in every one of them, so someone MUST have made some **misdiagnosis** somewhere.

You see a strapping twenty year old. Okay, but he is emotionally stunted in development, and is still in his very *early teens* emotionally. He has irrational thoughts, is immature, unstable, chaotic, and impulsive, and is not in control of his actions. He does **not** understand the cause, or the repercussions of what he does. He breaks a window then just stands there waiting to be arrested, as he believes that he **hasn't** done it. But he has.

He lacks foresight and cannot control his behaviour, or his unstable moods. **Oh, yes I have rights too.** The right to have Neil treated, to have Neil kept safe, and to safeguard the public. I don't care how plausible Neil is, or how he comes across to his solicitor or the doctor to give a second opinion (the solicitor being a new mental health solicitor to Neil from Bolton) the doctor, one of *their own,* Janice Short who saw Neil for ONLY half an hour, before stating that in her opinion Neil was *not mentally ill or suffering from an enduring mental illness.*

Neil said how **easy** it was to pull the wool over **her** eyes,

306

especially when the staff members on the ward were telling him what to say in order for him to get off his Section. I have no time for this particular psychiatrist, as later on she writes in a medical report that not only did the psychiatrists at Fernlea General find me a specialist doctor to diagnose and treat Neil for A.D.H.D., she also went on to say that I missed the appointment they were generous enough to find me. That as you can imagine is very hurtful to me and in absolutely terrible taste, as it's a **blatant lie.**

I have stated to you in this book, and have given you well documented evidence that it was me who found the doctor with the help of a solicitor, and I made the diagnosis for Neil. So you see, doctors lie, doctors write things down on medical reports that are untrue. Sadly these untrue remarks then follow the poor patient throughout their lives, to be changed and added to when the doctor chooses, but this is cruel and wrong, because it's not an accurate account on a document, WHICH IN TURN MAKES IT so frustrating and wrong.

I've never met you Dr Janice Short, but I'll **never** forgive you. I will make it my life's work to make people sit up and listen, and unfortunately if Neil is taken off his Section, and he does what I **know he will do,** it will add more weight to what I say. The trouble is when the medical profession makes so many mistakes, they **never** learn from them, and neither do the Social Services. Neil's case has been well documented in the press, and I will make sure it will continue to be the same.

****

I rang the ward on Wednesday 8th January; I expressly asked to talk to Dr Chaucer as I was worried about the phone calls I'd received from Neil the day before, and then by the staff. I knew Neil was severely depressed in the late afternoon of Tuesday 7th January, so when he lost control I wasn't surprised. It made sense to me, but not to staff to help this by giving PRN medication BEFORE he gets into such a state, but I've tried to tell them this before, but have been told by Paul Harper (staff) that Neil **isn't** depressed. He obviously thinks he knows Neil better than I do.

Belinda (staff) told me that Dr Chaucer was coming to the ward when I said I would shortly be visiting Neil. She said that I could see Dr Chaucer in person. We left the ward at 4.30pm having been there

307

for nearly <u>three hours</u>. We didn't see Dr Chaucer and neither has Dr Chaucer been in touch with me as I was told he would, if I didn't get to see him on the ward.

****

Neil's behaviour didn't endear him to staff. They were still making the *same* mistakes, in that they were saying he can learn to pull himself together; then they could turn him around. THIS IS NOT SO AT ALL! Neil was NOT able to learn or change his behaviour; this was **completely beyond and outside of his capabilities**.

The criminal system makes you pay for your mistakes, 'make amends' but Neil acts on impulse, he hasn't planned it, so he will **always** be 'paying back'. It's the same now on the ward they would take Neil's 'stuff' off him time after time, just as Fernlea General did, as a punishment. They must all read from the same manual; they mismanaged the situation. They would empty his room, but this didn't work, it wouldn't EVER work, because Neil did NOT UNDERSTAND cause and effect. They needed to act differently in his case and not just PLAY by the book.

Neil was an individual with rather *different* needs, so alternative strategies needed to be put in place for him, but they NEVER listened. Patients with an intellectual handicap can be treated like this as you would need to treat them like naughty children. Not all of them though, as each one of them is a unique individual too, but I would say *most of the time* you have to do this. They needed boundaries and actions, such as removing their pleasures in order for them to behave. They were able to recognize that if they misbehaved, action would be taken, and privileges would be removed. They would be able to change accordingly, but Neil WAS NOT ABLE TO CHANGE NO MATTER WHAT THEY DID AT HIM. He was powerless to change his behaviour, **<u>as it totally ruled over him</u>**.

****

My sister works with the intellectually handicapped in Australia, and they use this method of 'tough love' and it works. They even having an electrical switch that they can use to turn off the TV sets and other electrical items in a person's room. It does work for them, but this **does <u>not</u> work for people like Neil**.

There was a time when they took Neil's clothes off him,

308

expecting Neil **not to go out,** but he still did, and he would be sat at the bar of a pub in his pyjamas. It is not the right way for Neil as it is totally beyond his comprehension.

We had already worked this out for ourselves through years of experience with bringing Neil up; that is why Neil responded when he was locked in, as he felt safe. He reacted much better when he knew that *someone else* was in control, but naturally only when he trusted them. He would settle down then.

The situation now at the hospital is that they have Neil's 'stuff' **more than he has his own belongings.** You cannot turn Neil around. He will always set alarms off. It was cruel to keep *expecting* Neil to pay for his mistakes. It was exactly the same with the criminal system, as it stands to reason that it *doesn't work* for Neil, and this frightens people. Why do they do this over and over then?

No, he wouldn't commit murder or a *serious crime*, so it wasn't a case of him 'getting off' with murder or suchlike; it just wasn't like that. It was just that his brain didn't work properly, so he does loads of daft stuff and really petty things. These were done without any thought first, they might be provoking stuff to others, but to Neil they were simply *impulsive* stuff, and were never serious. **He was ill!** Should he therefore be <u>punished repeatedly</u> for being ill? He was made to pay though, and as he can't EVER change, then he'll always be paying.

He broke a window on the ward and was arrested, yet he was assaulted three times by the *same patient,* but that wasn't thought of as being so bad, so they did nothing until we kicked up a fuss. Neil is locked in, and suffering because he's not getting the help he needs. He is completely misunderstood, which makes him feel so frustrated with his situation. He can see the misery ahead of him, as he's not going to get better, so naturally his feelings run high.

Neil's review of his Section 3 was made on 27th November. The purpose of the review was because Neil appealed against his Section. *Reason for Decision.*
(The Panel is obliged to discharge the patient if the answer to either of the following questions is **No.**
1. Is the Panel satisfied that the patient is suffering from a mental illness, psychopathic disorder, severe mental impairment or mental

impairment of a nature or degree which makes it appropriate for the patient to be liable to be detained in a hospital for assessment/treatment? **Yes.**

2. Is the Panel satisfied that it is necessary for the health and safety of the patient, or for the protection of others, that the patient should be assessed or receive such treatment. **Yes.**

3. If the answer to **both** of the above questions are **No** does the Panel consider that this is a case where it is appropriate to discharge the patient. **(Nothing entered)**

Recommendation

1. The decision for the move to St. Andrews is made as soon as possible.

2. For medication to be reviewed at the request of Mr Green.

Decision of the Panel.

To continue detention under Section 3 of the Mental Health Act 1983.

****

Neil's solicitor had a Psychological Report prepared by Brian Newscombe, Forensic Neuro-Psychologist, for the Tribunal on 11th February 2002.

Mr Newscombe **didn't make appointments** to meet with Neil on the ward, and neither was Neil prepared for him. Instead Mr Newscombe turned up at different times on different days. He supplied an in-depth report that was made over time.

Neil *tried to pull the wool over his eyes,* but in the main he **couldn't** do it, as Mr Newscombe saw through a lot of Neil's behaviour. He came to our home to interview **us too.** We weren't happy that he came to see us, knowing how dead against this action we were that Neil was trying to get off his Section. After all this man was acting for the solicitor who was trying to get Neil out of hospital, wasn't he?

We gave our comments, and Mr Newscombe prepared his report. A report in fact that Neil's solicitor **couldn't** use at the Tribunal, because it was **too damning,** and if it was shown to the Panel, Neil would **never** have got off his Section.

We were given a copy of the report that we copied for Ben (care worker, *Making Space*). He made Community Mental Health aware of the contents; and Dr Janger while he was with us. However Dr

Janger didn't want to know; he waved us away and got in his car.

I contacted Mr Newscombe and he recommended the Spinney that Dr Blake ran to help Neil, so we were on the same wavelength, as we'd asked for this too, and Dr Blake had asked Bob Gardner for him to take Neil there, but he was refused.

We went to the Tribunal meeting at Chorley Hospital. I felt sick with worry, and so did Steve having stayed up yet again after working the night shift. The Panel asked Dr Chaucer if Neil was mentally ill?

"No!" he answered.

Within minutes Neil was released off his Section. The solicitor said that he didn't need to speak at all, and it was the *easiest Tribunal* he'd ever won for a patient. He was amazed, but even he knew it was <u>wrong,</u> even though he knew he was representing Neil, he knew Neil **should not** have been allowed off his Section.

It was a travesty, but it was down to the psychiatrists at Chorley and Burnley that had allowed it to happen yet again, simply to get rid of Neil.

He never stood a chance against them. These aren't doctors. Doctors in my personal opinion **would be ashamed to be called doctors** if they were put into the <u>same league</u> as these inhuman people.

We couldn't control our tears Steve and I. After all this, Neil had to go back to Fernlea General on an open ward.

CHAPTER TWENTY-ONE
Fernlea General Wash Their Hands of Neil, Again

We were absolutely devastated. We had found out that yet again we'd been lied to, that **no referral** to another psychiatrist or hospital had been made for Neil. Why? How is that we've gone from Neil needing 24 hour care with a strict regime of Cognitive Therapies and Supervision, to Neil being released off a Section, to **nothing?** Was the Section even *legal* in the first place?

How can you say that all of a sudden Neil **wasn't** mentally ill, when he'd been <u>**incarcerated for nearly a year,**</u> yet his health wasn't any different at all, as there was absolutely no improvement to his health whatsoever. He *wasn't* given a miracle cure at Chorley, so how could this possibly be? Things **hadn't** improved in the least, so we were at a complete and utter loss to understand what was happening. What game were they really playing with our son's health? <u>**Furthermore how dangerous and harmful was this to Neil's well being?**</u> We could NOT answer or understand any of this at all.

We'd visited Neil on a regular basis, but it wasn't easy. Chorley is miles away from our home, and it was always such a rush to visit him in the evening and then for Steve to get back for work on time. We also had to work around Mum. We borrowed Barry's car because it was smaller and cheaper to run than our big car. We arranged for others to go, when we *couldn't* visit Neil. We always did our utmost to help Neil and the staff, so we felt so let down by everything.

We felt quite cross with Neil also, for him going against our wishes; but having said that we could understand him really. When we really thought about it from Neil's point of view we could see that he thought that they were doing <u>nothing</u> for him, just simply 'holding' him, without giving him any proper medication and no therapies, just promises of treatment and help that never ever materialized. It was all so tragic and sad, and Neil had just suffered enough.

After all who could blame him, he wasn't an animal, but he surely felt like one, caged up and to all effects ignored. **We all felt cheated.** We knew that Neil would go back to Fernlea General, but then they'd get rid of him as soon as they could. However we didn't expect it to be **the very next day.**

God! Nothing should surprise us anymore, as to how these people were. Neil always played into their hands. It wasn't *actually* his fault, he just didn't *know* any better. All Neil ever wanted was to be 'normal', and to be like his brother. He strived to do all the things that so called 'normal' people did, but he always failed miserably due to his illness.

What made matters worse was the fact that Neil was telling the staff he was moving down to Horsham to be with Kelly, whom he had met on Charnock Ward. They were writing all this down, and telling him they could see no reason why he s*houldn't* do it. They truly made me sick for the ways in which they played around with Neil's mind and life like this. They just wanted rid of him, so they had him play his own part to that end, making him believe that he could live away from us his lifeline, for a start. It was all pure fantasy. Neil provided *enough fantasies of his **own**,* so how could they do this to him, and keep feeding him more of the same? How could they be so terrible with him, and why wouldn't they ever help him? Yet we only had to look at what they'd done so far to answer that didn't we? Sadly yes, it does get worse!

For readers who even dare to think that we were parents who wanted to tie our son to our apron strings, please think again! No matter how much we loved our son, and we BOTH totally loved him; we could **not** cope with him properly when his mental illness kicked in hard later on in his life, at all.

At first we DID NOT KNOW what needed to be done for our son, but through our own previous trial and errors, we most certainly knew what things did NOT WORK for him. He needed real help from TRULY fair, qualified and caring psychologists; those real professionals who knew and had been trained to deal with patients like Neil, and those who cared enough about their patients to treat them in a respectful and honest manner. Those people in fact, who would work ONLY in the best interests of their patients, by doing the very best possible that they could for each and every single one of them. We needed QUALIFIED DOCTORS who would treat Neil on his own merits. We had thought that ALL doctors STUCK TO THE BELIEFS AND PROMISES THEY HAD MADE AND SWORN TO, AS WRITTEN IN THE HIPPOCRITIC OATH. Why else would they promise to do this; then ignore it?

Without one single exception ALL doctors should do their absolute best for every single patient they encounter during their whole professional working life. If they could see that some treatments that had repeatedly been offered had never worked for a particular patient, then they should either try something else, or allow that patient to be seen by another doctor or consultant who might just possibly find a solution.

All doctors should also treat ALL their patients, without one single exception, with respect, and an open mind, in order to do their very best for each one. Whilst it should naturally be taken into account what another doctor has written about a patient in their notes; it should NEVER be written in STONE, as it is always possible, that it might not always be a truly accurate account.

Doctors should therefore be **honest and humble enough** to accept that no one is God, in fact they should resist falling into the trap of ever doing this, and therefore consider when appropriate, that they might possibly be wrong. This idea should always be brought to the forefront, and be pondered on as a matter of routine should one of their patients always be coming back without any sign at all of improvement. Sadly good and caring doctors, who go that extra mile out of their way to help each patient, are often in the **minority**; so therefore are few and far between.

Those Consultants who have been practicing for many years, should allow their younger colleagues to make suggestions for particular problem patients, without any threat of loss of their jobs, or being downgraded, or thought of badly in any way if they intervene, or possibly suggest a different approach on his/her behalf. All patients could then be discussed with open minds, but NEVER with closed minds or old ideas being deemed as ALWAYS being right.

After all medicines, diagnosis, particular conditions, new ways and treatments are evolving every single day, so no **closed doors** should therefore ever be allowed.

Each doctor/person is fallible after all, so no one should ever play at being God according to the Hippocratic Oath; so second opinions should be actively encouraged as an ongoing possible improvement to the health of each patient, without one single exception. In fact those doctors who do NOT ALLOW this, or discourage others from looking into things for themselves, are *actively breaking* their sworn oath every single time they do this. Anyone blindly following a doctor along a path or route that they feel is wrong and NOT good for the patient, whether it be treatments, medicines or otherwise, yet do not speak out, <u>are equally wrong and therefore also equally guilty</u>.

Hospitals are a place where all staff should work in harmony together. Suggestions should always be actively encouraged; speaking up on something they feel strongly about, should never lead to being dismissed. It is the patient who is always the most important person in their care, so the correct treatment and diagnosis should always be the most important finding. Incorrect diagnoses lead to wrong treatment, prolonging the illness, and at worst suffering and death. After all the first rule of medicine is FIRST DO NO HARM.

Medicines are deemed to be given at certain times of the day and night, and these times and doses should always be strictly adhered to. Giving medicine too often, or at the wrong times, too much or too little of a dose, or stopping it immediately when it is one that should be weaned off gently, can do FAR more harm than good. When this involves the treatment of children, the elderly or the mentally ill; those people often MOST incapable of speaking up for themselves, then it is wrong. However when these wrong doings are constantly being repeated, there are NEVER any reasonable excuses, and the doctor in charge should be made to answer for his errors.

They say that doctors bury their mistakes; in 2009 this is absolutely totally and utterly unacceptable. No one should be left suffering and in so much pain that they wish to kill themselves nowadays; nor should a suicidal patient be turned away from hospital for any reason. No one should ever be allowed to go straight from intensive care, jump out of a window dressed in only a gown, and then the staff members on duty be allowed to walk away and wash their hands of that person, without first checking that the person is well and has NOT sustained any injuries. People should only be

315

discharged when they are felt to be well, not after an event like this. No one goes from intensive care, then straight through a window out of the hospital. This was an obvious sign that the patient was frightened, and he should have been put onto another ward until he was deemed well enough to be discharged. With physical, elderly or mental illness the same respect for the patient should always be given. There should NEVER be any discrimination to these groups most at risk - those who often do NOT have a voice of their own.

We would look and see that a dog or other animal was okay after jumping out of a window, why then do we ignore a man? The doctor in this case had no conscience whatsoever. Mental illness does NOT perhaps endear us to those around us; however where is our sympathy and our care in society to those who probably need it the most?

In other words as said so often before in this book, why can't we make a doctor, doctor? More importantly though, why should we have to do so? <u>Shouldn't every single person in this profession WANT to do their ABSOLUTE BEST for every single one of their patients?</u> Why would any one of us need to **beg** for help, when it is just not their job, but also their CHOSEN DUTY, to do their best and act professionally for every single one of us?

******

Neither Steve nor I were medically trained at all, however we could **easily judge** that by keep repeating over and over the same WRONG TREATMENTS, and either prescribing him with the WRONG MEDICATION over and over again, often at the WRONG TIMES and inappropriate strengths, despite labels and advice to the contrary, they were in truth **not only making him worse, but they were actually putting him and others in EXTREME DANGER.** They were also ignoring the first rule to do no harm.

Repeatedly they let Neil out of hospital when he was very ill, and in fact when he was not only a danger to himself, but to the public in general. How many suicides are taken as the LAST AND ONLY WAY OUT, by poor misunderstood patients such as Neil? The Government in their 'wisdom' have closed down so many homes for the mentally challenged, and so many of them have been placed into society at large, where they are at **best** taken advantage of, and at **worst** allowed to kill themselves, and are also blamed for loads of

316

things that they NEVER ever did.

Some of them are gentle like Neil, and direct their frustrations inwardly by self-harming, whilst others either deliberately or through the directives of the voices that they clearly hear, listen to, then actually harm others. The question though is where can they go? Who will help them to get the correct help to aid them to lead a better life that would be much safer for BOTH them and the general public?

****

Dr Newscombe said that his present assessment suggested that Neil suffered impairments consistent with a finding of A.D.H.D. Additionally, he said that there was a finding of non-dominant personality disorder, which is reported as described.

Collectively the information gathered suggested that Neil has neither the cognitive abilities, nor the emotional resources, or the practical skills either to control his behaviour, or to provide for himself.

*Neil might indeed understand the notion of right from wrong, but appears incapable of controlling the impulses that drive him to undertake his acts of misconduct. He could easily have ended his own life on several occasions, or indeed the lives of others, had it not been for timely interventions. In order to address these issues Dr Newscombe believed that Neil would benefit considerably from a combined cognitive behavioural and psycho-therapeutic programme, which he believed **required a more structured and secure environment than is currently available to Neil.***

He summarized that although no evidence was found of psychosis or other severe mental illness, there was considerable evidence to support a finding of severe behavioural disorder co-morbid with personality disorder, either or both of which amount to mental disorder consistent with Section 1 of the Mental Health Act (1983). As such, he said that he believed that discharge from his Section Order at this time would be inappropriate.

****

We were happy with Brian's findings, it was an in-depth report. It is true that Neil probably didn't show any psychosis at the time he saw Brian. However Neil was very clever at keeping some control over his thoughts, and being in a safe environment he didn't display

317

this as much as he did when he was in the 'outside world'. But yes, I felt that he was starting with schizophrenia and suchlike conditions, but he would become much worse later on, but at that time Brian gave a **true** account of Neil's illness, and even though he himself didn't see the evidence as we did; it was there, and the future looked bleak.

Neil's solicitor I believe gave us this report because he knew Neil *shouldn't be released*, and he expected us to *show it to all involved,* but he was acting for Neil and what **he** wanted. The doctors, Dr Chaucer, Dr Janger, staff on Charnock Ward and Social Worker Donna Castle Calder all knew about the report, but they chose to ignore it. Therefore they very coldly and calculatingly turned their backs on Neil. There was no doubt that Bob Gardner, the Nursing Manager at Fernlea General knew too, as he always had his hand in everything.

****

They said on that day 12th February 2002 that Neil was too disruptive on the ward, reminding me of the time when CPN Angela Moore told Social Worker Harriet Keith, that she thought the young lady Harriet was investigating and writing the statement for Burnley, Pendle & Rossendale Magistrates Courts, in regard to whether or not she was fit to look after her *own child* in the matter of the Childrens' Act 1989, and needed to consider her choice of friends and partners as she had been witnessed the previous evening, giving oral sex to one of the '**most dangerous patients**' on the ward. By this, she had meant Neil.

The other patient had an alcohol problem, and was the person she had drunk with on Sunday. I have this statement in front of me. This is what they thought of Neil, and yet they were content enough to release him into society. I feel sorry for this young girl who could lose her child if you have to rely on these people. I have already touched upon what was happening on the wards as far as being highly sexed on medication, especially with drink and drugs being on tap there too. The girl hardly stands a chance, does she? Ms Moore ends up being Neil's CPN for a period of time later on.

Neil's solicitor told us that he was assured by Bob Gardner that Neil would remain on the ward for a period of time until they sorted out his aftercare package, and in that was finding him somewhere to

318

live. *What they did do in fact, was put Neil into a Bed & Breakfast place that was full of alcoholics and drug users.*

They all had their meeting and decided that Neil was **not entitled** to 117 aftercare, so he was discharged off a Section because he had no mental illness.

Keith Deighton (manager) CMHT Leeds Rd Nelson, stated that from this meeting they would have no further involvement with Neil. Social Services would NOT get involved. He told us this days later, after they'd had their meeting, **and we just walked out.**

They told Neil that he had to sort out his **own** benefits; he had to go to the Town Hall Housing Department for temporary accommodation because he was homeless. He had to go and get emergency medication from his G.P. and self refer himself to Bull Street, because he had an alcohol problem.

They'd done it again!

****

Ben tried to help, he ran around after Neil just like we did. To expect Neil to do **all this himself was ridiculous**; he didn't have the means or the capability, and by now he was in such a state, and was deeply depressed about his situation. He was all bravado, but now that it was reality and he was facing life 'outside'; he was very frightened.

How I cried when I saw the B & B. Don't get me wrong, it was a decent place for some (and I'm not being nasty) but Neil was a sick, young lad mixing with older men, a lot of them were alcoholics and drug addicts too, but that I would only find out about later on.

The lady who ran the place with her husband was a very decent caring woman, who did more than put a roof over these poor unfortunate men's heads; she cared about them. She fed them well and housed them when no one else would. I liked her, she was a good woman. However this was no place for Neil.

****

Neil contacted the newspapers himself, and again his plight was written about in the *Telegraph* and local papers. Neil said he couldn't cope and he was pleading for help, because he'd been dumped and left to live in a B & B. It was stated that the way Neil was treated prompted an outcry, and the local M.P. vowed to take up his case and asked that we get in touch with him.

319

I told the journalist that I was absolutely terrified for Neil, so much so in fact that I was expecting a knock at my door to tell me he was dead. I said we were back to square one after he'd been in hospital **for a year.** They called it a catalogue of neglect.

****

Things were getting pretty bad with Neil's health; he was becoming really depressed and withdrawn. He was so insecure. We had him home on a regular basis which wasn't easy because he was unstable, emotional and depressed, but he had to return to the bed and breakfast every evening.

I took him to Bolton to see the solicitor who had got him off his Section. Neil wanted to get back into hospital, and wanted him to help him to this end. There was no way that this could be done. Our only hope was to get **another opinion,** and for that to be done outside the area. We already knew that, but we couldn't get the psychiatrists at Fernlea General to refer Neil, and another Consultant psychiatrist would <u>not see him</u> unless they did so, which they obviously knew. We were simply in a catch 22 situation.

Even if we went to see someone *privately,* the psychiatrists at Fernlea General would *not acknowledge their findings* as they didn't with Dr McKewen when Neil was in Lancaster Farms, or in the future when Neil was seen by Dr Samuel Plackett a Forensic Psychiatrist from The Guild at Preston. (One of Lancashire Health Authority's own).

Dr McKewen was one of Dr Plackett's team. Not only **wouldn't** Fernlea General psychiatrists acknowledge their findings, they **wouldn't treat Neil afterwards,** and although Dr Plackett outranked Fernlea General's psychiatrists <u>on all fronts,</u> they said *his was just an opinion as if he didn't matter*. Should this be called honour amongst thieves? I don't think so. After all Neil would always have to come back to Fernlea, so we really stood no chance at all, and Neil was left with nowhere else to turn.

In fact the Hippocratic Oath sworn by doctors, regarding referrals actually states: *"I will not be ashamed to say "I know not", nor will I fail to call in my colleagues when the skills of another are needed for a patient's recovery."*

They had us tied up in knots, and no matter how many solicitors we saw (and we did see quite a few) not one of them could do

anything to help us. We just kept hitting yet more brick walls all the time. This was naturally so frustrating for us, but how do you think Neil felt? He was the one living in hell.

Here I was, like a headless chicken, going to see my M.P. ringing up everyone I could think of, (my phone bills were horrendous) and seeing solicitors, Ben, and going to meetings where I would come away feeling worse than when I went in. I was forever feeling deflated, and then there were the letters I wrote, and ALL for what? **Nothing**!

****

Philip Porter M.P. wrote to me requesting that I took Neil to see him urgently, to see if there was anything he could do to help us. I made the appointment.

David wrote to tell me that Brian Newscombe's report would be useful in the future, as the conclusion to the report says that whilst Neil understands the notion of right from wrong, he appears *incapable* of controlling the impulses that drive him to undertake his acts of misconduct. **That is effectively what we have claimed all along,** namely that Neil does understand it is wrong to act in the manner in which he does, but is incapable of preventing himself from actually acting in this manner.

As I've already told you, I spent most of my time seeing to Neil's needs, which included taking him to all of these appointments he had, as if *I didn't,* he probably wouldn't have got there. It was no good giving Neil any appointment unless they told me as well, which in the main is what everybody did including our G.P.'s. They were good enough to keep Neil on at my address, because he moved about so much that they never knew where he was.

I had a good relationship with my G.P.'s especially Dr Guardi, Dr Spercer, Dr Wells, Dr Fleashman and the lovely Dr Parsons who always listened and rang me when I asked her to. She was particularly understanding, and they all knew as Neil was telling them often enough.

"Tell my Mum," Neil would tell everyone for he trusted me completely.

He knew that I would never do or say anything that wasn't true in order to get him help. He might not have liked me being so honest on occasion, but I told him that he couldn't have it both ways. I've always been honest all through my life, and Neil respected me for it.

"There are three women in my life, my Mum and my two Grandmas," he would say.

Our closeness was uncanny. I knew Neil like I have said before, like no other. I could read him BETTER than a book, which is one of the reasons I'm suffering now, because I should have been listened to at the beginning, shouldn't I?

As I said earlier, giving Neil an appointment was ludicrous as Neil wouldn't remember, or he would set off to go then he'd move off in a different direction entirely, if some other thought popped into his head.

****

At this time Neil had disappeared. David wrote in his letter that he needed to see him urgently, but we couldn't tell Neil because we didn't know where he was. It was a worrying time because he was going downhill fast, and becoming desperately ill.

Neil in fact had gone down to Sussex to be with the girl he met on the ward at Chorley. We were just waiting for the inevitable time bomb to hit us.

David said that the court case would go ahead for Neil breaking the window at Chorley Hospital. Dr Chaucer insisted that he be prosecuted and pay compensation, which I found inevitable, but really quite disgusting.

David had also received a letter from the Council about the cost of repairs to the house that Neil was in, before he'd attempted to jump off the motorway bridge and then ended up in hospital. The cost amounted to hundreds of pounds, and was one of the reasons why the Council *wouldn't* allow Neil to rent another one of their properties in the future.

I can remember that terrible night vividly. I asked Barry to go up to Neil's house in the early hours of the morning. He found the house doors wide open. All the water taps were running, and the gas was turned on. It was a right mess, and it was also very dangerous. Naturally we didn't know if Neil had left it like that, but if he did, it just showed the terrible state of mind he was in, and served to emphasize the fact that he shouldn't be living on his own. Also because the police had left it insecure, as they were so worried about Neil, and rightly so as he was their priority, did someone else go into

322

the house and do these things whilst the property was left open?

It was a strong possibility, as the people who surrounded Neil were awful people. It's no wonder Neil ran away with all this on his tortured mind.

I told David to send the bill to C.M.H.T. (Community Mental Health Team) at Nelson. It was their fault that he was put into a house to fend for himself with no help from them, or anyone else in the 'Services'.

They said, *he was quite capable of managing on his own.* YOU WERE WRONG. YOU HAVE ALWAYS BEEN WRONG!

Philip Porter M.P. wrote to tell me saying that he had spoken to Neil on his mobile phone, and as he was no longer in Burnley but in Horsham, this meant that he was no longer his M.P. but he gave Neil the name and number of another M.P. for Horsham saying that the Horsham one would contact Neil if he didn't contact him first. Philip told me that he had written to both Social Services and the NHS Trust, and upon receiving their replies he would get back to me. He asked me to get in touch with the Community Health Council.

****

Neil in fact at this time was in hospital in Horsham. On the 8th March the police rang me up to tell me they had to take him there because of his 'strange' and 'disturbing' behaviour.

I was then called by a doctor at the hospital asking me about Neil's mental illness. It was all a bit vague, the doctor was foreign and I couldn't understand a lot of what she was saying. I don't think that she could understand me either. However she did say that they had been in touch with Fernlea General Hospital, and they had told her that Neil was *not suffering from any mental illness* and for her to discharge him.

They must have got in touch with Social Services, because a Social Worker gave Neil money out of their 'petty cash' to get him back home. In fact we went to pick him up from Manchester Railway Station.

They wanted Neil out of their hair. It was 14th March 2002 and we'd just had a garbled message off Neil.

"I'm in a mess Mum," he said.

As always we dropped everything and went to Manchester to pick him up. I wasn't prepared at all for what I saw though. Neil was unwashed, in need of a shave, and looked scruffy. He'd been drinking, but worst of all he was disturbing, he was agitated and defiant; in fact he tried to jump out of the car on the motorway while we were travelling at speed.

Steve had to go to work again worrying about Neil being with me because of the state he was in. I could control him better than his Dad, and although I could understand my husband being worried about me, I knew if Steve stayed in the state he was in, then the whole situation would get much worse. As I've said I could shoulder Neil's behaviour to both safeguard Neil and others around us, including Mum who was crying in her room. This was more for me to worry about as she knew how tormented I was.

I said, "No love, you go to work, I'll be O.K." Naturally enough though, **I wasn't.** I was terrified, and for the first time I wondered if I could cope with Neil and defuse the situation. I was awake all night. It was awful and Neil took off in the early hours of the morning, but he did come back. He was accepted back at the bed and breakfast the day after.

CHAPTER TWENTY-TWO
Stop the World I Want to Get Off

It was a bad time for me. There is nothing worse than watching your child deteriorate before your eyes. God only knows how parents cope with a terminally ill child. What made it worse for me was knowing that Neil could have so easily been helped, but the people who <u>could</u> have helped him didn't care. They were systematically killing my son. It was so hard to deal with what we had to cope with day in and day out. There were too many people relying on me, I couldn't give up, even though I felt like doing so, as it was all just too much to bear.

No matter where Neil went in the country he says the 'Bishops' were there, or the so-and-so's. He thought people were after him; he told Ben the same. He was in hospital in 2006 and he cowered down in his hospital bed, because he said the man who walked past was this particular person. It wasn't, but then it never was!

He'd been turned away so many times from Fernlea General when he was frightened, hearing voices, covered in blood because he'd either self harmed, or he'd been injured in some way and blamed it on the so-and-so's who were after him, when maybe he'd fallen, or in fact had been attacked by somebody else. You didn't ever <u>really</u> know, because Neil didn't know himself.

The police would take him to the hospital themselves, using the powers they thought they had on a Section 136 for his and the public safety. They would stay with him, and insist that a doctor saw him, only for him to be turned away *without* a psychiatrist even seeing him. Then he was told he **wasn't** hearing voices.

In the main the police did this for Neil's safety, even taking him to another hospital, but all the other hospital then did was to ring Fernlea General, so that would be it. It became a vicious circle and he was turned away yet again.

A ranking policeman told me this year to take Neil to a hospital somewhere **else** in the country, and leave Neil, there. Tell him to give a false name, so at least he would be seen by a doctor, get a diagnosis, and by the time he was found, we would have got what we needed. We might have to one extent, but STILL even after that Fernlea General **wouldn't have** treated him. Neil would have to come back here, because he couldn't live away from his family unless he was in a Secure Hospital getting all the help and treatments that he was promised, but **never** received. My argument all along was how did he ever change from **needing** that, to **needing nothing**, and especially so when he was becoming a lot worse too. It was coming to something though if we would have had to resort to dumping our son in this way. I don't know if I could have done it. We'll never know now, will we?

****

Back to March 2002.

Neil was found unconscious and he was taken to Fernlea General Hospital by the police. He came around while in A & E. He actually left the hospital with a needle still in his arm when all the nursing staff were told to get rid of him.

He never had any money although he received benefits, and this made his money add up to a lot more than a lot of the men at the B & B got, so they were forever borrowing off him. It made little difference really, as Neil didn't know where his money had gone anyway. As soon as he got his benefits he'd spend all of his money on the same day. He was a real nightmare, because if he was agitated he'd become threatening if I **didn't** give him the money. His money I mean, because I tried to keep some of his money back from him until the end of the week, so he'd have some money to fall back on; but he wouldn't have this, so I would have to give it him all anyway. It wasn't as bad then in 2002 as it got in later years, but there was a reason for that which I will tell you when it happens later on.

****

I wrote to Philip Porter M.P. on 1st April 2002 because things were getting much worse. Pat who ran the B & B had told Neil that she couldn't cope with Neil any longer, so she was seriously thinking of throwing him out. I already knew this as she had told me the same, saying that it was ridiculous what they expected of her, as she had already told Neil's Social Worker Donna Castle Calder that she

326

wasn't a Social Worker.

It was their job to take care of Neil NOT hers. Neil's erratic behaviour was very disturbing, and she shouldn't be expected to have to watch Neil and care for him as much as he needed it.

Donna had said at one of the meetings that, "Neil was a 'model' guest and that Pat had no trouble with him."

So now we know that to be a lie. She was in fact threatening to throw Neil out. It was the self harm that she found the most difficult to deal with. She was worried about finding Neil with a serious injury. It was also true that the local police beat officer in her area was giving her worries about Neil, telling her that he was trouble.

He was trouble, so I don't blame Pat, because I couldn't cope with Neil, and he couldn't cope in the community either, so I would have been a complete and utter hypocrite if I called this dear lady for trying so hard when she was actually at the end of her tether.

Neil hardly slept; he wandered at night, and this in itself would put him into situations he had no control over. Control – that's a word. Neil had **no control;** his life was chaotic. Neil was changing alarmingly. I put a lot of this down to the situation he was living in.

I'm going to sound a real 'snob' now, but Neil was brought up in a loving, caring family. We provided him with the 'designer' clothes, the nice home and the care that he needed, plus lots of attention. We lived with rules and boundaries. I was on Neil's back all the time and he responded to that; now though he had **all this freedom**, but he'd no discipline whatsoever; he was just floundering not living. He was simply going through the motions.

He was a twenty year old child, who had been dumped in a place that wasn't a bit like where he had come from. He was mixing with people who neither he nor we would have ordinarily given the time of day to, but it was marginally better than living on the streets. He saw no way out for himself, and neither did we. He would NOT live at home with us as he wanted his freedom.

I was his 'Appointee' for his benefits, which was something that I never wanted to be, but **had to be** because Neil couldn't control his money. It was a real headache, as it meant dishing his money out to Neil sensibly, and included taking him to the supermarket, which I hated because I had to watch carefully that he didn't take anything without paying for it. Maybe this was because of what had happened in the past when he was a child. He might not now be the same as he was then, but it had conditioned me into thinking he was. I couldn't help it. I took him for clothes, trainers and everything he needed. He didn't like me questioning what he wanted money for. It was always a battle. He thought it was his money, so only his business. In a way this was true, so I could never win the arguments when he blew his cash on rubbish or on other things that he could never even recall.

I had his benefit book, and I must admit that if he did need money for something genuine and specific, I would lend him the money to buy it, and just take it out of his benefit the following week. The trouble with this was that it was coming about too often. He was **always** asking for money, and he would make up elaborate reasons for me to give some to him. I started putting my foot down, but in doing so I then had to put up with the consequences of that.

****

I was at Kathleen's one day when Neil knocked on the door. I could see by his manner that he was in an agitated state, and that there was no getting through to him. He was **demanding** money. I refused him, so he then asked his Grandma for some. She refused and he left after a lot of shouting, saying he was going to my house to ask his Dad.

I told him not to, but he wasn't listening; his Dad was in bed after working the night shift. I locked the door behind him, but no sooner had I done this than he was back pounding on the door. I told him to go away and he started kicking the door. I could do nothing but ring the police, which was not at all what I wanted to do, as by this time the police thought they were dealing with someone, who was **not** mentally ill at all, but a complete 'bad un' who was dangerous and out of control. At this moment he was out of control, but he was also displaying symptoms of *serious* mental illness. He didn't know what he was doing, and he wasn't taking any medication.

This wasn't Neil, just as it wasn't Neil when he broke every window at his Grandma's flat showering her with glass in her bed. Why should a loving boy who knew that he was loved, and was treated so well by his frail and ailing Grandma, who doted on him and smothered him with love and kindness as Grandmas do; why would he intentionally do such things, and more often than not be in the vicinity to be seen?

328

At that last time, probably the third time, we'd realized it wasn't anyone else. Neil had said it was those people who were after him. They knew his Grandma lived in the top flat. They were doing it to get at him. Why would anyone do such a thing? Why would Neil do such a thing? At that time none of us knew for certain. We couldn't, or wouldn't blame Neil; he wouldn't do this. He didn't know he had done this because he hadn't!

Now we were beginning to realize **it was** Neil, and knowing this to be true, this meant that we also knew that he was terribly ill. It was as if he had seen the person doing the deed next to him, just as if he was watching **someone else** doing these things. Yes he was chased on more than one occasion, but not caught though. What would his reply be if he was caught? *It wasn't him?* He was never caught. If he was confronted with his terrible deed though, and we made him believe it was him, what would that do to someone as mentally ill as he was? Would he **ever** believe it was him?

I know I'm not explaining it very well, and it's no good me telling you now that a psychiatrist would know, because we know in Neil's case that they were 'crap' so *I will be the psychiatrist in Neil's case,* and say that I thought that it would send my loving son over the edge to think that he could harm the people that he loved most in the world.

I believe Neil was so ill, suffering from delusions, schizophrenia and such that he did tell the truth. Well what he **believed** to be true. It wasn't him. I know I'm not explaining all this very well, as it even took me a long time to realize what was going on. If we had caught Neil with a brick in his hand, obviously we'd have known sooner, but we didn't! Neil was a decent, loving, caring lad; he would never intentionally do such things. We were always there for him, and he knew that. He <u>truly</u> didn't know what he was doing.

I had a suspicion that he had done the £2,500.00 damage to my car, but I couldn't prove that either. I said the same to Steve once, but he told me that I was being stupid. I knew he had smashed Ryan's car windows, and Ryan knew too, but we **all** shouldered it, and didn't report it to the police, because the police were treating Neil badly. They'd seen Neil turned away so many times from the hospital, so when they had Neil in custody and were supposed to ring the hospital or the Police Surgeon, they were told to ignore Neil and

his parents because there was <u>nothing wrong with him.</u>
****

So, back to where I was torn between ringing the police and protecting Kathleen's property, and also Neil, because by this time he was climbing up the plastic drainpipe up to the flat and I could hear it coming away from the wall. I did ring the police, but by the time they came Neil had gone up to my house. They came to the door and I couldn't open it to them because Neil had damaged it so badly. They left me and went up to my house.

Steve had been woken up by Neil banging so hard on the door. He didn't have time to find out what was going on because by the time he had opened the door and let Neil in, the police were behind him. He saw that Neil was in a terrible state, crying and agitated.

I will now copy a statement that Steve had to make when he and I went to Nelson Police Station to complain to Inspector Roberts about how Neil was treated upon his arrest on this day, and how P.C. Buckle and P.C.Pitt *lied in their statements* concerning that day.

*I am Stephen Green of the address overleaf. At around 13.55 on Tuesday 19th March 2002, police officers attended my home address and arrested my son. I have since read a number of statements made by P.C. Pitt and Buckle which I am **not happy with,** as they have <u>falsely stated</u> that I told them to 'Eff Off' on a number of occasions.*

Going through the statement written by P.C. Pitt, dated 19.03.02, on page 3 it is written, 'As we approached the door it was opened by Stephen Green who said 'Eff Off'. I can clearly state that I actually opened the door <u>prior</u> to any officer knocking, as I had already seen them through the window.

*A police officer asked to see my son and I shouted for Neil, my son, to come to me. I did **not** swear or shout at the officers, my manner was calm and certainly not aggressive. It also states on P.C. Pitt's statement that I slammed the door twice, I did **not** do this. I just shut the door to, but it didn't slam.*

*At the bottom of page 3 on P.C. Pitt's statement it is claimed that I said "Eff Off, I'll sort him out." This is **not true** I never used the 'F' word throughout the whole incident. All the other information on this statement is correct.*

On P.C. Buckle's statement it is claimed that I shouted "Eff Off,

330

what do you want him for?" before slamming the door.

*Yet again I did **not** say this, and didn't slam the door. I never use the 'F' word even when upset or angry. I had only just got out of bed when the police called round, and would describe myself as being calm and polite throughout this incident. Other than this the remainder of this officer's statement is correct. I did not stop the police from taking Neil away from the house, as both me and my wife feel that Neil desperately needs help for his mental condition.*

I do not know why the two police officers have <u>lied</u> in their statements.

On the 3.04.02. I visited Nelson Police Station where I spoke to Inspector Roberts and P.C. Edgeworth. I have asked that Inspector Roberts investigates this matter. However, I do not want to make a formal complaint. I will co-operate with the Inspector throughout this matter and I agree with any further action the police wish to take.

S. Green.

This is why Steve detests the police and is why he wouldn't have any police officer over the doorstep if it were not for me inviting them in.

I had been the one throughout Neil's tragic life who has dealt with the police, and in the main I have been especially treated reasonably well. I think that it is because if they had me in front of them telling my side of things, they would believe me about Neil and his bad treatment by the so called 'medical experts'. The trouble was that I couldn't *always* be there.

Neil was confronted by different officers all the time, who were in the main so frightened of this tall, well-built man, that they used to 'get in there' first. Probably they'd been told that Neil was a 'mad man', and unpredictable, when they rung in on their radios.

Steve is a very quiet, mild mannered, **decent** man. He was terribly hurt when he read the lies in those statements, and they *were lies,* and no, I wasn't there, but he would no sooner swear at a 'bobby' than I would, and I don't swear. No one has ever heard that word pass my lips.

We used to have respect for everyone in authority, and we brought our kids up to be the same, so it really hurts us to see that respect thrown back in our faces by these two men wearing a uniform and acting in this way.

David didn't even flinch, he said, "It makes it sound better in court if they write things down like this."

Again though, call me naïve, but this is supposed to be a document of the 'truth' so this is very wrong. Some people out there would think this was nothing, but to Steve and me it was 'something'. I felt angry, not only that the police **lied,** but that they were so needlessly rough in the handling of Neil. Then on top of that they were treating Steve with contempt too, when he could have quite easily have talked calmly to Neil and let the police take him without there being any trouble at all from him. The police would rather throw their weight about though, because they have all this adrenalin running through their veins, add to that the fact that they know that they can.

****

A friend of Neil's came around to my house in June 2006 and told me that the last time she had seen Neil he was being jumped on by all these police officers. He was screaming and crying, as they were really hurting him. There were about SIX officers she said, and he was doing *nothing* to warrant such treatment. She came out of her house with her husband who was shouting at the officers for what they were doing, and he was told to shut his mouth or he'd be arrested too.

She said it was crazy, and showed the police in a bad light, as there was no need for it. It was the last time she saw Neil, and the memory of it still 'haunts' her.

"Neil didn't deserve to be treated like that," she said.

We knew that too. They were like us, decent law-abiding people. We did realize that keep putting Neil through the criminal system was doing nothing but giving him a long record of arrests that made him look, *on paper at least,* like a **real** criminal.

Inspector Howes had said to me that putting Neil through the courts would make people sit up and listen and do something. Do what? Put him in prison? They couldn't do **anything** to make doctors treat him. Who could actually make a doctor, doctor? It was a vicious circle.

SOMEONE, ANYONE AT ALL, PLEASE HELP US!

No one did, because no one could!

****

2nd April 2002

Neil was in a terrible state when he came to my house. I had to take him to A & E. I knew the response would be the same. We'd be shown the door, ignored, left to 'stew', hoping Neil would get fed up and leave. I was determined whatever the outcome, as I couldn't stand seeing him like this, pacing, anxious, depressed and suicidal. They made us wait over SIX hours to be seen, but no, it **wasn't** because they were busy. It **hadn't** been busy for hours, but they did this all the time.

The security man told Neil to drop his legs from the chair, as he was waiting so long and was in such a state I'd put his head on my lap to comfort him. I surprised myself as I snapped at him and called him a 'heartless bastard'. I guess I'd had enough too. He went away.

Dr Yearwood saw him *eventually*, and by the time she'd admitted him to Ward 20 we'd been at the hospital's A & E for EIGHT hours. I knew as soon as Bob Gardner, or Dr Janger got wind of what Dr Yearwood had done, that they'd get rid of Neil as soon as they could.

Neil had cut himself; he was shaking, angry, depressed, lethargic all of these things, but on the ward he'd calmed down a little, but he was withdrawn. This was a constant roller coaster. He had to be made to stay in hospital. At that moment he was desperate for help, and clinging to the hospital, but he can suddenly change and then he would turn to drink.

****

Primary Health Care rang me about Neil; they told me that *mental disorder is mental illness.*

I rang the Emergency Team at Social Services and they said *that mental disorder is mental illness.*

MIND say mental disorder is mental illness. Dr Newscombe says Neil's illness is progressive, and he believes the psychotic episodes will get closer, so Neil will deteriorate quickly. He's not surprised at the failing in Mental Health, but he says he is sorry for Neil as he deserves better than this.

Wednesday 3rd April 2002

Neil rang me off the ward to tell me that his Ritalin was written

333

up as 10.00am 2.00pm and 10.00pm. This was totally <u>unacceptable,</u> so I told him to **refuse** the 10.00pm one. Staff members were all offhand with him; they wouldn't listen and said they'd note down that he had *refused* the medication. He wasn't covered by his Ritalin this day, and the gap of more than four hours between the first two doses (as he was made to wait longer) and a gap of over eight hours, and then having to wait again after 10.00pm for them to actually give it to him, they knew that you **shouldn't give a stimulant** at this time of night. Yes, they knew <u>exactly</u> what they were doing to make Neil worse, probably sitting back and waiting for him to blow up, so that they could then say that he was disruptive and badly behaved. They **wanted** Neil worked up. Probably they'd been told to do the same by Bob Gardner. He was usually behind *everything* that went on, as he was the Nursing Manager. Neil did of course become agitated. He asked for PRN medication, and it was refused him.

I was told on this day 3rd April 2002 that there was to be a meeting between East Lancashire Health Authority, Philip Porter M.P, and Fernlea General Hospital.

I was rung on the morning of 4th to be told by Janice Throup that the meeting had been cancelled. She told me that this was due to last minute Trust business. I went to the East Lancashire Health Authority's office building on the Lomeshaye Industrial Estate, Nelson. I wanted to know the **real** reason, as no one involved believed this, as arrangements had been made. The truth she told me, was because I had got the newspapers involved, and Philip Porter had been told the same.

It wasn't **me** who had done this at all, but Neil himself who had done this deed, and who could blame him? If they had **nothing to hide,** why would they **not** talk to the press? They all kept telling me to back off, to let Neil stand on his own two feet. I would have loved to have done that, believe me, but then Neil would have been totally at *their mercy,* and although I couldn't <u>make</u> Fernlea General treat Neil, at least we weren't taking it lying down and we'd stirred the waters up a bit. I did try to back off years later, because my own health was deteriorating, but I couldn't for long as they did even less for Neil. (If that was indeed possible).

****

Neil rang me at 9:00pm to say that he was told by Norman (night

334

shift) that if he went out (Neil said he needed to get some fags) he **wouldn't** be allowed back on to the ward. Neil went anyway with another patient who they said *could* go out, whilst Neil couldn't.

Neil said, "If he can, then I can."

Neither of them were Sectioned, and it was normal for them to come and go like this. I did ask Neil if it was because of the time, he said it wasn't because it happens all the time. He'd also told me that he had cut his arms, and the staff had told him to look after it himself throwing a bandage at him.

Neil sounded coherent, fine really, maybe a little frustrated at his treatment but otherwise okay.

At 11:45pm there was message left on my telephone answering machine. I had just gone to bed, but I came down when I heard the phone ring. It was Norman and he said that Neil had discharged himself, and he was just letting me know.

I immediately rang Neil on his mobile phone and asked him, "What on earth was going on?"

"They **forced** me to sign a bit of paper Mum, but I don't know what I'm doing."

He sounded completely out of it. I asked him, "Why did you sign it then?"

"I don't know Mum," he whispered.

In fact he had signed it, he said he didn't know, **but he'd actually tried to hang himself.** He'd also taken pills from the patients as he needed something to settle him down, and the staff <u>wouldn't</u> give him anything to help him. They wouldn't listen to him, and had told him to go away, but the other patients had helped him. They had given him their medication, valium and co-promazine.

"Have you been drinking?" I asked him.

"Some," he replied.

I asked Neil to give his phone to Norman.

I asked Norman if Neil had been hurt? Has he tried to hang himself?"

Norman answered **no** to both questions.

I said, "How can you discharge someone at midnight, it is so wrong. Can't you wait until tomorrow? How can he possibly get into the B & B at this time?"

He said nothing.

335

Neil took back his phone and he told me that they had rung for a taxi.

I rang the police, the operator rang the hospital. She rang me back, saying that the hospital staff had told her that there was *nothing wrong* with Neil; he wasn't mentally ill, he had behavioural problems.

Pat at the B & B told me later that the police had rung her to tell her that Neil was on his way, and she wanted to make sure that he could get in, but she wasn't pleased at being woken up at that hour.

Pat rang me up the next day (Thursday) at 8.00am to say that she was extremely worried about Neil; his bandaged arm was black and soaked with blood. It was coming through the bandage; she said that there was blood everywhere.

Steve wasn't here at the time, and I didn't have a car. I rang Ben. He went straightaway to the B & B to see Neil. He took him to Fernlea General A & E, but he had to leave him there. He rang me, I told him it was alright, I'd managed to get a hold of Steve and he was on his way.

Ben went on to Ward 20 where Neil had been discharged off. I rang A & E and insisted that they got a psychiatrist to see Neil.

The nurse took off Neil's bandage that he had applied himself. Steve said that she nearly passed out at the sight of Neil's arm. Neil had cut it really deeply. The nurse said that it had been left too long, and that it had needed stitches, but it couldn't be done now or it would become infected. She steri-stripped it and bandaged his arm.

The psychiatrist came down, a Dr E. Ross. Neil told his Dad that the ward had sent a lady member of staff home last night because she was so traumatized at seeing Neil hanging.

Dr Ross rang Ward 20; he hadn't seen Neil's arm as the nurse had already bandaged it. The ward told him that the cuts were SUPERFICIAL. They also **denied** that Neil had tried to hang himself.

By this time Ben had left the ward, but he told me later personally, that he had indeed been told that Neil had tried to hang himself. He told me that he had also asked on the ward for Neil's benefit book. They told him that they had already sent it to my address.

****

There was a young girl who had committed suicide by hanging herself on the Psychiatric Ward. In fact she did this in the showers with her 'Doc Marten's shoelaces. This was years earlier, but the hospital supposedly had the showers altered after that, but they had already brushed it aside before, when Neil had done this by saying, "You can't hang yourself with laces."

It was a miracle that Neil was still alive. He came to our home later on in the afternoon. It was obvious that he had had enough.

I received a letter off Philip Porter M.P. stating the reason the meeting had been cancelled was because I'd informed the press and the doctors wouldn't go to the meeting.

Ben went to the doctors' meeting on Friday at 3.00pm it was supposed to be with Dr Janger. Steve went, but Ben said it was best that I didn't go. Dr Janger refused to see them, but he sent another doctor in his place, Dr Chan.

He didn't want to talk about what had happened on the ward. He said he was the one that was bleeped when Neil had cut his arms, but Neil had refused treatment. They need to get their stories straight don't they, because the ward said Neil's cuts were SUPERFICIAL, in which case <u>he would NOT have been bleeped,</u> and Neil was refused treatment, not the other way round.

When I had spoken to Norman he said that Neil had NOT hurt himself. Neil told Dr Chan he was *telling lies.*

Dr Chan said that he wouldn't talk about it any further. Ben tried to talk to Dr Chan, but he wouldn't talk to him either.

Steve told the doctor that **he didn't believe him** and he wanted an explanation for everything that had gone on the ward leading up to Neil being in this terrible state. He wouldn't talk any further, and he brushed them aside. Ben got a hold of Steve's arm and told him to leave it as Neil was becoming very upset.

Dr Chan gave Neil a hospital prescription for one week's Ritalin, and said that after that the G.P. would do it. He also said that Dr Janger would see Neil as an out-patient in six month's time. He also went on to say the hanging incident *wasn't serious, you **can't** hang yourself with laces.*

Monday 8th April 2002

I still haven't received Neil's benefit book back from the hospital

337

after they had said to Ben that they had already sent it to my address.

Tuesday 9th April 2002

I still haven't received Neil's benefit book, so I will have to report it as missing. I know you find all this unbelievable, don't you? I do myself on reading this all back from my diaries, but it is true, **every word** and Ben did the same, he noted everything down. My poor sick deluded son had to suffer all of this while being so mentally disturbed; the future sees more of the same as Neil is getting worse.

CHAPTER TWENTY-THREE
Self Harm

I am about to write about something that I know very little about, or understand. Neil told me that he started to self harm while being on the Psychiatric Ward at Fernlea General Hospital. He said that he had copied others who had done it for 'relief', as they had told him to try it. I wasn't sure of his explanation, because Neil would start a form of compulsive behaviour because he got into a habit.

When he was on the ward at Chorley Hospital I told them to keep his razor away from him, so that he **couldn't** get at the razor blades, because if you broke the 'cycle' and kept the habit formed article away from him for a prolonged period, he would stop doing it. We had tried the same tactic successfully for other habit formed behaviour in the past.

The members of staff at Chorley Hospital **wouldn't** listen or do as I asked, so Neil continued to harm himself. We therefore asked for his razor back, so that instead of it we could give them an electric shaver we had bought for him. He was still able to get at sharp items though, but it did get a little better.

I dealt with all of Neil's problems, but this one turned my stomach, and I couldn't cope with it very well. I was ashamed of Neil's arms, I must admit that. It sounds awful I know, and maybe daft when you consider that Neil was always being arrested, but I always found a reason for that, in that he didn't know what he was doing, and it was down to his illness.

I suppose the same could have been said about his self-harming, but Neil had told me it was truly a relief to cut himself. I still have my doubts. I know that is why other self-harmers do it, but Neil was *never* like anyone else. I wouldn't take Neil out with us unless his arms were covered up. He said it didn't bother him; let people think what they liked. The trouble is people see this, and with Neil it was deep scars all the way up both arms, because he'd not got treatment and stitches when he should have.

It did bother him when he was thinking straight. I knew that, and other people would stare then turn away, and then they would look down on him, treat him differently, and their views of Neil would then be tainted.

I did take Neil to see a Consultant to have Plastic Surgery or a skin graft. I knew the scars not only on his arms but on his mind needed treatment, as he looked upon them as punishment for being bad. He would have no chance of stopping forever, or people seeing beyond them to get to like him, before they were to judge him if he couldn't get the scars covered up.

Neil hadn't self-harmed for a short while and I really had to fight his corner to get the doctor to listen to Neil, and to do what we asked, but she was prepared to go ahead. Unfortunately Neil's health deteriorated so badly that I couldn't get him to go to the appointment which by then was at Chorley Hospital. I rang the doctor's secretary to explain, and she said that she would tell Dr Lattern, and they could see Neil at a later date. I would have to get my G.P. to refer him again though.

Sadly things beyond our control took over, and we never did get to see Dr Lattern. Neil was *never well enough*. I still believe it was a way of Neil punishing himself, he said that the voices told him he was bad and not worthy of living. I think that was more the case than him getting relief from the injuries he caused himself.

Having a mental health solicitor wasn't making any difference at all in getting Neil treatment from the hospital, or indeed receiving a second opinion; as no matter what Consultant Psychiatrist Neil had from Fernlea General, none of them **would** make a referral for Neil to be seen by **another** Consultant Psychiatrist. All that was left open to us was to hope that the court would make a Hospital Order to get Neil into safe surroundings while getting an *unbiased opinion* and treatment.

David told me in detail the rules and regulations governing the making of Hospital Orders, and in particular he advised me that whilst we were seeking to deal with the shortcomings of the Mental Health Services through the back door, and by means of use of the Criminal System, he could **not guarantee** that this would ultimately have the desired effect, as the Hospital Order is a criminal sentence which has to be imposed by the court, and they would not agree to do that at a Defendant's request.

There were also practical difficulties surrounding the obtaining of two reports that are required as a precondition to the making of the Hospital Order.

At present, as advised to him by Dr Blake, David requested a report from Dr Leister at Fernlea General Hospital. In reality he didn't expect that he would provide that report, in view of the difficulties that had arisen previously. If the report was not available by 12th April, then he would make arrangements to speak to Dr Blake again, in order to see whether or not he was then prepared to undertake the preparation of the report. If he was, then David would have to obtain authority from the Legal Services Commission to incur the expense that would be involved, that would take in the region of 10/14 days, and David anticipated that it would then take Dr Blake at least four weeks to prepare his own report.

In the meantime David would have to ask the Magistrates to order the preparation of a second report, and while he would obviously explain to them we did not want the report to be prepared by anyone associated with Fernlea General Hospital, we would *not* in fact have a free choice in that respect, as ultimately it would be up to the court to determine where and by whom they felt the report ought to be prepared.

If both reports ultimately concluded that it was appropriate for a Hospital Order to be made, that is to say that they both accepted that Neil was suffering from a mental illness as specified in the Mental Health Act, then the court would be invited to make the relevant order. In those circumstances David expected that they would make the order, although further difficulties could then arise as regards the location of the hospital at which Neil was to be detained. Again whilst we could make suggestions or representations to the court, they would have a limited amount of discretion and could not necessarily order a particular hospital to provide a bed for Neil.

In the circumstances it had to be recognized that difficulties could arise with regard to the making of the order, and indeed the mechanics of it once it **had** been made.

David did speak to Dr Blake and he was prepared to see Neil and make a report. It would take the Legal Services Commission about

341

ten days to give their authority, and maybe about two weeks for Dr Blake to prepare the report.

****

I went with Neil to court on 22nd April and although David pleaded with passion as always on Neil's behalf, he was told that the offences Neil had committed and pleaded guilty to, were not sufficiently serious enough to consider the making of a Hospital Order, so they gave Neil a Conditional Discharge.

Neil was upset and crying, and he shouted out to the Magistrates, "What do you want me to do, commit murder?"

He was so let down, again. It's all a game, a terrible game. I can remember Eddina, Neil's CPN, later on in this book telling us, and fully knowing the ins and outs of the system, that Neil could go to court and get reports done, and they could make an Hospital Order, but knowing that this *couldn't be done,* because Neil never did anything serious enough to warrant a long stay in prison in order to get that done. The hospital just had to carry on **ignoring** Neil and waiting for him to make the moves. They were in a win, win situation, and smug enough to know that they had us all trapped. They knew that *we couldn't beat the system,* no matter what we did, or which way we turned, or to whom.

We just kept hitting brick walls. Neil wanted to go into hospital, he was desperate. He wanted to be locked up, he wanted support and treatment. We wanted the same for him. We were downhearted and our hopes were ripped apart. We left the court and Neil went back to the B & B.

****

On 2nd May Neil received a letter from the police stating that the man who had assaulted him on the ward at Chorley Hospital was found guilty of Occasional Actual Bodily Harm.

He attacked Neil more than once and eventually he was arrested.

Dr Kuwait came to see Neil at my home to make an assessment. He worked at Calderstones. Doctors from Fernlea General asked him to make an assessment.

In his report he stated that he had read the psychiatric notes held at Fernlea General Hospital, and in them it states *that Neil is **not** suffering from Mental Impairment or Severe Mental Impairment.*

The question of evidence relevant to the presence of mental

illness he wrote that Neil had suffered from A.D.H.D. since childhood, for which he is receiving Ritalin. In addition he is also diagnosed as having periods of depression and transient psychosis. He said that Fernlea General Hospital had diagnosed Neil with Personality Disorder.

He stated that Neil's A.D.H.D. was well controlled. (As you have read, Neil's A.D.H.D. was **never controlled,** because they **never** gave him his medication on time, and later discarded it altogether).

Dr Janice Short recommended that his personality difficulties were not treatable, and he is not detainable under the Mental Health Act. (That horrible psychiatrist who first saw Neil at Chorley and Neil said she was a walkover as he saw her for only thirty minutes, before she said he *wasn't* suffering from mental illness, and she was the one who lied in that medical report).

His findings in his short assessment? That he agreed with the other doctors. So there was no surprise there then.

****

I didn't know that Neil was using heroin, but after I visited him at the B & B and went into his room that he shared with someone else, I had found needles. I told Ben, and I also told him that we had to get him out of there. Then things took a terrible turn.

****

On 28th May 2002 we received a telephone call from Fernlea General Hospital telling us that Neil had been brought into hospital by ambulance after a road traffic accident.

We arrived at the hospital to find Neil awaiting surgery. The ambulance crew that picked Neil up told us that Neil had wanted to kill himself, as he had driven the car a short distance at speed, and hit a lamppost deliberately. They wrote down the same on the accident sheet.

Neil had to be cut out of the car. He looked a terrible mess. He had *severe* leg injuries, because his legs had been trapped under the dash, and one of his knees was totally smashed. He also had horrific facial injuries. I've seen enough motor accidents to know that it always looks worse before the person is cleaned up, but when it's your own child lying there, it's heartbreaking, and to know he'd done it on purpose, and he's back in the hands of that *terrible* hospital, made me feel even more sickened than I already was.

343

I know I shouldn't condemn the <u>whole</u> hospital for what the Psychiatric Department had done to Neil, but we had Bob Gardner who was still the Nursing Manager, John Duggan, Service Director, Chief Executive Foster Roberts who have all had input into Neil's case, and written me stupid letters, that I look at now with hateful passion in my heart for the neglect and cruelty they dished out and put my son through, just to prove a point it seems to me, because even if you take out the stupidity of the psychiatric doctors, you can still see the evidence of Neil being *seriously ill,* and yet these inhuman people still turned their backs.

If I could put a curse on these horrible excuses for human beings, I would gladly sell my soul to the devil to do so. So yes, I do blame the hospital as a whole, and I wouldn't want to be treated there. I have even become distrustful of my own G.P's. I am left with a fear of doctors, because they lie together, and <u>are not to be trusted,</u> as too are many Community Mental Health workers such as CPN's and other staff and Social Service workers. We all know how inept they can be, because we often hear about their cockups in the press and on T.V.

But that remains a long list, and you would think because it is such a <u>long list of mistakes and neglect</u>, that they would **learn** from their mistakes; but they never do, so naturally they still continue to make them. You all disgust me. Break the habit of a lifetime and learn by your mistakes, why don't you? My son lies here battered and broken, seeing the only way out of his misery is to kill himself, but all you lot say is, **"Get on with it!"**

I see the look on the nurses' faces seeing Neil's cut arms and the needle marks. I can see what they are thinking. I want to cry out, it's your fault, but it's not just <u>their fault</u>, **it's my fault, and society's fault for allowing these people to get away with it**.

My son wasn't taking drugs until you Fernlea General Hospital turned your back on him, and put him into a B & B with drug addicts. You threw him out of hospital to fend for himself, as if he was a piece of rubbish you could just discard, and now your nurses and others in society look down on Neil, because the only ways out for him are to go to a better place inside heroin, to get away from the demons inside his head, or to kill himself.

This is the lesser of the two evils for him; and now because he woke up with a needle in his arm, it sickens him to see what he has been brought down to, and he'd rather **die than live like this**. His own mum, who he thought could move mountains, <u>couldn't</u> help him. No, I will never forgive you all, and I know I will never forget because it's **not** today 28th May 2002 that my son dies, but a few years later after even more pain and misery at your hands, because you never do help him. <u>**You should all bow your heads down in shame.**</u>

****

After Neil's surgery he is put on to a Surgical Ward to recover from his injuries. As soon as he was, in fact the day after, Pat the owner of the B & B had all of Neil's belongings brought into the hospital and dumped at the side of Neil's hospital bed. We were left to pick up the pieces again, but who could blame Pat? Certainly not me! How on earth was she expected to deal with all this chaos that surrounded Neil? She knows he needs help, but **she** cannot be expected to cope with this, no matter how much she likes Neil or feels sorry for him; *she* has **no expertise** in dealing with mental illness. The hospital staff and the Social Services didn't care a jot about <u>her</u> either, or they wouldn't have put Neil there in the first place.

I asked for psychiatric doctors to become involved with Neil, as he was still telling everyone that he wanted to die, and he would try again as soon as he was able to. The psychiatrists at Fernlea General **would not** get involved with Neil, and in fact wouldn't even come down to see him on the Surgical Ward he was on. <u>They totally ignored him.</u>

<u>**When someone has tried to kill and self-harm themselves to an alarming degree on several occasions, and is still threatening to do so again, isn't this TRULY a psychiatric problem? If NOT, then PRAY DO TELL me whose problem it really is? If someone is that ill – don't they NEED and DESERVE as much help as possible? WHO CAN THEY AND THEIR FAMILIES TURN TO FOR HELP?**</u>

****

They got rid of Neil from the hospital as soon as they were able to with a full length pot leg, crutches and a smashed up face. They knew he found it difficult to eat, because of the broken bones in his

345

face. In fact he had to have ALL his food pureed so that he could eat anything at all, but still after just ONE week they discharged him into a house to fend for himself all alone. This was simply to get him out of the hospital and out of their hair. Again, you disgust me!

He had a new CPN. Angela Moore. I will never forget her sitting me down on a bench outside of the hospital, outside of Neil's Surgical Ward, and telling me that she and the Mental Health Services need **not** get involved with Neil, as he **wasn't mentally ill,** but she would help Neil on this occasion to get accommodation.

It was a first, and although I told her that he was *still voicing suicide*, and wasn't fit to look after himself after the accident besides that, all she did was shrug her shoulders, and said **it wasn't her problem,** but mine and Neil's. She implied that it was good of her to even find him accommodation as she didn't need to.

I'm supposed to be grateful, I don't think so; as far as I was concerned it was *her* job, although she did her best to make me think that it wasn't. **If it wasn't her job, why then was he even allocated a CPN?**

We were then left to furnish yet another house, and help Neil with his everyday needs. It was futile to expect anything else. At this time I had been registered as disabled and had been pensioned off from work due to ill health. It wasn't easy running around like I was having to do, but I JUST had grit my teeth and get on with it.

****

The Chief Executive Foster Roberts had written to my M.P. and he had passed the letter on to me. It was riddled with lies, as always, when these people write to M.P's, solicitors and doctors. It always looked good on paper, **but the reality** was always very, very **different.**

At the start of the letter he said that Neil was currently on Ward 23, but he was **not,** as they had already got rid of Neil before this letter was even written. It said that Neil remained an inpatient at Fernlea General Hospital. The letter was dated 20th June 2002, Neil had the accident on the 28th May, and he had been in hospital for only **one week**, and even I can work out those sums. They were saying that Neil had been kept in hospital for a further SIXTEEN days at least at that point, which was yet another untruth!

He said that Neil was making a good recovery from his injuries,

346

and that Dr Janger was working closely with his colleague Orthopaedic Consultant Dr Saaul, to make sure that when Neil was fit for discharge, which hopefully would be the following week, (to make it appear that Neil had been in hospital for a whole month, instead of ONLY the one actual week they had kept him). In other words, written down on paper **was what they should have done**, but it was not only untrue, it was a downright and utter lie. Oh yes it looked good, and it appeared as if they were still caring for **and** looking after this badly injured man, yet they had in fact **already discharged** him much earlier. In fact after just SEVEN DAYS Neil had been thrown out to fend for himself, when he wasn't able to feed himself.

Mental Health Services would continue to follow up Neil's care. He said that they had already arranged his benefits, which was **news to me**, as it seemed that I needn't have been chasing my tail after all. Local Mental Health Services have had a long period of contact with both Neil and his mother to manage Neil's problems (Oh they have, have they, well this was indeed *yet another piece of news to me*) and they have arranged for a variety of specialist's assessments to ensure that every opportunity has been taken to provide him with appropriate care.

I am banging these keys on my laptop so hard that I have visions of them all pinging out. I'm so mad at the disgusting way in which these people do this, **write these lies down, in order to have other people believe that they are <u>doing so much,</u> when in TRUTH they are doing nothing, or on a good day only the *absolute minimum.***

He continued by saying, that they were looking at the possibility of Neil receiving long term psychotherapeutic services at the Henderson Unit, which is a nationally recognized Centre of expertise.

This was yet another *empty promise*, as **this isn't the sort of place** that would even take someone with serious mental illness, and so it is totally unacceptable to even mention it. Like I am forced to say so many times, it all looks good on paper though.

He mentioned the mislaid notes. Neil's records had gone missing on the ward, and he says fortunately duplicates were available, and these records were relating to Neil's recent physical care following his accident.

(Wait a minute; shouldn't this have been, following Neil's **attempted suicide?**) Neil's entire mental health record is kept separately, and I can assure you that it is complete.

****

What a load of RUBBISH! Regarding the notes that went missing? Neil had been reading his notes when they had been left with him, and he'd read about things unrelated to his ACCIDENT, about his mental health. They then disappeared suspiciously, and this year NOW 2006, four years later than the letter above, Dr Musto said he'd **not** seen medical reports that were supposed to be in his notes, but were not. I remember thinking he <u>should have been better prepared,</u> especially when seeing Neil for the first time, as he wasn't well versed at all about Neil's mental health.

Neil said that they **lied** about the notes, all his notes were together, including mental health assessments and records. He even told me about one from Dr Mallard and that had been written years earlier. That one in particular I would have preferred Neil **not to have seen.**

****

It was October 2nd 2002 and Neil was in the local papers again telling of how and why he had driven into a lamppost.

I rang Calderstones just after Neil had done this, and I spoke to Joe Calder who was the man who dealt with the findings of the assessment made by Dr Kuwait, Dr Grey and nursing Staff Iris North. I told him about Neil crashing the car at speed to kill himself, and how seriously injured he was. He stated that it was very serious indeed, and although he will not be popular in telling me the findings of the assessment, and what Dr Kuwait's findings were, he knows of the urgency in getting Neil help.

*He said that Fernlea General Hospital **are** responsible for Neil, and **have** to find him an appropriate hospital, and he said that there must be a hospital somewhere to take him as it is a desperate situation, as that the lad needs help. He told me to contact my M.P. again. He stated that Neil **has** mental illness, because TRANSIENT PSYCHOSIS **is indeed a mental illness**. (Also Adult A.D.H.D. being different to childhood A.D.H.D. this too **is** a mental illness. He has psychopathic disorder, which form is treatable, and he is suffering from depression. He also said that he feared that Neil had turned to*

348

*drugs in order to **self-medicate**, as too was the **alcohol**. He commented on Neil's self harm, and the fact that he wanted to die because no one would help him.*

****

My solicitor said that dumping Neil in a bed and breakfast, revoking his 117 aftercare was **unlawful,** as he was still in considerable need. I had told Fernlea General psychiatrists many times about the drug addicts and needles at the bed and breakfast, and also Bob Gardner and Social Services, stating Neil was to say the least, extremely vulnerable, but they didn't care. To say that they were cruel and uncaring is an absolute understatement!

Again I asked for Neil to be referred to **another psychiatrist** and **another hospital** and asked why this couldn't be Dr Blake at the Spinney, Atherton?

They said that this was a *private* hospital, but I knew Dr Blake had already asked Bob Gardner to let him take Neil, as he knew that he **could** help him. So for Dr Blake to even request this in the first place told me that indeed this could have been possible.

Fernlea General refused him again and again; they refused to do the right thing, and continued to ignore Neil's considerable needs. Neil had spent six hours in surgery after the accident, and had to be defibrillated and brought out of the anaesthetic because of water on his lungs; then he was re-anaesthetised to continue surgery on his badly crushed leg. He had broken bones in his face and could only eat pureed food. He was in terrible pain, his pot leg was full length and heavy to move around, he felt faint with every step.

Yet he was discharged from a Surgical Ward just over a week later, because they wanted rid of him, and the psychiatric doctors wouldn't get involved, and they never saw him in hospital at that time. He had both chest and facial pain. He was distraught, depressed and tormented, but what does our wonderful health service do? They discharge him to live on his own, and left it to me to run around after him when I was struggling so much to manage with my **own** disability. I did take it on myself, because I was the only one who really understood Neil and could get through to him, besides no one from Fernlea General Hospital would help him, so what other choice did we have? He needed me and I would be there for him as always.

****

349

I did as Joe Calder said to do, which was to get in touch with M.P. Philip Porter. I told him what Joe had said. All credit to Joe Calder for being so open and understanding, and for telling me the **true facts,** and not for doing what the other doctors and psychiatrists do, stick together no matter what, and cover up and lie for one another.

I found him open and honest, and he would do the very best for anyone in his care. If he was the one faced with a patient that he couldn't treat, **he wouldn't play God** and deny that patient to anyone else who might possibly be able to help them. We had a doctor like that in Dr Blake; dear Dr Blake who is no longer with us, and I dream about him being with Neil, and possibly being his doctor in another life, where Neil perhaps for the first time in his tortured life is without pain, confusion or worry.

****

Philip Porter sent me a letter saying that he would at his earliest opportunity raise Neil's case urgently, because Neil needed help and support, but he was away in Scotland but would contact me on his return.

The Community Mental Health Team at the Resource Centre on Leeds Road Nelson isn't far away from my home. The accommodation that was found for Neil was a rented house on a street not far away from CMHT. At first Neil would go there for a very limited period of an hour only one or two days a week; in that time he would see his CPN, Angela Moore. I thought it would be like a drop-in centre for Neil, for him to access a team that could help him to make a meal, as there were kitchen facilities there, or to facilitate some form of therapies or self-help groups. There were clients going that sat around, chatting, and playing pool and suchlike, but Neil was never asked to do any of these things and we had asked for it. They **never wanted** Neil to go there, and they made it quite plain during the short time that he was there, that he was only there under sufferance. His time was short and pre-arranged. It was a pathetic and useless exercise.

Neil wasn't welcome, so the members of staff were horrible with him. I told Angela of this, and she said that the staff 'out front' were not qualified staff, so they couldn't be expected to deal properly with Neil. It was those staff members who were the first to see Neil, and

350

criticize him, then talk to him in such a manner that he felt unwanted. They talked about him within earshot of other people, and Neil was always upset about that.

He'd ring to speak to Angela, but his messages weren't passed on. This was happening a lot with me too. I told Ben; he told me that I had to tell them to write it down that I'd rung and for whom. I will give Angela her 'due' she always got back to me whenever she did get the message. Neil was a drain on them though as he was very needy. He was always popping into the Resource Centre because he did need so much; they were fed up of him, especially when he did his usual party trick of mastering the digit codes on the doors.

Inevitably he'd have had a drink which made it easier for them to disregard his needs, but harder for Neil to obtain any help. Neil didn't plan it this way; he was simply foolish enough to play into their hands, but sadly Neil was always this daft. He couldn't plot or deceive. This was Neil; he was so open. So they banned him completely from the Resource Centre. For what little they did provide for him there it wasn't a great loss, but it was still the place his CPN was at and he **needed** her.

Angela said once that she could spend all day, every day with Neil and it wouldn't be enough. **This was true!** Ben said the same of his time too. Neil was a drain on all of their resources but surely it was a need, not because it <u>wasn't</u> warranted.

****

We were getting nowhere with the solicitors we'd used. They couldn't get the hospital to treat Neil properly, nor could, or would they start any sort of proceedings against the hospital for their mistreatment thus far, and after the letter we had received from Philip Porter M.P. we had to review the situation. He said that involving solicitors makes it more difficult from his viewpoint as the Hospital Trust would only answer him with caution taking the position of legal challenge into account. He would try once again to contact Lancashire County Council and the Lancashire NHS Trust and he would get back to me in due course.

I could see that all these people we had contacted to help us could see no way of giving us that help, as it was so frustrating for them. I'd seen it with David, Ben and his predecessor Daniel Pounder. You can't fight doctors; <u>they do not have to refer you to another doctor</u>

351

and if they don't refer you, then **another doctor will <u>not</u> see you**. This I know would *generally never happen* because the doctor takes the Hippocratic Oath to do the **<u>best</u>** for their patient, and he would generally do that, but not in our case with Neil, because Fernlea General doctors would NEVER refer Neil.

There isn't a single thing that could be done to make them do it, but what if for instance <u>you don't agree with your doctor</u> and what he says is wrong with you, or even if you don't like his manner, or something like that. If you feel that your needs *aren't* being met, or the doctor failed to facilitate a type of treatment for you that would help your illness, then just **try putting yourself in Neil's position!**

It wasn't as if there wasn't enough evidence of need. We had care workers, legal people, courts, police all trying to get Neil help, but they like us kept hitting brick walls because the GODS that are the psychiatrists, managers, staff, Trust, PCT, executives and suchlike at Fernlea General Hospital, need not do a damn thing. All they had to say was that Neil ***didn't*** have an enduring mental illness.

They kept medical reports under wraps like the one that was made in Lancaster Farms, and the one that was done at their own request by Dr Kuwait from Calderstones, when Joe Calder *exposed* the contents to me. They have systematically tortured my son to his death, and in my eyes have committed murder, but not one of them will be brought to task for it.

There is another kind of sin, **a sin of omission**. This is a treatment to help their patient that they <u>could have done</u>, *might have tried,* but DID NOT DO. They refused to help Neil over and over again.

Justice! There's no justice. A child, a man, a mentally disturbed person, they don't matter. This is my son yet no one cared about him. YOU SHOULD HANG YOUR HEADS IN SHAME.

Chief Executive, Foster Roberts sent a letter to M.P. Philip Porter stating that at the moment it is correct that there is no active involvement from Social Services staff with the Community Health Team. This was a decision made by the care team who are involved in Mr Green's care.

WHERE IS THERE REASON OR JUSTIFICATIONS FOR THIS?

Did they have no obligations to give any? IF NOT, WHY NOT?

352

CHAPTER TWENTY-FOUR
Police

I have already touched on the fact that the police had a tendency to bully Neil, as they saw him as an easy target. There were a few decent coppers, but they were few and far between. I guess it was mostly the policemen who had contact with me and knew of Neil's history, that treated him with respect and more fairly, but a lot of how Neil reacted to them was down to their treatment of him. The fact that he *wasn't* on the correct medication; if indeed he took any at all, or because he'd been drinking with his medication or without, naturally made a great deal of difference.

A case in point was on this day 12th September 2002. Neil, as I have told you before, had a tendency to walk into the road without looking. He's always done it ever since I can remember; only when he was a child he'd have my hand or his father's to hold onto, but not as he got older. If he was with me I would link up to him, as he always made me feel nervous when we were approaching any roads. I know that it was because he didn't think first; like with everything else, he'd just set off without any thought at all. We were amazed that he had escaped being run over. He could have been seriously hurt, and it would be the motorists who we would have to thank for that. It's a good job no one got hurt when swerving their vehicle to avoid this jay walker.

****

I am now going to copy you the statement that was read out in court:-

I am Police Constable 345, Michael Adrian Keith Grant of the Lancashire Constabulary currently stationed at Nelson Police Office.

On Thursday the 12th September 2002 I was in a uniform patrol travelling along Scotland Road Nelson, in the direction of Barrowford.

At approximately 9:50am I approached the traffic lights at the junction with Leeds Road. The lights were at green, and on seeing an elderly female crossing the road I slowed down. As the female reached the footpath, I was aware of a male who suddenly stepped out in front of the police vehicle. I braked sharply to avoid an accident.

Through the open window I said to the male who was standing about three to four feet away from me, "Watch out, you nearly got run over."

The male was a man I know to be Neil Green. He suddenly turned and shouted, "Eff off," and gestered with his arm in an aggressive manner.

I alighted from my vehicle and said, "Stop swearing."

Green turned away from me and said, "It's effing police harassment."

At this time several young children and elderly people were within earshot, and appeared visibly distressed by Green's behaviour.

Green suddenly turned towards me in an aggressive manner, his eyes were bulging, and he adopted a fighting stance, and said "Effing what now."

Fearing that Green was about to use unlawful violence towards me at 9:55am I said, "I am arresting you for section 4 public order," and cautioned him.

He replied, "No effing way."

To prevent injury to myself and for safety reasons, I took hold of Green by his right hand to apply the handcuffs. Green resisted by pulling his hand back, but I managed to gain control and handcuff him to the front, double-locking him. Green was then conveyed to Colne Custody in the section van. The facts were related to the Custody Sergeant and detention authorized.

At 12:10pm I was on duty in Colne Custody and charged Green with the offence as per MG4 to which he replied, "Harassment, police harassment."

Now I carefully checked out the time that they had put Neil into custody. This was simply the policeman's version of events; however the **true and accurate version was very different indeed**. I knew that what he was saying in his statement was **untrue** and filled with embellishments to suit him, for reasons known only to him, but BOTH I (his truthful Mother and my own Mother, also very honest) remembered this actual day very vividly.

In fact Neil had been to see his Grandma at the disabled centre, not far from the incident. He had been in a very good mood, telling his Grandma that he was meeting me at Kwik Save Supermarket to help him with his shopping, and then I was taking him home.

He would NEVER swear at a policeman (unless they were doing something wrong to him) as I had brought my two children up to respect the law and other adults. I could well believe that Neil would walk into the road without looking first, as this was something he *always did* right from being child, so that part of the statement would be correct. However the rest of it was deliberately added to, in order to make this into a crime, when no crime had in fact been committed. If Neil is accused of something that he has NOT done, then he gets angry, just as anyone else would.

Even my Mum doesn't believe the policeman's version at all, because she said, "Neil was fine that morning, in good spirits, and looking forward to meeting you."

My Mum was always so intuitive. I suppose when you are totally blind you develop good instincts.

Reactions from the police had become worse after Neil was seriously assaulted in the cells at a time BEFORE this incident, when Neil broke the officer's glasses, and Neil ended up severely beaten and bruised because of it. He did not hit back THEN either, even when he was being severely beaten, nor did he gesture or try to fight back. In fact Neil has **never** hit out at the police even when he was provoked.

Neil did say that, (as we knew would have happened) "I had stepped out in front of the vehicle, which resulted in the driver having to brake hard, so this made the copper quite mad. I did not realize at the time that it was a police vehicle. I always walk into the road without remembering to check first, so this incident was no different than usual. I had my headphones on listening to my walkman, which was my usual thing."

Walking into the road without looking first, was simply part of Neil's medical condition, and something he has done since he could

355

walk, particularly if not watched over all the time. It was NEVER ever done on purpose. He simply did NOT remember to look first, no matter how many *thousands of times* we told him to do so. Nothing registered about the dangers of doing this with Neil. It was pointed out that he was at risk for the DLA, as he never recognized or was aware of common dangers.

Neil also told me, "How could I have told the copper to 'eff off', when I hadn't even heard him speak to me. I did not realize that he was even there until the policeman confronted me face-on out of the blue, as far as I was concerned."

Neil continued, "I did not put my hands or arms up in any way towards this policeman. It is just a lie Mum, he is trying to fit me up for something that I NEVER did."

So in fact our son was arrested for walking into the road without looking first. They could arrest him every single day of his life for doing this, for he had no learning curve, so he would always continue to do this. The officer was cross that he had to brake hard to avoid him, which was fair enough, but the police knew that Neil had many problems, so this was grossly unfair to pick on a man with an illness over which he had NO control.

The police officer in question should therefore have made allowances for Neil, certainly not have arrested him. He made up stories of Neil swearing and going into a fighting stance quite simply in order to justify Neil's arrest. Neil in fact was **not aware** that it was a police van he had walked in front of, nor had he heard the policeman talking to him as he had his headphones on and was listening to his music. It was only at the moment of arrest, when the handcuffs were placed on Neil, that he knew anything about it at all. Naturally this came as a complete shock to him. He had neither been abusive, sworn or acted violently, or in an aggressive or threatening manner whatsoever; he had NOT even seen this policeman.

****

This incident was probably in retaliation for Neil breaking the Sergeant's glasses some time earlier, for which he had apologized in court, as he knew that he was totally out of order in doing that. Yet they had locked Neil in a cell from early morning until the next day when he went to court. The worst thing about this was that Neil had been **totally resigned to the fact that he was ill-treated in this**

way, so obviously it had happened on many other occasions. Police brutality should NEVER happen, they are neither the judge nor jury, and any punishment due to anyone is for the courts to dole out, NOT the police themselves. There is NO excuse for them beating people up at all, for they are simply there to enforce the law, to escort the prisoner to jail, not to beat them until they need hospital treatment. Neil was NEVER aggressive, so why would they need to punish him in this way? He never even told the doctor how his body was beaten with some kind of weapon; he only lifted his tee shirt up in front of the Custody Desk at the Police Station for me to see. Yes they called a doctor, but Neil had facial injuries to show him, the other bodily ones *he just expected to receive*, which makes me feel so very sad. Wrongly it seems, I brought my boys up to respect and help the police, as they represented justice.

Just how would Neil, who suffers from mental illness think, when I had drummed into him since he was a child; that if you needed any help at all, then ask a policeman, as they will always be there to help you? It just upsets me now too much to speak about. I state now what I have said before, NOT ALL POLICEMEN are bad or unfair, but sadly a large number are! I thought that these men and women joined the force to make a difference to making the world a better place for us all to live in. Sadly I was wrong, for there are in the police force, just as in any other job, a few bad apples who then spoil it for everyone else!

Steve and I already knew that the police lie, and like to throw their weight about from our OWN previous experiences, as we have learnt this to our cost in the past. The police had accused Steve of swearing on another occasion, yet Steve NEVER uses that sort of language to anyone at all. So this was yet another lie told by the police to another member of our family. Are lies so rife in the police force?

****

Back to Neil's arrest though, there was a lot of bad language in this police statement, and Neil **genuinely isn't like that**, and especially so when he was in good spirits according to Mum. He had money to spend, and was looking forward to seeing me, and this happened early in the morning, so it didn't sound to me that it was true, especially as I know Neil so well, and I can always tell if he is

357

lying. Indeed it was quite clear to me that Neil was telling the truth!

Neil wasn't like this with the police, especially so as he knew he'd always come off worst if he was; he wasn't that mentally ill, that he didn't know how bad *some* policemen were with him. They labelled Neil, and they picked on him and pushed him, disliked him, especially with what had happened before. No I don't believe the officer; I do however believe Neil.

David said, "There are cameras in Nelson Centre."

Neil quickly retorted, "Good, then we'll see who's telling the truth!"

Whether you believe the officer or Neil it doesn't matter, the fact is this all happened because Neil stepped out into the road. To say the officer could have handled it better is actually an understatement.

I am **far** from being anti-police, but I have seen first-hand how *some* of the police act, and I don't like it. They are not beyond fabrication and telling lies, to make what they do and say appear better. No, I don't trust them. They themselves are <u>not above the law,</u> but **they** will be believed **before you and me,** and there is no one more honest and law-abiding than I am. This all makes me so angry because I know my son.

****

We were having the 'normal' CPA meetings at the Resource Centre. Nothing was ever coming out of them; we were just going through the motions. Bob Gardner was there to oversee and make sure that no one said anything that they shouldn't, or offered Neil any help and support, as he is quick to speak out, if ever anyone did. They were always guarded, smug, and a complete waste of time. Every time we asked for anything at all, we got slammed down.

Neil really needed to be somewhere, doing something with his time. They made sure that they got in all their remarks first in order to deter anyone from doing anything for Neil.

They said how disruptive he was, he drinks, takes drugs, keep him away! He's got behavioural problems, he is *not mentally ill*, we don't have to do anything, he's not on 117 aftercare, but he's taking antipsychotic drugs, co-promazine and promazine and the rest, but he's **not** got mental illness?

If he <u>wasn't</u> mentally ill, he wouldn't be <u>there now</u>, and they wouldn't even be going through the motions would they?. Yet he

358

was there, but they were *not **doing** anything*, except <u>trying to look to some</u> as if they were <u>actually</u> doing something. Naturally though, they were always telling us that **they didn't need to**. Is that pathetic or what? It looks good on paper for them though, doesn't it?

"Oh! We are giving a lot of time to Neil and his Mum," they'd tell people as they were going *through the motions*.

Neil **should have had people going into his home to give him his medication**. He <u>should</u> have been able to go somewhere <u>during the day</u>, where they could make him a hot meal, and someone to take him shopping. Somebody **should** have been helping him to look after his money, and help him to budget, to make sure his bills were paid, and check that he had heating and lighting. There should have been someone to check that he was alright, and had food in his cupboards. He needed to talk to someone when he got agitated and stressed.

He'd ring me up often, sometimes twenty or more times a day for reassurance and guidance. Yes, he was needy, very needy indeed, but being in the community, where was the care in the community? There was little to call anything. One hour twice a week, and that's it; it's quite ludicrous.

Neil needed to be living in a <u>safe environment</u> with people who lived in the same place, on tap, so to speak, so that he could always go to someone, even if it was just to talk. It was all that he needed sometimes, for someone to simply <u>be there</u> for him.

Sadly we could not cope with Neil when he was mentally ill later in life. We often had to try to pick up the pieces when Neil was dumped from the hospital and left out to fend for himself, whether injured or without medicine. Financially we must have furnished several houses for him over the years, we had to borrow whatever we could. Obviously this drained us of our cash. We had to visit him wherever he was placed, whether it was hospital or in jail. Naturally all this took its toll, and the house we once owned outright, we have now had to get a mortgage.

Other people lived at home with me, my husband Steve, my Mum and my other son Ryan. Wherever Neil lived, trouble always followed. We could not cope with all the complaints, the broken windows and the steady stream of harassment from our neighbours. Neil himself would not live on so much cash a day; he wanted and in fact demanded ALL his money at once. It was impossible to teach him to budget, so he blew his money in one day every single time. He would argue that it was his cash (which it was) and then he'd make trouble until he got every single penny. Both Steve and I were very down and depressed all the time, as it was so unrelenting, trouble LIVED at our house, whether Neil was with us or not.

Steve and I got very little sleep, and we were both in pain on a daily basis ourselves. As we got older, naturally we had less energy, more pain, yet the problems continued. My Mum was blind and whilst she had been very pleased to come home at Steve's invitation, it was only then that she knew the real extent of what went on. Even though she was blind she picked up on the atmosphere and could kind of smell trouble from ten paces. Ryan had loads of friends, so they too would get roped into Neil's problems on occasions. I am wondering just how we ever managed to get through each day. It is so difficult to comprehend that we ever did, when I think about those days now.

****

Neil was severely depressed so we went to see our G.P, Dr Parsons. She prescribed him anti-depressants, which he very much needed as they did help him. I was horrified to learn that Dr Janger had been in contact with her to tell her **to stop** prescribing them to Neil.

On one of our regular visits to her, she told Neil that **she would continue prescribing the anti-depressants**, as in her opinion he needed them, but she was **being pressured** by Dr Janger. They didn't want Neil to be showing a need of anti-depressants, as they were constantly saying that Neil wasn't depressed, yet Neil was *always* depressed, not only was it within his illness to be so, but with the **lack of proper treatment** and the contempt he always felt was directed towards him by the Mental Health Team, especially Ahmet Ahmed the Manager of the Team, who by this time had rung the police to eject Neil from the Resource Centre many times.

Ahmet wouldn't even come down from his office to talk to Neil, even from behind a screen. If he felt so threatened, but no **it wasn't that**, he just didn't like Neil, so he had no time for him. The staff would wind Neil up then tell him to go. Neil just wanted to talk to his CPN.

"She's not in, but Ahmet is," he was told. But Ahmet wouldn't talk to Neil.

Ahmet said, "Neil threatened to damage my Mercedes which is parked outside."

Neil didn't damage his car. Ahmet was lucky, because after the meetings we had with him involved further input from him in Neil's future care; I would have felt all the same frustrations as Neil. Ahmet held a grudge against Neil, and boy did he use his powers to block help for Neil from ALL the other agencies.

****

Dr Janger and the Mental Health Team tried to facilitate a referral to Webb House, a therapeutic rehabilitative facility in Crewe. At that time I couldn't believe what they were doing, because this was definitely the *wrong place* to send him, and probably one of the reasons they didn't want him on anti-depressants, because to be admitted there Neil would have to be drug free, and by that I mean prescribed medication.

Neil needed antipsychotic drugs as well, so I really don't know what on earth they were playing at. In fact I found this totally ludicrous, as I felt they were pulling the wool over the eyes of the Centre too, which they surely were. The Centre *couldn't* have coped with Neil's mental illness at all, and Neil needed the co-promazine and the other medication, including the anti-depressants and the sleeping pills.

I know the Centre would be appalled even now, if they found out what they were trying to do, in putting Neil in their facility, as it would have been turned upside down. Everything at the Centre that they had previously managed to do for their *other* patients who they were helping, all their good efforts, would have been put at risk and possibly disrupted. If Neil had been sent to them, their past help with suicides, self-harm and suchlike in other patients would have been spoilt.

What therefore where the psychiatrists at Fernlea General thinking about? Obviously they only had a one track mind – to offload Neil to anyone and anywhere else, and to this ONE END they had no thought at all for the welfare of others only themselves. Is this EVEN a caring and respectful attitude, let alone doing their BEST for EVERY patient? How can they be ever called professionals?

361

Why they did not send Neil to another hospital for a second opinion is a mystery on one side, as this might have moved Neil on out of their hair. However it WOULD have also shown up given time, that what they were continually doing for Neil was the wrong treatment, and the wrong diagnosis from the start, and once this had been proven they could possibly have faced a Tribunal for their wrong doings. Other matters might also have come out of this, and Neil would have benefitted greatly, his illness could have been improved, correct drugs could have been given to him at the right strengths and times, and they certainly did not want this or anything good to happen for Neil. No they preferred him to have a lifetime of suffering. However they would have got Neil out of Fernlea General's hair possibly for good, so this never made any sense to us.

I bet the Centre weren't told about Neil at all, just as later when Neil went to 'Rehab', they weren't *told enough* about Neil's illness, or how he was affected by it, and they couldn't cope, because Neil needed intensive one to one care by people who were qualified in mental health, not just drugs.

These people ought to have at least been given the *correct* information. How totally *unprofessional* it was to do this to other professionals. What an arrogant disregard they held for them, and the other patients in their care. We were told that this was all that was on offer, and they were telling Neil how marvellous Webb House was. They had things to offer Neil with other therapies.

I have no doubt that it would have been a **crime** to put Neil there, as it would have failed miserably, and I know that would indeed have been the case. We went through the motions though, which meant that Neil was once more given high hopes, because they were telling him that it was the *perfect place* for him. It was disgusting!

****

Angela Moore CPN escorted Neil to what was described as an introductory meeting in Crewe on 29th September 2002. We had already taken Neil to Manchester for an interview. I felt like a liar and a cheat as I knew it was <u>completely wrong</u>. They were setting Neil up to fail, but they also had a total disregard for the professionals at Webb House, and their patients, to want to put this **disruptive force** into their hands. Luckily for Webb House they refused Neil, which was only because they thought that Neil wasn't ready to leave the people that he relied on. They had a very lucky escape. There was no way on this earth that Neil would have been able to comply with their wishes at any time. It was a farce, and showed me yet again to what lengths Dr Janger would go.

****

They sent Neil a letter saying how sorry they were that he wasn't able to go to Webb House at that time, but he could be re-referred in six month's time. Some group members said that they identified with Neil, and were impressed at his withdrawal from heroin. Yet Angela knew that Neil was **still using heroin**. They also said that they were impressed by Neil's ability to manage his behaviour. He was being thrown out of the Resource Centre all the time. They were well and truly stitched up. This was a deliberate wind-up for Neil, as they had **no intentions** of ever sending him there, as they knew that he was not AT ALL SUITABLE. They would NEVER send him to any place that had even the slightest chance of getting Neil better. They weren't prepared to help Neil, but nor were they prepared to ALLOW anyone else to help him either.

We were left to pick up the pieces. I *applaud* Webb House for denying Neil a place, because it would have been wrong, and this isn't very easy for me to say. As to Neil and ourselves it would have been better than nothing as it was nothing that we were left with. For Webb House, it was to save them a lot of grief. It made it all much harder though for Neil, as once more he was being rejected.

Ben had gone along with the idea as well. I hope it was in his case as in ours, that it was 'something' rather than the 'nothing' that we always received; but I still say that it was the *wrong place* for Neil and Neil was the *wrong person* to admit for them. We were grasping at straws, but his CPN Angela Moore and Dr Janger must have either told lies, or **omitted** to tell them enough information about Neil, for them to even contemplate a place for Neil at all. Why then if I say it **isn't true** did Foster Roberts (Chief Executive, Burnley NHS Trust) write these pieces in a letter to M.P. Philip Porter about Neil's behaviour?

****

The Leeds Road Resource Centre had experienced difficulties in providing a service to Neil over the last nine months or so. The most significant problems occurred on 31st July last year (this letter dated

363

4th February 2003) when Neil reported to staff that he had accessed the entry code for the Resource Centre and was intending using the information to his advantage. (What a drama queen you are Mr Foster, if that **was** the case, Neil **wouldn't** have told the staff he could get in. It was enough for Neil to let them know; and for them to have to remember another lot of digits). He was asked to leave the premises on this occasion and eventually did so. (This is when they called the police; the police asked Neil to leave, and Neil went with them very calmly, but Ahmet wanted Neil arrested, and the police **didn't** do that).

He said that Neil returned during the afternoon of the same day, intoxicated and making a number of threats to staff, and in particular to Ahmet Ahmed the team manager. He was again asked to leave the building. His responsible Medical Officer Dr Janger, along with the team manager reviewed the situation the following day, and decided that Neil should no longer attend the Resource Centre, and he was informed of that decision. Support continued through one to one sessions with Angela Moore *away* from the centre.

I remember this incident, as I wrote things down at the time, as I always felt I had to do because of the way they treated Neil who was asked to leave the Centre, and he came to tell me. He told me that he could have entered the premises to go and play pool with Aidy his friend if he wanted to, but he didn't. Instead he asked nicely if he could come in, he was refused and told to go away, as he always was. He'd **not** been drinking and he **wasn't** agitated, he just wanted the same chance as everyone else, including his mate Aidy who was a drug user; the opportunity to socialize and play pool.

****

Neil was down again because they had put him down, they knew he'd respond by drinking to ease his pain; they always knew this, and then they'd call the police on him, which they usually did to put him back into their hands. They decided then that he no longer should attend the centre; well they wouldn't let him anyway.

It sounds so pathetic, and it was. Angela saw him **once** for one hour over many weeks, but this went to **once every three months** at the CPA meetings which we attended. Neil needed **daily** support. He was always asking to attend the centre, but they'd say he could go; then he'd be wound up by them, turn to drink then play right into their hands, so that they could easily revoke his admission.

He couldn't stop himself. Neil did feel victimized, and both Ben and I felt the same, and also Neil's friend Aidy, because he was well aware of what was going on as he'd heard the comments made by the hospital staff. They didn't like Neil, so they tried to get him arrested whenever they could, in order to take the pressure *off them*, just so they could then say that Neil was just 'bad', and had criminal tendencies, **but was not sick!**

Yes, it wasn't anything to do with any 'clinical decisions' that they made, but UNLAWFUL **personal ones,** made especially by the team manager Ahmet Ahmed. I believe that he TRULY victimized Neil.

****

Foster Roberts the Chief Executive, also refers to other issues at the CPA meeting on the date in question, and information received from the Community Mental Health Team, as he says they provided clarification on the points I had made.

The Resource Centre's staff denied having said that, "They couldn't stand him."

Angela Moore, at the same meeting stated that the reception staff at the Resource Centre, were not as experienced as the clinical staff in dealing with Neil.

I have already mentioned this before, how horribly the staff treated Neil, and even when Neil asked to see Ahmet Ahmed or his CPN, he was told to go away. No one 'clinical' would see him, even if it was for a *genuine* reason that Neil needed to see someone.

I refer to the time when the reception staff didn't know me as Neil's Mother, and I would be standing behind him. Yes, they were extremely offhand with him, and sometimes downright nasty, and yes, they definitely talked about him within earshot of others, **including me,** so yes, Neil was telling the absolute truth.

****

They tried to get Ben to provide accommodation through *'Making Space'* as they had supported accommodation. He wouldn't do this, as he knew at the time just as we did, that Neil needed a lot more than they could provide, as he needed a lot of structure which Mental Health Services **should** have supplied to him.

Foster Roberts also talked about my request to refer Neil to Dr

Blake, and this was so upsetting to me. He said that although Dr Blake had some involvement with Neil in the past when he worked for Burnley Health Care Trust, he was now involved in the private sector at the Spinney Psychiatric Services in Atherton, which was a facility which accommodated patients with **severe mental health** problems which could not be handled by local services.

The Spinney is a high dependency unit which was EXACTLY WHAT NEIL NEEDED in our opinion, but in Dr Janger's opinion, would most definitely **not** be appropriate in Neil's case.

No explanation for Dr Janger's opinion was either given, or as far as he was concerned, ever deemed as being necessary.

If there was one comment by Dr Janger that would make me hate him more at this time than I already did, it was this comment. Dr Blake broke their rules in asking to take Neil in. He knew, just as did Mr Newscombe the Forensic Psychologist, that the Spinney was the *right place for Neil.*

They **lied** when they told us and everyone else that they had referred Neil to St. Andrews in Northampton, which is a residential placement, offering much the same as the Spinney. So now they are denying Neil this chance too, when they knew how much we wanted it, and our son needed it, and also how much we held Dr Blake in high esteem, yet they too refused, thus denying this honourable man any opportunity to help someone who TRULY needed so much help, when all Neil EVER wanted, was to TRY TO BE NORMAL.

The whole thing was way beyond belief. If a doctor cannot help a patient, why on earth can it not be ENSURED that they HAVE to pass that patient on to someone ELSE who MIGHT just be able to make a difference? Do the contents of the Hippocratic Oath that every single doctor SWEARS to, NOT mean a single thing to them?

I know that if Neil had BEEN ALLOWED to go to the Spinney, and was looked after by dear Dr Blake, he could have been saved. I know in my heart that this would be true. He would then have been given supported accommodation, regular treatment and a proper structured regime of medication. To say that these people who were involved with Neil could handle his needs, is an **insult** to even put down on paper. THEY COULDN'T, THEY WOULDN'T AND NO ONE COULD MAKE THEM DO ANYTHING THAT THEY DID

NOT WANT TO DO.

They would lie, or omit the truth to aid their case. They would give EXACTLY THE OPPOSITE TREATMENT, or NO TREATMENTS AT ALL, to help the patient react and show that he WAS NOT ILL, when in fact he was EXTREMELY ILL. I am NOT just talking about Neil here either.

Dr Janger you should not be a doctor and I am extremely ashamed that you STILL are. How many of your patients like Neil are you still being allowed to destroy?

GP's ARE SOON GOING TO BE CHECKED UPON REGULARLY BY LAW; this MUST be extended immediately to include all hospital doctors, and specialists. After all doesn't every single patient deserve the very best treatment, irrespective of whether or not their illness is physical or mental in origin?

At the **same** CPA meeting Neil begged for supported accommodation. Kings (a private sector care in the community agency) was talked about by Angela Moore.

She states, and it is written on the CPA Review Sheet, "That it was felt that Neil's presentation is **too complex** for an inexperienced worker to deal with, and different personnel leads to inconsistency, which is unhelpful to Neil."

What they mean is Neil my love, you are getting nothing as always, and you **have to make do,** because you can't have Kings as they are not qualified enough.

I say therefore, "THEN GIVE HIM SOMEONE THAT IS QUALIFIED ENOUGH."

They can't do that because, "He's *not mentally ill,* so we can't provide that."

So he got nothing, seeing Angela once a week was granted, yet it **never was EVEN once a week**, because she was ALWAYS on a course, or off sick, or doing someone else's job, or running late. **Surely if someone is away for whatever reason; then someone else takes their place, don't they?**

They did get Kings later, but that is another story. You will be amazed.

****

I wrote this letter in reply to Foster Roberts, Chief Executive. Dated 14th February 2003:-

Dear Mr Roberts,

I am writing this letter direct to you this time instead of getting your letter via Philip Porter M.P. although I will send a copy of this letter to Peter and Neil's two solicitors and his support worker.

I really find it so hard to understand the cruelty Neil receives from all concerned with him at Fernlea General Hospital, and how in the position you hold, for you to do the same, in the obvious 'backing' you give them.

It sounds so much better doesn't it the way you write down that this person, or that person is doing so much for Neil, when in reality it's <u>nothing at all!</u> So let's go through some of the points in your letter.

*Yes there has been a long history with Neil, because I've battled with him to get some help because the medical help has been lacking on all fronts. In fact the help he **should** have got years ago is still as bad now. We've moved on, as in fact Neil has caused injury to himself, and all of this could have been prevented. Yes, indeed Fernlea General has a lot more to answer for than ever before. As far as we are concerned, you have **not** provided a service, and the little you have given has nowhere near met Neil's needs.*

*Neil was grasping at straws when he was told of Webb House that this was it, as no more could be done other than this. Angela, Dr Janger, and everyone else knew that Neil and I were of the opinion that it **wouldn't** work. I more so of course, because being no fool and **not** mentally impaired, I could not be lulled into thinking that Webb House would work.*

*We kept Neil positive, but I'm glad he didn't get in, because you would again when Neil failed, have made him feel worthless, just as they did at his last CPA meeting in January. It's a real pity that minutes **weren't** taken, and Neil's solicitor wasn't allowed by Dr Janger to attend, but never mind, as I know what was said, and so does Neil's support worker, who like me **<u>was disgusted</u>** when Angela did say that Neil wasn't liked or welcomed at the Centre.*

She remarked directly to Neil, "You know they don't like you, so why do you want to go somewhere where you are not wanted?"

Neil continued to ask to go there, even after that terrible and quite unnecessary rebuff. It doesn't bother me how many times you go on about Neil being so distressed that he turned to drink, and even in drink, still begged to be allowed into the Resource Centre. With what I have just said about Angela's comment, this shows how he was treated by staff; he was victimized. This was nothing new though, as at Fernlea General they did the same too.

*The last occasion when the staff felt fit to ring the police, well I spoke to the officers involved personally, and they told me a **very different story**. Neil was already going out of the Resource Centre when the police arrived. He came back inside to speak to them. They say he was **not** abusive and he **was calm**. They had no problem with him at all.*

It does look good on paper though doesn't it? Neil is his own worst enemy, because he isn't that devious as to do things behind other people's backs. He does get upset and shouts his mouth off, but what else is there for him to do when he's so cruelly treated by you all?

However he states that he hasn't threatened staff. Professionals or at least 'so called' professionals should be above all this anyway, but they took it as personal, which in truth just shows me how inadequate they all are. I don't think ONE hour a week is classed as being caring from his CPN. One hour a week, when he wasn't looking after himself, and he'd become so very thin? All alone, when he's physically looking so very ill and he cries incessantly? When he didn't bother to wash, so became unkempt, instead of his usual careful and particular ways of dressing. It was obvious to so many others, but NOT to professionals, what does this tell you?

*Oh! Yes you can see all that in one hour, can't you? Oh! He **wasn't** depressed they said, and noticed this in one hour also. Yet outwardly he was showing so many of the symptoms of being totally and utterly depressed.*

*Dr Janger saw that in a half hour session months apart. Dr Janger did tell Neil's doctor to stop prescribing antidepressants to him. **This is a fact though**, as she rang me and told me so personally. She also told me that she would continue to prescribe them, **as she believed Neil to be depressed,** and she was right, so what does that tell you?*

Dr Janger is a disgrace, he told us all at that meeting that Neil was not depressed, and if Neil continued to receive antidepressants

369

he would finish being his Consultant.

To that Neil said, "Good."

*I told Neil's doctor, and even knowing that Dr Janger would refuse to be Neil's Consultant, she **still prescribed the antidepressants.***

*By the way, Neil's felt much better on them. So this was yet another mistake made by Dr Janger. We personally felt that Dr Janger would do anything he could to STOP Neil from getting better, as that's the way he always seemed to work, never **for** Neil, always **against** him. What for? Just to prove that he was right and we were wrong? What about the oath he swore to help ALL of his patients.*

****

*Neil and I went to see the drug team in Burnley and we were told that Neil didn't have a drug problem (although Dr Janger and everyone else there would like to think so). He was **self medicating**, but a member of staff at the Resource Centre told Neil to stay on heroin. **Do you really think this was helpful?***

*At the last meeting we were told that Neil would **not** be allowed into the Resource Centre at all, and yet you said in your letter that it was decided he could go for an extra hour. Which of these is REALLY true? I was confused myself, so no wonder Neil didn't understand their ever changing rules.*

*Neil needs help **every day**, he needs to see **someone every day**, he needs help with shopping and money matters. He needs help with taking his medication as his forgetfulness has caused him to suffer terribly. He needs assurance every day. His DEPRESSION needs constant monitoring. He needs help to avoid the pressure of people forcing drugs on him. Neil drinks to blot out his life, the pain he is suffering and the abuse he's received. In a lot of aspects the very people who **should** be helping him, have made him to turn to the bottle for solace, and then they **dare t**o sit in judgement.*

Angela Moore was on holiday, and Neil NEVER did get even one hour a week during those weeks. I rang the support worker when Neil was severely depressed, and he told me to ring the Resource Centre, as surely someone would 'cover' for Angela and go and see Neil, but despite them knowing about it, no one ever did.

Neil's own doctor was worried because he couldn't gain entry, so he contacted me, but no one cared about that at the Resource Centre.

370

The two hour group session you mention, **wasn't available** to Neil, because it clashed with his appointments for Physiotherapy, so he cancelled his much needed Physio, but then he was banned from the centre anyway. Neil had the decision made for him months ago, that he'd <u>never be allowed</u> in the Resource Centre, although it was stated on many occasions to his solicitor that it was under review. His support worker was told he wouldn't be allowed back in, so these were lies too.

I know what Bob Gardner meant, and so does he. We have shouldered every aspect of Neil's needs, because the hospital **denied** him services. Neil's needs are great, and in that case they have let us down too. We have supported Neil to the degree it has made us ill, and that is unforgivable.

Dr Leister turned his back on Neil and put him into police hands, so Neil would suffer the consequences of the doctor's actions for that. How on earth can we expect any more from Dr Janger, we do not trust him, and this fact has been proven to be correct on many occasions.

Of course we think back to the truly good doctor Neil saw years ago, whom we admire and trust, because he **proved** his worth to us. It's a pity you lost such a wonderful doctor, and indeed man, for Neil and replaced him with so little. Yes, if Dr Blake had Neil in his hands a year ago, we would not be here now. Even mental disorder is treated in his clinic, and we have 'experts' who say it would have been the **right** place for Neil.

So what is it, pride, prejudice why you won't let him see Dr Blake, although Neil could have been helped and Dr Blake was willing to do so? You all left my son deeply depressed, knowing you would never help him, or give him the medical care and support he should have. I wouldn't treat a dog the way you have treated Neil. **Were you afraid that you would be <u>proved wrong</u>, or did you just hate Neil so much for being so needy?**

So Neil has run away from the <u>inadequate care</u> you supplied, as you say that ONLY ONE hour a week to you is adequate! You are all to blame. Anyone would think that because Dr Leister made such a **grave mistake**, that you would do everything in your power to help Neil now, but you didn't do that did you, instead you all continued to turn your backs.

371

*There is no sense in it all. Is it right to ask a patient to continue to see a doctor who he feels is mistreating him, a man whom he <u>doesn't trust,</u> who makes mistakes that cause him further pain and anguish, a doctor who **won't refer him** to another doctor who he knows could help him? The very thought that he thinks this way, makes you halfway there. Did Dr Blake leave under such a cloud that you refuse him a patient?*

Like many doctors have said to me, "You'd think Fernlea General would be glad to see the back of Neil."

Apparently not though, you still want to dig the knife in deeper. C'est la vie!

S. Green.

CHAPTER TWENTY-FIVE
General Medical Council

On the 2nd April 2003, I made a formal complaint to the G.M.C. At the top of the form to fill in it says. 'General Medical Council. Protecting patients, guiding doctors.'

The form asks me for my details:
The full name of each doctor that you are complaining about.
I write, Dr Mark Leister, Clinical Director/Consultant Psychiatrist .
Dr Janger, Consultant Psychiatrist.

The address each doctor works at:
Fernlea General Hospital.

Details of your Complaint:
We had a wonderful doctor at Fernlea General called Dr Blake whom Neil our son, saw early in 2000. He was Neil's Consultant for too short a time, but he was a superb doctor and human being, As a family we all had great respect for him, as he was wonderful with Neil.

He knew little about A.D.H.D. but he contacted Neil's past doctors and read much about this condition, and also contacted the Support Group and other A.D.H.D. Specialists. We couldn't fault him! Then he left Fernlea General to start his own Private Clinic.

We were left in 'limbo', as Neil wasn't referred to anyone else. A Dr Kumar saw Neil at Fernlea when he was admitted to the hospital when he went chaotic. This doctor took Neil off his Ritalin in one single swoop. Neil was <u>uncontrollable</u> after that, and I had to take him out of the hospital.

I was told you **should NEVER stop this medication like that.** They knew nothing! Neil was confused and at risk. I couldn't leave him like that. We tried to control Neil's illness. We coped up to tea-time, but when he had his last medication he rebounded and went chaotic. We needed specialist help.

I found out about Daniel Pounder, a support worker for '*Making Space*'. We'd also found out about the mental illnesses on my husband's side of the family, schizophrenia (two Uncles), manic depression (Granddad), psychosis and two suicides by other family members. Neil had begun to talk to himself, he thought that people were after him, and he heard voices. He got stressed out and became psychotic.

Daniel Pounder contacted Dr Leister. We had high hopes, but they were very short-lived.

This was what followed:-

28.03.01.   Neil admitted to Fernlea General by Dr Leister, Neil anxious and depressed.

02.04.01.   Neil talks to Donna Castle Calder (Social Worker) regarding his feelings of suicide.

O3.04.01.   Donna organizes Section 2, but Neil left the ward and ended up on a motorway bridge. (Police called). In the papers as a suicide attempt.

07.04.01.   Neil left hospital again, chased by police, attempted suicide again by jumping in river. More police involvement.

30.04.01   At last, Section 3 Dr Kay. We were tormented throughout because the doctors found Neil difficult. They couldn't control him, taking him off his Ritalin which helped his behaviour. He could kick the door to get out while on Section. They didn't like him or us. I knew about A.D.H.D. I even wrote about it for them, giving pages of what I knew to Dr Leister and the Social Workers and other people involved in Neil's care, as I thought this would serve to help our son.

Dr Leister insisted on being in charge, but he **wouldn't** refer Neil to an A.D.H.D. Specialist. He organized Neil to go back on his Ritalin

374

only **after** he deteriorated so badly that he was bouncing off the walls. We were told by him that A.D.H.D. doesn't carry on into adulthood, as it's only a child's illness.

If this is really true, "Tell me please then at what age is the cut off point?"

Once more they knew nothing. Dr Leister put Neil on a very **low** dose of Ritalin which didn't even touch him. Our son is 6ft 4ins, and built like a body builder. They gave it to him when they *felt* like it, going hours over the times he *should* have been given his next dose. They also gave it to him at 10:00pm or 10:30pm at night which is absolutely the **wrong** thing to do as it is a stimulant.

We all tried to talk to Dr Leister but he wouldn't listen, as he thought he knew it all. After all he is GOD, isn't he? Dr Leister saw his opportunity to get rid of Neil, and had him sent to prison for kicking a wardrobe door off its hinges. It was not even damaged either, and he was **never** convicted of the so-called offence.

Neil's Section was still in place. The man (I can't bring myself to call him a doctor) ruthlessly refused Neil treatment that he should have got under Section, to be kept safe. Instead he *refused* to take him back on the ward and had him arrested.

Dr Leister **lied** to the police and told them Neil had been *discharged* off his Section and *discharged from the Hospital.* He **hadn't** done either one of these at the time he said he had done so.

The police tried really hard to get Neil back into hospital. They thought it was *disgusting* and couldn't believe it. They wrote notes saying the same on the charge sheet. They rang Dr Leister. He **lied** through his teeth. They were appalled, and we were also appalled.

Neil went to Lancaster Farms Young Offenders for nearly three months, as there was just no other alternative available to him. In there they had to keep him on the block, because they couldn't cope with him; he was hearing voices; they put him on Co-Promazine. He was anxious, agitated and severely disturbed. **He hung himself and technically DIED.** They had to resuscitate him, saying that it was a **serious attempt on his life**.

They got Dr McKewen a Forensic Psychiatrist from The Guild, Preston. He told the prison staff that Neil **should be** in a hospital, and Fernlea General **were responsible** for him, so he had to go back there.

Do you honestly believe that we wanted Neil to go back there after what they had done to him? Did we really want us and Neil to be constantly told that <u>there was nothing wrong with him</u>? **Don't only ill or severely depressed people try to kill themselves?**

He's got behavioural problems they told us, when we knew that he was very seriously mentally ill. Yet they insisted, no, he's not suffering from any mental-disorder or mental illness.

The police have witnessed him, and so have two support workers, besides my husband and me and his solicitor also.

22.09.01   Back at Fernlea, but they wouldn't Section Neil, even though he'd just tried to kill himself in prison. Many, many suicide attempts later, they did section Neil and moved him to Chorley Hospital I.C.U.

The first time Dr Leister said he'd referred Neil to St. Andrews in Northampton, was when Fred Clough and C.H.C. got involved. I rang them to be told he **hadn't** referred Neil. So there were no surprises there then.

All throughout this terrible mess we've had three solicitors involved, Fred Clough, two Support Workers, Philip Porter M.P. and Gilbert Price M.P.

What I've learnt is letters go back and forth, but STILL nothing happens to help Neil. There's never been 117 Aftercare, although Neil's been on numerous Sections. Social Services would <u>never get involved,</u> because the 'doctors' at Fernlea insist Neil **has no mental illness.**

Back at Chorley. Neil's sent there just to be held. They are referring him to St. Andrews. **This never materialized**. They didn't even come to assess him. Dr Janger knew in December it *wasn't* going to be. They didn't tell us, and Neil got fed up of waiting and appealed against his Section.

He was never treated by Dr Chaucer at Chorley, he just told him that he was looking after him for Fernlea. I wrote many letters to try to get Neil kept at Chorley until the Tribunal.

Neil's solicitor had a psychologist's report done, we weren't happy about it, we'd lost all faith. Neil told us it was a foregone conclusion that he was getting off his Section. He blagged Janice Short the psychiatrist whom he saw for such a brief time. They gave him drugs to calm him and <u>told him</u> what to say. It was so easy he said.

He couldn't do the same though to Brian Newscombe the Forensic Psychologist, as Neil's own Solicitor brought *him* in.

He came at different times, spending hours with Neil; they didn't know he was coming, so they couldn't prepare Neil. He couldn't 'blag' him.

To my utter amazement, because I truly **didn't trust him** to come up with the goods after such a shameful bunch of inadequate doctors, *he did.* He worked correctly to a tee. It's the most honest opinion by anyone, and tells the whole shocking truth.

However it was **so absolutely damning**, that Neil's solicitor wasn't going to use it at the Tribunal, as Neil would not have got off his Section. As it turned out his solicitor said it was the *easiest* Tribunal he'd been to, and the *quickest.*

They asked Dr Janger if he could see any reason to keep Neil in Hospital, he said "No."

He asked the same of Dr Chaucer, he said "No."

So that was that. Neil was told that they'd kept him **falsely** on a Secure Ward and he could sue them. He later went back to the same solicitor who got him off his Section to get him back <u>into</u> Hospital.

11.02.02.   I could understand Neil to a degree. They weren't doing anything for him. What a mess! His solicitor through my tears told me that he was assured that he'd go back to Fernlea General straightaway, and he wouldn't be allowed out of hospital until they'd sorted out 117 Aftercare, and somewhere for him to go.

I laughed, as I knew that he'd be thrown out. I was right. Neil misguided as he was, had played right into their hands.

They discharged him straightaway into a B & B with no 117 Aftercare. He was left to his own devices. He could ring Donna, the Social Worker.

He has the mind of a twelve year old. He was put into a dive of a place with lots of men suffering from various things, including mental illness, alcoholism, and drug addicts.

02.04.02.   Neil is admitted to Fernlea General Hospital pacing, anxious, depressed, threatening suicide. This is laughable, as it's Neil who we are talking about here. We were always told that if Neil presented himself as **needing** treatment to Casualty, then he'd get it. He never did, even when the police took him, as soon as they knew it was Neil he was shown the door. The police even tried to get him arrested *out of the area,* in order to give him a better chance at another hospital.

Even <u>they</u> knew that this was wrong!

03.04.02.   Neil is discharged. What's new?

28.05.02.   R.T.A. Neil took a car from someone at the B & B who'd already stolen it. He was in a room with needles all over the place. **He didn't want to live**. He had purposely driven the car at speed into a lamppost hoping to kill himself. He told the paramedics the same. Firemen cut him out of the car. He had <u>severe leg and head injuries</u>.

The owner of the B & B had all of Neil's belongings dumped at his bedside. She didn't want him back at the B & B.

They put him on a surgical ward, as mental health WOULDN'T get involved. They discharged him with a full length pot on his leg just over one week later.

We had told Dr Janger that we had no faith in him, and we were sick and tired of asking for a referral to **a Specialist in A.D.H.D.** at least. **It always fell "Upon Deaf Ears."**

He is indeed a sad excuse for a doctor. In his hands Neil has made several attempts on his life, made so many self harm marks upon himself that it truly sickens and disgusts anyone who sees them. Except those members of staff at Fernlea General of course.

Dr Janger has treated Neil with contempt and not treated his illness at all. They just throw pills at Neil when <u>he doesn't know</u> what he is doing.

My G.P. made several attempts at getting a referral for Neil; she contacted Preston Guild's Dr Plackett. He wouldn't see Neil, telling her (Dr Parsons) that it had to be done through the hospital psychiatrist.

So what do we do, because Dr Janger wouldn't do it, and neither would any other psychiatrist at Fernlea General Hospital?

I rang Dr Plackett's secretary, and I was told the same. My G.P. then rang Dr Blake, who stated the same, but he went one step further for us, as he always told me Neil had mental disorder that was treatable, if not the mental illness as he might now have, because he had not seen Neil for a few years.

(I could never understand the difference between mental illness and mental disorder, some doctors refer to one, some to the other, as some say it's one and the same, and that it means the *same thing.*

I tended to look at it this way; Neil when young had a diagnosed A.D.H.D. a form of which was very acute. I would say that was mental disorder, and then when he became delusional, psychotic, depressed and schizophrenic, I would say that was mental illness. I'd always said to my doctor, that Neil was mentally ill.

A mother knows, especially a mother who was as tuned in to their child as I was. I wrote in a visitor's book in a church in July 2006 that I will never be loved the same again. The loss of my son is just so extreme.

379

Dr Blake contacted Fernlea General Hospital and he told Bob Gardner that he would take Neil on as a patient at the Spinney. Bob Gardner refused Neil this lifeline. Dr Newscombe told me that when he was making the report on Neil, that all the while he was thinking that The Spinney, Dr Blake's Private Clinic would help Neil. He told me this, not even knowing how much we regarded Dr Blake, and yes it **could** have been done, but again *they refused treatment* to Neil, and wouldn't let any other doctor have any input in Neil's care. WHY?

I know this though, Neil has a **right** to be treated for his illness, and you would have thought that the hospital would have an **obligation,** wouldn't you. WRONG!

He has a right to a **second opinion.** WRONG! He was refused BOTH by the incompetent doctors at Fernlea General. I do truly believe that these doctors should have been 'struck off' for the inhumane way Neil was treated by them, or should I say **mistreated.**

The doctors are a law unto themselves. They were playing GOD with peoples' lives. The effect it had on my own health was phenomenal, having to deal with all these inadequate people but it had to be done, because if I didn't try to take them on, to fight for Neil, then I think that our son would have died sooner, and dear readers that is so hard to write down, but as always I tell the truth.

It's a good job we didn't hold our breath when we asked for a crumb of care and decency. I know as many do, NOT to have a nervous breakdown, because all there is for people in my area is Fernlea General, and the Mental Health there is chronic.

In Dr Leister's OWN words, "I know the staff are rubbish, but it's all we've got." **If that was his honest opinion, how bad is that!**

"God help us," I thought then, and STILL think the same now.

Doctors at Fernlea General tried to get Neil transferred to Calderstones Hospital in Whalley. In order to do that they said Neil had 'Learning Difficulties'. When I rang Joe Calder who is in charge of sorting out the referrals and reports, with whom a meeting had to be arranged with in order to progress, told me that Neil was **TOO Mentally ill for them to take, as he had transient psychosis** and he **should be in hospital** as he was **depressed** and he had **psychopathic disorder.** He told me that Fernlea General was obligated to find Neil a hospital somewhere in the country. But that's NOT what they thought at Fernlea General, Joe.

****

Where are we now?

Neil is residing with a girl in Chorley. A girl he met in Chorley Hospital, she too has mental health problems. Neil went there after again being refused a second opinion, and the help he would have found with Dr Blake. He went to get away from Dr Janger and the man into everything, Bob Gardner. He managed to find a very good G.P. practice in Chorley. After his new G.P. made an 'urgent' referral to Chorley Hospital Psychiatric Department, Dr Chaucer refused to see Neil after the appointment had been made for him, on the <u>very day of the appointment</u>, he said that Neil had NO Mental Illness.

Neil needs help and support NOW! His G.P. tells me she isn't qualified to give out co-promazine and other drugs that he is on. He needs a mood stabilizer which she can't prescribe. He is unstable, and volatile. He is at extreme risk, so too is his friend and her five year old son. He's not on the correct medication, and his severe A.D.H.D. remains untreated.

He's depressed. Before Neil went to Chorley his G.P. put him on antidepressants, although Dr Janger said he *wasn't depressed,* with him being qualified enough to say this, after seeing Neil for just one half-hour every six months or so, and going off a CPN who saw him for half an hour once a week **if** Neil was very lucky.

They refused him entry to the Resource Centre saying he wasn't liked, and asked should he go somewhere where he wasn't wanted? He became unkempt, cried all the time, and could never remember to take his medication on time, which in turn made him become deeply depressed. His G.P. RIGHTLY gave him antidepressants. Dr Janger said that if she continued to prescribe that, he wouldn't see Neil again.

He tried to get the G.P. to stop, but she wouldn't, and she continued to prescribe. Dr Janger then made an **even bigger mistake,** when he said that he didn't think Neil had A.D.H.D. either. That man is a joke; it managed to turn me against him even more, if that was possible. I felt like hitting him.

After that meeting when his **CPN** told Neil to **continue taking heroin,** Neil was the first one to walk out, followed by us. They tried to say that Neil's problems were the result of 'drink' then 'drugs', but in reality it was neither. **His illness was <u>inevitable</u> because it was in the family.**

Neil used drink then drugs only to self medicate. We went to see the Drug Team at Burnley. They said categorically that Neil **didn't** have a drug problem, he was self medicating. <u>It was down to inept medical attention.</u>

They even tried to get **her** to say differently, and say that Neil **did have** a drug problem. However Caroline knew her stuff, she'd been in the job for a long time, and she couldn't be leaned on. She also resented them for trying to persuade her to **tell lies**, to make them <u>look as if **they** were telling the truth</u> about him. They would resort to any means to turn people against Neil. Most people could see through them, especially when we showed that we were loyal to Neil and kept up a united front. However those at Fernlea just simply followed their leaders and aided and abetted them in their lies and wrong doings.

****

Neil went missing for days, then turned up at Chorley. Now Dr Chaucer says he would stand by Fernlea General. (He had no option to continue to be this way, as it was because of him and his hospital that Neil was suffering further, because Neil was on a Section on his ward when he had agreed with Dr Janger that Neil had **no mental illness,** and therefore should be released from his Section to try and further kill himself, and for him to be introduced to drugs when Fernlea kicked him out of hospital straightaway into the B & B. Yes Dr Chaucer, we know what a wonderful doctor you are **<u>NOT</u>**. They stick together, thick as thieves, and it's no wonder <u>I will never trust a doctor again.</u>

They ignored Dr Newscombe's report which came after Janice Short's, whom they had Neil see to further 'back' them up. Neil always said it was easy to 'blag' her. Yes, they all stick together.

Dr Blake states Neil has mental illness in the letter I am sending you a copy of. That was years ago, believe me he would be sickened to see how much Neil has deteriorated now. Dr Newscombe's report came after Janice Short's but that was ALSO ignored. They all have a copy of that.

There's been a lot of solicitor input, C.H.C. input, comments and statements from his support worker, who backs us all the way. Input from TWO M.P.'s. I wouldn't treat a dog the way that Fernlea General has treated my son. The police and the courts believed **me** and not them; they tried to sway them, but the evidence was too vast. I will continue to fight. *One in four of us is supposed to suffer from mental illness at some time in our lives, according to the latest statistics.*

They tried to put Neil in police hands three more times but they refused, turning on the hospital. They lied, and the police found them out time after time. The police put Neil on **wrongful arrest,** and they made sure that they wouldn't do it again.

I am sorry dear readers for repeating 'stuff' I've already written about, but I am writing down what I wrote to the G.M.C. to give a truthful and accurate account, and to also ask the question. Why? Why didn't the G.M.C. do what they say on the front of the form, remember? **Protecting patients, guiding doctors.**

Back to the complaint form:

Do you have any documents (for example, letters or medical records) which might back up your complaint? If you do, please send us copies and list them below. If you ask us to, we will return all original documents after taking copies.

1.   Letters from Dr Leister to my G.P. Dr Spercer.
       Daniel Pounder (*Making Space* Support Worker)
       Paul James, solicitor, Farnworths.

2.   Letters from Community Health Council.
       Letter from Philip Porter M.P.
       Many newspaper stories, sending you ONE only.

3.   Numerous diaries of Neil's stay in hospital.
       I have many, many, many more letters, two files full of correspondence.
       Psychological report Brian Newscombe.

Are there any other people who saw and heard the things you are complaining about? If so, please give their names below, and how they were involved in the events.

Police, including police doctors (Throughout)
David Woodman, Criminal Lawyer (Throughout)
Daniel Pounder (Retired) passed on to Ben Law, who was by my side throughout it all. He made notes, sent letters, had copies of my letters.
Fred Clough, made appointments and came with us to meetings at the hospital.
Community Health Council.
Telegraph Newspaper, wrote about Dr Leister and the hospital's lack of care.

Would these people be prepared to make written statements to us.
Yes.

We try to deal with most complaints through correspondence but, if it becomes necessary, are you prepared to be a witness at a public enquiry into your complaint.
Yes.

Have you complained to any other organization about this matter (For example, an NHS Health Authority or Board, a Hospital Trust, or the general practice where the doctor works)?

If 'No' go to question 18   Yes

If 'Yes' please say which organization you have complained to.

Give us brief details of what happened to your complaint, and send us copies of any letters between you and that organization.

Community Health Council are *currently* chasing up a complaint letter with many of the correspondence I've sent to you, that I sent to Karen Wilson, Director of Clinical Services, New Mental Health Trust. Recorded Delivery in June last year, she rung me in the evening, asked for more information. I rang her Secretary, Sandra, she says she received everything, but she completely **ignored** it and me.

I sign the form then send to:

Fitness to Practice Directorate General Medical Council
178, Great Portland Street
London
W1N 6JE

I wrote this above mentioned letter to Karen Wilson, Director of Clinical Services, Sceptre Point, Sceptre Way, Walton Summit, Bamber Bridge, Preston, Lancs. The letter is dated 11th April 2003. She eventually replied to this letter ONE YEAR LATER. Yes, one whole YEAR LATER you read that right.

Dear Karen,

I have today received your letter skirting over the issues as usual. I am truly incensed by your lack of understanding, and that of the doctors and care staff associated with Fernlea General. I have for two years + done nothing but complain of the lack of care for Neil. Shall we again go through it all, as I am going to copy this letter to Ben Law (Support Worker Making Space) Philip Porter M.P. C.H.C. and the G.M.C. to whom I have made yet a further complaint.

*Neil has **not been treated** for having any mental illness which he has, or for at least the mental disorder that is, and was treatable under Section. We have been tormented throughout Neil's association with Fernlea General, that Neil suffers from **no** mental illness, therefore they will not treat him as such, or detain him under Section to obtain treatment. To gain Social Services back-up, 117 Aftercare. Neil was put into custody by your Dr Leister while under Section, when he should have been receiving treatment from a hospital. Dr Leister lied to the Police putting Neil in **extreme danger** where **he hung himself, and very nearly died**.*

*He suffered seven more times of coming back to court to be sent back to prison. It was inhumane. We suffered the anguish of visiting our desperately ill son in prison, knowing he was there because your doctors didn't, or wouldn't, or couldn't give him the treatment he has a **right to receive**.*

385

His A.D.H.D. (Severe) remained untreated. Dr Leister or Dr Janger would not seek the Specialist help Neil needed for this illness. Therefore they mistreated it by giving him Ritalin at the wrong doses, wrong time; it being given at night, which is completely the wrong thing to do.

*Neil was **refused treatment** when he was brought to the hospital by the police. He was sent away **with a needle still in his arm** when staff members were told to get rid of him. He made <u>countless suicide attempts</u> and a very serious one last year, when he hit a lamppost at over 100mph trying to kill himself, telling the paramedics, then the doctors at Fernlea General, that **he didn't want to live,** YET STILL your mental health doctors <u>wouldn't</u> get involved. They kept him on a Surgical Ward then released him with full pot leg into a house to care for himself. It is absolutely inhumane.*

*Don't tell me he's had CPN input at an hour, sometimes half an hour a week, because more often than not he's had **none** at all, as his CPN was on holiday, sick or somewhere else, so he got **no one** at all. Don't tell me that trying to refer him to Webb House was the **right** thing to do, when we all know it <u>wouldn't</u> have worked because of his mental illness. Don't tell me that all the rows we had at the meetings with Dr Janger and Bob Gardner did Neil **any good.** Don't tell me their constant resentment of him **helped** Neil.*

*I have never been at ease with anything that was said to have been done for Neil, because **<u>nothing</u>** has been done for Neil. We are still the same. Neil was mistreated on the ward, not given treatment for a deep self harm incident, as they said that it was superficial, but in fact it had 'needed stitches', according to the Casualty doctor when he was brought in by his Support Worker, having been found in a pool of blood by the B & B owner. Yet despite this he was sent back to them after midnight, after he had been discharged from the hospital **<u>after trying to hang himself.</u>***

*In fact a member of staff had been sent home because she was so traumatized when she saw him. Yet the police had been told there was nothing wrong with Neil. (He had behavioural problems) This was all well documented by the police as was anything to do with Neil, because they knew it was **wrong** what Fernlea General were doing.*

Ben Law has documented nearly as much as we have, and cannot believe the inhumane treatment of Neil. Your doctors lie through their teeth, and we have the evidence to support this. Don't send me stupid letters saying you didn't know I was complaining; how dare you? Don't say John Duggan was told to take care of things when he's the same as the rest, and doesn't give a 'toss'. I am sick and tired of repeating myself. I am sick and tired of these stupid letters that are being sent to solicitors and M.P's, saying we the NHS Trust have given a lot of time and effort to this family. It's rubbish, as talking to you lot is like talking to a brick wall.

Neil will **never be treated appropriately** or fairly by Fernlea General Hospital. We have asked throughout to be referred to Dr Blake, somewhat sickening when he used to be at Fernlea General and treated Neil, that you won't allow him to do the same now. He has actually said he'd take Neil on, and try to address what Fernlea General's done to him. As I can tell you they've done a lot more harm than good, and there's a lot more to do now, as that was two years ago.

You should have had an internal investigation into Dr Leister's management of Neil, and the fact he sent Neil to prison when he was under Section. While a lot has been done in different areas at Fernlea General, the mental health department is still chronically bad. I think all your doctors need to go, as well as the staff on the wards. You cannot undo what you've done as a hospital to Neil, but you are still causing damage now to others.

"Neil is doing fine," you say. How the heck can he ever be fine? Listen to yourself. Neil has **not** received treatment for his A.D.H.D. or the mental illnesses he now suffers from. Dr Chaucer has <u>refused</u> to see Neil, because he's got Dr Leister's, and Dr Janger's recommendations in front of him, that he is **not** suffering from any mental illness or disorder. What's A.D.H.D. then?

Oh yes! It stops in childhood, and now Dr Janger says he doesn't think he's suffering from that either. Dr Janger probably still thinks the world is flat too. So Neil has no psychiatrist, he's depressed. His moods are all over the place. He's breaking under the strain of a mentally ill partner and her hyperactive five year-old. The balloon will go up soon. It always does. Now you've made me skirt over the issues of Neil's **lack** of medical care. He won't go away Karen, no matter how hard everyone at Fernlea General wants him to. **<u>Is this</u>**

387

in your opinion a complaint?

*Dr Leister should be struck off as he's no doctor. A doctor tries to do **the best they can for their patient** to get the medical care they need. He has left Neil to rot. He's no doctor. Dr Janger is as inept and uncaring of the treatment of Neil, but does the fact he's frightened of losing his job if he doesn't do as he is told by Dr Leister or the Trust make him as bad? Yes, I think so. Should the cruel staff on the wards be still working in mental health? NO I don't think so. I cannot find the words to describe my feelings about Bob Gardner, John Duggan, so it is best to leave that for now.*

*Is this letter strong enough for you Karen? **Don't bother!** I expect what I've always got from Fernlea General. NOTHING!*

S. Green

****

Neil went missing for days before I found out he was with this girl he'd met in Chorley Hospital. We weren't happy at all that he had moved into her home. It was good of her to think of him in a time of need, because it was Neil who was so depressed and being pestered all the time from people selling drugs; he knew the only way to deal with it in his vulnerable state was to run away.

He wasn't fit to go to this girl though; she was older than him and more worldly wise, and was quite manipulative. I couldn't understand what she saw in Neil, and I told her so, but that was before I saw her fondling his private parts, while she was sat down on a chair in my living room, and he was standing beside her.

I told Neil that I didn't like her after that. I knew exactly what she saw in Neil too when she told me that she'd not known what it was like to have a baby.

"Her child," she said, "was brought up by her devoted husband, and she hadn't known what it was like to care for a baby."

I knew she'd get pregnant by Neil. It's exactly what she wanted. It sickens me to know that's all she saw in Neil.

Neil was a pathetic, chaotic wreck. Although she had been on a mental health ward herself she was nothing like Neil. He would never hold down a job like her, marry, or run a home. She was lucky! I told her to end it with Neil, as he wasn't able to form a realistic relationship.

She allowed him to drive her car all the time, knowing that Neil

388

had no license. I can remember going to her house and seeing Neil driving her car to her Grandma's, which was not far away, just to park it in her drive. He was involved in an accident with another car, and her car got dented. She lied to her Dad about how the damage was caused, but Neil told us the truth.

Neil was drinking far too much with her, and I told her off about that too, but she wouldn't stop doing these things. I was worrying what if her son was involved in an accident when Neil was driving, what would happen then? Her father didn't want her involved with Neil. Snap, we didn't want Neil with her either, but she was the grown up. She needed Neil to give her sex and a baby; she allowed him to drive her car. They were BOTH so wrong.

Neil got into a confrontation with her dad, and while struggling with a crate, her dad ended up with a tiny gash above his eye. If Neil had wanted to hurt him, he'd have done more than that. Neil was in turmoil, not taking his medication, drinking, trying to cope with someone with problems and a child. Something had to give.

Her dad was following Neil, trying to get him to leave his daughter alone. Neil didn't understand. He couldn't cope with what she thought he could. The feelings Neil was dealing with, the maliciousness of her father and his confrontations were all too much for Neil to handle.

Neil was seriously mentally ill, and he was put at risk by having his illness go unrecognized and untreated. Because of this, so was everyone around Neil, including family or girlfriends. He wouldn't have meant to hurt her dad; he was like a rabbit caught in the headlights, he just wouldn't have known what to do. He didn't plan it. He was in such a mess.

I told this girl to leave him alone. He came home, but she kept ringing him and then she came to pick him up. We couldn't do anything to stop them; as they were really **both as bad** as one another. We knew there would be trouble; she didn't get on with her Dad, and I think this was yet another reason why she got off on her Dad not liking Neil. There was no way that Neil could cope with a girl like that, he was stupid, naïve and childish.

Mental Health found Neil a B & B at this time. Amazingly for someone with a *drink problem*, it was in a Public House in Preston not far away from where this girl lived.

The first time Mental Health found him a B & B they put him in with alcoholics and drug addicts, and now with a drink problem, he's placed in a Public House. **What a ridiculous state of affairs!** There was no chance. Now it was a downward spiral.

The one good thing about Neil being in Leyland was meeting the lovely Stella Barmforth, Support Worker for *Making Space*. I liked her straightaway, and boy did she know her stuff. She was wonderful with Neil and she really understood him. Ben had looked after Neil here while being a go-between with Neil and the hospital. He'd heard views on Neil by psychiatrists and CPN's, but Stella had just viewed Neil, and it was a case of her getting to know him first, and we liked what she had observed, as well as what she did to help Neil, and how quickly she grasped his illness. She knew he had mental illness and we talked about schizophrenia.

Stella wrote this letter to try and get Neil more suitable accommodation. Dated 15th April 2003 to Sandra Rowan.

Dear Sandra,

I am writing a letter on behalf of Neil Green who became homeless from his previous address on 14th April 2003.

I have supported Neil for the past few months in my capacity as Family Support Worker for Making Space, but I knew him prior to this when he was an in-patient on the Psychiatric Wards at Chorley and District General Hospital. As an organization, we support families and people who suffer from serious and enduring mental illness problems, offering them both emotional and practical support whenever needed.

Previously to this, my colleague Ben Law, Family Support Worker of Pendle, Making Space, supported Neil. Ben still supports Neil's parents in Nelson. Neil suffers from A.D.H.D. with associated serious mental health problems that have caused Neil to become extremely vulnerable to any negative stresses and pressures.

Neil moved to the Leyland area, to make a fresh start in a new relationship that was both emotionally and practically supportive to Neil and his ex-partner, following a very long period of mental ill-health. Unfortunately though, the relationship between Neil and his girlfriend, who also suffers from serious mental health problems, has broken down, despite many attempts to keep it working.

To remain together any longer has deteriorated to the point that Neil himself now feels, that staying together could have serious consequences for them both.

*In the past Neil has been easily influenced when pressurized by his peer group, and adopted negative coping strategies that led to a massive deterioration in his mental health, further exasperated by not receiving the correct care and treatment when he was previously unwell. This **dual** combination means that it would be detrimental for Neil to return to Nelson on health grounds, and necessitates that it would be in Neil's **best interests** for him to make a fresh start in Leyland, where he has begun to make positive health and social connections. At present Neil is working very hard in order to move on positively, and deserves our continuing support in which to do so.*

****

I did wonder though how could Neil make a fresh start when the psychiatrist his understanding G.P. sent him to, and made an urgent appointment for Dr Chaucer, **wouldn't even see him**. Neil did manage to facilitate wonderful G.P's in Leyland, but hit a brick wall with Chorley Hospital. He didn't do much for Neil anyway before, so it wasn't a great loss. Is there any psychiatrist with honour? Apparently not! God help my son as the damn psychiatrists won't!

On 15th April 2003, I received a letter from the G.M.C. thanking me for my completed 'complaint form'. I have been sent a consent form authorizing me to act on behalf of Neil, so he has to sign it. Also a medical record consent form to enable them to obtain copies off Neil's G.P. and hospital records from 1998 to date.

****

On the 2nd June 2003, I received a letter from G.M.C. telling me that they had passed my complaint on to a senior caseworker who would report on it, after medical reports were received from the hospital.

I have told you that the girl, or woman I should say, because she was much older than Neil, had discarded him because she was now pregnant; therefore he was surplus to requirements. This didn't stop Neil from wanting to be with her though. He didn't understand why she tossed him aside like a dirty duster. He cared for her and needed her. The woman was so manipulative and clever, she prided herself on it.

391

Neil said that she liked to get into his brain. She knew what she was doing, and he said that she would cry wolf to get what she wanted from the psychiatrists.

Neil said, "How is it that she gets help, but I don't". He didn't deny that she was ill, but she knew how to play the system.

Neil didn't. He was just so open like he was. He didn't understand his illness, and hardly anyone helped him. Stella Barmforth was doing her utmost, she went to see another doctor, a psychiatrist, she asked as a favour to her, and it showed just how much commitment she had towards Neil, that she put her own reputation on the line, because the doctor did see us. He obviously held Stella in high esteem.

He listened to Neil and me, and read the reports and documents that we had taken to show him. He backed off, and said that although he sympathized with our predicament, he **couldn't** get involved. In fact he did seem quite *frightened* to do so.

****

This is something that even now in **2006** I can't get my head around. How can a doctor close ranks and **deny a person** medical help, especially so someone like Neil, who was begging for help, but the doctor had to 'side' with another doctor.

I know I may not be being realistic. The police stick together, they won't stand up against another officer, not all of them of course, but I know the majority stick together. A doctor does the same. But with a doctor though, all a doctor has to do is to refer them to someone else. **Why didn't they do this for Neil?** Why didn't they save my son's life? Why did they commit him to a life of torture and the end result of it, a death sentence? Where's the logic? How can they do this? I know in all honesty that this is NOT just confined to Neil. He is not alone in suffering like this. There are others, many others still suffering out there.

****

It was another slap in the face for Neil, he was so depressed. He broke into the woman's house and hid there to wait to see her, to beg her to take him back. He'd taken her car keys, and drove her car as he'd always done before, but this time she said she'd **not** given him permission. He parked the car later on her sister's drive. Now he was to be arrested for trespass and breaking and entering, on top of taking her car without permission and driving without a license or insurance.

Meeting her was the worst thing that had ever happened to him. No doubt she will say the same, but she has what she wanted. She screwed him alright in more ways than one.

Don't get me wrong. I don't condone anything Neil did, but he was desperately ill. So totally out of control in fact, and he didn't plan these things. Trouble followed his chaotic life that he couldn't manipulate. He was full on, living his life in total chaos. He didn't know any different, as he couldn't think or reason, like you and me.

****

The police wouldn't let Neil go back to the Public House which is one good thing, and again after going to court he had no bail address so he was sent to Preston Prison.

We had the same problem with the police in Leyland. They were told that Neil **wasn't ill,** so they weren't as helpful as they could have been. The woman got all the sympathy, whilst Neil got none. They weren't interested in Neil being sick; he'd committed a crime so that's all they were interested in.

Neil was in danger and at risk again, because the police wouldn't be thinking Neil was *suicidal and depressed.* He'd probably had a drink but not had any medication. I rang the police to tell them to keep a close eye on Neil, and so did Mr Clarkson, the solicitor that David had found for him, who was a colleague of his, because David couldn't commit his time to Neil in Leyland, because he had clients here. We understood, and Mr Clarkson was really nice and a very good solicitor.

We had to go to Leyland to pick up all Neil's belongings from the Public House. We didn't know what kind of reception we'd get there, because we didn't know how Neil's problems had rebounded on his surroundings.

It wasn't as bad as we thought. They were all really nice and helpful. They had packed Neil's stuff for him and were careful with it. They knew that Neil had severe mental health problems; in fact the cleaner said she could sympathize with him, as he told her all about his life and not getting medical help. She liked him, and with the lady who cooked the meals, they helped looked after him. They sort of mothered him together. Everyone liked Neil, especially so the

393

ladies. It made it so hard to listen to all the bad stuff they used to say about Neil from here at Fernlea General, and the Mental Health Team, because he was such a nice lad, very caring, genuine, loving and thoughtful, with a twinkle in his eye for the ladies, and he was such a good looking lad with a body to die for. Stella met us there. We'd miss her. We'll always be grateful to her; she believed in us, and knew just how ill Neil was. You were right Stella. (He was).

We crammed all of Neil's stuff into the car, we weren't going to go back and do two trips, as it was too heartbreaking. The car was full to the roof. In fact there was so much stuff, that we actually **damaged** the inside of the car. We've still the holes in the doors and lining, as a reminder of yet another heartbreaking time, and another mess. We were in bits. Would we ever get any peace? Was this it for us? Would we always be left picking up the pieces, for the rest of our lives for Neil? Yes, we were afraid so!

CHAPTER TWENTY-SIX
Prison

Neil was with the criminals of society, the big boys. He was mixing with murderers and rapists and everything in between. We were terrified for him, but we were frightened of Neil living the way he was too. He was in prison for a driving offence, that wouldn't normally have put anyone in prison. Where was the justice in that?

He really should have been in some place where he could get help for his illness; if he'd have been in some form of supported accommodation, he could have gone back there, but with him being in a B & B in a Public House there was no other place for him. He didn't have the capacity to care for himself, he should not have been forced into doing so, as always it came crashing down, and everyone involved with Neil at these times was always caught in the 'fall out'.

Neil sent us a Visiting Order for the prison. It was a frightening experience for us, totally alien to us, as you find yourself being herded from one place to another. You feel like second class citizens, and it is part of the offence your loved one has committed, that has to be rubbed off onto you.

No one tells you anything, so when you do something wrong they tell you off like little children in front of everyone. We wanted to hold our heads up high, but it was so demoralizing. It was a TRULY terrible experience. We'd experienced the like before, when visiting Neil in Lancaster Farms, but this was quite different. This was a man's prison, so the rules were far more rigid.

First of all you have to queue outside the prison, which is on a very busy street corner, with traffic lights right in front, which give the people in the cars plenty of time to stare at you. We felt like goldfish in a goldfish bowl. They won't let you in through the gate until the time that has been allocated to you, and if it's pouring with rain you get soaking wet. You go through the gate and into a room with lockers, and you have to put everything in there.

You are allowed to take in a few pounds to buy a drink, and a chocolate bar or crisps. You have your photo taken; then you are searched. You then go through another door into the yard that has a narrow path with high fencing which makes you think of being a herd of cattle lined up for slaughter. Then once again you are outside, and if it's raining you are getting wet again, because you have to wait for an officer to come from somewhere else to let you through into the next part of the prison. They eventually come; then you walk in line keeping to the left of the yellow line. There might be a dog to sniff around you, so you go forward and stand on a numbered spot, around five of you at a time.

Then you go into a waiting room, which is very basic, very bland and wait again until you are allowed in to see your loved one. On this occasion Neil's arms were bandaged as he had cut himself again. We had to look past it, and make the most of our visit for Neil's sake. We were always upbeat for Neil. We acted well enough to have won an Oscar. Then when we came out we'd both cry, and not talk all the way home.

It was really hard, but then we'd pick at one another, including poor Mum, but she understood the reason, so always tried her best to lift our spirits. It was so draining! We felt like our hearts were being chipped away little by little. Neil wrote to us nearly every day. He was always telling us how much he loved us all, and how sorry he was for keep putting us through it. If I'm brave enough I'll find you a letter and copy what he writes, but I will have to be brave now, because my son is dead, and I loved him so much, and to write this book is bad enough, but to see his handwriting will be hard for me, but this book is about my son and the truth, so I will go and find that letter and I will copy it word for word if I can see to do so through my tears.

I plucked up enough courage, so one of Neil's letters is copied out for you to read as below:-

Dear Mum & Dad and Grandma,

Well I have good news; I am getting my second opinion. Probation Services are asking for me to see a psychiatrist, so finally we are getting what we want. The downside is it will take a couple of months, so I am in here until then.

And yes I will be honest, that I promise you.

I have put you all through enough, I will tell him about my past ie the voices, the reason I turned to drink and the drugs. I have also seen a psychiatrist last week, and I am also seeing him again this Thursday.

He has upped my medication, he is thinking about changing it if it does work.

He is thinking about that drug Clozarill where you have to have regular blood tests.

He seems really nice, so yes things are getting better.

How are you all? I hope you are all O.K.

Can you send me some photos and a letter?

I am missing you loads so the contact would be great.

I have had a bad weekend I have been so depressed.

I am listening to Century F.M. at the moment, and it's just gone 10:00pm on Sunday evening.

I am also wondering would you be willing to come and see me, as I am going to be here for a couple of months?

I am missing you, and it would be nice to see you, it would cheer me up.

So please consider it please.

Thank you for that £100.00, you can do that every Tuesday if you can, I will save my D.L.A. up.

Remember I need my money to purchase things like fags, toiletries and my treats, you know I like them.

Please remember I am grateful for all you do for me, and I do LOVE YOU very much.

*Yes I know I have **not** shown it, but in my heart of hearts I do.*

Mrs Percy is on tonight she is really nice.

Anyway I am going to go now so take care.

Take Care, Love Neil XXXX

I don't care what anyone in Criminal Justice may think, but to put someone with mental illness in prison is **fundamentally wrong,** this is not a case of keeping the public safe, Neil wasn't a risk to society. It was **not** in the public interest to criminalize my son. The REAL criminals were the psychiatrists who **wouldn't** treat him, but the justice system (so called) allowed it to happen, and we saw no other way out but to try to use it to our advantage, and that was to keep Neil in prison to see a psychiatrist who might just give him that much needed second opinion. It was cruel, so very cruel, but it was also disgraceful to expect Neil to be able to fend for himself. He was becoming more anxious and more depressed. It was a rollercoaster, and we feared for our son, at least he was away from drugs; well that's what I thought at the time, but this wasn't true.

On our visit there was a lad telling an older gentleman visitor how easy it was to get drugs into the prison. He looked across at me and raised his eyebrows. Neil had said the same. They throw it over the walls, and there are other ways which I witnessed on another visit, but wasn't absolutely certain that I saw what I think I saw. It was a young girl with a baby buggy; she pulled out the stoppers at the end of the buggy frame and pulled something out of the tubular steel. I wasn't going to say anything, as I couldn't believe my eyes. It's rife in prison Neil was telling me. Is this the reason that Neil wanted me to send him so much money? He said it wasn't.

He said that he would lend money to such a person, as he has no one to send him money. He was Neil's cell mate, and he had no money, and his cell mate looked out for him. I couldn't argue with Neil, but it did cross my mind also that someone could be leaning on him for cash or goods, or he was paying someone to look out for him. Neil's strange behaviour would draw attention to him, and he wouldn't be liked for it. There were a lot of hard cases and the same goes for the prison officers. Neil was a pest and a 'nutter' as far as they were concerned.

I cried on one of the visits; I couldn't help myself. I thought they would kill him, or Neil would hang himself like he'd done in Lancaster Farms. I was so frightened.

Neil said, "Don't worry Mum, they look at my arms and think I'm mental, so they tend to leave me alone."

Bless him, but he didn't really make me feel any better. My heart was in my stomach and it was doing somersaults.

Steve was as bad as me. I've often said how I tended to shoulder everything and try to keep a lot of Neil's problems away from Steve, because I knew he *couldn't* deal with them all the time. I didn't want him to hurt like I did, but now Steve was hurting very badly indeed. He was the 'man' yet he couldn't protect his son. It hit him pretty badly. We both suffered greatly with stress, it was beginning to show on our faces.

My dear Mum used to go to the Disabled Centre and cry to her friends, because she felt our pain, so to do it in front of me would add on some more stress, so she kept it for the centre and shared it with her friends.

"My poor daughter," she would say. "She has so much to deal with, and she's not well herself, her poor legs. I don't know how she's managing to walk on her poor legs, how does she cope with it all, and that poor kid, **no one helps him**, he's a sorry little bugger."

Mum used to say that she'd get the papers to come and see her and tell them what they were doing to him at Fernlea General. I miss my dear Mum. I did tell a lie at the very beginning of my book. It wasn't really a lie though, because she was alive when I *started* this book, but she didn't get her wish of me finishing it before she died. I'm ahead of myself again, back to June 2003.

****

Neil was to see Dr Samuel Plackett from the Guild (Formerly Whittingham Hospital in Preston, where Steve's Uncle was incarcerated for many years). He's a Forensic Psychiatrist and David says that he is a good man, who has earned a lot of respect in his job. The prison respected him too. David had arranged for a Medical Report to be done for the court, and also the prison had wanted Neil to be seen by him too, as he acted as psychiatrist for the Prison Service. I was told by letter by Andrew Green, the Governor, that he would see Neil on Tuesday 17th June. An appointment had to be made.

Dr Plackett **didn't** see Neil, and he was due back in court on the 8th July, and without the report David had to adjourn the court date until 21st July. Poor Neil it meant his agony would be prolonged. I became so worried about Neil's depressed state; that I wrote to Andrew Green and again to Philip Porter M.P. They tried to reassure me, but I knew my own son. The prison was finding Neil difficult. I told them to find him something to do, he was hyperactive and he needed to work off some energy. Did they have a gym? They didn't understand, they weren't used to anyone like Neil, and yet they were *so complacent about having so many mentally ill men in prison*. So it **wasn't** just Neil.

Our hospital did and could do this to other poor mentally ill people, but was it true that others the length and breadth of the country were having it done to them too? **It's completely insane!**

****

Neil sent me a heartbreakingly true story that was in a newspaper that he had read headlined *'Failed by the system'* about a young lad who was suffering from mental illness. He had barricaded himself into his council house, and had smashed up all of his furniture, set light to it, and had then sat on his bed waiting to be burnt to death because he wanted to die. He was rescued and taken to hospital, he had suffered mental health problems for over fifteen years, and had been fighting for the help he needed all that time. The most *unbelievable* part of this poor man's story, was that he was arrested and charged with arson, with intent to endanger lives.

It isn't so unbelievable though is it, because Neil is in exactly the **same** situation as the poor young lad in this article. He's been dragged through the criminal justice system too, time after time, when like this other man he should have been given the help from Psychiatric Care. This man was told like Neil from the psychiatrists that he had seen that he would be better off in prison, where he would be better helped. For God's sake, these are human beings who are ill. **<u>Does anyone reading this agree with me that this is wrong?</u>**

Prison is certainly not the *right* place to put these poor, disturbed people. All this is doing is prolonging their illness anyway, because of their bad treatment by ordinary *unqualified* officers who know nothing about mental illness. Is it right to bang them up in prisons and throw away the keys? We are in 2009 not in the dark ages.

It was typical of Neil to be upset by reading this, he was always thinking about others. I will never forget about a young lad who was in Fernlea General at a time that Neil was there, when he was so cruelly treated by the staff when he was on Section. His name was Andy. He was a lovely lad, who was a bit younger than Neil. He had a lovely loving family. I used to talk to his mum and his sisters. Like me they were at their wits end.

Neil said one day, "I don't know why they can't help Andy, he's **not** like me, he could be helped so easily."

I will never forget that, Neil knew. He always knew about how

400

people portrayed themselves. It was so profound. Andy had lost his way and started to take drugs. He had a watch that could turn the T.V. station over when he twiddled it, and this annoyed people. We knew it was him, but it was only a harmless joke, and he had this twinkle in his eye. It broke the monotony and he didn't persist with it. Yes he was a lovely lad, but I'm afraid there isn't much hope for him if he is still in the hands of Fernlea General. I know that as I live and breathe.

Too many people in prison who suffer with mental health problems are **not** receiving the help they so desperately need. Or for the little they do receive, they have to wait weeks, if not months to be seen by a psychiatrist, and it is often left to officers on the wing to deal with these prisoners, even though they have had no formal training, and there is an ever growing list of prisoners who have committed suicide. They don't mean anything though do they; these people? They don't *matter* to society at all! Throughout their lives they have been shown that they don't matter by the doctors, Mental Health Social Workers, hospitals then the police, courts and the criminal system that they are inevitably pushed into. Well I'm telling you that they **do matter, and very much so!**

These are *sick people,* and just because they take more time to deal with, and are more trouble, is it right as a Society that we let them be treated in this way? It is disgusting, and I for one don't want any part of it. All *decent* people will be of the same opinion. So why don't we do something about it together? What about you the mental health charities, surely you can stand up and be counted? Get off your backsides and do something BECAUSE these people are TRULY getting away with MURDER. Ask yourselves if Britain truly is a civilized and caring society? Bear in mind also, that one in four of us can get mental illness at some time in our lives. Shouldn't that FACT alone, be of interest to every single ONE OF US?

I defy anyone not to be moved by this story of a man's plight to get medical help. Isn't our country supposed to be held in high esteem for our 'wonderful health service?' Our chronic mental health system **cannot** be included in that, can it?

****

To the gentleman who has written his story I say, "You are articulate in the way you write about your illness, and the issues

401

surrounding your illness. This is reality, showing the bigger picture. My heart goes out to you."

I'm afraid though that he and Neil are just the tip of the iceberg. Well we think so. No, we **know** so. We promise you that we will do our best to promote your issues about the mental health problems as a whole, and the fact that people like you and Neil should **not** be sent to prison just because the Mental Health has failed you. It is *unjust,* and a travesty of our criminal justice system, to allow it to happen. Prison is not a Holding Centre for *mentally ill people*; it is for criminals, whereas these people's only crime is being mentally ill.

You, the criminal justice system complain that the prisons are full. **Well obviously they will be**, because a vast majority of those prisoners **shouldn't** be in there. I do **not** believe in justice anymore, it's a complete nonsense, and a sham, but I'd LOVE TO BE PROVEN WRONG BY YOU, for the sake of everyone's future.

Get rid of the poor mentally ill; gas them in those chambers like the Nazi's did during the war, because **at least then they would be put out of their misery.** That would be one way of getting rid of them. You wouldn't do this because it's inhumane. Yet, so is what is being done to these poor sick people now. What do they do instead? Slam the door shut on them and hide them away. For what use are they, they are nothing, so they don't matter! **They don't have a voice**. Well I for one am speaking up for them! Please join me!

Remember though that they are also our children, mothers, fathers, brothers, sisters, granddads, grandmothers, aunts, uncles, cousins and dear friends. They are **not the dregs of society**, so why do you treat them as such, as if they don't matter. Stop it. Stop it NOW!

****

Neil made a formal complaint on a pink form, headed, Form Comp 2, Prisoner's formal complaint, Under Confidential Access.

Why are you using the confidential procedure?
Because it's a medical issue.

Your complaint is?
I have suffered from mental health problems for a number of years. My case is well documented, and my Mother has contacted

you over her concerns. My medication prescribed by a psychiatrist has been stopped. This medication is supposed to keep me stable. I can only see problems arising from this action, and I feel that my medication needs to be immediately restored, to prevent problems from arising.

What would you like to see done about your complaint?
Immediate restoration of my medication.

Response by the Governor, the Area Manager or the Chairman of the Board of Visitors was that because Neil was on Promazine and Chlorpromazine, they decided that he *needn't* be on the two, as they thought that they were the *same* drug, but as Neil said a psychiatrist had prescribed it as such. Neil certainly didn't feel as stable when they took one of them off him.

I had regular contact with Neil and the staff on the hospital wing, and the staff allowed Neil to ring me when they needn't have done. I have no complaints about Preston Prison. My only argument was that they were **not able or qualified** to take care of Neil. His mental health problems were difficult to deal with and quite complex. I didn't want them to be lulled into a false sense of security, by the past incompetent psychiatrists still having input to the prison about Neil, as this always put Neil into a very dangerous position. I had to make them listen to me, and believe me, and NOT believe his so-called doctors.

All I could do was write letters, copy documents and medical reports that I had in my possession, and that they didn't have knowledge of, because they *weren't* given the information by the so-called doctors and Mental Health Team. They did copy what I sent, and they did put these documents and letters into their records, and then they approached Neil differently. They began to ask him the relevant questions. Neil was *treated fairly and with respect* the majority of the time. The blame and the faults still lay with Fernlea General. I will not taint Preston Prison at all.

****

Philip Porter M.P. had written to the Area Manager of the Mental Health Team, Liam Marsh. He told Philip that Neil was no longer in the area, and if he was to be released from prison and returned to

403

Chorley he would be assessed by their Mental Health Team. Yes! Right!

We've heard it all before, nothing changes; it was all as unhelpful as ever. All we could do was to hope that Dr Plackett came up with something that we could throw at them to 'FORCE' them into helping Neil, because they won't do anything for him otherwise.

We got what we wanted from Dr Plackett eventually, but they still wouldn't do anything.

****

Read on:

A further adjournment was made at court because Dr Plackett didn't have the Psychiatric Report ready until 30th June.

Dr Plackett asked Neil about his family background and the mental illnesses in the family. Dr Plackett then said that this would indicate a highly significant and immediate family history of **serious mental illness.**

Neil told him that he could not remember much of his childhood, only that he couldn't settle as a child, and couldn't concentrate on anything. He was reckless and had a lot of energy. He said his mind would wander, and he was **always** very anxious. He told him that he was into everything. He said he was moved from school to school. Dr Plackett thought that Neil had some degree of intellectual impairment, because his comments were childlike at times.

Neil told him that he was often bullied at school, and that the teachers couldn't cope with him. He said that he tended to block out a lot of the 'bad' things that had happened to him. He said that he was happy at his last school Eden Grove, but he missed home and his family, so had a tendency to run away from school.

He told him that since the age of eighteen he had lived on his own, although he received considerable input and support from his parents, but he said, "They can't always be there."

He said that he tried further education, but his life was too chaotic to continue with it very long. He told of his relationships, but said that his partners couldn't cope with his moods. He would be 'high' for a period of a few days, and then needed sleep, and then he was 'buzzing', and then he'd feel 'down'.

Neil said that he would drink when he was feeling 'down' as this helped to block out his feelings. It helped to make him feel better, as

404

it would take away his feeling of anxiety. He told of his drug taking, but at that time it wasn't like it was later. At this time Neil was smoking cannabis/heroin and had injected, but they were nothing like the doses he did later. At one time he did stop without supervision, and without a withdrawal programme, but as I say he wasn't using it as much then. I know that he had used 'crack cocaine' too.

Neil did **not start** to take drugs until he had left home at the age of eighteen. I know he used cannabis while on the ward at Fernlea General Hospital, because as I have already told you, a man used to deliver it directly to the hospital doors, and the patients used to buy it from him. This was a regular occurrence. Neil started to inject heroin when he was dumped in the B & B with drug users by the hospital, and because he awoke with the needle still in his arm, it was this that had sent over the edge enough to want to try to kill himself, because he was so ashamed.

****

The psychiatrists from the hospital would have you believe, and they had probably written this down in Neil's notes knowing them, that Neil started taking drugs from a *young* age. Yet we can state categorically that this is **untrue,** as while we had control of him when he lived under our roof, he did **not** take drugs, and neither would he have felt that he would need to do so. The psychiatrists though would have you believe differently, because it looked better for them to label Neil, and blame him for bringing mental illness upon himself. This is rather a contradiction on their part isn't it, because they denied he even had *any mental illnesses.*

****

Neil told Dr Plackett the truth at the time he wrote the report. Neil was using heroin on and off in his darkest hours, when he couldn't stand what was going on in his head. He could have stopped as he did with the drink. We were, up until he went into prison, going regularly to Westgate to see Caroline on the drugs team.

Dr Plackett said that Neil's psychiatric history was extensive, and he had to refer to previous psychiatric records, because Neil's account wasn't entirely useful. The problem with that being that there are things entered in his records that are **untrue,** especially if it was from his records that Janice Short had used, when she said that Fernlea General referred him to the A.D.H.D Specialist that **I had**

405

personally found for him myself.

It had been said too that I had complained about Neil being nasty and violent, **but this was totally untrue,** and can easily be proved as untrue, because it was <u>always</u> asked of me, and I had always denied it. Neil was **never** abusive, nasty or violent as a child. He didn't have that side of A.D.H.D. He was a caring, demonstrative and loving child.

Dr Plackett also referred to the fact that we got the Psychology Service in to Neil. Yes we did, but not when he was aged twelve, but very soon into his Primary School years, when he had started at junior school, not for his aggressiveness though, but because he was being assaulted by teachers. My G.P. asked the psychologist to go into the school, so they got that wrong too.

I was incensed at reading some of the comments that Dr Plackett had written. It was from previous medical records that he had got his so-called information, and as such was not his fault. Neil was never nasty, violent or aggressive and **I won't have this said about him**. No doubt if I had said this, we might have been seen quicker by Fernlea General. I never said this though, because **it wasn't true!**

The psychiatrist lied about this, because he knew nothing about A.D.H.D. and when he was told by me after the diagnosis of A.D.H.D. by Dr Stevens, he <u>mistakenly</u> thought that A.D.H.D. sufferers were **all nasty, violent and aggressive**. This alone shows how little this psychiatrist actually does know.

I can relate back to all the changes of schools, and all the input by doctors, as well as teachers, BUT not **one** person ever said that Neil was like this, because **he wasn't**. I won't have them lie about Neil again.

I told Ben Law that this infuriated me, and he also knew it *wasn't* true. I suppose the hospital wanted to dignify their lies when they said that Neil was aggressive on the wards. Yes we remember don't we, when they accused Neil of attacking a member of staff, and called the police in, only for it to be found out later to be a <u>total lie.</u> Neil was **not referred** to an A.D.H.D. Specialist by the hospital. We saw her privately ourselves.

Dr Leister said that he believed Ritalin could bring on psychosis. Neil was a very acute case, and he responded well to the medication to treat this illness. We didn't give him this medication lightly. I

406

would honestly say that I personally think that Neil would have become psychotic *without* it, because it runs in the family, but I don't think it would bring on schizophrenia. We always knew Neil didn't just have A.D.H.D. Ritalin helped his condition, there is no denying that, and his life would have been a lot worse had he tried to live **without** it.

Neil did develop a range of symptoms as Dr Plackett said, and dramatic self harming episodes. He did have manic depressive episodes and paranoid ideas. It was funny (peculiar) really that he found all of this in Neil's records, when the psychiatrists at Fernlea have continually stated that Neil **does not suffer from any of the above.**

They would like us to believe that Neil has a personality disorder because this is untreatable, whilst Neil's illness is not! They have also said that Dr McKewen fully agreed when he saw Neil in Lancaster Farms but the prison staff told me differently. I know that this was the start of Neil's demise, when the self harm became catastrophic, when he didn't get the help he needed, and he was so frightened of the voices in his head. He tried to keep it in, because no one believed him; he was fighting against them himself, all alone and trying to deny the voices.

He didn't trust anyone that had anything to do with Fernlea General but he did trust Dr Plackett. In his company I heard Neil open up, but he too turned his back, and Steve and I had both expected much more from him.

Anyway his was just an opinion, so said Dr Janger and the Mental Health Team, including his CPN Angela Moore. Dr Plackett's report was just an opinion and they discounted him too. You may all stick together you doctors, but you are hypocrites also, to discount a psychiatrist with the esteem of Dr Plackett. We asked to see Dr McKewen's report, but they *lost it,* then they *found it again,* but still they didn't allow us to see it.

Dr Plackett said that in 2001 a diagnosis of effective psychosis with paranoia was offered, and further referrals were made to the specialists in A.D.H.D.

There you go again with the referrals. Dr Plackett, for the very last time, PLEASE DO LISTEN! Neil was NEVER referred to anyone who specialized in A.D.H.D. or otherwise. No matter how many times we asked. We did ask, and ask, and ask, and ask, and ask, and ask AGAIN. Our solicitors asked, asked, then THEY ALSO asked again.

Dr Plackett did believe that Neil was suffering from a **schizophrenia-like illness**, and he said that although Neil had told him about the severe mental illness in the family, he did not know if this was so. However I have already told you that Dr Leister treated two of these family members himself, so surely that <u>should have</u> been put into Neil's notes, and then Dr Plackett wouldn't have had to rely on Neil to tell him. Dr Plackett went on to say that if it was true, then this would strongly support a speculation that Neil may indeed suffer from a schizophrenia-like disorder.

Yes Dr Plackett, my son did suffer from schizophrenia. I would stake my life on it, and with all the schizophrenia and psychosis in the family, and manic depression too, Neil didn't stand much chance did he?

A matter of weeks before my son died, Dr Plackett I begged and pleaded to your secretary for you to intervene, because Neil had become so ill.

He said that he believed that Neil had treatment needs, and he was to assess his response to antipsychotic drugs while in custody.

My views as Dr Plackett skirts around it, is that prison is holding my son, and Dr Plackett is going to treat him by giving him antipsychotic drugs. The point is that prisons are **not** there for this reason, **but** members of the medical profession **are** using prisons for this reason. Why then do they push the mentally ill into them, if what I am saying *isn't* true?

They did it with Neil when they purposely put him into police hands when he was still on a Section. They saw their chance to offload him, and they took it. Dr McKewen more or less said the same when he was in Lancaster Farms, in that he was already being held in a place of safety, **so why put him in hospital,** but instead use this opportunity of using antipsychotics on him and assess him.

It is wrong to use the prison for this, prisons are for criminals, so what are the medical profession doing? They are simply criminalizing the Mentally ill? Prisons are *dangerous places*, and the prison staff officers are <u>not qualified enough</u> to treat these people. It is ridiculous and it is also inhumane.

408

Just because the NHS has seen in their wisdom to close long term hospitals for the mentally ill, they've decided to use prisons instead. **It's a scandal.** My guess is that the Government is well aware of this, because the Prison Service definitely is. I did think it was because if the hospitals off-load patients into prison, then money isn't coming out of their budgets. Then I thought, surely the Prison Service cannot be that stupid, so then I thought that maybe they ARE simply in league with the devil.

Dr Plackett said that Neil's complex needs would warrant some form of monitoring and support from various agencies, such as Probation and Social Services with an overview from Psychiatric Services.

We were pleased with Dr Plackett's report when he was using his *own observations,* and I think he too would have had a better understanding if it weren't for the fact that there were a lot of things **omitted** from Neil's records and an awful lot written in them that was absolutely untrue. Did you know for instance Dr Plackett that they had **refused to say** that Neil had a mental illness? Did you also know that they refused him a second opinion or referral, yet they mistreated him in hospital, and withdrew his medication? Did you know that they made our life hell?

We were to see Dr Plackett again, outside of the prison, when he kindly saw us at our request. We liked him. Funnily enough he reminded us of Dr Blake, both in his looks and manner. The best thing though was that Neil liked him. Most importantly though Neil also *trusted* him, so he opened up to him. Neil had been kicked so many times by psychiatrists, Bob Gardner, hospital staff and the Mental Health Team, all to do with Fernlea General, but he was like a dog that would trust its owner even after it had been caused so much pain.

So to trust Dr Plackett actually took a lot, and was such a big step for Neil, as he very much distrusted the people who were involved with him from Fernlea. Everyone who knew Neil, be it, our G.P's, care workers, solicitors or whoever else, knew that the only way Neil would receive treatment from Fernlea General, was to have Dr Plackett involved with Neil's mental health.

To oversee his treatment, Dr Plackett was very much of the opinion that he *couldn't,* or *wouldn't* be able to do this over a long period of time. We would have preferred to have had Neil seen only by him, but he said it <u>couldn't</u> happen, because he would eventually have to have his needs met by Fernlea General. In other words he **had perhaps unknowingly signed Neil's death warrant.**

We thought that at least his report would help, but it didn't, as once again the psychiatrists at Fernlea General ignored it. They said it was only an opinion, as they had done previously with others, and they continued to say that Neil <u>didn't have mental illness</u> therefore they did so little for him, that all in all it really amounted to nothing.

We saw help that we thought we had with Dr Plackett slipping away from within our grasp. We felt all our hopes evaporating! I knew what would happen, and I sadly, frustratingly and very worryingly was proved right.

Neil was still in Preston Prison when I had a knock at my door...

CHAPTER TWENTY-SEVEN
Hello, I've Had Neil's Baby

There was a knock at my door. I opened it to see a young girl standing quite a way off from the door. I **hadn't** seen her before.

She said, "Hello, I've had Neil's baby."

I stood there for a minute or two as it took time for me to register what she had just said. I asked her in, and she told me that she'd had a boy and he'd just turned four months old.

"I thought I should tell Neil," she said.

I asked her, "Why didn't you come sooner, before your baby was born?"

I didn't really get any proper answers off her because she was rather slow; she only spoke after she'd thought long about what I'd said. Then she talked about her son and the fact that Social Services had him, but she wanted him back.

"Would Neil want to see him? By the way, where is he?" she asked me.

I couldn't tell her that he was in prison. I told her that he was living in Preston. She said that Neil had forced himself upon her, and I thought that the next thing that she would be telling me was that Neil had raped her. I couldn't believe that of Neil, but why on earth was he having sex with this girl, she was undoubtedly 'challenged'.

She was slow, but a bonny girl, but not at all the kind of girl I would have thought Neil would choose to go with. He had mentioned her name though, and apparently she had been to my house a few times with him, but I had never met her before. I can remember some photos that Neil had of her, that had been taken outside my house.

I asked her, trying to clarify if Neil had forced himself on her, "How many times did Neil and you have sex?"

"About nine times," she answered.

Her reply put paid to that myth then. Neil said she was a friend, who was always hanging around. They gave one another comfort,

411

this was true, but he never had to force her, and he said that I shouldn't have had to ask, because I should know him better than that. He said that her mother was very strange, and that she had given her a hard time for just being *seen* with a boy.

He said, "I regretted it for her sake, but I did like her, and I'm so pleased that I have a son. I will stand by her."

I knew that this would indeed have been the case if he had been allowed to do so, as Neil was kindness itself.

I felt so sorry that she has had to deal with this all by herself. She told me that she had no one, and she didn't know a thing about childbirth. I would have been there for her had she told me. Poor kid, it was obvious that she couldn't possibly care for a baby on her own. I once went to her Mum's house, but she barely opened the door to me, but I could see beyond her that there was little in the way of furniture in the house. Her Mum was very strange and obviously so fearful of people. She had major problems of her own, that was obvious enough.

The girl had no chance of getting her baby back, and rightly so if she had no one to help or support her. Neil went to see the baby, and the baby was brought to him to see how he would cope with him, as Neil wanted access. Neil meant it too, he was wonderful with children, but sadly Neil had his own problems, he was chaotic, mentally ill and a drug user.

While I knew he could have stopped the drug habit, he just couldn't cope with a baby with his mental health problems, especially as they **weren't** being addressed and treated. He was becoming more ill. I couldn't and wouldn't back him to look after the child with our help. It would have been a nightmare, and I would have had to deal with Neil saying this was **his** child, and having to argue with him all the time.

There was no doubt that if I had have persisted, and I had wanted the child, I would have been given the chance of adopting him. I couldn't do it though for the child's sake; he was better off being adopted as a baby by a loving family. It was the right thing, although it was heartbreaking for us all. I never saw the baby; I didn't think it was right to do so, as he would have pulled so much at my heartstrings.

They said he was a real bonny baby who looked like Neil. I told

412

Social Service Social Workers to make sure that it was well documented about Neil's illnesses, as it was probable that either this little boy, or the other child yet to be born by the woman in Leyland, would or could, inherit any of the illnesses that Neil had, so they needed to know to look out for them, and not to be kept in the dark as I had been for a long time.

This was my first grandchild, yet I would never be able to cuddle him, smell him, or love him. I felt sad for BOTH Steve and me, but also and more especially for Neil too. It **wasn't** his fault that he had mental illness and *didn't* get treatment, or any help and support so that he could have had input into this child's life. He lost out, and so did we. All Neil wanted was to be 'normal', live and have the same chance as anyone else had. He was robbed. We were all robbed, and indeed robbed will be the last chapter of my book.

****

It's now 24th September 2003. I received a letter from the General Medical Council telling me that someone else has taken over the management of my case. All the papers relating to this matter have been carefully considered by two members of a team of screeners, one of whom is **not** a doctor. They are members of the G.M.C. appointed to consider complaints and information about the conduct and performance of doctors at the initial stage of the first Fitness to Practice procedures. The decision was explained to me as follows:

Their main role is to license doctors to practice in the United Kingdom. Although they provide guidance to doctors on what constitutes good medical practice, not all alleged breaches of that guidance will warrant formal action by them. They have powers to take action against a doctor, only where his or her behaviour justifies the restriction, or for the removal of his or her registration. In legal terms such behaviour is described as 'serious professional misconduct' or 'seriously deficient performance'.

They said the screeners could understand my reasons for writing to them. However, having carefully considered all of the information that I had submitted, the screeners did **not** consider that **all** of my allegations against Dr Leister and Dr Janger, if proved, would justify an allegation of serious professional misconduct or seriously deficient performance, and thereby possibly lead to action to restrict or remove his/her registration.

The screeners were satisfied that Dr Leister and Dr Janger had *undertaken adequate assessments* of my son's condition, and provided appropriate care and treatment to him. They also found **no** evidence to suggest that Dr Leister had *deliberately* acted without my son's best interest in mind, by signing him off his Section in July 2001. (When he sent him to Lancaster Farms and his Section was withdrawn the day after his arrest).

When considering allegations about misconduct by a doctor, the screeners may only refer a case forward for further consideration, if they are 'satisfied from the material available in relation to the case, that it is properly arguable that the practitioner's conduct constituted *serious* professional misconduct'.

This screening test essentially breaks down into two component parts. Firstly, taking the allegations to be true, they consider whether they are so serious that they should think about taking action to remove or restrict the doctor's registration to practice medicine, in order to protect patients.

They said that they take **all** complaints seriously. However, there are inevitably some allegations, which although understandingly viewed as serious by the complainant, do not warrant further investigation by them. This was **not** the case they say in terms of my allegations. Taken at face value, these were felt to be serious enough to raise questions about Dr Leister and Dr Janger's continued registration.

The second part of the screening test requires them to consider whether a proper case could be made to support what the complainant alleges. It is against this second element of the legal test that they decided to close my case. Having taken all the relevant information into account, the screeners were not satisfied that a proper case could be made in respect of these allegations.

They said that they recognized that this may not be the decision that I had hoped for, but they thanked me for bringing the matter to their attention.

****

On 1st October 2003 Neil received a letter from Jimmy McKay telling him of his 'Action Plan' upon his release from prison. He was to visit Neil to explain it in more detail.

He said that he would remain his 'contact' person, and he would liaise with Social Worker Andrea Robbins, whom Neil had met at Fernlea Hospital. Neil had said that he was intent on moving back to Nelson. He said that upon Neil's release, a multi agency forum should be convened as soon as possible, to facilitate a reassessment of needs, under the CPA and a care/package formulated and implemented. Jimmy would take an active role in this process. Consideration was in place to call a MAPP meeting which was to be discussed at the planning meeting. In regard to Neil's medication arrangements, these would be made for faxed prescription, details to be forwarded to Neil's G.P.

I received a letter from Philip Porter M.P. saying that it appears that we are moving in the **right** direction for Neil to get the care and attention he needs, and he hoped that this would continue.

Dr Plackett said that he had reviewed Neil in prison, and that Neil had demonstrated a significant clinical improvement following treatment with antipsychotic medication when combined with a mood stabilizer, but he had only started this recently. He said that he would be happy to review him at Guild Lodge as an out-patient in the months following his release from custody. However this would not be a long term clinical commitment, but he felt that he thought that he should show some clinical support to the other clinical staff who might be involved in Neil's care for a more extensive period of time. He said that he would only be prepared to offer such input once Neil's referral to Community Mental Health Team had been accepted, and once he had made contact with a local psychiatrist, as he didn't intend to act as his 'nominal RMO'. He said that he understood that Neil's presentation continued to cause concern and frustration.

He said that he was unsure how Neil's accommodation was being met.

Neil was prescribed:

Depakote 250mg three times a day.

Chlorpromazine 150mg at night and 50mg in the morning.

Venlafaxine 150mg at night.

Promazine 150mg.

Hydroxyzine 25mg at night.

There was talk of stopping the Chlorpromazine and replacing it with Olanzapine.

This is the list of medication Neil was on when he left prison; surprisingly as you may have noticed, he was **put back on both** Chlorpromazine and Promazine. Neil was right then when they withdrew one of them, and he had to complain because he felt unstable.

However significantly you will notice that on this list there is absolutely **no mention whatsoever** of Ritalin. Seemingly they had withdrawn this medication from Neil many months earlier in fact. However Neil was still suffering from this condition, yet he was NEVER prescribed this medicine again!

Our questions were never answered regarding the withdrawal of this necessary drug for our son.

****

Neil came out of prison in December 2003, and again as before, nothing was put in place for him for when he came out. Why was it that the court would release Neil on a Friday, usually around 5:00pm which was then too late to get a prescription off the doctor, as the G.P's surgeries are shut at the weekend? Tell me how my son could get much needed medication like antipsychotic medication to sustain his tortured mind?

The police would take his medication off him when he was arrested, so he would never have any left in the house. Then the prison would change his medication, and they would **not** give him any or give it to Group 4 to look after in case he was released from court; therefore he would be suffering terribly by the time he had waited all day at court, as by then he would be in great need. So what would Neil do then? Buy heroin of course, so naturally the rot sets in again, and he's soon back on the merry-go-round.

Why don't these people ever learn? You can talk until you are purple, without any effect. What's happened to the care package? The prison should contact Neil's CPN, or anyone in Mental Health Services to prepare a prescription ready for Neil to pick up.

I ring Community Mental Health Team (CMHT) and ask if they have done it? Naturally they say no! So I then do it if I have time to, but I'm not even with Neil sometimes, or it's just too late, and everyone from CMHT has gone home. I should be able to rely on the prison to inform CMHT to get things in place for Neil. The prison said on occasions that they had done this, and even faxed CMHT,

416

then the CPN tells me that the prison have **not done either of these things,** and it's their fault. I don't care whose fault it is, I just want my son on his medication so that he doesn't turn to drugs.

No one thinks about Neil, they are just ready to blame someone else, in order to pass the buck. Sadly this is a typical and usual state of affairs. On this occasion Neil was told to go to the Town Hall to ask for emergency accommodation. It's ridiculous that they ask so much of Neil, given the state he was in every time that he left court, after being incarcerated for a good length of time too.

The Town Hall said there was nothing, but the Manager from CMHT Ahmet had told Neil to go to the Town Hall, because it was sorted. It was not; so Neil was on the streets. He ended up staying with a 'druggy' friend, and you can easily guess what happened next.

Oh! Yes Dr Plackett it did look good on paper. Oh! Yes Philip Porter M.P. it did look like we were going in the right direction. In fact the same direction as always – on the road to NOWHERE!

It was always the same offer, much on paper, then nothing or the very minimum of help, which meant in Neil's case absolutely not ONE thing to make any difference to him at all.

Neil made arrangements for both him and me to meet his new landlord. He was so proud of himself for having found a rented terraced property in Colne all on his own, but his landlord wanted to meet at least one of his parents before he'd let him have the property. I said before that I wasn't happy to get involved in such things, because I'm a very honest person and no hypocrite, but Mental Health *wouldn't* find Neil some sort of supported accommodation that we frequently asked for, and although I knew things would come crashing down, I still found myself in this same position of supporting Neil then waiting for the fall out. The house was a neat little place, and his landlord was an extremely nice man. I told him that Neil had mental illness but we supported him. He was fine with that, and at first he made regular visits until he was satisfied that Neil was looking after the place.

I had saved Neil's money up for him when he was in prison. This was to make sure that Neil didn't waste it all, as he usually would have done. I took him furniture shopping. He bought a new cooker, fridge freezer and washing machine. Kath bought him a lovely microwave and a vacuum cleaner, and we bought him a second-hand suite that we picked up from a lovely couple in Burnley. The settee turned into a bed, which he used until he got himself a double bed. I gave him some bits of furniture, and for his birthday we all clubbed together to buy him lovely light fittings, a standard lamp and tie-backs all in wrought iron. I made the curtains and blinds. When we had finished he had a really cosy-looking home. We went to our local electrical store to buy him a widescreen T.V. which they allowed Neil to pay monthly for.

As I had control of his money at the time, I was willing to allow this, and I would make sure that it was paid for, as the people who owned this shop were a lovely family, and we had bought most of our electrical equipment off them as they have been exceptionally good to us.

Having 'things' and making Neil comfortable didn't make any difference though, because Neil couldn't cope with living on his own. He came to my house daily, but he hated having to go back home to be on his own. He wasn't taking his medication, so it was hit and miss for him. He'd been off his Ritalin a long time now, and he was making do with the cocktail of antipsychotic drugs and sleeping pills.

After only a matter of weeks Neil was wandering at night, and I'd see him in the early hours around my home. He'd sometimes climb over my garden fence and he'd make me jump; in fact I found it very disturbing at times.

On a number of occasions I'd be driving, when seemingly out of nowhere, Neil would jump out into the road, right in front of the car. It happened that often that I was always looking out for him.

He'd shout, "Mum," at the top of his voice.

It was so uncanny at times, as it happened that often no matter where I was in the surrounding towns. He would then jump into the car, and he'd want to come back for his tea. Most times we didn't mind, but sometimes we were going somewhere and we didn't want Neil with us, so instead we'd simply abort the idea. We were very 'tied', as it wasn't possible to have friends round, because we didn't know what Neil would be like when he came. Sometimes he'd be very agitated and anxious.

I have never been able to even think of getting a passport, because I wouldn't be able to leave the country. I'd always be called back because Neil needed me or he'd attempted suicide or was hurt. He got into so many scrapes. He was truly a nightmare and we never had any peace. Neil was fighting me to get his own money via his benefits. I had to let him have his way. He wanted independence, but we knew that it would all end in tears. He tormented us until he got his own way. He couldn't handle money at all.

He ticked over for a short while, but the elements around him wouldn't leave him alone. He didn't have friends, just 'druggy' mates who aren't REAL friends at all; they wanted Neil to be a drug user because he had regular money coming in, and most of them were on the dole and living in grotty conditions. They used Neil, ate his food, and dossed down at his house. Neil was vulnerable so they took advantage of him.

Neil found out that the woman in Leyland had a little boy too. I just hoped that Neil wouldn't go near her, as she would have caused him real trouble. He had no option but to try and get on with his own life, but this news further tortured him. Neil was a loving boy and children loved him, he was childlike himself, so I know he found it very hard knowing that he had two little boys, but he couldn't be involved with either one of them.

He was wise enough to say, "When his children were eighteen years-old they could find him, and he'd be there for them. He wrote letters to his first child, and gave them to Social Services to give to him when he was of age. He had settled down to the idea that he would be better off with a loving family. At least we hope that is what he got. It took a while for Neil to admit this, and he did blame me for a while for not wanting him.

He said, "You'd have got him, if you'd wanted."

This was probably so, but I had good reasons why I didn't 'want' him. It was the right decision, and Neil eventually realized that. He knew that I would ALWAYS do the right thing, and this was one of the reasons why he loved me so much.

****

Neil's depression was becoming a lot worse and I feared that he'd be caught in the loop again of using heroin on a regular basis. We found ourselves searching his house for ANY signs. We didn't have to look too far. Spoons and silver paper were lying around the house, but when I found needles and a tourniquet, I then knew to what

419

depths Neil had plunged.

Going to see the Drug Team at Westgate was a real eye opener. I was learning about things that **I didn't want to know about**. I was involved in a world that I didn't want to ever experience.

Neil was always open and honest with Caroline, it was so matter of fact on her part, she told Neil to smoke heroin rather than inject it, as there was a chance that he could lose an arm or leg. It amazed me where they could inject, in the groin, in between the toes, but after you've used the veins to a large degree, they do pack in. I saw lads who had lost a leg, but *still* they continued to use. We all know that the world is full of drug users. Some people take drugs who have everything in life, those who you would never think they'd need to use drugs. I've learnt **not** to judge people.

What made it all more difficult for me though, was that Neil used heroin to self medicate, to help take away his pain. This was the pain of his tortured mind; he was trying to relieve the voices in his head, when they were telling him that he was bad and no good. It's what they said about him in hospital, and it's certainly how they treated him.

"They **don't want** to help me Mum." This was what he always used to say about the psychiatrists, CPN's and Mental Health Team.

It's true they did as little as they could, and ignored him completely in the main.

****

Things came to a head at Christmas. I've dreaded being with Neil at Christmas, yet there was never any question that Neil always came first at Christmas. He *had* to be with us on this day, but more often than not he'd use it as an excuse to drink.

"It's Christmas," he'd say.

I always go to a lot of trouble at Christmas as I love this special time of the year. I enjoy trimming up and making things nice. I get all the best crockery out, cutlery and glasses, tablecloths, runners and napkins, and lovely candles.

Kathleen and Barry would come, and Mum would enjoy herself. It was a pleasure to give them all a lovely day. Ryan would be with his girlfriend at her house. We waited for Neil to join us on Christmas Day. He knew what time we had dinner, but I was just about to dish out the meal when he arrived.

420

He was agitated and anxious. I thought that he'd been drinking but I couldn't be sure, but he was definitely 'wired'. He hardly ate a thing. In fact he never ate well at all these days. He picked an argument with his Uncle Barry; he was so argumentative.

Neil stood up and 'fronted' Barry; he stood up and his chair went flying. Christmas dinner was ruined! I had eaten nothing. Neil started fighting with Barry, none of us could constrain him, and they all went out into the hall.

Neil was there smashing up pictures and ornaments as he went, then somehow he was in the living room. I'd taken Mum in and sat her down on her chair, and Neil with all his weight knocked me over my glass-topped coffee table. It was lucky for me that it had a strong wooden frame, and the glass wasn't in one full sheet, but consisted of four pieces slotted into the frame. I went straight over it, and hurt myself very badly. I was black and blue all over.

Steve and Barry managed to grab Neil. Mum was screaming at Neil to stop, but in the state he was in he **didn't** even hear her. She was also swinging her arms about trying to hit him, but with being blind she failed miserably. They managed to get Neil to the front door and managed to get him out, and then they told him to just go.

We rang the police because we were worried about Neil and people that he might come into contact with, but we wouldn't have him charged with the damage that he had caused. It ruined Christmas for everyone, and Kathleen and Barry said that in the future if Neil came at Christmas, they wouldn't!

I don't know why Neil was like this, no one said anything wrong to him; he was *already* agitated when he came. It wasn't at all like Neil. He kept away for a few days after that, he rang me but he couldn't remember what he had done. I went to his house to show him some of my bruises.

He cried, and he vowed not to drink, and he **never did** drink again after that. He would never have hurt me intentionally, but I did get hurt as others would if they got in his way. I do think it was a mixture of things, drink, drugs; his tormented mind with medication or without. I don't honestly know. He was severely disturbed, so I asked for an emergency CPA meeting.

****

Neil had got into a lot of debt over this period and he hadn't a

421

clue as to what he had spent the money on. There were a lot of undesirable people hanging around him. Things were going missing out of his house, electrical stuff and things like that. A guy up his street was taking them off him, and giving him a low amount of money for them, but then if he wanted them back he had to pay a lot more cash for them. This had been going on for weeks.

When we found out Steve went to the man's house but he was belligerent and said, "A junkie is always a junkie, I'm simply providing a service. If Neil is daft enough to use drugs then he has to pay the consequences." Steve couldn't get through to him so he never stopped doing it.

It wasn't just Neil he was extorting money from; he must have been on a good earner. We were fighting a losing battle. The next thing that we found out was that the man who owned the local corner shop was doing the same, and he had Neil's video recorder. Steve went into the shop blazing and he got it back.

Then we found out that this *same* man had Neil's benefit books. Neil had wanted money, so he gave Neil £100.00 and told him to give him the benefit book and he would draw his money. He did and he gave Neil a few pounds back out of the £250.00 he got from the book.

What made it worse though, was that when we got the books back and we had reported what was going on to the D.S.S.; on looking through the stubs in the book it showed that sometimes this man had gotten the money **before** the due date, therefore the post office that he had gone to was *fraudulently* giving him the money. Wherever we seemed to look these terrible things were going on. It was unbelievable.

The next thing we knew was that Neil was pawning his goods at Cash Generator, while they gave him more money for the stuff he pawned; it still wasn't enough for the decent stuff he was pawning. I managed to get the paperwork off him and we'd buy the goods back and keep them at our house so he couldn't do it again.

****

We had the CPA meeting. It is written on the form that the meeting was called to review Neil's care plan following concerns expressed by Neil's Mum about Neil's ability to cope.

Neil had been using illegal drugs and also getting into debt by using his benefit books as collateral. A referral to drug services was discussed and agreed by Neil. His Care Coordinator was to liaise with Probation and/or Westgate. It wasn't a case that Neil was spending all of his money on drugs, he just *didn't know* where his money was going. Then when people were pushing money at him, then wanting an exorbitant amount of cash back for what he had borrowed, things soon spiralled out of control.

I have no doubt that some of his undesirable 'friends' were using him as a soft touch, because he wouldn't see anyone without, if he could help them. Yet his money was always spoken for, so at times he didn't know which way to turn, which further exasperated his panic and stress, leading to feelings he had of there being no way out, plus him still having the need for heroin.

When we went to Westgate I was told that Neil's drug habit **wasn't in the extreme**, and Neil certainly didn't 'use' all of the time; only in times of real stress, which by now was a regular occurrence, but the amounts he used weren't excessive. I was told by the drug team as when Neil went on to the methodone programme, this was regulated to the amount of heroin he used, and Neil didn't have the need to steal to feed his habit, as it wasn't as bad as that. Even at this time we knew that Neil *could* have been 'saved' and turned around with the right help, and the main thing was the fact that Neil shouldn't be on his own trying to cope alone. He didn't feel secure, he never did, but now he had other pressures that he just didn't have the capacity to deal with.

Phil (Kings) spoke about not being able to support Neil with budgeting, as Neil's books had been given to a local shopkeeper. When the books are returned, I told Phil that I would again have to act as appointee for Neil's money, in order to stop this happening again, as it was obvious that it would, but I really didn't relish the thought of having to do this. I would then be in a position to give Phil some money each week to buy groceries with Neil.

Antony Brown had offered outreach services from Oak Villas on a Monday or a Thursday. This was scheduled to begin in the week of February 23rd.

The list was made as follows:

Kings will meet with Neil on Tuesday, Wednesday and Friday.

Neil will continue to see Probation on a Monday afternoon.

He will see a worker from Oak Villas on a Thursday afternoon. (For outside activities).

Care Coordinator will contact Neil by phone.

Do you remember that at one of these CPA review meetings it was stated that Kings were not qualified in looking after someone like Neil, with such complex needs? I agreed with this, but they used them anyway.

Phil was a very good Carer; but he admitted that with Neil he was out of his depth and he wasn't with Neil for long. What we had with all of these carers was that they could see things weren't right with Neil, he was depressed and frequently in an agitated state and he wasn't eating properly. There was little or no food in the house, no gas, no electricity, his phone was cut off and his goods were going missing, yet no one ever informed us.

It was me who wanted this meeting, there were occasions too when Neil wasn't in, or answering the door, and they would just go away. Phil was good with Neil, but he *wasn't qualified* to look after him. I asked on numerous occasions for more input from his CPN; she did ring Neil on occasion, but unless Neil went to these meetings every three months, she or other CPN's didn't see Neil.

I wanted **them** to visit Neil so that they could see for themselves at first-hand how he was living, and I wanted *them* to take him shopping. No, they wouldn't do either one of these things.

We saw Antony Brown from Oak Villas once, but he never did allow Neil to go into Oak Villas to socialize or to get a hot meal. He used the excuse of Neil taking drugs, but this wasn't truly valid, as other drug users were going into Oak Villas, including Neil's friend Aidy. He never did get this service. Neil's CPN couldn't contact Neil by phone, because by this time he didn't have a land phone, or a mobile phone either.

If I had let them refer Neil to a drug worker it would have taken many months. I contacted Caroline at Westgate and pleaded with her to take Neil. These places are so in demand as there are so many people on drugs, and it is so badly under-funded. Neil did jump the queue because of my intervention. Caroline was brilliant and she always felt, that Neil's problems were fired up because of his mental illness.

****

Neil was allocated a new psychiatrist but was yet to see him, and Dr Plackett had written to him about his concerns after we had seen him with Neil at Guild Lodge.

He told Dr Baddiel that we were very concerned about Neil's welfare, and that Neil was living alone in a manner which seemed to be chaotic and isolated, having spent a lot of money and having sold a lot of his possessions. He had told Dr Plackett that he had started reducing the drugs that he was taking, and was only taking one bag a day. He had told Dr Plackett that he was injecting heroin in a safe manner, and that I was supporting this by making sure he had clean needles, and I was also disposing of his old needles. We told him that we were deeply concerned about Neil's vulnerability, but we felt unable to provide the intensive level of support which we told him that Neil had needed since his release from custody.

Dr Plackett did detect a great sense of frustration from me; he said that I had expressed my frustrations in various ways in the past, in a manner that greatly affected Neil. I am not too sure what he meant by this!

Yes, I have had to fight and complain about Neil's ill treatment, and I wondered if he had meant that this wouldn't have endeared Neil to the 'Services' that were providing Neil's care. The fact was though that Neil didn't, wouldn't, have the care as little as it was, if I *hadn't* intervened; so I completely missed the point he was trying to make with this statement. My intervention hadn't turned Neil into the state he was in now. I probably prolonged the time that it took for him to get into this state, because I doubt that Neil would *have still been alive at this date* had the rest of his family and me **not** been there for him.

We had told Dr Plackett that Neil was in trouble with his peers due to the increasing debts he was incurring, and he felt that this may be promoting an increasing sense of social sensitivity and paranoid ideation. Neil did express to Dr Plackett his frustrations in relation to the care he was receiving, although on paper he thought that it did seem fairly complex and comprehensive. He knew though that Neil *hadn't* been seen by his psychiatrist since he had been released from custody, and he also knew that Neil had seen him twice, so he told Dr Baddiel that he was <u>very keen</u> for Neil to be made an appointment

425

for him to be seen by Fernlea General's psychiatrist, and to make this as soon as possible.

Neil told him that the small amount of care was only put into place recently, as when he came out of prison there was **nothing** in place and he had already gotten into a mess before anything was done. He told Dr Plackett that he only had occasional contact with his local coordinator, but he was finding all of this hard to understand, as Neil's care plan actually suggests *a much greater degree of multi-agency involvement*, than **was actually** in place.

Dr Plackett said that it would seem however, bearing in mind the anxieties that Neil had expressed around the time of his release from prison, that arrangements **could** have been put into place earlier to provide support, and to identify and communicate Neil's needs. Dr Plackett was concerned that he was the one that we identified as Neil's first point of contact if things were to go wrong for Neil, and Neil needed to be encouraged to use and develop the resources around him. **(What resources around him?)** Just what is he referring to? The empty promises and lies on Neil's records? The help that was **supposed** to be given to Neil, yet hardly ever was?

He said that he could see on the whole that Neil seemed low. Neil told him that he was *not* coping very well on his own, and he was avoiding crowds and other busy social gatherings. He reluctantly admitted to the doctor that he experienced intense persecutory experiences, believing that a group of men were following him. He didn't want to explore this matter further with the doctor, but he said that he had noted from me that the description may well be psychotic.

I did tell Dr Plackett that Neil was speaking on his mobile phone when he hadn't even got it switched on. Neil told him tearfully that he had strong suicidal thoughts on a daily basis, and this the doctor had said was of **great concern** to him. He said that he thought Neil was at high risk of serious, and potentially suicidal behaviour, and he intended to highlight this in his correspondence to various agencies.

He told Neil that he would see him again to review him when he had the minutes of the care plan meeting which would need to involve his psychiatrist from Fernlea General. It was relevant, bearing in mind the complex needs that Neil demonstrated. He asked for details of the treatment service that were providing help for Neil with his drug addiction.

Dr Plackett summarized what his feelings were, and what Neil's needs were, and he said that he couldn't rule out the presence of psychotic illness process. The vague abnormal mental experiences Neil was reportedly suffering from, **were not** in his view, fully attributable to Neil's use of heroin, and indeed had been clearly evident to him when he was in custody and <u>free of illicit substances</u>.

Dr Plackett had written to the psychiatrists at Fernlea General before he was released from prison, and he had said in that letter and indeed to Neil, that he thought the use of the prescribed drug olanzapine would have been of benefit to Neil, and although in the letter to the hospital he hadn't explicitly told them to put Neil on the drug, he was asking them to think of doing so, but like everything else they **chose to ignore it** (after all it was only an opinion, and the GODS that are the psychiatrists at Fernlea General know everything, and need not take the advice of any other doctor).

He thought that this antipsychotic drug would help Neil in order to rationalize the medication he was currently receiving.

Dr Plackett said that he had **serious concerns** about Neil's vulnerability, and his inability to manage in a fully independent manner, and the **risk of suicide,** which he felt at that time, was *fairly significant*. He thought Neil was socially isolated, and was involved in illicit substance misuse, and was possibly experiencing persecutory phenomena, but because he had a limited repertoire of coping strategies, and a reduced tolerance to frustration, he wasn't able to cope with it all.

He also said that in his opinion Neil had a number of needs that might be difficult to meet (he realized that because of Neil's use of illicit substances it may prevent his needs from being met). Neil used illicit drugs BECAUSE his needs weren't being met, and now Dr Plackett is stating that because of his use of illicit substances it may be hard to deal with Neil's problems.

Dr Plackett still said though, "That Neil needed more monitoring of his psychotic symptoms, the identification of more suitable accommodation, the monitoring of Neil's suicidal thoughts, support and accessibility from the drug dependency services, a rationalization of his medication with the possible use of olanzapine and the identification of suitable vocational activities, even on a voluntary basis. Dr Plackett said the next time he would see Neil it would only be **after Neil** had seen another psychiatrist from Fernlea General, and that would be in the region of three month's time.

As usual, <u>every single recommendation</u> made by Dr Plackett was totally ignored.

****

Neil felt, and so did we, that Dr Plackett had thrown Neil to the wolves.

The only way the psychiatrists at Fernlea General and the Community Health Team would do anything for Neil, was to keep Dr Plackett involved in the loop, and for the Probation Service to be involved also, to keep the pressure on for Neil to receive treatment.

After a terrible time over a matter of weeks, and not getting anywhere with the Community Health Team, Ben gave me the name and address of Mr Nicholas to complain to.

****

I wrote this letter dated 26th February 2004.

Dear Mr Nicholas,

*I really didn't expect that I would have to write a formal letter of complaint so soon after we were told that this was a 'fresh start' for our son Neil Green. Relationships in the past had become strained, as there could be no doubt that Neil's illness **wasn't** taken as seriously as it should have been ie; stating that Neil suffered **<u>NO mental illness.</u>***

Our only support has been Neil's support worker from 'Making Space', Ben Law, who has been a tower of strength to us; he stated on many occasions to 'give the Services a chance'. We have done this, but we are still confronted by an appalling failure to support us.

I was then, and am grateful for the organizing of 'Kings' to see Neil three times a week, of asking Oak Villas to become involved once a week (although this cannot start because of Neil's present problems).

I was told by Neil's Probation Officer that she was told in no uncertain terms that Neil would be contacted by phone EVERY Wednesday by his CPN. Neil has been left hanging on his phone on Wednesday for this to happen. I explained to her that promises have to be kept, as Neil relies so much on them doing as they promise. I also told her that I had asked for Neil to be rung on Mondays, as this

428

is always such a 'bad day' for Neil, so because the CPN couldn't do this, she most kindly did it herself and rang Neil to motivate him into getting up, washed, ready to feed himself and then to get dressed ready for his interview with her in the afternoon.

Last Monday I rang Ahmet Ahmed at the Resource Centre because he had returned a call I made the previous Friday. He was in a meeting, so I left a message that I had returned his call, and could he ring me back. He didn't ring back Monday, so I rang him on Tuesday afternoon and left **another** message for him to ring me.

He didn't ring me Tuesday, Wednesday or even Thursday. In the meantime Neil was deteriorating fast in his health, he was not eating, had become unkempt, most of his electrical goods were gone, as also were his personal belongings. We needed help, and Neil needed a lot of help. Neil rang me on Friday, sounding very abusive, asking for money, threatening to call on me with his care worker for some of his belongings to sell for money.

I refused; he was ringing me on his support worker's phone. I tried to ring Ahmet to at least ring Kings to stop this. After five calls on the landline and more then on mobiles, I'd had enough. I rang Kings myself. I asked her to ring the support worker to stop him from lending his phone to Neil. I was obviously in distress when I rang the Community Centre, and left two messages for Ahmet to ring me leaving my mobile number, but yet again he didn't ring.

That was _four messages_ left last week, yet he never did ring me back. Neil says that they do it with **him** all the time, but **I'm** not as used to be treated so rudely. It really annoys me to see with what little respect we are thought of, or dealt with. It is very disrespectful to say the very least!

We went to see Neil's doctor. Dr Plackett on Monday 23rd February. I had taken the care-plan to show him. It is stated in that care-plan that Neil didn't want to go to the Resource Centre because he feels that certain members of staff treat him like something they've got stuck to their shoes.

He told Dr Plackett that, "They don't give me a chance; they talk to me like dirt."

Dr Plackett asked that "Neil needs to do 'something', to get out, couldn't he go to the Resource Centre with his support worker?"

He did so yesterday, Roberta Wilson (staff) denied Neil and his

429

support worker entry. She was offhand with Neil in front of his support worker. Her attitude, as has happened before, was confrontational. Neil asked to see someone else.

*She said," No, **I'm** telling you."*

Neil felt as many times before that he was discriminated against. She was the one recently who stated Neil had alcohol in his back-pack, which he denied. Neil wasn't confronted about this at the time, but she had used this as an excuse to deny him entry before, when she didn't even ask him to show her what he had in the bag, but she STILL told his CPN he had alcohol, not that she had <u>thought that he might have.</u>

*It's **not good enough** all this. It's not just Neil, we feel totally let down too. Dr Plackett said that in this time of chaos who is helping us? Again I rang the Resource Centre and asked for Keith Deighton to ring me. He was there, in **no meeting** but again no one rang me back. I would have made a verbal complaint to him about how neglected we feel at his staff's attitude problem to Neil. It really doesn't take a rocket scientist to work out why Neil can talk to Dr Plackett about his illnesses, but cannot talk to his CPN's. We feel totally let down. I copied this letter and sent a copy to Ben, Neil's G.P. and Dr Plackett*

*******.

We had a CPA Review meeting on 20th April 2004.

It was stated that the Crisis Plan remains unchanged from 2nd February 2004. Neil was still being supported by Phil from Kings three times a week. It was said that he had support with shopping and activites. Neil had asked for extra time on Friday to do some social activities such as going to the cinema. It was agreed that an extra hour could be made available on a flexible basis every month. This would involve Neil informing Kings in the week before, so that extra time could be made available. The care coordinator was to contact Neil on a weekly basis. His care coordinator was to be changed.

Tracy Farron would be leaving Lancashire and Neil was to have Angela Moore back as his CPN. She would take over when she finished the course that she is on. There will be a **gap of one month** and in this time it was to be the manager Ahmet Ahmed who was to oversee Neil's care. Neil was seeing his Probation Officer on a fortnightly basis. They said Neil has contact with his CPN on a

430

weekly basis, but he was aware that if he needed any help outside of these times he could make contact.

Neil was still having contact with the drug team and he has been prescribed methadone. Neil would have regular out-patient appointments with Dr Baddiel. These were to take place every three months.

I had asked if there was anything Neil could do to fill his time with, like a course of some kind, because Neil was not active enough during the week. They asked Neil in such a way to make it sound like his decision, when they said that they thought he had enough on in the week, so Neil agreed.

It was said that Neil lived alone in a rented house and that I had stated that *this wasn't the best* environment for Neil. The team agreed to keep accommodation as an ongoing issue for Neil.

It is true that on paper it looked like they were doing so much. Neil **wasn't** taking his medication, so I asked very early on for someone to come and give out his medication. Care workers from Kings (which changed their name to Cedar Rose, same company) were going in to Neil for one hour, three days a week, but then this changed to only two days a week.

It wasn't long before they stopped going into a cosy home, to going in to find nowhere to sit, and to no fridge freezer, so Neil could only get 'perishables' when he was able to use them straightaway because he couldn't 'shop and store'. He didn't have a cooker or a microwave, so what did they do for him? He didn't have money to do the shopping because he was in debt. They left him like this for eighteen MONTHS and they **never** tried to get him any other accommodation.

I tried to motivate Neil, I wanted him out of the house to stop him thinking about what he had lost, but no one would help me to do this. He was living a miserable existence, yet they continued to allow it to happen.

The meetings were a complete waste of time, nothing came out of them and Neil would drug himself up before we went. He did finally get C.M.H.T. to take over his money and be his appointee. They tried to help Neil to budget, but it was a non starter as he was having to go into the Resource Centre to get his money *where he wasn't welcome*, and where Ahmet would **rather call the police** than come down to

431

even talk to Neil.

Angela tried hard to cope with Neil, but he pushed her to her limits, as he kept changing what they'd agreed, as to how much he'd get on a certain day. I'd found it really difficult myself so I knew they would. We didn't think it would be as easy though for him to do it with someone he **wasn't** related to. We didn't think that he would send them to distraction, but he did, and it made his relationship with his CPN very strained indeed. He was driving Angela up the wall. I asked for her to pay up front out of Neil's money to a café or something of the like so that Neil would get **at least one hot meal a day.** So she went to Neil's local chippy without asking Neil his preference first. Unbeknown to her though, Neil was banned from this chippy. This further frustrated her, so she **wouldn't even** try anywhere else.

We were all frustrated, <u>failing him</u> and everything was snowballing out of control. Angela saw that I was getting really down with it all and she told me to back off a bit. I tried, but when I did they'd do even <u>less</u> for Neil and he'd get into *more of a mess*, so I'd end up being dragged back into the mess.

He was given a new care worker from Cedar Rose and we not only found out that this person was selling drugs, but he was also taking Neil's furniture for payment, and he'd taken Neil's 28 inch widescreen T.V. to the Cash Generator. We had gone into the shop to explain that Neil had a mental illness, so for them <u>not</u> to take any more goods off him. Sometimes though they continued to do so because Neil got someone else to take his goods into the shop, and tragically one of these people was this care-worker.

As soon as we found out Steve went over to the care-worker in his car and told him to go and get the T.V. back, which he did, but then he leant on Neil to pay him back the money he had to pay to get the T.V. back. This man had been doing this for ages, and taking half of the money. I told the Mental Health Team what had been going on and that I wanted this man sacked, not just for Neil's sake, but for everyone else he was going to and ripping off.

This **didn'**t happen, so Ben and I mentioned it again a lot later on and then they told us that he had been sacked, but it took a long time and constant pushing for them to do it. Who checks up on these people? How many more vulnerable people did he do the same to?

432

Kath from Citizens Advice Bureau had Neil's debt to Royal Bank Scotland cleared like she had done before with a different bank. It was simply more of the same. Will it ever end?

The police are **not allowing** Neil to have an <u>appropriate adult</u> AGAIN after the desk sergeant put the phone down on me yet again after I'd asked that they did this.

I returned home one afternoon to find the police at my house. Two officers were looking over my gate, whilst another officer on seeing me pull up in my car, came over to my driving side window and told me to hurry up and let them in, before they smashed my door down.

Again I complained to the police as to what rights do they have to threaten me like this. I knew nothing as to what they wanted, but they were looking for Neil.

Every police van passing near to my home gives me a deep sense of dread. An ambulance siren, the police helicopter in the air, it was like living on a knife edge.

Neil wasn't living; he <u>was just existing</u>! He was given the chance of Rehab at The Diana Princess of Wales Treatment Centre in Norfolk. While Neil needed this very badly for the treatment of his drug addiction, he had also deteriorated not only in his physical health but also in his mental health. He was though full of hope that he was getting this chance to be free of drugs.

His mental health seemed to be always fuelling his need for drugs. Surely it was a *combined strategy* that was needed, and the main problem which was his mental health, should be taking priority. I could be wrong but I did think that the Princess Diana Treatment Centre were expecting it to be more the drug issue, especially when we had no faith in the hospital and CMHT passing on to them the **full facts** as to how bad Neil's mental illness was, and if they had told them Neil's problems were brought on by drugs, because if they did say that, <u>it wasn't true</u>. I just *didn't* want them taking Neil there without them knowing all of the facts.

Neil needed help for BOTH his physical and mental health URGENTLY by this time.

CHAPTER TWENTY-EIGHT
Rehab

I have had to stop writing this book for a few days because I've had a particularly bad week, starting from when the Coroner's Office rang me to tell me that they **couldn't** find any reason for my son to have died. I have since received the Post Mortem Report and that too is a very upsetting thing to read.

****

It was in April 2005 that Neil was allowed to go to the Royal Princess Diana Treatment Centre in Norfolk.

I had been the one who got in touch with Social Services knowing that we would need their 'backing' to fund Neil's stay in a Rehab Unit, as the funds would have to be split between Mental Health NHS and Social Services. I was also *mistakenly* under the belief that having **more** people involved in Neil's case would further help us and our son.

I was wrong, because no one could influence the Mental Health Service into providing treatment for Neil, or even to first acknowledge that Neil had mental illness, and that he was self medicating.

I will always remember seeing Dr Plackett, afterwards, as he had said the same, telling Steve and me that he could understand why Neil used heroin, because it would calm him, and help to stop the voices in his head. It reminded me of Ritalin, as that is also an amphetamine. Usually amphetamines are used by drug users to give them a 'high', but in Neil's case they had a calming effect on him, as they acted in *reverse* on Neil's medical condition.

Isn't it really sad that my poor tormented boy had to use drugs to either stop his torment, or to give him a small chance of a normal life, even if for a little while?

The children who suffer with A.D.H.D. have a chance to lead a normal life with drugs. To assist them as parents, we will do anything we can to help relieve our childen of this heartbreaking

434

condition. We do not however allow our children to take *unnecessary* medication. We put a lot of thought into this, because **not** to do so, was in fact far more catastrophic. You have to weigh everything up together.

My son did much the same when he used heroin, but the sad thing is, that he only resorted to do this because he **couldn't get** the much needed help he so richly deserved, and in truth had the <u>right</u> to <u>receive.</u> He was so ill, yet the services out there not only turned their backs on him, but then proceeded to treat him as a <u>nuisance</u>, before cruelly and quite unnecessarily turning their backs on him, which resulted in him feeling that he was nothing, and didn't matter. He had the voices in his head telling him this also, so what chance did he really have? We tried to keep him safe; we tried to access help and services. We also **failed** him, and we have to live with that fact.

I will leave it to you, the reader of my book, to judge who is **truly** to blame? I will summarize my feelings about that at the end of my book, although you will now probably be well aware who I blame, but more about this later.

******

Norfolk is a long way away, but Neil managed to get there all by himself. He was taken to Preston with all of his belongings; then he got on a coach that would take him on the rest of his journey. For Neil to have done this on his own, to even be <u>able</u> to do it, ill as he was, showed us just how *truly committed* he was. He did try to help himself every time; the reason he failed so regularly was the fact that he was mentally ill, and the illness simply overtook him. **<u>We were so proud of him.</u>**

He rang us often, and as time went by I noticed a wonderful change in Neil. I felt that they were getting through to him. Like I said before, he would listen. He would try and put into practice what they asked of him, but what **they** didn't realize at the time, was that the therapy would have to be 'full on' and very intensive if it was to be beneficial to Neil.

This was a *dual* diagnosis treatment centre; they were to tackle his drug problem but <u>also</u> his mental illness. What they did **not** know, and what they told me when I rang the manager on Neil's unit, was just how much of a challenge Neil's illness was. They were not prepared for this at all, but they **<u>should have been.</u>**

435

Neil needed far more help than was on offer for him, but this had never been set up for him at all. It was obvious to them that Neil needed more one to one help, with much more input. They didn't have the resources there to cope with Neil, and they needed to re-structure the help surrounding him, which would be more costly, as for a start we were talking about more *qualified* staff.

Neil couldn't cope with his illness without that help, and when he didn't have the drugs and the alcohol as a substitute, he easily became very anxious and agitated. I was so very pleased at what they had managed to achieve with Neil in such a short time though. In fact I wondered what they <u>could</u> have achieved, had they had the *proper resources* in place to meet his needs.

Yet again CMHT **hadn't** come through with the right information or the correct package of care for Neil. They *should* have put an intensive package together for the treatment centre. Yet again they failed Neil. I got this from the manager of the centre, from the horse's mouth, so I knew that this was true.

Neil did get alcohol, and he did mess up, and he did break a window. The thing was though, that they were STILL willing to give Neil another chance DESPITE THESE PROBLEMS, and they actually told him so. After six weeks Neil was asked to leave, *but to return at a later date* when they could put into place an intensive package of therapy and care. He left a lot of his belongings there. In fact that is where they *still* remain, because Neil was **not allowed** to go back.

As far as Ahmet and his CPN and the team at Community Mental Health, Neil had had his chance and he'd blown it. This is a letter I wrote to Ahmet Ahmed on 7th October 2005.

Dear Mr Ahmed,

*I cannot put into words the deep regret I feel at this time as to the fact that you have decided **not** to fund Neil's stay at Rehab (Princess Diana Trust). I hope this is a <u>professional</u> decision on your part, and not a <u>personal</u> decision, as I know how deep your feelings run about Neil as you've told me so on more than one occasion.*

If it is therefore a professional decision on your part, I hope you can relay this to me in writing, and explain why and how you've come to this decision, when everyone else involved in Neil's welfare *says it is the **correct** thing to do, **including** the Rehab Centre themselves, who I have also contacted.*

*Could it be breaking the habit of a lifetime for you to do something **right** for a change after all the mistakes Fernlea General have made, and others including CMHT, which in turn have all served to turn Neil into the mess that he is now?*

In fact in a paragraph of the book that I am currently writing, I actually *say that Neil would be **better off dead**, than being looked after by you lot. I would have preferred to be told by you also, and not to be fobbed off by Eddina, when the decision had already been made.*

*When you have sent me the letter stating the reasons why you think Neil **is not committed** to helping himself change from his drug addiction, which will be quite interesting, as it TRULY must take some commitment to put yourself in prison.*

*Yes, it was **actually Neil who did this to himself**, and what's more he could not be dissuaded either by me or his solicitor, because in his words, "I need help!"*

*Help, which by the way has **always been lacking** when he's asked it from you. So he has done this to try to get off the drugs and stop offending. It will be interesting to hear your reasons.*

*I asked Neil why he didn't make his meetings with Eddina and the doctor. He said he couldn't, as he was 'banged up' at the time, so you've used this as an excuse that Neil was not committed. I put it to you that it's **you** who is not committed to helping Neil.*

*OK Ahmet I agree that Neil is difficult, and he's had a chance, but things weren't put into place for him at the Princess Diana Trust, but even so he made a **serious** attempt to work with them. In fact they were making giant strides towards helping him. Both Angela and I saw a marked improvement, so what could they achieve when things are **properly** in place? He tried really hard, did his life story and all of his homework, and he was the **only one** who did some of the work he was asked to complete.* **Isn't that making an effort?**

You know that I have banged on about Cognitive Behavioural Therapy for years, and the fact that it's because of Neil's mental health, that he takes drugs, which Dr Plackett himself recognizes, and the terrible disorder he's living with. It is therefore the responsibility of the mental health services to help Neil with his addiction, and more so to help with the therapies that he needs for his mental health which the Princess Diana can provide, and are **willing** *to put the work in to achieve.*

I will appeal against the decision **not let Neil go** *to the Princess Diana Trust, and I will copy this letter to everyone involved in Neil's welfare towards that end.*

Neil will be released on 25th October and I would appreciate an urgent meeting with you, Eddina, Neil's Consultant and other parties involved in Neil's care, including the drugs team at Westgate, which I had found years ago, and pushed them into taking Neil, thus seeing Caroline. Now they had tried their utmost, with **little** *concept of Neil's problems,* **unlike you** *who know him so well. Maybe that's it; they are willing to give him another chance, but you are too bogged down with Neil's* **past** *to do anything for him.*

I am also asking for more help with Neil regarding therapies, more contact with Eddina (Neil's CPN) and other services, housing, money and suchlike, and also for you to sort out the fact that The Princess Diana Trust are holding Neil's belongings, There are a considerable amount of articles there, (including his clothes) that Neil needs back, as **you have decided** *that he will not return.*

I await your earliest reply.

Susan Green.

****

Sadly Mr Ahmed never even had the decency to reply to my letter, either verbally or in writing.
****

It was true that Neil was in prison again. In fact Neil's health had deteriorated to such an alarming degree, that he couldn't cope with being alone in his house or looking after himself. Our son had gone from being a lad who always looked just 'SO', and was immaculately dressed in all his designer finery, with spiked bleach tipped hair, smelling gorgeous, clean shaven with his head held up high and looking confident, to now looking so dishevelled, unkempt, thin, unshaven and dressed like a tramp. His clothes were full of holes where he had burnt them because he shook so much. He dripped with sweat. He was always bent down, with his eyes looking at the ground, he wouldn't look up at anyone and he'd constantly rock himself to and fro. He'd also be extremely suspicious and wary

438

of everybody, and had turned into an absolute shadow of his former self. He hardly ever went out as he was so very frightened. He didn't eat, and by this time all of his furniture had gone.

We'd bought him *another* cooker, microwave, bed, and he'd got my leather suite that I replaced, just so that I could store it at Neil's for Ryan who was now engaged, and about to move into his new home. But that too, like the other stuff was taken or sold by Neil or more often than not by the undesirables who watched and haunted his every move.

****

I have told you throughout this book of Neil's distrust of the police, and how they *weren't* always sympathetic towards him, and even treated him quite badly at times. This now shows you how badly Neil was presently feeling, that he chose to run to **them** in his hours of need. They treated him *better* than the psychiatrists and Mental Health Team, and he'd understand that if he committed a petty crime they would have to lock him up, then he'd tell them if they let him out he'd do it again, so they **had** to send him to prison, where he felt much safer. He liked being told what to do, he needed to have structure in his life, and stay where he was fed, with no one tormenting him or taking his drugs, or always stealing his money, or forcing him into getting his money to give to them out of cash machines. He hated living with no furniture, and where he was so afraid and unable to cope or defend himself. He stayed in his bedroom where they couldn't look through his letterbox and see him. He always had his curtains closed, but they would knock on his window and his door, repeatedly. He took to leaving a note on his window saying that he was in hospital, but still they continued to pester him. Those people such as Neil are such an easy touch, and low-life's are especially drawn to them as they make such easy pickings and wonderful targets. You see them everywhere, people like Neil who are always being taken advantage of, when what they truly need is Mental Health help, as well as someone to stand up for them and help them to lead their daily lives in a decent way.

Neil's so-called care worker would come twice a week for an hour, but he **wouldn't even go into the house**. Instead he'd simply beep his car horn outside for Neil to get into his car; then he'd take him to the drug team meetings, or somewhere similar. How could he

439

possibly report on what Neil's home life was like, <u>when he did not even enter the house?</u> It didn't really matter though as his CPN already knew how he was living, not because she'd seen it for herself, God forbid that she'd actually get up off her backside to do that, no – she knew because I was telling her, as also were Neil himself and Ben his care worker from *Making Space.*

Ben did enter the house because he really did care about Neil.

No it didn't matter that this excuse of a care worker didn't report back to CMHT, because they would just have ignored him anyway, but having said that why were they not doing the job which they were actually being paid to do properly? What in God's name was their excuse for leaving Neil in such a pathetic and ill state?

We understood that he couldn't even take Neil food shopping very often, because Neil hardly ever had any money, because whenever he did get his cash, it might already be owed, or else someone had got to Neil first to borrow or steal it off him. More often than not the care worker would shove a prepared note through Neil's door saying he'd been.

Neil was often <u>just too ashamed</u> to even open his door, so was left to make some excuses yet again. All in all it was a complete and utter farce. His care worker was not interested in Neil or his welfare at all, if he had have been, then **detailed and URGENT reports** should have gone in every single week during this period especially.

****

Matalan was the store that Neil ran to most often. They had in fact **banned** Neil from the store, as he had also been banned from most of the other stores in Colne, which also served to make it much more difficult for Neil to shop for his food. He knew that going into Matalan would sound the alarm quickly. They had a camera faced towards the front main doors and he was well aware of this. He'd grab the most **useless** items, so ridiculous in fact that he couldn't even sell them.

He took things like old DVD's that were cheap to begin with, but he didn't <u>want</u> to sell them; he desperately simply wanted the police to come for him. He <u>needed</u> to be arrested; he <u>wanted</u> help and to be taken somewhere where he felt safe. His self-preservation urge was strongly in force. Despite his treatment he was still a human being after all.

440

He'd go to the back of Kwik Save and take a very large batch of toilet rolls or suchlike. He could hardly even carry them, which meant that he was so very obvious, so naturally he'd be picked up by the police again.

It was all so pathetic really, and if he *wasn't caught* he'd sell the stuff. Once he even asked an old lady on a friend's street if she wanted to buy some Always panti-pads.

She laughed, "Neil, I'm seventy-two years old."

He replied, "Do you have daughters, or friends?"

Neil's list of crimes, petty though they were, ran into so many in total. At *long last* we had the police beginning to ask questions. It had all **finally hit home** to them. Still it didn't help him in the main though, because even though they were mostly feeling sorry for Neil, they had to do their job and send him to court, hoping that perhaps the powers there could help Neil. However the court simply sent Neil into prison.

I ask you, who other than Neil would get his shopping in the trolley at Kwik Save, then walk through the checkout with the shopping, not pay for it, but pack it carefully before walking out with it, thus giving the security staff there plenty of time to realize what was happening right in front of their eyes? He'd actually wait to be mob handled as he left the supermarket, knowing that they were ready waiting for him outside. **This showed how ill Neil really was**.

****

I'd told his CPN that she should shop with Neil. He was either without his medication, disturbed or had too many drugs this day, and I mean *prescribed* medication. He was most certainly in no fit state at that moment in time, yet he was charged with theft. The Mental Health Services wouldn't stick up for him, and neither would the psychiatrists from Fernlea General, as they preferred Neil to be kept well away from them, and prison always suited *them* best. If Neil was in police hands, then that was good in their eyes, but if he was actually sentenced to prison, they actually looked upon this as a bonus, as this kept him out of their hands for a longer period. It was always the same which makes the law look so stupid. They didn't want to treat Neil themselves, but neither would they pass him on to any other doctors outside Fernlea to be looked at. It doesn't make any sense at all does it?

The extent of that stupidity showed itself when they gave Neil an A.S.B.O. on one of his very last appearances at court. They'd gone completely mad. I was sure of that and I couldn't get over it. Do the courts not take on any of the responsibilities of adding to my son's torment? I would have thought that theirs would have been the voice of reason. They were well and truly stitched up by these so-called doctors, and sadly Neil just played right into their hands. **Think about this the next time you have a mentally ill person before you, and then don't let it happen again.**

How many thousands of other <u>never diagnosed</u>, but mentally ill patients, spend years of their lives going in and out of prisons as they are scared to live in the outside world as they are not getting proper treatment? Surely someone should notice that the SAME people keep coming back again and again and wonder why?

****

I took Neil to see a solicitor in Bradford after we had another typically disastrous CPA meeting.

This is the reality of what they expected of Neil, and he couldn't meet any one of their demands, as they already knew because of his very real and continuing descent into much more **serious** mental illness. They would move the goal posts, and tell Neil he'd have to meet all of his appointments, have drug tests, anything to prolong the time, so that Neil would fall by the wayside. **They continually held a carrot in front of him; then whipped it away.** Thus they were actually beating him with the proverbial stick, as they were always asking the **impossible** of him.

****

However we had a truly wonderful drug worker from Inwood House in Colne. Mick was so committed to Neil, and he knew his stuff. In fact he'd taken drugs himself, been a 'bad' lad when young, stealing cars and suchlike, but he, with a lot of hard work, had turned his life around and he gave of his time to both Neil and me. I had never known anything like the way that he was with Neil. How understanding he was, how he knew all the excuses, he never let up with Neil. He was **exceptional;** we trusted him to have a key for Neil's house, so that if he wasn't able to get a response off Neil when he'd deteriorated so badly or was so frightened, he'd enter the house to make sure that he was alright.

442

He was man enough to care, and conscientious enough to do an exceptional job of looking after someone in **great need** who also had a drug problem. I cannot tell you how excellent he was; we had never had it before from anyone, and he meant so much to us. Unfortunately he had to re-apply for his post, but it was given to someone else. We were so very sorry. They were stupid to let Mick go. He was so good because he'd been there himself, so he truly understood the problems of being on drugs from an insider's point of view.

Whoever employs him in the future is onto a winner. I'd recommend him to anyone, and what's more I'd trust him to give 110% at whatever he does. We have him for a little longer and while we do he acts as the appropriate adult at the police station, after they assure me yet again that this will happen again in the future, but I've heard it all before.

We have another disastrous CPA meeting.

It was the *usual thing*; the emphasis was placed on Neil to meet his appointments, which was very difficult for him to do. Neil never was aware of the time even when he was younger, if he wasn't reminded, as he was just so forgetful. Even if you did remind him he'd set off to go, and then something else would come into his head then he'd set off in the *wrong* direction.

We had told the drug worker **not t**o make appointments for Neil in the morning because he couldn't make them. He would probably have been up all night wandering, and then he'd take his medication which would make him drowsy and totally out of it, sometimes when he'd got it wrong and probably overdosed on them.

It made no difference though, as they continued making the appointments to suit **them**, and if Neil still missed keeping them it was yet another black mark for them to say that he <u>wasn't committed</u>. We were always saying the same things Ben and I about Neil's environment, and that he **shouldn't** be living like this. We wanted him to live in a more secure environment, sheltered, with help on hand for him. At this meeting I was asking for Neil to go to the Princess Diana Drug Rehab Unit.

I rang Westgate and they said that Neil had been taken over by another drugs team, yet we knew nothing about it at all. They had passed Neil onto Social Services' drug team, to this woman who kept giving Neil morning appointments knowing full well that he could NEVER make them. This was <u>such a bad move</u> because Westgate were exceptional in their care.

Neil's Probation Officer was at this meeting, and again she put the emphasis on Neil to stop his offending. **He would if he could! Why could she NOT understand this?** He would have been able to stop taking drugs as well if he had been given the right treatment and medication, and been given the medication by someone, rather than him having to do it himself when his memory failed him so often that it was always rather hit and miss.

They asked Neil to continue seeing Rick Fisher and for him to work with Neil on relapse techniques and to remain drug free. They all said that they wanted Neil in another Rehab Unit. This was naturally a non-starter as they **wouldn't allow** it again, and if they did they couldn't do as before and give the *wrong* information about Neil's mental health, or indeed **omit** telling them how severe he was, so they thought it best not to bother at all in their eyes.

His CPN Eddina went on AGAIN about Neil going to Oak Villas for therapeutic activities and listed below what was deemed necessary:-

To increase Cedar Rose to two sessions per week.

Dr Porter at Guild Lodge will review Neil's mental health and may consider placing Neil on Clozaril.

To meet appointments with her every two weeks.

To have regular drug screening and to look at a suitable Rehab Unit.

She would monitor all appointments.

She would send Neil appointment times.

It just shows what nonsense is written down so that it looks like 'on paper' (at least) that they were doing something.

****

Neil saw Dr Porter in prison, but he hadn't to attend any appointments to see this doctor, so *how on earth* could he be put on Clozaril?

Oak Villas, again? They'd been promising Neil the same thing for nearly two years but without fruition.

Rick Fisher was **not** Neil's drug worker anymore, he'd seen Neil once when he came to my house for their *initial* meeting, then he left

Inwood House, and we never saw him again as a drug worker that is. I was the one who had to contact Inwood House to ask for someone else, thus seeing Mick, but this was <u>after</u> the meeting at CMHT. This being the case, how on earth could we possibly have an appointment for someone **who no longer even existed** at Inwood House?

If Neil didn't go to see Eddina, and he **didn't** a lot of the time because he was too ill, chaotic or locked up; she just put another black mark against him and left it at that. She wouldn't ever dream of contacting Neil or going to his house, or doing anything to see if he was okay. God forbid for her to ever do that, or give Neil an extra inch even.

****

I've told you about the other drug worker from Social Services, insisting that Neil visit her in the morning when Neil couldn't get up because of his medication. This was the Social Services Social Worker, who had replaced the drug team at Westgate Burnley who were wonderful. So on this day of the meeting she gave him another appointment for *yet another morning.* No one at these meetings ever listened to us, no one made allowances for Neil; instead they did what THEY wanted to do at times to SUIT THEMSELVES. Neil's needs as the client were always ignored. His tremendous efforts were marked down only as failures, because he would do as much as he could at times, but never *quite* be able to succeed, as they seemed to move the goalposts to that end.

Everything they did conflicted with Neil's real needs; they never served to <u>help</u> him. Is this fair? Is this the SAME Mental Health Service that all of us might be under at some time in our lives? Isn't this a truly horrific future for many of us to look forward to?

****

It's at this point in my book that I would like to tell you about Aidy McMahon, (his real name). Aidy was Neil's friend who he met when he came out of hospital, after he'd been in there for nearly a year, and he went to live near the Resource Centre.

Aidy lived nearby too, but he was always at Neil's house, they both used drugs together, but in a safe way, and they looked out for one another. Every time we went around to Neil's, Aidy was there, so we found ourselves providing food for the two of them when we

445

went to the chippy or to Morrisons for pies or chickens; *Neil loved their cooked chickens.*

We didn't mind, and Kathleen and Barry did the same, and even took them out together. We went out with Aidy and his lovely mum Lily, and we took them for an enjoyable pub lunch. I had a lot in common with Lily because of her relationship with Aidy, as he was hard work too and a real worry for her.

Poor Lily, she suffered with a back problem and Aidy doted on her. He gave her money when the D.S.S. took away her D.L.A., quite mistakenly so, because they didn't believe her illness, which turned out to be tumours that had formed in her spine. When she did finally find out how ill she actually was, she died within six weeks of going into hospital.

Lily was such a lovely lady who suffered terribly, and was let down by her doctor. We always used to talk about our lads. Aidy used to be a body builder; in fact he came second in the Mr Pendle competition and won a trophy. You would never think someone as dedicated as he was would abuse his body with drugs.

He was a lovely quiet lad, older than Neil by about ten years. This is why you should never judge people by what you see on the outside. Why Aidy went into the drug scene was unknown to his family. He had a warm and loving family; they were so close knit. His sister Johannah lived next door to his mum with her husband and their two 'bonny' lads. I've told her that I wanted to mention Aidy and she gave me her permission to do so.

Like I said before, they don't know why Aidy turned to drugs, he had a relationship that broke up, but they didn't really know if it was that that actually set him on the road to destruction. He'd been using drugs for about eleven years. The thing was with Aidy that the use of drugs over a period of time had brought on a form of mental illness, such as the paranoia, which can be a usual occurrence.

His illness was certainly different to Neil's, and he knew it to be so. Drug users are not in the main <u>stupid</u> people, but it is an idiotic thing to do. As I said we liked Aidy, he was a really lovely lad who wouldn't hurt a fly. Other drug users tried to use him, but he avoided them, though he knew that Neil wasn't able to do this. Neil was always sought out and taken advantage of.

Aidy chose to be alone with his mum or with Neil. However there

446

came a time when Neil drifted away from Aidy because at that time he was trying to get off drugs, and he couldn't be around Aidy whilst he was doing this; also Aidy didn't like the sort of people who used to seek Neil out, because he was an easy touch and so very vulnerable. Aidy also **hated** needles. He'd tried them once and reacted badly to a needle, so he stayed clear of them after that.

On Tuesday 29th June 2004 Aidy was found dead in his home. No one had told his mum or his sister; it was left to an elderly neighbour to inform them that their son/brother had been found dead. They said it was an injection in his thumb, which even I think sounds far fetched, especially so when coupled with the fact that it was not only through a needle, which Aidy completely hated, but also with being into a thumb on the same hand that he would have used to hold the needle to inject. Isn't it so that you have a pulse in your thumb, therefore it would go straight to your heart? Not sure of this though!

I found the whole thing very 'iffy' to say the least, very far fetched and so much out of character for Aidy as I knew him. I really don't believe it of him; he would **never** have done this, as he did **not** like needles at all.

Neil said he knew who had killed Aidy, and who had injected him with this lethal dose, and this bloke had Aidy's mobile phone. He also had Aidy's wallet and he had bragged about killing this lovely, thoughtful lad who took care of his mum and doted on his nephews, and especially liked art and was a keen drawer.

Where's the honour amongst you drug users, like there is honour amongst thieves, why do you not turn him in? Aidy was a sick man, but it was easy to get into his house; he was probably fast asleep having taken his medication and had a drink more than likely, he'd be out cold, so would therefore have been an easy target.

This is what Neil thought, because he went into the police station every day to pester the police, asking them if they had picked up this man, who was around forty years old and lived with his mum. Neil said that there was also talk that this man messed with kids, and Aidy's sister told me the same. What an all round sick individual he sounds!

No, Aidy didn't deserve to die. He harmed no one but himself. Lily became terribly ill after Aidy had died. He was cremated on 8th July and Lily died on 14th October of the same year.

She always said, "It's good that Aidy went first; I know that he wouldn't have been able to cope with me dying, and he would not have been able to cope at all after I died, as he'd have been so lost without me."

I feel so sorry that Johannah had to suffer the loss of her mother and her brother so close together. This was something else we have in common. God bless her and her family.

Neil, although deeply saddened by Aidy's death, still continued to 'dabble' with drugs, and we were terrified of finding Neil dead on a daily basis. Sadly Neil *couldn't* stop the voices any other way, and even the loss of his dear friend wouldn't keep those voices in Neil's head at bay.

Neil continued to visit Lily until she died, and Johannah's boys loved him, and they told me some lovely things about him. I just wanted to tell you a little about Aidy. He was a 'druggy', but he was also a very decent human being.

Neil was different to Aidy, he had been mentally ill from being a child, so he used drugs for a totally different reason. Even so though, Aidy needed help, and although he got the services that Neil couldn't get; his mum said she too pleaded for help for him and got very little.

****

2004 was a terrible year and while we are talking about doctors that get it wrong; it was also this year that we found out my sister Pauline had cancer. Her doctor was treating her for 'piles', whilst in fact she was suffering from cancer of the bowel. The bleeding she reported that run down her legs while in the shower like a tap was turned on, (her words), was cancer. Finally she had an operation in which a wonderful surgeon saved her life, and when she was struck down with M.R.S.A. after the operation, the truly wonderful nursing staff that had treated her on Intensive Care for months brought her back from the brink of death.

Dear Pauline, so like my mum in being both generous and kind. She wanted so little out of life; yes she was just exactly like Mum. We were so relieved when she came through the operation. Our euphoria though was short-lived. We visited her in Bolton Hospital as much as we could as naturally we still had our own nightmares going on at home. In between visiting Pauline on Intensive Care while she was attached to all of the machines keeping her breathing, keeping her alive, it was always touch and go. Visiting her on Christmas Eve; then giving Neil a Christmas where it was repaid by ruining our Christmas Day and me actually getting hurt was just too much.

This was followed by me visiting my beloved sister on Boxing Day while the snow fell behind her out of the hospital's windows. I was talking to her all the while, holding her hand, wearing my most sparkly scarf just in case it caught her eye, as if it would, laughing and joking with members of staff who were full of Christmas cheer, lifting our spirits.

Dai, whose name I can only remember because I rang in every day and I was told by the nurse it was Di I spoke to the last time.

I said, "No it wasn't, because it was a fella."

"No," she replied. "That's Dai, he's Welsh named."

Ha! Ha! Yes. All the members of that nursing staff were wonderful. I thank you all for looking after my sister.

We all have in our lives some pain, but ours was always overshadowed by Neil's problems, so ours appeared to be tenfold at these times.

****

We have always had wonderful dogs that have helped us to keep sane. Pets are wonderful as they give us so much, yet ask for so little in return. They know when you are down and they give you unconditional love, and while I write this book, crying on and off, it's Mac our dog curled up on my settee that looks at me with his big brown eyes and comes to put his head on my lap for a love.

There was Katie before Purdy, who grew up with Ryan. Tess my best friend was another border collie like Mac. She was tragically taken from us when a taxi driver lost control of his car and knocked her down. She used to run past Neil's bedroom door; she was extremely wary of him; probably she knew what he put me through. Our latest dog Mac has brought my husband and me a lot of love after the pain of losing our other dog.

A recent photo of Steve
pictured here with Mac on his knee.

CHAPTER TWENTY-NINE
No Christmas This Year

We got through Christmas 2005 in a dream. We were prepared for a scary time because Neil was so very down, depressed, anxious and pacing. He'd completely lost his appetite. Neil normally loved my roast dinners; he famously told everyone in his company about them. He hardly ate a thing on Christmas Day. We were prepared for Neil to stay for a few days over Christmas. We would take it in turns to keep a vigil over him, we could do it together.

Steve told me, "We can't let him be on his own like he is."

True to their word, because of what had happened the year before, Kathleen and Barry *didn't* come, and Ryan was again with his girl and her family. Here I was cradling Neil, and feeling very worried about him.

Neil left just as quickly as he came, leaving us both very worried about him. He was jumpy and was not really with us at all. He seemed so suspicious. He needed to go, but I had really wanted to just tuck him up safely in bed whilst we watched T.V. and we were all on hand in case he needed us. Mum was crying, in fact we're all crying. I hate Christmas!

Whilst it was always difficult for everyone, we would have liked Neil to stay with us, especially now when he was so very ill and miserable. However Neil often preferred to do his own thing, he really only wanted to be like others of his age. He longed for true friends, he missed Aidy so much, as in a way they had understood each other's problems.

However when it came to money matters, Neil would never let me help him apart from his shopping usually. At the moment however he had completely lost his appetite, and was living more inside himself.

Steve and I were both afraid to let him go, yet also unable to stop him. Mum was so upset to see Neil this way, we all were, and the only choices we had at that moment were to either let him go of his own accord which is what he wanted to do, or to try to make him stay against his wishes. He was after all a grown man, and though it broke all our hearts we just had to let him go. Neil could NOT live with us any more, but neither could he stay away from us for long. The draw of home and his family always brought him back. Neil loved us all just as much as we loved him. His faults were due to his illnesses, not because he ever *wanted* to hurt us. The voices he could hear in his head, he could no longer ignore, for by now they were ruling his whole life.

****

I have started to have 'panic attacks' and I can feel my heart banging inside my chest. I am coming to the end of my book and Neil's life, so this is especially hard for me to do, but do it I will!

I have no doubt that there was a lot going on in Neil's head around this time; the voices he was experiencing were getting worse in what they were saying, and his thoughts of suicide increased so much, as he told me this was it, because it was his **only** way out.

He was constantly battling with the voices in his head. He needed constant reassurance, which in turn meant that he really needed to be with someone 24 hours a day. We often said that at times Neil needed locking up and the key throwing away. We meant that in these times of dire need; he needed to be somewhere with a tight regime of care therapy to pull him through. He had bouts of being able to cope with life, but because he'd **not** got the help when he should have done, these were now very few and far between.

The only way that he thought he would get that help was to keep putting himself in prison. He needed the structure; he should have been in a *secure* hospital because this was totally necessary for him, but foolishly Dr Plackett said that he couldn't justify locking Neil up in his secure unit at The Guild.

If this wasn't the answer, then somewhere else should have been found for Neil. It **wasn't right** that Neil had to be locked up in prison either. Neil **couldn't** cope with life, as his mind was in complete and utter turmoil. He was absolutely shattered and at the end of his tether, yet still the powers that be were NOT concerned enough to really help him.

****

He was back in police hands shortly after Christmas. I wasn't surprised. If Neil was so bad with his drug habit, would he really keep putting himself into prison and thereby going through a very fast and painful detox?

I don't think so; it wasn't the drugs that were causing him to steal in order to support his habit, because Neil was actually not really a criminal, (except on paper that is.) In fact he **wanted** to be caught; he didn't ever steal anything of great value; he always stole as a cry for help, never ever for monetary gain. For him it was purely a means to an end. His drug habit wasn't that bad, and he could have pulled away from it, but he needed help to do so. He wasn't a 'druggy' in the accepted sense of the word.

He was self medicating, and the need for that wasn't the same when he was in prison and being taken care of. Doesn't it sound *disgusting* to you all that the only way my son felt safe was in prison? No one wanted to change things for him, the prison, the courts, or the police. They all knew what Neil was doing, yet they let it carry on over and over again. They must have also known that they were being used by the hospital, so that they would be let off from doing anything for Neil. Sadly therein lay the **injustice** and the crime.

****

On January 2006 Neil was released at court after ten days. I knew Neil was coming out on this day and I rang Rose at the drugs team at Westgate, she told me that Neil was being taken care of by another drugs team and that he would be well taken care of, and what I was asking for would be done by them before Neil was released. It would all be put into place.

Yeh! I've heard that before but I live in the **real** world. I expected in that case to take Neil straightaway to the drugs team and get Neil a methadone prescription if that is what he needed. I was being told that this **wouldn't** happen now upon Neil's release.

This was rubbish of course, for yet again Neil was given no medication upon his release. Without prescribed drugs Neil is here shaking, frightened and withdrawn. Neil said it was a bad day. He didn't have a coat so he was freezing. It was indeed a very cold day, so I asked him where his coat was.

"The police have it," he answered.

I was sick of this; they had taken his coat as they had many times before for forensic tests, but they **never** gave him his clothes back. He'd lost numerous coats and shoes in this way. I took him to the Army and Navy Store in Burnley to buy him a coat. I rang Eddina, his CPN for her to ring his doctor to make sure a prescription was ready to pick up.

Once again this was a Friday, with only one hour to spare to pick up the prescription before the surgery closed until Monday. She should have <u>already</u> done this; it's 'supposed' to be her job, but she **never** does. She says she'll do it though.

Why didn't she ever do it *without* me asking her? The prison told me that they informed CMHT when Neil was to be released. If this was so then things should be in place but they NEVER are. Eddina always blames the prison. I asked her to ring me so that I knew it had been done, but she didn't ring me; when I rang her I was told that she had already left to go home.

I therefore rang Dr Brown and I told him that Neil had no methadone and no medication.

He replied, "This is disgraceful. If you had rung me I would have made certain that Neil was scripted for methadone."

I didn't know that he would do that, and I was told it would have been done, but no one had contacted me to tell me who in the drugs team was looking after Neil now, if it wasn't Westgate.

Dr Brown checked if indeed Eddina had ordered the prescription, he asked Lorna who was on reception; she knew of Neil's problems and I know her mum and she always went that extra mile with Neil as she likes him, and also Neil knows that he can rely on her. She told Dr Brown that no antipsychotic drugs had been ordered.

I couldn't believe it and neither could Dr Brown. These were the most important drugs of Neil's medication, besides the Ritalin I would add.

Neil still suffered from this ADHD condition, but he was told that he didn't need Ritalin now as he was on antipsychotic medication. It's actually a plain but true fact that the psychiatrists from Fernlea General denied Neil this medication, even though he had a true diagnosis and was in truth still suffering from this condition. Yet Neil was NEVER again allowed to receive Ritalin.

Dr Brown told me that he would write another prescription and he said that I could pick it up straightaway.

I said that I couldn't.

He said, "You should, because Neil needs them now."

I said, "Well I know this, but he's now in that bad a state knowing that they had done it to him again, and lied about having it sorted out for him after they promised him that everything would be arranged, that he's now gone off to 'score'."

I was told by Mick his drug worker from Inwood House that this was a very dangerous time for Neil. He'd been incarcerated, so had been off drugs for weeks, so was now extremely vulnerable and upset, so he could easily overdose.

I had no option. I had to leave without Neil. How did I feel? (I'm reading this excerpt from my diary that I wrote on that day).

I feel mad, angry, weary, deflated, gutted and that things will never ever change.

I was waiting for the phone to ring, but worried as by whom. Would it be the police, Neil, or the hospital? It was out of our hands, as the tornado called Neil, never ends. Of course we see Neil in between these times. He comes to our home, to his Gran's and to the disability centre to see his other Gran.

Personally I cannot go into Neil's house as it makes me physically sick to see how he is living. I know that I'm a coward, and he's my son, but the memories of the lovely things that he had, and being worried of who he had in his house, I was scared to go there. I didn't want to meet up with the undesirables who had their hooks deeply imbedded into Neil.

I had already been threatened in my car twice and was run off the road on one occasion by people who were after Neil for money. The other time there had been trouble, Neil had been with me in the car.

When I stopped, a car parked close to my door, so that I was unable to open my door. Someone got out of this other car, and then stood at the passenger side of my car right next to the door. This ensured that I was completely blocked in and could not move my car.

Now every single time I turned into Neil's street, my heart would always leap up into my mouth, and my stomach would be forever churning and I'd start to shake.

'Would this be the day that I would find my son dead?' That thought always ran through my head, and other thoughts too, terrible thoughts!

****

27th January (Friday) 2006.

Neil rang me; he had been arrested again for theft the day before from Matalan. The police were talking to Neil about thefts in December. He'd probably own up to them too, even if it *wasn't* him. He went to court on Saturday and was sent to Preston Prison.

I wondered, 'Do they keep a cell ready for Neil's return?'

I'm chasing around again for his solicitor, who never rings me back. He's not like David. I asked custody to put me through to Group 4 and they let me talk to Neil's solicitor, who was with Neil.

He asked me to write a letter for court to get Neil out of prison for a pre-arranged meeting at the Resource Centre with yet another new psychiatrist Dr Musto. No one wanted to get involved with Neil because of all the controversy surrounding him. The real fact was that they didn't want to know, having closed ranks with their colleagues and the Hospital Trust.

We'd seen Dr Baddiel and he started off by saying that he didn't want to get involved with the past problems, and he hardly lifted his head to look at Neil or myself. There was no eye contact at all. I gave him the benefit of the doubt the first time, but the next time we met he was just the same.

I said to Eddina, "Would you want to go to a hospital and see your psychiatrist when it was obvious they *didn't* like you or want to treat you?"

She said, "No," and agreed that Neil would never be treated properly at Fernlea General.

It's the truest thing that she has ever said. Yet this was where the GMC had said that Neil had to be treated, by the *very same* doctors that I'd reported to them in that *same hospital.

So we are about to see another psychiatrist that will treat him just the same. The trouble was that we couldn't fight the system itself, so we had no option but to see these incompetent doctors with no feelings at Fernlea General, No one else would see us, as Fernlea General just **wouldn't allow it.** Why did they keep clinging onto Neil when they made it so obvious that they did not wish to treat Neil at all? Just what were they scared of?

It was so hard, especially with the way I felt about these people,

456

not to blow my top. I didn't even want to give them the time of day as they disgusted me. This meeting was the worst that we had ever been to, which is surely saying something after what we had previously been put through.

There was a lot of ill feeling in the room by everyone that wanted something done for Neil. They were trying to address the **same** issues that we tried to do for years. Ben was so disillusioned with it all. He knew like we did who was to blame for how Neil was.

That day Ben said, "Doesn't Neil look so very tired and gaunt and extremely frustrated?"

I will tell you more about the meeting later. Meanwhile I have written a four page letter which was read out in court.

I couldn't be there, as it was too distressing for me to see Neil in the 'dock' going through the same, when I knew he shouldn't be there, but there was nothing I could do to change things, no matter what I said. I'd already had a heart scare just before Christmas and Steve's was yet to come. I was depressed and felt so inadequate that I couldn't help my son, and couldn't make anything happen to make things better for him.

The court was always sympathetic, but it couldn't do a damn thing except to apportion blame to the hospital and the services, but it was just talk, and as we all know talk is so cheap. I never held back though, I always told the truth, and let them see just how things were.

Neil was released from prison on 30th January at 5.00pm. I lent him some money when I picked him up from court as I didn't want him to have his cash card. I would get him some money tomorrow and then take back the amount that I had lent him. I shoved £20.00 through his door on 31st January and told him on a note not to get drugged up for the meeting later with Dr Musto.

Mick from Inwood House met me at the Resource Centre and gave me Neil's risk assessment form as shown below:-

Clients Details, name and address. Dated 24th January 2006.

Risk Specification.   Assessment Risk (Score 1 - 5)

Risk		
1. Self Harm	YES	5
2. Accidental Overdose	YES	3
3. Harm to Others	NO	2
4. Child Care	NO	0

5. Personal Safety   NO   0

6. At Risk to the Community YES   2   **Total 12**

Is a full risk assessment and analysis required?   YES

1. Self Harm - Deliberate and Suicide

   Depressed Mood   YES

   Impulsivity   YES

   Suicide plans made   YES

   Previous suicide attempt: Cut arms and wrists.

   Dangerous method   YES

2. Accidental Overdose   Yes

   If yes, how many times   ONCE

   Regular intravenous use YES

   History of past overdose   YES

   Overdose witnessed by others YES

   Alcohol involved   NO

   Injects alone   YES

   Drugs Involved   HEROIN

3. Harm to others   NO

   Past history of violence to others

   (may include sexual violence) NO

4. Child Care   NO

5. Personal Safety - Self Neglect   YES

   Past History   YES

   Long Term Institutional   NO

   Reliant on others   YES

Cannot cope with, or needs help prompting in:
Budgeting/handling money/accommodation   YES
Doing Weekly Shopping   YES
Taking care of personal hygiene YES
Cooking for self   YES
Homeless/no fixed abode   NO

Have there been any major events or issues in client's life or those around client in last 12 months?

YES, Self Harm and Depression.

6. At risk in the community   YES
  Drink-drive conviction   NO
  Drives/operates as part of occupation   NO
  Drives/works while intoxicated NO
  Uncaring/indifferent to risk   YES
  Chronic intoxication but still drives and works   NO
  Risk, threat from others   YES, Dealers

Level of Risk:
  For Self Harm   HIGH
  For harm to others   NIL
  For personal safety   MEDIUM

Category of Risk:
  Risk to staff, clients or residents   NIL
  Risk to the public   MEDIUM
  Risk to self   HIGH

Is there any significant evidence of risk in the following areas?
A. Risk of violence, harm to others
  Past   NO
  Current   NO
B. Risk of suicide
  Past   YES
  Current   YES
C. Risk of other self harm (please state), Overdose, Self Harm
  Past   YES
  Current   YES
D. Risk of neglect/vulnerability YES
E. Risk to staff   NO
F. Risk of medication   YES

Further action recommended:
Discussion with manager.

Risk history - Describe (include details of most serious harm caused description Account to self or others)

459

Client states he's self harmed at least 12 times whilst in custody for 8 days.

At CPA meeting. First impressions of Dr Musto:
He says that he is broad minded and he listens. He wants to talk to Neil on his own which is a good start. He says that he will refer Neil to Dr Plackett. I apologise as I have no faith in any doctor from Fernlea General. He says that he has only Dr McKewen's report from five years ago, not Dr Plackett's or any others. We find it funny that, and I look at Ben Law who rolls his eyes.

What we are asking for can't be done he says, no resources to accommodate Neil in some form of assisted, structured residential accommodation. Mick speaks up forcefully about Neil being at risk, and **you're** offering him **nothing.**

Dr Musto said that he would see Neil again in a month's time, which **isn't true** because he's on annual leave for a month, which is what we were told later by letter.

Mick says, "It's too long to wait, Neil's at **serious risk** NOW!"

No change. Nothing. The drug worker makes Neil another appointment **in the morning YET AGAIN**. It's all a farce.

Eddina says that she *hasn't* omitted olanzapine on Neil's prescription. I believe that she did because Lorna, the receptionist at Neil's doctors had told Dr Brown the same, and Neil was known personally to her, so she made a point of knowing what medication Neil was on.

Eddina also said that the prison **hadn't** told her that Neil was to be released on 18th January, and they **hadn't** told her that Neil had badly self harmed in prison. **Yet the prison said that they had contacted her personally about both.**

She then went on to say, as if it didn't matter, and of course too it being a lie, "Neil only self harms in prison anyway."

Mick was the first to tell her what he thought about that comment, then Ben speaks up. Next I say in front of everyone including my drugged up son.

"I feel like getting a gun and shooting Neil to put him out of his misery, because none of you want to help him, and you are all a disgrace."

We all came away from that meeting feeling deflated and
460

couldn't honestly believe what we had all just witnessed.

****

Weeks went by. I rang Dr Plackett's secretary and she stated that no referral had been made, and I told her that Dr Musto stated categorically that he would make the referral **within 48 hours**. However despite him saying this no referral had been made.

We received an appointment for Neil to see Dr Musto on Tuesday 13th June when he said on 31st January he'd see him in a month's time. (All of this being witnessed by a room full of people.)

Neil was **actually dead** by Tuesday 13th June. So they had really all helped him, hadn't they? **Helped him to die that is!** Their lies and false promises over many years served to end his life at the very early age of just 24 years.

****

We receive review care plan:

Mick Turbeck, the support worker from Inwood House, expressed his concerns that Neil was incapable of self medicating or self caring. He announced that Neil needed 24 hour support, and his Mental Health difficulties which need assessing (addressing is the term he actually used Eddina).

Mrs Green, Neil's mother also feels that Neil is mentally unwell and requires a comprehensive assessment and does not want him to live alone or go to Rehab. Dr Musto has agreed to contact Dr Plackett at Guild Lodge and request an opinion on Neil and to send this referral **within the next 48 hours**, though he did explain he could not guarantee that Dr Plackett would see Neil.

(There is rather a contradiction here, as I've been told that an opinion is not a referral, and as it turned out eventually Dr Musto did ask for an opinion, so he said over the phone, and he knew damn well what we were asking for. He did say that he would refer. He is simply another doctor who lies through his teeth).

Dr Musto has also requested that he sees Neil alone within the next FOUR weeks, to which Neil agreed, and to which THE DOCTOR lied about again.

Neil continues to use heroin and steal to pay for his addiction. Do you know something it's about time I make it quite plain. Neil NEVER DID steal to pay for drugs. **What Neil did steal wouldn't EVEN have paid for a good meal, never mind any drugs.** He

461

never had money for various reasons, including the fact that he couldn't handle money, so would spend it all in one day, and he would ALWAYS have it taken off him for various reasons. I suppose them saying this would make Neil sound worse than he actually was, and give them yet another excuse to deny him help all the time.

Neil has received a drug rehabilitation order and one of the conditions was that he attended appointments with the drug team, but as he failed to do this, as he is often offered **morning appointments** which he finds great difficulty in attending these due to his medication making him drowsy. The drug worker said that she would pursue this, and try to arrange a later appointment. *In fact she never does get round to doing this though.*

Due to Neil's chaotic lifestyle and difficulty in engaging with services, Eddina has referred him to the Mental Health Assertive Outreach Team. (They only deal with the **mentally ill** Eddina, you are tripping up here dear, as Fernlea General stated in a letter that Neil suffers **no enduring mental illness**.

Crazy aren't they? Because they wouldn't be attempting to show all this support and regular meetings that Neil's too ill to attend or else in prison. You can't have it **both** ways. (If you think you can, then you are maybe the mental one's).

Unfortunately due to staffing difficulties the Outreach Team don't currently have any capacity to take Neil on, but will keep his file on the waiting list. **(Until he dies, but still it's down on paper, isn't it?)**

Eddina told Neil to attend the **morning** appointment with the drug team to be scripted for methadone to reduce the risks associated with heroin. He was to receive continued support from Inwood House. A referral would be sent to Dr Plackett at Guild Lodge forensic services this week for further assessment.

Mick wrote a letter to give to anyone supporting Neil like Ben Law. He also sent one to Dr Plackett after knowing Dr Musto didn't refer Neil to him when he promised to do so within 48 hours and now weeks later Neil is deteriorating fast and **we are absolutely no nearer to getting any help for him at all.**

I rang Dr Plackett's secretary again, and I was crying and telling her that Neil was going to die; he was so very ill, and she said that Dr Plackett *couldn't* possibly see Neil unless he got a referral from Dr

462

Musto. **I told her that Neil was dead then!** She said that she could do nothing.

In the letter Mick told them how long he has worked with Neil, and in the time he had been with Neil he had been arrested three times, and while in prison he had seriously self harmed **each and every single time.** Neil had told Mick that he did not feel safe in the community, and he knew what his needs were, and that was hospitalization, where he could be watched and have daily support by *professional* people who understand mental illness, and who can also ensure that the appropriate medication was being strictly administered as and when required.

Neil forgets to take his medication and as these drugs are given to him to keep him stable, so this current way is <u>not working</u> as Neil forgets to take it because he has a tendency to lose track of day to day things.

Mick said that in his opinion Neil needed one to one daily support in a secure unit to achieve his goals. These goals being, to be drug free, stable in the community, which he certainly is not at the moment. He said that prolonging this treatment could be catastrophic for Neil and also to us all as a family.

****

Dr Plackett wrote to Mick and said that it was **impossible for him to intervene with Neil's treatment** as a referral had to made to him before he could see Neil. He said that I was frequently in touch with his service, and I acted as a strong advocate for Neil, but he said that it would be wise to go through the normal pathway in order to avoid confusion.

What was normal about any of this Dr Plackett?

The hospital were as pedantic as ever, delaying tactics I would say, in that they wouldn't give me any information, by quoting privacy to a patient, when in fact Neil had *already given them his permission years ago* for all or any information to be given to me about his health. They were always the same; they didn't want me poking my nose in, they wanted to be able to just walk all over my very ill son. I didn't make much difference as they walked all over me too, but I still intended to stir them up even if I got nowhere, and now while I look at all the documents and letters I've received over the years I can put it 'out' there for **all** to see, because they want to hide things, cover them up, so that they can do the same to someone else. So PLEASE EVERYONE OUT THERE let us make it harder for them by 'outing' them.

Ben asked me to write letters for Neil to sign saying that he allowed information relating to his health to be passed on to me. I did so for Fernlea General, Dr Plackett and Neil's G.P's who have always been good about that as Neil gave them his permission years ago.

Dr Brown wrote to Neil's solicitor on 7th March 2006 at her request. He quoted from Mick's letter what he thought Neil's needs were, and he agreed that Neil should be further assessed by a Forensic Psychiatrist. He also quoted from another psychiatrist that Neil had a VERY long standing use of heroin, WHICH IN FACT WAS TOTALLY UNTRUE.

Neil's use of heroin *only started* when he was **discharged** from hospital and put into the B & B. This was in 2002 but AT THAT TIME it was very much on and off. Dr Brown also stated that in his opinion Neil should be assessed by a Forensic Psychiatrist. I would like you to remember that, because a letter that I received from Fernlea General, in fact the Trust itself, states that Dr Brown was **not** of this opinion. In fact it was the final letter that I received from Fernlea General.

****

On one of Neil's visits to the drug team at Westgate, he saw Dr Kerr who then wrote to Neil's G.P. about his concerns over Neil. He firstly explained Neil's drug history and what they had decided was the best way to tackle his drug problem. He was more concerned about Neil's obvious decline in his mental health, and suggested to the doctor that Neil should engage actively with the Community Mental Health Team. He thought that Neil's adherence to prescriptive drugs was suspect, and he needed help with that to make sure he was taking his medication. He wanted his C.P.N. to see him more often, at least once a week and he suggested that **DAILY** supervision of his prescriptive medication and his methadone was warranted. He wanted Neil to be reviewed by his Mental Health doctor as soon as possible.

Everyone was saying the same. We all wanted the same things for Neil, but Fernlea psychiatrists, the Trust, and CMHT didn't, so they wouldn't do a thing to prevent Neil's decline, or alleviate his pain and suffering in any way at all. Instead they preferred him to either go away, be locked up in prison or for him to die. He gave them two of those things. I was sitting in a room at Burnley Magistrates Courts on my own, looking out of the window. I'd been there for six hours waiting for Neil to be put before the court. I wrote down my thoughts on the back of an envelope.

****

On the 2nd February 2006. Neil rang me from Burnley Police Station stating that he'd been arrested. I'd made his tea and I had asked him not to come too early because his behaviour was so irate and unstable that I couldn't cope with him all day on my own. I didn't expect him to be arrested so soon, having only been released two days before from court. I took him tobacco, filters and papers, £10.00 and a McDonald's Big Mac Meal to Burnley Police Station. It was the same thing as it had been two weeks earlier. Theft - I didn't even ask the details. The desk sergeant said that he could have given him bail, but he would only go out and do the same again according to Neil. He thinks that putting him through the court procedure will get him medical help. If the court had the powers to do so it MIGHT, but they don't. So to say that is really just hot air.

At court on the 3rd February. I've come here with a letter from Mick stating that Neil needs to be in hospital. His solicitor is at a loss to know what to do, and he has gone to see the prosecutor.

"It's really hard," his solicitor said. "Where's the solution? I can't in all honesty see one."

He tells me that the police do their job and arrest Neil. If they did like the medical profession are doing, and did nothing, then where would Neil be then? He said that Neil was obviously under the *misapprehension* that getting arrested was his best chance of getting help.

Well, we've tried everything else. I didn't want this. **Has the world gone mad or what?** *Are the hospital and his doctors beyond reproach?* How can they get away with mistreating and denying a patient his right to medical attention and a referral to another doctor? It is those people who are the real criminals, not Neil! Neil is simply extremely ill.

CHAPTER THIRTY
Mistakes After Mistakes

I wrote the following letter of complaint to Ms Pearl Boothman at Trust Headquarters. It was dated 28th February 2006.

Dear Ms Boothman,

*As I write this letter of complaint, I find myself on familiar ground, as four years on I'm **still** writing letters of complaint, and making numerous phone calls to try and get help for our son.*

*Neil suffers from severe mental illness, and this was the issue with Fernlea General, as before being treated there he did **not,** although the evidence was there and he was sectioned three times.*

*He was also held at Chorley Hospital on a secure unit awaiting a referral to St. Andrews in Northampton. A referral in fact that I am told was **never actually** made. Having as evidence two different Consultants and Bob Gardner stating the same, yet quoting different references as to who <u>actually supposedly</u> did so, which tells me that it would have been beneficial to them to get their heads together **first**, then they could have quoted from the same hymn book if they wanted to lie to us.*

*Oh yes, I've lots of evidence of neglect and cruelty inflicted on my son by the staff at Fernlea General, which I won't go into detail now to you, as I'm saving that for the book I'm writing, other than to tell you that Neil told his G.P. last week that he's still having nightmares about what was done to him. You see Ms Boothman he's a lot more understanding of his illness, and he's more adept in speaking about it and asking for help, but despite this he's still shown the door and told that Fernlea General **cannot** accommodate him.*

*At one time I was fighting to get treatment for him, and he sometimes said he heard voices and was mentally ill, whilst at other times he could blag doctors like Janice Short, who saw him for half an hour and stated he **wasn't suffering** from mental illness. He still* *states how easy she was to fool.*

I was left having to deal with that kind of thing from our son Neil, and various problems arising from the staff at Fernlea General, so I had it <u>twice</u> as bad. Despite this though I kept on, because I knew then, just as I do now, that Neil suffers from the same mental illness as do numerous members of my husband's family.

It was easy therefore for doctors to turn their backs because Neil himself played into their hands by saying he <u>wasn't</u> suffering from hearing voices and other such things, when very clearly he was.

Now though, we actually have Neil **begging** *for help and treatment, yet still the doctors, CPN's and others involved, just think that if they ignore Neil he will go away, or better still kill himself to save them from getting involved with a* complicated individual *who causes them nothing but trouble.*

We had a CPN meeting at Leeds Road, Nelson on 31st[t] January 2006. In that meeting Dr Musto stated he would make a referral to Dr Plackett at the Guild, Preston **within 48 hours**. *In fact this was only done last week, <u>which is in fact quite a few weeks later than promised</u>. What's more to the point though, it was NOT a referral we'd asked for, because we made it quite plain after Dr Musto stated that they* **couldn't** *accommodate Neil at Fernlea General, that we wanted Dr Plackett to treat him.*

This was because Neil trusts Dr Plackett; he has a reverence for him, opens up to him; but most importantly, Neil respects him. Fernlea General have done too much harm to Neil, so much so in fact that he will **never** *be treated properly or fairly there. If the truth be told, they* **don't want** *to treat him, and* **Neil doesn't want** *to be treated by them. (That's if you can even call it treatment that they give out).*

We have long said that the Consultants don't doctor, as they are told what to do by the 'Trust'. This is actually not just **my** *opinion either. I've heard it said many times by a few people I respect. It won't make me popular with you for saying this, but <u>I believe it to be true,</u> because I cannot believe that the doctors we've been in contact with at Fernlea General having once taken their 'hippocratic oaths' would have treated Neil so badly as this, as this would make them into deliberately EVIL persons.*

At this meeting on 31st January it was also stated by Dr Musto *that he'd see Neil **within ONE month**, yet we only received that appointment the other day, and it was for the 13th June.*

****

Neil is currently in the worst state of health that I've ever seen him. He's begun to wander at night again, and constantly paces up and down. He cannot engage with anyone or anything as his mind constantly lacks concentration. He doesn't eat or wash or take care of himself in any way whatsoever. He is currently living in just one room where he hasn't even got one light working.

There are containers around everywhere, each one is filled with *ash and his room smells awful. His clothes are all piled up into the middle of the room, looking just like a bonfire. They are all unwashed. He has a kettle and a cup in this room and a bed that is capable of walking all by itself.*

*He **doesn't** take his medication properly, and it's all a very hit and miss affair. He's paranoid, psychotic and very frightened. He has a carer provided for him by his CPN for ONE hour twice a week. But Neil actually sees them a lot less than that, but this fact **doesn't ever get back to Social Services.** Also neither does the fact that he was without heating for weeks in the cold weather, because his pilot light had gone out. Shouldn't the carer always make a report on their findings to someone? His cupboards are all bare. All in all he's not living, in fact he's <u>barely surviving;</u> and he's only just managing to even do this at the moment.*

*Maybe this carer is as inept as the last one, who was actually selling his furniture for him, and getting cash rewards when he was taking Neil's personal goods to Cash Generator in Burnley to pawn. I thought I'd beaten Neil with that one, going to the shop, having him blacklisted, but instead his carer took his goods to sell for him, and what's more and even worse, he benefited from Neil with goods for his family. I NEVER thought of that happening! **<u>I always believed that carers were kind, trustworthy and helpful people who cared for their clients. HOW WRONG COULD I BE?</u>** I always believed that EACH CARER would be checked up on before being allowed to deal with the most vulnerable of people in the community. Surely as an employer Social Services **should** check up very carefully on those people that they are about to employ BEFORE letting them loose into people's houses?*

468

*You may ask how is it that **I don't know** all that's going on until it's too late? Well this is because we've furnished Neil's house beautifully, not once, but twice. I cannot bear to go into that house, as it quite literally makes me sick to my stomach to see how he's living **without** a cooker or fridge. He couldn't make a hot meal even if he did have any food.*

People bang on his door to get at him, because they know that he has regular money coming in. I was very ill before Christmas and had a heart scare, so too did my husband a couple of weeks ago. I've started my book by stating that by the time I finish it, I don't know if my son will be alive to read it.

I even told Dr Musto and the rest of the people there at that meeting that I feel like getting a gun and shooting my OWN son to put him out of his misery.

*Yes, he is taking drugs, I, like my G.P. would be very surprised if he **wasn't,** taking the fact that he is left out in the cold to fend for himself. I wouldn't treat a dog the way he's being treated by the people who **should** be caring for him. Care in the Community? THERE IS NONE! – Well Neil gets none of it.*

*He needs to be taken into a place of safety, to be detoxed, put on a regime of medicine that is **seen** to be working over time, and he should NOT be put into a house to fend for himself because he CAN'T look after himself, he just is NOT able to do so.*

*I told Dr Musto that holding a carrot in front of him like they were prepared to do for Rehab, knowing fully that Neil **could not** meet the criteria, was just prolonging his misery. There was never any intention of them providing this for him. They knew he'd fail, and I stated that he'd become very ill if they left it too long. So there is no surprise there then.*

Neil is self-medicating; it is a symptom of his mental illness. You can't treat him at Fernlea, so get him to someone who can help him, like Dr Plackett. The only way that he can see him though, is for him to be referred by a psychiatrist from Fernlea General – so why not get on with it – after all you don't want to help Neil yourselves.

Do not continue pushing my son into the criminal system so that he feels safe. It's coming to something when a 24 year old ill man wants to be in prison to feel safe and secure so much, that he commits petty crime, then goes and hands himself in to the police for them to lock him up.

Fernlea General's treatment of Neil is a disgrace, and the after-care there is a complete but very unfunny joke. No one is laughing; as this is a **very serious matter**. This is a <u>complaint</u> just so that you know it.

To explain in <u>the actual words of Dr Leister himself</u>, in front of myself and care-workers, "I know the staff here are rubbish, but it's all we've got."

In his next breath he continued, "He'd be better off in prison."

Which is EXACTLY where he is now, so maybe on the one hand he was right. On second thoughts though, in both respects, because it's only where he's ended up, because the staff were rubbish, and he feels he's better off in prison than living in hell. Nice one Dr Leister!

If you take as long as Karen Wilson did in replying to my letter of complaint years ago. I will hear from you in 2007 because it took her 12 months to reply to me. I have all the letters covering about four years and I'm finding them while filing for my book. The thing is I've asked I.C.A.S. to help me this time, so you won't forget me because <u>they</u> won't let you.

I will copy this letter for my G.P. and Neil's care workers who do help him, the ones that I have personally found for him.

Neil is self harming to very large degree, especially in prison because he has no drugs. Also Neil's veins are packing in due to injecting, so he could lose limbs, so DO please regard this as urgent.

S. Green

The reply to this heartbreaking letter, that I really thought you'd have to have a swinging brick instead of a heart not to be moved by it, **came over two months later**. It probably only came then, after they knew that they had Neil in hospital after an overdose.

Her letter was the same as the ones that I had received in the past stating that they will respond fully to Neil's needs in the best possible clinical and most ethical way. She said that my comments about Neil's G.P. backing up my feelings about Neil's mental health **were untrue**, as he had **not** said such a thing.

I had told you about this earlier when I said I wanted you to remember, because when he wrote to Neil's solicitor he said that he felt that Neil should be fully assessed by a Forensic Psychiatrist, and he quoted Mick's Risk Assessment, and the fact that he thought Neil should be **hospitalized as a matter of urgency**.

She said that part of Neil's ongoing care programme involved Neil's G.P. and he was fully aware of all that was being done for Neil. He was also of the *same* opinion as them, because Neil's G.P. was kept informed by Neil's CPN at every step of the way, as also were the police and the Prison Service, and they had **not** indicated any concerns, or that Neil suffered from a severe and enduring illness.

I know that these are **lies** because I have all the correspondence, far more than she does, and I know that she is as corrupt as the rest of them. This woman has also quoted Dr Plackett as saying that Neil <u>did not suffer from schizophrenia</u> and that he said that he had seen Neil in a psychotic state, and she fully implies that Dr Plackett is of the opinion that it is his drug abuse that has brought on this psychotic state.

She should really check up on her facts, as Dr Plackett actually wrote in a medical report prepared for Neil's solicitor that he had seen Neil in prison *free from illicit drugs, yet* his symptoms were still the same, and that if it was true about Neil's family suffering from severe mental illness (and it is), then he had no doubt that Neil was suffering from a schizophrenia type illness.

I cannot continue picking out all these lies and cover ups in this woman's letter as it is far too upsetting, and most certainly **isn't** worth it. You now know what I have had to deal with all these years. This reply with its lies and its cover ups is just a total disgrace.

I would rather poke BOTH my eyes out, than contact Bob Gardner as she has asked me to do. I will not speak to this horrible little man ever again, as he is the one that I detest the most for what he has done to Neil.

I've told you of Dr Plackett's report where he states that he has witnessed Neil first-hand having delusions, and being psychotic while **free** from drugs while being in prison. Yet they continue to write these God damned awful patronizing letters and put the blame on the patient.

You are to blame for my son taking drugs, because you stuck him in with drug addicts in the B & B, but if he then chose to take drugs because you **wouldn't** treat him and care for him, then is it really any wonder? You have *neglected* my son, denied him a second opinion and a referral, and withdrawn medication for a diagnosis of A.D.H.D. In fact you have blocked us at every move. You have continued to lie and cover up, which makes you utterly contemptible.

If Dr Plackett, the police and H.M.P Preston want to be tarred with the same brush, and be seen to be in the same league with you all at Fernlea General, then so be it, but they would be very silly to do so after they have all read the truth. Everything I have written is the **truth** and what is more to the point I can prove it. So think very carefully before you speak out. You make me sick.

In another story in the local paper after Neil was jailed for his petty crimes. It was said that he was sent to prison for two weeks in the hope that the urgent treatment he needed would be available when he got out. He told the court that he took heroin because it was the *lesser* of the two evils to ease his suffering. The bench hoped that treatment would be ready on his release. His solicitor said that his problems far outweighed his difficulties that were before the court. He took drugs to alleviate the burden of his mental health problems, and that we felt let down by the medical and social agencies, and we were desperate to get some help for him.

His solicitor told the court that Neil needed help, and he needed to be in an institution which caters for his specific problems. He also said that Neil was one of the nicest and most polite men he had ever spoken to. He said that this is **not** at all a normal case, and neither is this a <u>normal</u> young man. To <u>have</u> to take heroin because it is the lesser of two evils is actually quite astonishing.

It wasn't that long ago that the headlines in the local paper were about the case of another young man who was mentally ill, and had hanged himself because services had let him down. He was on the *same* ward as Neil at one point. His sister was a nurse, and she and her family slammed the Psychiatric Services in East Lancashire.

There was another story in the local paper entitled, FAILURE OF OUR HEALTH SYSTEM, where a judge had to put off getting help for a mentally retarded man for 'the seventh or eighth time'. He had again hit out at the mental health service for dragging their heels.

****

The thing with Neil was that he **wasn't** a danger to the public for he harmed no one but himself. His crimes were petty. On many

472

occasions when Neil was at court and held his hands up willingly to the crime, I felt that he really *wasn't fit to plead*. I know my son. He looked normal, displayed a thoughtful charm, but inside he was struggling. He'd self harm to an alarming degree. I do believe that a doctor's view would be tainted by what Fernlea General had stated, that Neil was **not** mentally ill, when he MOST TRULY WAS, and then Neil was denied his rights at court.

It would seem to be the same with the police and the courts, but that wasn't **totally** their fault, as they weren't given the whole truth, or the correct information. Social Services in Neil's case were as lacking as the medical profession.

How long will this carry on? The medical profession needs a kick up the backside, but much more than that, because they are getting away with **murder.** They stand there elevated on a pedestal acting God-like, where no one can touch them. Not the Law, and not us – no one! Why is this situation ever allowed, when according to statistics, one in four of us can suffer mental illness at some time in our lives? There are also no boundaries. You can be young or old, man or woman, black or white, none of it matters in the least. Do we not deserve better than this?

The police, the courts, the Prison Service need to get their houses in order, and stop defending the CRIME that is happening in the medical profession. I bet you would never in a million years believe as in Neil's case that a doctor would deny him his rights to see **another doctor** as a referral or second opinion. Nor would you even realize that another doctor/psychiatrist **would not see you** unless the first doctor/psychiatrist allows it, and thereby gives you a referral, or is asked by your present doctor to see you.

In actual fact, if they won't refer you, you **cannot** see another doctor/psychiatrist, we know the truth of this as we tried to do so for years. Our own GP tried to do it and could not. **Tried very hard, but failed I think would be on our report.**

We thought that seeing another psychiatrist like Dr Plackett who was still under the remit of the area's NHS would be easier and couldn't be denied to us, but it was. They played GOD with Neil's life, and under their care he suffered years of hell, and while we looked on heartbroken not being able to do a thing, our son Neil deteriorated before our very eyes; but what makes it so unbearable is the fact that Neil <u>could have been saved.</u> **He need not be dead!** He was neglected by the services, but he was cruelly treated by all at Fernlea General.

Another story in our local paper was, A CATALOGUE OF ERRORS AND MISJUDGEMENTS LEAD TO THE DEATH OF A BURNLEY BABY who was thrown into the canal by her mentally ill mother. This was revealed by health bosses. An independent enquiry commissioned by East Lancashire Health Authority identified failings in the care provided for the thirty-year old mother.

Yet another story in our local paper was that of a young man, which was headlined as, TURNED AWAY TO DIE. A man who was frightened and hearing voices in his head was turned away from Fernlea General just days before he hanged himself.

This particular story is so like Neil's, as this is what they did to our son all the time. This had actually happened three full years **before** Neil's death, yet the lessons were never learnt AT ALL, for it was the very *same* hospital, the *same* doctors, *same* staff and their *same* uncaring attitude towards mental illness that led to this young man's death.

I was heartbroken when I read this in the local paper, as it so mirrored Neil's predicament. This young man had slashed his wrists and was trying to cope in a B & B in Colne, in yet another place that was well-known for its drug addicts. This young man took drugs, probably for the same reasons as Neil did, to help him get rid of the voices from out of his head. He was even possibly trying to avoid the drug scene but being continually drawn back into it, because no one in these places will leave you alone. He was vulnerable just like our Neil.

The Chief Executive of the Trust Foster Roberts said that he, **"would look into this urgently,"** after he had heard the coroner's verdict.

Yes, of course you will. I don't really think so. This could so easily have been Neil; it was so uncanny how it mirrored him. Neil himself was turned away from Fernlea General on so many occasions, and like this man Neil was hearing voices and he was self harming. **How many more neglected people are there out there?** I would sack the lot of you and close down the mental health unit at Fernlea General. The trouble is, as we saw when Neil took the overdose in March 2006 (yet to write about), that the staff from Fernlea General who Neil disliked so much were at Blackrodd Hospital working on their psychiatric wards. Sadly they were also passing on their failings to yet **another** hospital. It is so obvious that an immediate shake up is needed in Mental Health, but that is an understatement to say the very least!

Another story headlined in the local papers said, CHAOS IN HOSPITAL WARDS. A scene of complete and utter chaos greeted Community Health Council representatives during a surprise visit at Fernlea General Hospital. Staff ran around like headless chickens. Yet still it continues to go on and on, time and time again.

EACH ONE OF THESE HEADLINES REPRESENTS A HUMAN BEING, PROBABLY BEING LEFT TO SUFFER AND COPE WITHOUT SUFFICIENT, OR THE CORRECT HELP FOR FAR TOO LONG.

CHAPTER THIRTY-ONE
Robbed

My very good friend Pam tragically died on March 22nd 2006. I had known Pam for such a short time, nearly a year. I met her when she came on our caravan site after she and her partner Ray bought a static caravan. I was selling tickets for the village 'duck race' and I was just on my way down to the local pub to sell some to the landlord, staff and the 'locals'. It was all in a good cause for our Village Hall. We all do our bit for the village as we are a close knit community.

This lady came out of the site office; she had three colours in her spiky hair, wore very colourful clothes and bright stripey socks.

I looked at her, she looked at me and then I said to her, "Do you want to buy a duck?"

She laughed, and we have been close friends ever since for far too short a time, if that makes sense. I loved her to bits; she was so full of fun and with a heart of gold that we just clicked. God love her and keep her, because our loss is your gain. She was a loving brave lady. I miss her.

****

On March 27th 2006 Neil was admitted to Fernlea General Hospital having been found unconscious after taking an overdose of pills. **I wasn't surprised.** I was waiting for something to happen because of the terrible state Neil was in. We went to see him on the Medical Ward. Steve had been on this ward weeks earlier.

Steve and I had been on the way back from our dear friend's Chris's house in Prescot near Liverpool. We'd had a lovely day with Chris and on the way home Steve became ashen. We were in the Shogun, not in my car which is an automatic, when suddenly Steve couldn't change gear. He had pins and needles down his arm and he couldn't grasp the gear knob.

I was very worried about him; I was already grieving for my

friend, constantly worrying about Neil, now I was facing losing my beloved husband. It was no wonder, the stress we were under with Neil. Things were as bad as ever they could be; we were terrified every day of something happening to Neil and I was crying most days.

Steve was rushed to hospital with a suspected heart attack. He looked dreadful and I was terrified. He was admitted onto the same Medical ward as Neil was now on. They looked after Steve very well. Luckily Steve was okay, but we both took this as a very serious warning. He has to be very ill to take time off work, and he went back to work very soon, before his doctor and I wanted him to do so. He was scared, but I think he wanted to get back to normal.

We saw the same doctor while at Neil's bedside who had treated Steve and he smiled at us. Steve pointed to Neil and told him that this was the reason that he had told him about. You could see that he understood. Neil was in good spirits surprisingly. I thought it was the fact that he felt safe.

We stayed for quite a while and then we went to the shop to buy Neil some pop and other goodies. Neil was just like a child in many respects.

****

On 28th March 2006 a staff nurse off the ward rang to ask me to come and sit with Neil, because he was very disturbed and hearing voices. Of course I went to him and stayed there all day. We saw Dr Moore and Dr Guerlain both psychiatrists. We also saw Andrea Robbins, Social Worker (who was known to us all off the psychiatric wards at Fernlea General. She had input into Neil's care and was as useless as the rest), and the Crisis Team. Neil spoke well about his mental illness and we were both so proud of him. Would they listen this time? Or would they show him the door as usual?

On 29th March 2006 Neil was moved to Isaac Ward at Blackrodd Hospital. On 31st March we went to Pam's funeral.

****

On April 3rd Neil was able to get off the ward which we were not happy about. He'd gone for a drink and then he set off the fire alarm. They called the police and had Neil arrested. The police kept Neil for a few hours before taking him back to the ward.

I spoke to the ward manager Kate about Neil's drinking, because they hadn't told me about it, and she said that she wasn't prepared to talk about patients.

This was said after they had told us that they wanted us *to work together,* and after I was rung about the incident over the weekend when I'd been to see Neil, yet no one had told me about what had happened **until** <u>after</u> the weekend.

I told her that the ward should have told me about it sooner. She replied that there would have been nothing that I could do, because Neil was an adult.

I said, "Well I wouldn't have given him any money, which I had done, but if I had known that he was drinking again, then I wouldn't have done so. In this way he just would NOT have had any money with which to buy any drink. I also wouldn't have given him packets of cigarettes for him to *sell* either."

I rang Elizabeth Shinns the Manager of the Probation Service in Nelson. Carla had sent Neil a nasty letter because he'd missed an appointment with her, when Neil had **already** rung her while he was in hospital, which I was cross about. The fact that he was in hospital <u>having taken an overdose</u> and being **in a shocking mental state,** yet she was STILL the one who thought that he should ring her was just typical, but quite unbelievable.

One of the reasons he didn't want to see Eddina his CPN anymore was because she was *useless.* She didn't tell people anything about Neil, just like the care workers who persisted in putting notes through Neil's door whilst he was either in hospital or in prison, or simply lying there very ill; they never bothered to check properly if he was okay or not, so what use were they really?

Now there was this coming from Neil's Probation Officer. Anyway this awful woman Elizabeth Shinns was really off-hand with me when I rang being very polite to her, to ask her to tell Carla to stop sending Neil these threatening letters because he'd missed his appointments, because he was actually in hospital.

I was frightened at that time that if they did kick Neil out of hospital, then he would go home and read these letters, which perhaps would just serve to tip him over the edge again into doing something stupid.

Elizabeth Shinns snapped, "That's all you do Mrs Green, make complaints."

Can no one do their job properly? I guess with all I'd been through over a matter of weeks, I was very low and my guard was down, and Elizabeth Shinns caught me at a bad time. I was so upset by what she said to me, and I certainly didn't warrant such venom.

I've had to deal with all these *so-called professionals*, that have made Neil's life a misery, because they are so useless and uncaring, and when they are pulled up about the *slightest thing* they retaliate in this way. They were very much in the wrong!

Well you were right Elizabeth Shinns. I played right into your hands because I complained about you, and I was told by your District Manager that I **couldn't** complain about you, a Senior Probation Officer because **I am not** the client. Neil is though, and I was not only his Mother, but also had permission from him to be informed of all his medical and personal history, therefore it was a personal matter yet you denied being rude. I think it is Tommy Rot, but I didn't pursue it further because I had enough on my plate.

I hope Elizabeth that if you have children that they don't have to suffer as my son has, or even you or any members of your family have ever to suffer from any unsympathetic 'professionals' that are there to do a job of work. They must always bear in mind that they shouldn't *further distress the professionals* in anyway, whether or not their family member is as ill as my son was. I wouldn't wish that on you or your children. You were right though, that I have had to complain a lot over the years, yet you, and so many others like you, **have just added to my burden**, but unlike you I presume everyone will understand when they read this book.

****

Eddina rang me to tell me that there was a meeting on Isaac Ward with the doctors. She said that she knew that Neil didn't want her as his CPN, but the meeting wouldn't go ahead unless she was there to pass Neil over to Outreach who would be looking after Neil in the future.

Neil wasn't happy, as it seemed they were like a bunch of kids refusing to see us because we refused one of their own. It was up to Neil, his perfect right to change, as Eddina never once went to see Neil at his home as she should have, so naturally things got worse and worse, yet *she was the one* who was **meant** to be looking after Neil, and he realized this by himself.

479

Steve got up at 11.00am after working all the night before to go to the meeting with me. The room was full, but we had to wait over an hour before **we** were invited into the room. We went early so that we could see Neil beforehand. The meeting was at a certain time, but we weren't invited in.

Dr Day was the new Mental Health Chief Psychiatrist taking over from Dr Leister at Fernlea General, and he said that he was prepared to take Neil on. Then there was Dr Turner from Blackrodd Hospital and his assistant. Eddina, the Ward Manager, a lady staff member who Neil knew and could remember very well from Fernlea General, because he disliked her very much, and another member of staff who Neil knew from Chorley Hospital as Neil had once chased him in the car park of the hospital. There was someone else there, but I can't remember that person very well, and of course Ahmet Ahmed from the Resource Centre (CMHT) at Nelson. Our faces dropped when we saw him come onto the ward.

So there they were talking between themselves as they always do, deciding Neil's fate each time. *It's so God-damn ignorant.* They make their decisions on their own, but then tell you beforehand that **you are part of that decision**. So it's an utter farce. They invite you when they have *already* decided everything, and you are in the room a matter of minutes. You feel like dirt, not at all a *part of the process*, more a sort of afterthought. You feel like the dirt on someone's shoe that they can't wait to wipe away.

I'd encountered this many times before when I'd been at these meetings without Steve, but he'd never been to one of these meetings before, so when we left the hospital after the meeting Steve 'flipped'. He was appalled at the way we were treated. It was well over an hour before we were even invited into the room where the meeting was held, and that was well after the actual appointment time.

Dr Day went on and on about not having to deal with complaints from me, and for us all to make a fresh start. But then he says in his next breath that Neil is accountable for his behaviour, and he can't be there for him 24 hours a day. That was that, nothing more, they'd decided, so that was it.

Did we actually have to be grateful that we were seen at all? Steve and I were deflated. It was a complete waste of time. We had built ourselves up to talk about Neil, but we weren't given any sort of opportunity. We answered him when he asked a question, but that was it.

They all got up and we were ushered out of the room. We felt snubbed. Hence the reason that Steve 'flipped' when we got outside. We never could do anything but send letters of complaint about these people, but then they would use that as an excuse **not** to do anything for Neil. We really couldn't do a thing. They walked all over us. It was so disgraceful. It was always so very shocking and quite unfair.

I rang Ben when I got home. I told him I wasn't going to the ward round the day after, so he said that he would go. We could always rely on Ben. After we left Neil, he was told that if he went out for a drink he would be discharged.

We have these terrible, useless meetings where we achieve nothing. We don't get to talk, and then they hit it home to Neil not to drink. I was wound up, and Steve certainly was, so how would Neil be feeling? Just how bad would they have made him feel?

Naturally enough Neil went for a drink afterwards. Well surprise, surprise we might have even joined him.

My head was banging, Steve and I talked until we were both talked out. I put the phone onto the answering machine. Neil left three messages. He was only ringing to ask me when I was going to visit him again to fetch him cigarettes because the one hundred I had already gotten him, and gave him on Monday, (by now it was Friday), and the two large packs of tobacco, he'd sold for drink. No matter what we did we could never beat him. He would always do something though, whether we give him money or not, he'd sell something, or he'll borrow money off other patients always expecting us to pay them back.

Steve's mum had rung us because she had fallen. Kathleen is currently living on borrowed time, she's very ill with a serious heart problem so she falls for no apparent reason. Please God don't let it be that she's broken her hip again, or her arm or leg come to that. Please let her be alright.

I ran upstairs to wake Steve up again. It's just gone 9.00am and he's been in bed for only two hours. Poor Steve he never gets to sleep much, but I can't lift her alone, and we have to be very careful how we do lift her. We should ring for an ambulance, but she's adamant that she wants no ambulance, saying that if we were to go against her wishes, she wouldn't ring us again.

She doesn't want to trouble us as it is. Barry rang me once the day after she had had a fall, against Kath's wishes, but he knew how serious it was. I went straightaway and knew as soon as I saw her that she had broken her hip. I cannot tell you in words what the smell was like. It was omitting from Kathleen. She must have been in such intense pain.

"You have enough on your plate," she would say.

Oh! Mum, you are amazing; we have been so blessed with both our Mums. Of course I called an ambulance immediately. I think she would have died if she had been left much longer. This time though she was okay. She'd slipped down the bed onto the floor. I rang Neil, he said that Kate, one of the staff wanted to speak to me, she said they could have discharged Neil, and in fact it would really have been Neil who had discharged himself, if after it was agreed yesterday that he wasn't to drink, and he has, but they will not discharge him but give him another chance. The discharge will be in another couple of weeks.

I'm fuming because Neil should be on a ward that is secure, so that he can't get out in order to be allowed to buy himself any drink. It was the same thing over and over, but they knew that Neil would do this, so why is it always the same? Neil did say in the background while I was talking to her that he'd messed up again.

Recent photograph taken of
Kathleen, with her two sons Steve and Barry

Kate shouted to Neil, "Don't you tell me to eff off, as I don't swear at you."

I'm not criticizing her, but she had most certainly misheard him while she was talking to me, as I'd heard perfectly what he had said.

Neil is not, and never has been verbally abusive. He would never be abusive on the ward. What an outburst though from her, NOT Neil!

****

Saturday 8th April 2006.

Neil rang wanting us to pick him up as he'd discharged himself. We were at the caravan. I tried not to run after Neil, to not down tools and jump when he wanted me to, as he'd try to get me to do on a regular basis.

He did the same when we were out with friends like we were on my birthday. I never wanted to take my mobile phone when we went out, because it was quite rare for us to go out and enjoy ourselves, to keep getting it spoilt.

I'd say, "No Neil, we've had a drink, we can't come," but we always did.

Steve didn't drink, because in the back of his mind he'd have to drive somewhere for Neil. We lived on a knife edge, hating the phone, hating a knock at the door, dreading seeing the police vans pull up at the door, even if it wasn't anything to do with Neil our hearts used to race. We've never been without worry, fear or heartbreak.

Having Neil was one of the greatest joys we've had, but knowing that we had produced a child to suffer all of his life wasn't easy to live with. We felt that we always owed him enough to at least be there for him, because he was ill, and it wasn't his fault.

People looking on from the outside always thought we were fools, mugs, but they didn't know. We often kept a lot to ourselves about Neil's illness. If we turned our backs on our son, he'd have had no one. I tried not to make it easy for him though, so I told him that we wouldn't pick him up if he'd discharged himself, and the hospital would have to sort him out a taxi, which they did.

Naturally I was mad at Neil for discharging himself; that is until I found out the reason why he had. He told us that there was Crack Cocaine, Heroin, Cannabis as well as alcohol on the ward, and he'd already had the Crack and some alcohol. He knew that it would be him who they came down hard on, because they didn't want him there in the first place, but to stay on the ward with drugs on tap he wouldn't be able to resist them, and he knew that he would be playing right into the staff's hands.

484

It was quite a decision, a hard decision because the easier option would have been for him to stay and take it, but he wanted help and he wanted to get better. They told him that he would still get Outreach and it wouldn't jeopardize it to discharge himself.

Neil only used drugs to relieve him of his symptoms as part of his illness, the stress and fear, agitation and anxiousness were relieved a bit when he was in a safe environment, like a hospital or a prison, so his need for drugs wasn't as great.

Living in purgatory like he was on his own, in terrible conditions naturally exasperated his illness; but he couldn't get through to the psychiatrists who just wanted to blame him; they didn't want to help him.

They kept on saying that it was the drugs that were making him psychotic, but this was just a way they had thought of in order to get out of treating him. Neil has had mental illness ever since he was a child; it became much worse for him in his teens and now at the age of 24 it was full blown schizophrenia. We've seen it before in the family when the condition changes as the person gets into their late teens, so we had expected it. We were looking for the changes as we knew that poor Neil didn't stand a chance.

If you got BOTH the treatment and the care the symptoms may not be as bad. With Neil however, because he **didn't** get that treatment, care or help, and especially due to the ignorance of the medical profession, and the cruelty he encountered by the very people who *should* have cared for him, had served to make his condition much worse and made him feel worthless.

<u>To ignore him was bad enough, but to cause him more pain and suffering was quite unforgivable</u>!

I asked Neil if he'd told the staff on the ward about all of the drugs that were on their ward and he said yes, but they weren't interested. They were always quick to deny all this at the hospital, or they would blame Neil for bringing them in, but they could NOT do so on this occasion because Ben was visiting another patient on the same ward, and he was telling Ben the same.

Ben rang me to tell me that the patient's mother had made a formal complaint to the Trust. It would be a waste of time as that'll be it; she would just get one of their patronizing letters that completely skirted around the issue and blamed this on the patient like the letters that we received. I didn't need Ben to tell me that Neil was telling the truth. I already knew that he was.

I wrote a letter to Mick's boss. Mick had to reapply for his job at Inwood House to carry on being this area's drug worker. His care of Neil was exceptional and he was totally professional, and although I've spent most of Neil's life making complaints about how unprofessional, wanting and lacking the people who work in the 'Services' are, I have no complaints about the way Mick had done his job.

Maybe it's because I've had the bad for so long, that when some good comes along, it stands out to such a degree. Well he did stand out, and I respected Mick for turning his life around. He said that he wanted to give a little back if he could; he could understand better because he'd been there himself. What better person could there really be for a job like that?

This exceptional human being didn't understand about mental illness, but he knew all about drugs, and he knew immediately that Neil *wasn't a drug addict through choice*, but he was someone who was very ill and suffering with mental illness, so he used heroin to relieve himself of his terrible symptoms.

He thought his role for Neil was secondary to a psychiatrist, and he didn't stand a chance of helping Neil with a drug addiction unless the medical profession helped him first. They didn't! I have no doubt whatsoever that our son would die. Mick also understood that Neil was here only on borrowed time.

****

It didn't take Neil long to be arrested again. He went into the model shop, stole something; it really didn't matter what, for as usual it was simply a means to an end. He went and gave himself in to the police.

Neil rang saying, "I've been arrested, can you come to the Police Station and fetch me a McDonald's, biscuits, tobacco and money?"

He'd have given me his cash card so that I could get his money then send it to him while he was in prison, and then I was tied to him to get it back to him upon his release from court, or as now from the hospital. It was relentless, and we felt that we never had lives of our own.

While on bail for this he went into Matalan, as it was always a

486

safe bet for him there, as they always caught him quickly as they had cameras on the doors. The police could then clear up a lot of outstanding thefts because Neil would hold his hands up to everything, whether he'd done it or not. I was asked to go to the Police Station after midnight when they rang me. They sent a car to pick me up. Neil was asking for hot chocolate and a kind officer felt sorry for him and he made him another hot chocolate. It ripped my heart out.

Neil shouldn't be here. He was a mess. They showed him a photo of someone taken off camera facing Matalan's doors. I couldn't have said it was Neil for definite.

Neil said, "It looks like me. It must be me."

In fact the officer could have shown him a picture of a penguin and Neil would say it was him. Whether he knew what he was doing, whether it was a means to getting locked up, or whether it was a compulsive act he'd habit formed, I don't know. I didn't care really. It was so petty, especially as my son was sick in the head. He needed help and treatment. The police were out of their depth.

To me it showed the police in a bad light to see them pushing and bullying this pitiful human being. It was all so very sad and completely avoidable. It's no wonder I resisted going to the Police Station as this isn't what the police are there for; it's changed my perceptions of them.

I've told you how distasteful I've found the police at times, but most of it was through ignorance, but I was so tired of it all.

Neil had been allowed a McDonalds twice before, but when Neil asked me to take him one in while he was at Burnley Police Station on my birthday; we left the family at the restaurant to take him what he had asked for including his tobacco, filters and Rizla papers.

The desk sergeant was obnoxious. "He's not having that," he shouted pointing to the Big Mac, fries and drink. He could have looked through it but he didn't. It was up to his discretion, I know. I never spoke.

"If you say anything further he'll **not** get the tobacco either." He warned me before I could.

I couldn't argue, so we just turned tail and walked away. I'd never encountered such animosity before from the police. The sergeant might have been in charge, but he needn't have been so venomous and nasty. This hurt us all so much, especially so when we knew that Neil had actually **voluntarily** given himself up.

This sergeant was hard and callous, not because he'd refused my son a Big Mac, no, it wasn't that, but surely *I deserved some respect and thoughtfulness.*

He might well have thought he was a good 'copper', but a policeman's job is not <u>just</u> to catch and punish criminals. He'd probably have thought that Neil *deserved* all this.

He might have been the nasty 'copper' whose glasses Neil had broken. He might just know Neil from previous arrests, or he may just be of the 'old school'. I hope he feels a little bit differently if he ever reads this book.

Neil **wasn't** a criminal; he **shouldn't** have been treated as badly as he was on occasion by the police.

Maybe this sergeant thought Neil was a pain in the backside who kept on wasting police time. Neil was running to the police for **help**, where's the logic in that?

The outcome of it all was that Neil was sent to Preston Prison.

****

Mum wasn't the same after her friend Rennie died. He was my mum's good friend from the Disabled Centre, one of many really, because she had a lot of good friends at the Centre. She'd come home with such tales about her friends.

Mostly though she'd be saying, "You should see poor Ethel or someone else, she's a poorly soul; then she would tell me what was wrong with that person. Mum would be heartbroken that her dear friend would be suffering so, as my mum always thought about others before herself.

The Disabled Centre was a warm and caring place, a second home for her. There was an abundance of caring staff and dear friends that were suffering from some form of disability. I popped in to see Mum regularly and she would be sat with her friends knitting away. She knitted little tops that were taken by Oxfam, and sent away to poor countries to cover little babies. She'd been in the local paper because with her being totally blind, people were amazed that she could knit so well and wanted to do something for the little babies in a foreign land.

I hadn't really noticed how frail and tired Mum had suddenly

488

become. She had told me about her friend Rennie, there was always talk of a death at some time or another at the Centre. There were obviously quite a lot of sick, disabled and frail people who went there. It was inevitable, just as death itself is inevitable. She used to say how fortunate she was having me to live with, to be looked after and cared for. She knew this house like the back of her hand and she really loved it here.

I'd kick her out in the morning to stand and wait for the Council bus to pick her up. I didn't **really** kick her out, she chose to stand under the verandah because if the driver knocked at the door the dog would bark and wake Steve up. Mum was always thoughtful like that, and she adored Steve. It was a two way thing for the pair of them.

She liked a cigarette, she said that she had five a day, but it was probably more like seven or eight, but then who was counting? It was her only 'vice', except for the odd brandy, or two. We were okay me and Mum. She was my friend; in fact she was my very *best* friend. I could talk to her about anything and she would give me her last penny. My sisters used to send her money for Christmas and her birthday, and she'd always give me half. She said that she didn't need money, and I don't think she did. She was well provided for, but she was a soft touch, and I only gave her enough money for the day to day things at the Centre, because she used to give her money away. Yes, she was very generous and unselfish my mum; she loved me to distraction. Steve also loved her as much as he did his own Mum. We were blessed with two wonderful mums. Everyone loved my mum.

She was poorly and didn't go to the Centre. The last time she didn't go to the Centre was the time after I'd taken her to our Pauline's in Farnworth. She'd had a few brandies and she was 'hung over' in the morning. I rang her driver and told him and she told me off.

"You never told him that did you"?

I said, "Of course I did Mum, it'll give you street cred."

They had her 'on' at the Centre about that. We liked a laugh me and Mum.

She was complaining about a pain across her stomach. I was so torn the day I called for her G.P. Dr Masood to come, as I had told my sister Pauline that I would take her to the hospital at Bolton.

My dear sister Pauline needed to see her Consultant about having an operation to reverse the 'stoma' she had to have after her cancer operation. I needed to be with my sister, because she was terrified of going back into hospital. Even going to this appointment, she had a real fear, and who could blame her, for she was lucky to be alive. I couldn't let her do this on her own and I wanted to talk to her Consultant, to ask him to do it as soon as possible. Pauline would have kept putting it off. So I took her to the hospital on the 15th May.

Mum's birthday had been on the 10th May, she was 85 years old, but on the 15th May I had to leave her, so she had to see Dr Masood on her own. I left a note for Dr Masood and he kindly rang me to tell me that he had seen Mum and she had what he thought was indigestion or something of that sort, but he'd left her a prescription. I asked Barry to get this for me when he came home from work, so that she could have it straightaway. Mum wasn't ever one to complain or moan about illnesses.

When I came home Barry said that he had given Mum some soup but she wasn't feeling hungry, so she didn't really want it. Mum kept rubbing her stomach, just under her bust. She wasn't so good when she got up the next morning, and she didn't want any breakfast, but had a little soup for lunch. She complained about a pain across her stomach in the afternoon.

She said, "Help me Sue."

This was why I was feeling guilty. Should I have called an ambulance and got her into hospital? Was it her stomach or was it her heart?

I told her that she had to give the tablets a try that the doctor had given her. She loved Dr Masood, believed him to be a good doctor. He was a real gentleman. He hadn't been worried about her, far from it. I asked her if she would like some Lucozade? We had a ritual when we felt ill as kids. Mum would give us tomato soup (had to be Heinz) and Lucozade but not together of course.

She said that she would, and she went to lie down on her bed. We went to Asda for the Lucozade, poured her a glass of it and set it down next to her at the side of the bed. She said that she would just rest there for a while. We popped up the street to see her driver from the Centre at dog training with his new border collie. We were only away about half an hour, but we **shouldn't** have left her.

Steve went straight upstairs into her bedroom and shouted for me to come up. Mum had tried to get undressed to get into bed and she was undressed with her nightie still in her hand, but she was slumped on her bed. **She was dead**.

It must have just happened, she was very warm and her mouth was moving, so I thought she was still with us, but it was just her false teeth moving in her mouth. We laid her on the floor.

The lady on the phone after I'd rung 999 told me to give her mouth to mouth, we tried but we'd already lost her. The ambulance was at our house within minutes as the ambulance station was just down the road. They worked on Mum for ages, they were so gentle and kind but it was useless, she'd gone but it looked like peacefully.

I miss her so much. I said, "Don't go Mum, I'm not ready for you to go."

I would never be ready though would I? I rang Pauline who rang my sister Jean in Perth Australia, and she rang my other sister Christine who's in Adelaide, Australia. The police came, a lovely girl called Nicola, she was wonderful and she said all the right things and stayed with us for hours. I can't tell you how much we appreciated her at the time, and she was exceptional. We were ever so grateful that it was her who had come. I will never forget her.

The police have to come out for any sudden death. The ambulance men stayed until the Funeral Director came, and they too were marvellous, and so kind. We knew straightaway who we wanted to take care of Mum's funeral. Hamer's on Leeds Road in Nelson. It hadn't been there long as a Funeral Director's.

I used to pop in to the shop regularly when Joyce had it as a fancy goods shop. I'd pop in, look around and then chat to Melissa and Glynis, whose daughter works for my G.P. They were both such lovely girls.

That shop was turned into Hamer's Funeral Parlour. They've done a lovely job on the shop and I knew it was there that I wanted them to take care of my dear Mum. In fact the lad who came to take Mum was so quietly spoken and very tall. He was called Carl. He dressed Mum and put her into bed until the car came to take her away. It's the little things these lovely people do for your loved one, that make all the difference. He closed the living room door while they took her down the stairs.

Jim rang me up the next morning, he was the Funeral Director. He was also very quietly spoken. He sounded very nice. We went down to the funeral home. He was lovely with us. Even before I knew that they did Horse Drawn Funerals, I asked for one. I knew exactly what I wanted for my Mum, and horses and a glass carriage fitted the bill perfectly.

"Yes, you can have that. How about if I ask for Black and Decker?" he suggested. They were the two big black horses who were famous for being the ones on *Coronation Street* when Mike Baldwin had his funeral; it was even the *same c*arriage too. Mum would really like that.

We took her gorgeous silk nightie that my sister Chris had sent her from Australia, and her brand new embroidered blue suede slippers that Pauline had bought her for her birthday. Jim talked us through every stage, he was brilliant, a real gem.

Steve bought me two dozen roses, cream and soft velvet red with really long stems. I put them in the middle of my table and had candles at either side. We had candles lit in the living room too, on this the day of my Mum's funeral. The cards kept coming and the flowers.

On May 25th 2006 at 4.38am I got up and out of bed and wrote this:

Dear All,

As I can't sleep (again). I had this 'urge' to get up and write down, while fresh in my thoughts of yesterday, 'Mum's funeral'.

I did my crying when Mum died and in the days that followed, but I was determined not to shed one single tear yesterday, as I wanted it to be a celebration of Mum's life, and for one last time to put her first in thought, and not lessen the day in any way with grief and sadness.

Our prayers were answered, for the sun came out for her, which I knew it would, as the 'powers that be' could not deny this wish.

My gentle, kind (just like Mum) sister arrived with her two sons from Farnworth.

Margaret (her dear, dear friend) with Brian, her partner, who was also a dear friend, whom Mum found to be a real gentleman.

Paula, my dear friend, who, no matter what life throws at her, is always there for me, just as I will be for her one day.

Kathleen my mother-in-law, the absolute 'angel' that she is. She is also just like Mum, putting others first, and loving Mum as a dear and thoughtful friend (my mum loved her so much). Barry, her son, just the same as Kathleen, he is an 'angel' who cared for my Mum like she was his Mum, and he was always 'adored' by my Mum.

There was Chris, our dear friend whom we met on the caravan site and who wanted to 'be there' for us, having heard about my Mum all the time, but having never met her, only talking to her once on the phone.

Ryan, our son, who was deeply saddened and emotional with Lisa his 'rock', his pretty fiance. Leonard and Ethel our friends from 'way back' who knew everything that there was to know about our family, and who we regard as true dear friends. Margaret, our friend and neighbour, smiling always laughing, and such a kind friend who Mum always talked about warmly.

June, friend and neighbour of the same caring and thoughtful nature that we've known from the time that we moved here, but has grown in fondness as an honest, 'dear lady' whom Mum had the pleasure of knowing.

*Last but not least, Steve, my loving husband who thought of my Mum as **his** Mum, and was the one who 'wanted' Mum to live with us when she became blind, and was far too upset to leave her miserable in the blind home she was in at the time.*

He put her first and last, but always with love, and no one could have loved her more than he did, but me. My Mum was the 'rock' who always kept me sane in all of my times of sorrow and pain, and who will continue to do so now, only from the 'other side'. This I know from the bottom of my heart.

As the resplendent black and silver carriage, pulled by two tall black stallions came around the corner followed by the two black Mercedes limousines. I thought 'yes' this is 'fitting' for my Mum.

The horses looked so majestic and proud as they stood there. The Funeral Directors were so deeply caring to our needs, and with whom we will be eternally grateful, especially 'Jim' who is to video this day for my two sisters who are always this day in our thoughts, but who live in Australia, so could not be with us in person, but who must be feeling like I do today.

We set off feeling proud and uplifted. Neighbours were all standing outside to watch, and waving. All through Nelson Centre those wonderful horses clipped and clopped all the way.

Through the traffic lights to the Disabled Centre they strode out in perfect harmony, and what a sight there was for us all to see. Our hearts filled up and overflowed with all that wonderful emotion being directed at us, as we saw all of Mum's friends lining the pavement, some in wheelchairs, all deeply saddened to lose their dear friend. There were so many people it was truly amazing. We stopped as a mark of respect, and held up the traffic for a good few minutes allowing all her wonderful friends to offer up their personal and loving respects.

*Mum did so love them all. The Disabled Centre was her second home, where she was well provided for, and made all her friends, and to each one of them we will be eternally grateful for looking after her so well. We felt so proud that every single one of you honoured our Mum like this with such passion, waving, saying goodbye, blowing kisses. **Thank you so much!***

Off we continued, through Brierfield and Burnley Centre; cars stopped, lorries and ambulances gave way in order to let us get around the roundabout. People bowed their heads, and stopped to stare.

Through more traffic lights, up Manchester Road, the horses carried on. Oh what a pull it was for the lovely, and smart strong horses, down Rossendale Road into a freak shower of hailstones which quickly stop as sunshine follows us in the Crematorium.

All of Mum's friends from the Disabled Centre were already there and waiting, having been brought by the wonderful drivers that Mum had laughed and joked with all of the time in their Council buses.

You lift our hearts Ray. Dear Ray, our friend who had decided to come at the last minute, who sadly was still suffering the loss of his loved one, Pam; dear Pam!

In we go. Steve, Barry, Duncan and Ryan carrying Mum. Celine Dion was belting out the theme tune from 'The Titanic', My heart Will Go On. She was always one of Mum's favourite artistes.

*Phil Talbot, ordained, but who I had especially asked **not** to wear his dog-collar whilst officiating at Mum's 'Celebration of Life', and*

494

he was doing a fine job of it. Next it was Ronan Keating singing, 'If Tomorrow Never Comes' which was not only very apt, but also Mum's favourite song. We'd asked for Johnny Mathis 'Stoned In Love With You' because a part of that song said, "I'd give the world to you," and Mum always said that to me, but alas this was not to be as it <u>wouldn't</u> play on their sound system. Maybe Mum had decided she didn't want that one, but for 'My Heart Will Go On' to be played again.

Don't worry Jim, it wasn't meant to be. He'd wanted it to go off perfectly and he was mortified when he couldn't play this song for us.

It did all go off perfectly. We touched Mum's coffin to say goodbye. We said goodbye to friends from the Disabled Centre who wouldn't come to the 'The Golden Ball' for the reception, and we all enjoyed a wonderful buffet wake meal there.

We received lots of wonderful comments about Mum from everyone! Everyone said that it was truly wonderful, and remarked what a splendid send off it was for such a special lady!

"Truly the best funeral we've ever been to," seemed to be what everyone seemed to say, and also "She would have been so proud of everyone and everything."

What a wonderful day. Thank you one and all!

To my sisters Jean and Christine in Oz, I say, "We did her proud! Our Mum deserved only the very best, so that was what she got!"

I wanted my two sisters in Australia to feel as though they were there on the day at my side.

We know that they watch the D.V.D. of Mum's funeral, as do Kathleen and Barry.

****

Neil was in Preston Prison, he didn't know his Gran had died. The only blessing in that was that I could concentrate on Mum's funeral and be able to grieve for her in my own way. I prayed Neil wouldn't ring and ask to speak to his Gran as he usually did. He loved his Gran so much; she was the one who would talk to him for hours at a time. The good thing, or one of the good things I should say about Mum was that she'd talk to the boys when I was in no fit state to do so. She could step back and say it, as it was often too hard for me to try to get through to Neil. She *didn't* get through to him as

495

I've told you, as Neil couldn't stop himself, but he knew his Gran talked, and gave him so much of her love and understanding. Although he didn't like a lot of what she said, because she was honest, he knew that what she said to him truly was because she cared about him and me so very much.

Neil only rang me twice in the five weeks he was in Preston Prison. That in itself was <u>unusual,</u> it wasn't as if he didn't have the money to buy a phone card, he did. I was sending him £100 a week. When Neil did ring he was kind of detached as if he'd given up, or felt he had to give up on me. It was very strange and I rang to speak to a nurse that I'd spoken to before, to ask her if he was alright?

I knew it was because he was ill as if the voices and what they were saying to him were taking over. Neil needed me; everyone would tell you that. This was *very odd behaviour* from him. He didn't ask about Gran or anyone else, so I didn't need to lie, not that I could have done so. I have never lied to Neil or broken a promise, so he made it easy for me, but I was terribly worried. This was odd. This wasn't Neil. The same went for the day that we visited him on the 7th June.

I'd spoken to the nursing staff about the fact that his Gran had died, and also to the two Chaplains who said the same, that I should tell Neil while he was in Prison, in a place of safety, where they could keep a close eye on him. It made sense. We had an appointment made on that day in a room that was normally used for the inmates to talk to their solicitors in private.

We felt the same; Neil was detached, yes he cried when we told him about his Gran, but not like I would have expected him to do. We had some photo cards made up giving the date she died and a loving message, we gave one to Neil.

Something wasn't right though. We expected tantrums, shock, his sadness wasn't enough. Neil had a real fear of his Gran being burnt when she died, not a *logical* fear, and we had rows about it. He asked what we'd done?

We said a cremation, explaining how gracious and lovely it was. There was nothing to worry over at all; it wasn't a shock or anything like that. It was such a beautiful service.

Okay on reflection he did look a bit drugged up with medication, maybe they'd given him something to take the edge off him being frightened. Just how would he react when it finally sunk in, especially as I'd told them how he would probably react. Even given what I've just said I knew this was so different. He should have been *more* emotional. He wasn't allowed a drink or goodies. He didn't react at all though, which was all so very odd and completely out of character for him.

Steve said, "He took it better than I expected."

I was numb. Neil in the main was numb. This **wasn't** even anything like our Neil. What the hell had happened to him? We left and I talked to the Prison Officer who was looking after Neil; he assured and promised me faithfully that he'd keep a close eye on our suffering son for us. They knew what news he'd just had, maybe he'd react later when he was on his own. I also asked that if he was to be released on Friday at court, that things were put in place properly for him.

"It's all in hand. Outreach is dealing with him," we were assured.

I was told by Neil and his solicitor that he definitely **wasn't** coming out of prison. They both said that Neil was getting a medical report from a doctor at the Prison. He'd already been there too long so this must be being done.

I also received a letter from Neil's solicitor telling me that his case was adjourned off to the 19th June at 2.00pm. He had instructed the Senior Medical Officer at Preston Prison to have a full psychiatric assessment medical report ready for the 9th June for the next hearing. He said that unfortunately he was a little skeptical, maybe pessimistic given his experience, he said, trying to get psychiatrists to move within any time restraint. He said that he would see me at court on 9th June.

****

Neil told us that day at Preston Prison on the 7th June **not** to come to court on Friday because it was just a formality as he would be going back into Preston Prison because he was being fully assessed by the psychiatrist for a medical report for court, so naturally it was going to be adjourned.

Neil had been in prison for five weeks and they wouldn't have kept him in prison for so long if it wasn't for what Neil had said, and he'd said the same in a letter that he had written me. I didn't doubt Neil. We'd made arrangements to go for a meal with friends at the

497

caravan. Chris's friend was coming to the caravan to stay for the weekend because it was the Village Fete on the Saturday and Chris's daughter was coming to spend the day with us, she lives near her dad near Liverpool.

We were looking forward to it as much as we could but still grieving for Mum. In fact it would be the first time we'd been out since she died. Our friends wanted to be with us to try and lift us a bit. I knew what they were doing; and we greatly appreciated it. It was hard, but we'd have to do it some time.

Kathleen kept telling me to enjoy myself, "You've done so much for your Mum Sue, you've been the best daughter anyone could be, you're not tied anymore; do try to enjoy yourself with people that care for you."

We'd been used to getting up on Saturday to go home to make Mum's breakfast. We'd leave her a sandwich for lunch and a flask. Ryan would be at work. If he couldn't get back for tea-time to make her tea, one of us would come back to make Mum's tea, or I would have made her something at the caravan to fetch back. Steve and I took turns. Ryan was usually home for tea, it's the reason we had sited the caravan so close to home.

It wasn't ever a bind for us, don't think that, and if we did have somewhere to go we could always rely on Barry to look after Mum if Ryan was with his friends. We all loved Mum, she was no trouble, not demanding, fitting in with us, and not the other way around. We were still finding it very strange. We had, for the first time, not had to put Mum first, not to plan our lives around her. We were lost. It would take a long time to get used to.

Mum always said to lose your Mum was the hardest thing you'd go through in life, she'd lost hers when she was in her early twenties, in fact finding her dead in a chair.

She always said, "I don't want you to find me like I had to find my Mum. You only have one Mum."

She'd always said that, and told my boys the same and to, "Look after your Mum."

I felt so lost I know that. There's no love like a Mother's love. It's completely unselfish and unconditional. I know Steve loves the ground that I walk on; we are devoted, he tells me he loves me every day, but I was still broken-hearted and felt like there was something

498

missing. I can only describe it as being 'lost'. So we said O.K. to going out for a meal on Friday 9thh June with Chris and Rose and to going to the Village Fete on Saturday.

Neil rang me around 5.00pm on Friday 9th June he'd said that he'd been released from court, as they'd told him that they couldn't warrant keeping him in prison any longer. The solicitor was right, they'd **not** got the report ready to give him something to use in court, because they'd not got their fingers out. Neil had been released. He'd been in prison for that long for **nothing.** I couldn't believe it. Neil was so sure that he'd be going back.

I felt torn again, which was nothing new for me. Neil wanted picking up. Chris pulled up in his car to pick us up to take us for the meal. I told Neil that I would ask Barry to pick him up, but Neil needed money and I had his cash card.

"Don't worry Mum," Neil said, "I'll get a taxi, just leave my card under the step and I'll pick it up."

I asked him about his prescription, he said Outreach were dealing with his medication, it was sorted. I know that Eddina had made a mess of it all before, but this was before Neil went into prison. Outreach people were going into Neil's house every day to give him his medication. It was hard to get on Outreach's lists, because their care was supposed to be more intensive; it was a better form of care for Neil's needs.

Before he went into prison they were sorting his money out with D.S.S. to be his appointee. We felt better that they were involved at long last, so to know that this was back in place it made me feel a little better at least he'd be given his medication. The prison assured me that Neil had a full care package upon his release. They knew how worried we were about him.

Neil sounded fine not anxious or depressed, he said that he would take us out for a meal tomorrow and he'd get some new trainers. I reminded him that we were going to the Fete tomorrow, but if he were to give me a ring we'd sort something out. He said that he might go down to home himself, but he'd let me know.

I told him not to get a lot of money out of the bank, he said that he wouldn't.

"I'll get something to eat then get back for Outreach."

"Behave yourself," I told him.

499

He knew what I meant by that.

"I will do, and I love you and Dad," just as he always did every single time he rang us, no matter how many times a day he rang.

This was the very last time that I spoke to Neil.

Neil did pick up his cash card that I had left under my step.

We went to the Village Fete as we'd done for many years. We usually have a drink of Champagne or something, but I didn't feel like a drink because I felt a bit 'off'. I thought it was because I needed to eat something, so I bought a burger. I was still feeling a bit 'yuk' and my stomach was churning. We didn't stay long, it was nice to see our friends and the locals, and we had everybody coming up to us saying that they were sorry to hear about my Mum.

Maybe it was because of all this that I felt the way I did. Our neighbour Dave gave me some of his painkillers later on as I didn't feel any better. We came home on Monday. I felt a lot worse and I thought that I was coming down with something. I was sick and needed to be near the toilet. **Neil hadn't rung.**

I wasn't too worried about that as he did try to leave us alone when were at the caravan at the weekend, and he had plenty of money in his bank, so I thought that he would probably be spending his pennies. He'd be round Tuesday for his tea.

He didn't come, but I felt so ill, so I was too wrapped up in myself. 'I must have caught a bug of some sort,' I thought.

****

Neil didn't ring or come on Wednesday. I was still throwing up and I spent most of the day on the toilet, but by Thursday morning I felt that I would have to go to Neil's. I'd have to risk it. I still felt awful. I parked across the road from his house. I looked up at his bedroom window it was wide open, in fact as far as it could be opened. It had been warm though. I had his door key so I opened his door and my heart sank. The brown envelope, Neil's giro was still there and unopened.

'Surely he would have got that on Tuesday,' I thought to myself. Maybe it was because he'd been in prison; perhaps they were late in sending it.

There was another note off his care worker, he'd been yesterday. This gets me so mad. I had a drawer full of these at home. **What's the point of having a care worker who just shoved notes through**

500

the door?

I went to the bottom of the stairs and shouted. "Neil," then I went up the stairs. Neil's bedroom was at the top of the stairs facing the stairs, the bedroom door was open but I couldn't see into the bedroom because Neil had a blackout curtain up at the window, it was very dark. I tried to turn on the light but it didn't work as there was no electricity.

The double bed was straight in at the door. I don't know whether I touched Neil's foot or not, he was so big his feet often used to hang over the end of the bed. I rushed to the window. I was full of fear, which just came and overtook me. I pulled the curtain back, I turned quickly. Neil was lying on the bed on his head on the pillow his back with his arms outstretched.

He was black, no **he wasn't**, but **his veins were;** they'd risen to the surface. His head was massive, and his eyes had popped out and had mattered. He was extremely bloated. There was nothing coming from his mouth. I didn't want to look, but I had to do, as I was drawn.

My legs buckled from under me. I let go of the curtain. I couldn't breathe. I crawled out of the room.

I just screamed and screamed.

My phone was in my hand. I rang for the police and the ambulance. I had to get downstairs. I'd locked the door behind me, as I always did. I'd had someone follow me in once but luckily Neil was in the house. I hated being in that house. I don't know how I got downstairs. I was running this way, that way, like a headless chicken. I went back upstairs. I opened the bathroom door, I could see Neil's silhouette on the bed.

Oh! Neil it **was** true. I hadn't gone mad. "Hurry, hurry please," crying, screaming, I curled myself up on the floor. I was pulling my hair, digging my nails in my arms.

"Wake up Susan, it's not real."

But is was!

One policeman ran up the stairs, helped me downstairs, sat me on a chair; the other policeman went to a neighbour's to get me a hot drink.

"Who can we get for you love, you have to leave here."

"I want Steve, he'll be in bed."

501

"We'll get someone to go for him."

Barry only works around the corner but I couldn't remember, couldn't think. I wanted Steve, I needed him so much.

I rang Ben, "Ben, Neil's dead," I blurted.

"Bloody hell," he said.

The ambulance came and more police. They were joking and laughing outside.

I stuck my head out of the door and stared at this man out of uniform. "Who are you?"

He did tell me but I don't remember, but I'll never forget his face. I wished they'd go.

Bob, he's nice, he's a Police Dog Handler. He's Aidy's cousin. We talked about Aidy. He was very nice.

"Aidy was a lovely lad," I tell him.

Steve comes. He takes me to Kathleen's. We cry. I rang for Ryan to come home. I ring for Barry to come home as Kathleen's in shock.

I heard that. I needed the doctor as my heart was banging out of my chest. I walk out of there as I just could not stay. I needed to get home. God, help me, this isn't happening. Not Neil. I'd only just lost my Mum. Both of them were now gone in the space of three weeks.

I made Steve see him.

The policeman said, "No, I wouldn't advise it."

I told Steve that he had to. He stood at the top of the stairs. He didn't see what I saw, but why, why did I do it? Why did I make him see him? We owed him that, that's why. It was that, wasn't it? That wasn't our son; our son had gone!

What do they say? Shock, disbelief, anger, these are all the emotions that you go through when someone dies.

Well I'm angry alright. My son had no medication; he was relying on Outreach coming. He had told me the same, and also when an officer came to see me after I'd found Neil he told me that he'd seen Neil around 6.00pm near his home. He must have been the last person to see him alive, well, one of the last people, because Neil must have 'scored'.

If he'd had no medication he'd have got some Heroin. How could they have done this to Neil? They told us on the ward at Blackrodd Hospital that now Dr Day was taking care of Neil, the top man, then things would be so much better and Outreach too.

"You must feel better now Mrs Green," they told me.

He didn't have his CPN but she was useless anyway, they were to pick Neil up as they put it. To top it all Ben said Neil was to go and see his psychiatrist on the Tuesday.

Remember way back when we had that really awful meeting at the Resource Centre with Dr Musto and he said he'd see Neil within a month and we got the appointment for 13th June, which was months and months away? Well, that was the appointment that Ben was on about.

I had forgotten about it, but surely that had changed anyway, he was under Dr Day now.

"No," Ben said, "he should have gone, Eddina sent his care worker from Cedar Rose."

"Hang on a minute, not only are you telling me he *should* have had Outreach every day, but on Tuesday someone actually went round to see why he hadn't been to the hospital to see the psychiatrist? They knew he should have been at the hospital. I don't believe this."

All I could say to Ben when he came on the day that I'd found Neil, was that I *shouldn't* have been the one to find him. He'd been left to rot quite literally. Just as I said they would do. He had been left there for a full week on his own as he had died on the Friday. In seven full days, having just left prison, no one had been in to him at all. No one took him his medication. His carer had simply shoved a note through his door on Wednesday, not Tuesday when Eddina had told Ben that she'd sent someone round.

Neil was the worst I had seen him before he was sent to prison. I'd written to the hospital stating the same. I rang Dr Plackett's secretary crying and I told her the same.

"He certainly wasn't himself when I saw him on the 7th June in prison. They'd promised he'd be well looked after on his release. Well they gave him NO MEDICATION, not even a prescription for him to get his own. They'd just left him. They'd let him come home without anyone to see him, or give him his medication, or even to see how he was. We had been completely lulled into a false sense of security, thinking that someone was seeing him every day.

He missed his hospital appointment and Outreach would have been there, but still they didn't go round to Neil's or ring me to ask

503

me why Neil hadn't been, or at least to reassure them that he was alright. No, never that, **they didn't care**. They are to blame for the death of my son for they were the ones who had neglected him.

I was rung on the very day that I found my son by Gordon Nicks and I venomously told him, "Do you think that I want anyone to ring me from Fernlea General?"

So he wrote me a letter instead.

He said he was sending condolences on behalf of himself, him being the Adult Service Manager and his organization the Lancashire Care Trust. He said he was to hold a severe untoward incident review and offered my participation if I so wished.

Like I was offered to write to Bob Gardner that time, I would rather poke my eyes out. What a load of empty useless going through the motions dribble. Neil was in a long line of people that this 'Organization' had done this too and it was to continue. What a load of CRAP they were saying. **They should be showing urgent actions, not offering empty words and useless promises.**

I had believed them this time; I actually thought they were trying at long last, but because of that my son Neil died, and was left all alone and lying dead for a whole week.

I was ill, but what was their excuse? I had just gone through the death of my beloved Mother.

This was the *same* Gordon Nicks who Ben had spoken to months ago when Neil had deteriorated so badly, **before** he took the overdose. Ben had pleaded for his help and involvement, but he did *nothing*. No one from Fernlea General <u>ever</u> did anything. They didn't care; instead they turned their backs on Neil.

You should have listened to me Mr Nicks when you rang me on the day I found Neil, instead you sent me yet another one of Fernlea General's stupid letters, which just added insult to injury.

You should have done your job. You **all** should have done the jobs you were employed to do, and paid to carry out, and made sure that Neil was taken care of; but you **didn't** and you never would. You made my boy suffer. He was living in hell and every single one of you is to blame.

You, the psychiatrists, CPN's, Mental Health Team, Outreach, Social Services, all of you, and the 'organization' you speak of which is Fernlea General Hospital and the PCT that oversee it, I hate and detest the lot of you. You **murdered** my son just as if you had actually held a gun at his head, and I will **never** forgive you.

You robbed us of our son many years **before** he died, and made it worse for us to remember him without thinking how controlled he was by the voices in his head. My son **could** have been helped, he had a caring family to help him and back up the Services. All of Neil's life I've had to push and fight for help, services and treatment for my son. You ruined his life and ours!

Someone from the Coroner's Office rang me the day after I had found Neil. He told me that Neil was in a shocking state.

I said, "Have you noticed his badly scarred arms?"

He said, "Love, ring the papers, **this isn't right**! It's happening too often. We are sick of seeing people like Neil ending up on one of our slabs."

I did as he asked. It was hard, so very hard to do. Camilla Sutcliffe from our local paper came. I gave her a photo of Neil and she took it away with part of the book that I had started to write and she told me later that this book really needed to be written.

The headline in the paper was, **WHY DIDN'T THEY HELP MY SON? Mother's worst fear comes true.**

As far as I was concerned Neil was a 'victim' of neglect and cruelty. I wanted people to lay flowers for him as they did for other victims of crime *outside* his house; something to show that people cared for this loving harmless boy who loved his family and all he had ever truly wanted from life was to be 'normal'. **However no one did!**

****

Kathleen has fond memories of Neil visiting her in hospital every day when she broke her arm and smashed her elbow and it had to be pinned, and when she broke her hip he did the same. She told me of the time when he'd go at mealtimes just to feed the old lady across from her who was left her dinner, but because she *couldn't* feed herself, it was just left in front of her. Neil went just at that time to feed her.

Yes, Neil had a lot of good points; he'd get involved if he saw someone hurting, young or old and animals too. Kids loved him; he was generous, kind and thoughtful. He was the one who would buy me the sloppy cards, the fridge magnets.

'To My Loving Mum', and the teddies. You got plenty of hugs and kisses off Neil and I miss him for all that. We tolerated his illnesses because we knew that he <u>couldn't help</u> what he did, because of them and what he was made to do. Mental illness is **a terrible illness** and you are treated as if you don't matter.

Personally I've seen a lot of horrible things being done to these sick people, as if they don't mean anything or matter in the least. **It's NOT TRUE every single human being matters!**

I've tried to give the reader of this book the stages of mental illness to give you an insight, and to show you what we had to deal with from the person that is ill, as well as the Education, Social Services, Doctors, Psychiatrists, Mental Health Team, The Trust, PCT, as well as the police and the courts and Prison Service. I've written the whole truth, warts and all! We needed more understanding for the patient, and also for us as a family.

People who work with children also need to understand A.D.H.D. and we certainly need more doctors to specialize in this condition. These people all need to read my book to understand. How long are we going to put up with these young people dying, committing suicide, or being turned away from hospitals? We need to get these unfortunate people **out of prisons**, and that is a priority. They need care and treatment, not to be branded, labelled and criminalized.

We need to give the courts the powers to bring the doctors/psychiatrists to court in order to explain themselves, and for them to be able to assist these people into getting them urgent and proper medical attention from caring psychiatrists if the need arises. But most importantly of all, we **most certainly need it to become LAW that every single one of us should be entitled to get a second opinion,** from another hospital and another doctor, **without the influence of the first one overruling them.**

We need to be able to get a second opinion and to STOP ALLOWING the doctor`s to Lord over us, as no one can touch them. **They are just as accountable as any of us.** MAYBE MORE SO, AS OFTEN OUR VERY LIVES ARE HELD IN THEIR HANDS.

It is a crime to let them continue to close ranks. They are not GODS. My G.P. on numerous occasions approached psychiatrists for a second opinion or a referral for Neil, but was told it **couldn't** be done this way.

WELL IT SHOULD BE ABLE TO BE DONE THIS WAY!

Knock the psychiatrists and consultants off their pedestals, they are **not** GODS, so don't allow them to think that they are. We need secure hospitals that are run properly. Neil needed 24 hour supervision and care, and in order for them to **avoid** paying for it they **denied** that he had an enduring illness.

I'll let the readers be the judge of that. I hope that I have made you think about the issues that surround mental illness. In all probability one of your family members could suffer with it in some form at possible one time in their lives, or even you, dear reader. Would you want to be treated the way my son has been treated, or one of your loved ones?

He wasn't a **nobody;** he was my son and I loved him. His father loved him and his brother loved him as did his grandparents and our other relatives. He was a very precious and important member of our family.

Every single one of us is a person, and we should ALL matter. I've had letters off people, and people came to my son's funeral and **begged** me to write this book. There are thousands of people suffering out there. This story needs to be told. They say Society let my son down. Don't be one of them. Ask questions, fight for justice and don't forget my son.

This book has been the hardest thing that I've ever done.

I asked for a copy of my son's Post Mortem Report and it was horrendous to have to read it, but I had to know **why my son died**? The Coroner had said that if he had used Heroin on the day he died that he would have just drifted away without pain. I knew he **hadn't committed suicide** so that could be ruled out.

He said that in fact there wasn't a trace of alcohol or drugs in his body, and I knew that if he had taken Heroin on the day he died, it wasn't much, because I checked to see what amount of money he had taken out of his bank account and it was only enough for him to have paid the taxi fare, bought a chip shop meal and then paid for a bag of Heroin which would cost £10.

The verdict of Neil's inquest was Unascertainable. Which doesn't in fact answer any of the questions as to why my son died. I can only hope that he didn't die in pain at the time of his death, although he suffered pain all of his life.

Neil didn't deserve to die, but he had to die. I will let you be the judge as to who is to blame for my son's death but I don't want Neil to have died for NOTHING.

We must stop the way our mentally ill LOVED ones are treated by the Services that we pay to be put into place, for the treatment and care of all of us.

This is a diary of a very
special <u>Somebody.</u>

Neil Anthony Green,
Our beloved son.

You are in our hearts forever
We will always love you.

Last photo taken of Neil

The disk of this photograph of Neil on the previous page was supplied to me by Carol Collinson of Creative Gifts in Nelson.

I wanted her to put this photograph of Neil onto canvas, and change the background to a blue sky with fluffy white clouds.

It turned out with Neil's outline, that it appears to everyone who has seen it that Neil's in Heaven.

We can only hope that Neil is indeed finally resting in peace!

God Bless and keep you safe Son!

THE HIPPOCRATIC OATH
Modern Version used by Medical Students
(Written by LOUIS LASAGNA,
The Dean Of Tufts University in 1964)

I swear to fulfil, to the best of my ability and judgement, this Covenant.

I will respect the hard-won scientific gains of those physicians in whose steps I walk, and gladly share such knowledge as is mine with those who are to follow. I will apply, for the benefit of the sick, all measures that are required, avoiding those twin traps of over treatment and therapeutic nihilism.

I will remember that is art to medicine as well as science, and that warmth, sympathy, and understanding may outweigh the surgeon's knife or the chemist's drug.

I will not be ashamed to say, "I know not," nor will I fail to call in my colleagues when the skills of another are needed for a patient's recovery.

I will respect the privacy of my patients, for their problems are not disclosed to me that the world may know. Most especially must I tread with care in matters of life and death. If it is given to me to save a life, all thanks. But it may also be within my power to take a life; this awesome responsibility must be faced with great humbleness of my own frailty. **Above all I must not play at God.**

I will remember that I do not treat a fever chart, a cancerous growth, but a sick human being, whose illness may affect the person's family and economic stability. My responsibility includes these related problems, if I am to care adequately for the sick.

I will prevent disease whenever I can, for prevention is preferable to cure. I will remember that I remain a member of society, with special obligations to all my fellow human beings; those sound of mind as well as body as well as the infirm.

If I do not violate this oath, may I enjoy life and art, respected while I live, and remembered with affection thereafter.

May I always act so as to preserve the finest traditions of my calling, and may I long experience the joy of healing those who seek my help.

Please read the oath, boxed in red very carefully, so that you can take into account the true story and treatment doled out to Neil Anthony Green, to allow you to judge for yourself, whether or not the doctors and psychiatrists, treated him fairly in every way, diagnosed his condition correctly, or allowed him to have a second opinion, or did they as the oath itself warns – simply play at being God with the life of a sick boy, continuing through to a very seriously ill man?

Overleaf I have written a few questions concerning Neil and the PROMISES AS SWORN IN THE Hippocratic Oath, to see if the doctors did, or DID NOT treat HIM fairly according to their OWN sworn oath to care for the sick. I have made my own comments, but to be totally fair and honest, because that is the way I am, I will leave you the reader to judge THE TRUTH for yourself.

JUST A FEW QUESTIONS FOR YOU TO PONDER OVER!

Did ALL the doctors involved in the medical history and treatment of Neil, obey the oath which they had sworn to obey?

Did the doctors treat this patient, and his family, with warmth and sympathy?

Did they live up to their duties and responsibilities of looking after ALL their patients?

Did they call in one of their colleagues, when the skills of another were required for this patient's recovery?

Did they ever say, "I know not," when treatment repeatedly failed for this boy, then afterwards throughout his short adult life?

Did they prevent Neil's disease from deteriorating?

Did they remember that this was a sick human being?

Did they consider that this patient's illness might affect the person's family or economic stability?

Did they consider their special obligations to all their fellow human beings, whether sound of mind or body?

Did they in fact violate this oath that they swore to keep?

Did they ever aid the patient to recover, or prevent his illness from worsening?

WITH ONE EXCEPTION, I THINK NOT!

Could they have treated Neil Anthony Green better? - Absolutely *Yes!* – Sadly most did not care – and so Neil suffered on quite needlessly. One specialist made a diagnosis that Neil was simply a 'bad lad' seeking attention, when in reality he was crying out for help from everyone he could.

He was diagnosed as suffering from A.D.H.D. early on in his life, but sadly this *same* doctor did not believe at that time in this condition, and others simply followed his lead. They were also wrongly under the belief that an adult cannot possibly suffer from A.D.H.D. so Neil should have simply grown out of it.

How can anyone just be 'bad' who keeps attempting to kill themselves? Many of his attempts were almost successful. He was crying out for help, but not many medical people were listening to his pitiful pleas.

Sadly the few doctors, who occasionally did listen, were always over-ruled.

The main doctor had said that Neil was NOT suffering from mental illness, despite having treated other family members of our OWN family himself. He STILL would NOT allow Neil a second opinion elsewhere as he thought that he always knew better.

Neil was forced to self-medicate to try to escape the unrelenting voices and urges of his condition; he resorted to alcohol and drugs. He committed petty crimes, stealing things simply to draw attention to himself. In fact 99% of these items were absolutely of no use to Neil at all, he wanted treatment, but instead the doctors refused to treat him and sent him to jail without any help or medication.

I HOPE THAT THEY CAN LIVE WITH THEMSELVES!

I also hope that one in four of the rest of us, can fare much better, **as Neil should NOT have died in vain! He had his own rights to treatment <u>from the cradle to the grave</u>, just as it was promised to each and every single one of us!**

515